ONE NATION UNDECIDED

ONE NATION UNDECIDED

CLEAR THINKING
ABOUT FIVE
HARD ISSUES
THAT DIVIDE US

PETER H. SCHUCK

PRINCETON UNIVERSITY PRESS
Princeton & Oxford

Published by Princeton University Press,
41 William Street, Princeton, New Jersey 08540

In the United Kingdom: Princeton University Press,
6 Oxford Street, Woodstock, Oxfordshire OX20 1TR

press.princeton.edu

Jacket art and design by Alex Robbins

Library of Congress Cataloging-in-Publication Data

Names: Schuck, Peter H., author.
Title: One nation undecided : clear thinking about five hard issues that divide us /
Peter H. Schuck.
Description: Princeton, New Jersey : Princeton University Press, 2017. | Includes
bibliographical references and index.
Identifiers: LCCN 2016039948 | ISBN 9780691167435 (hardback)
Subjects: LCSH: Political culture—United States. | Poverty—Political aspects—United
States. | United States—Emigration and immigration—Political aspects. | Campaign
funds—United States. |Affirmative action programs—United States. | Religion and
politics—United States. |
BISAC: POLITICAL SCIENCE / Public Policy / General. | POLITICAL SCIENCE /
Civics & Citizenship. | LAW / Government / General.
Classification: LCC JK1726 .S37 2017 | DDC 320.60973—dc23 LC record available at
https://lccn.loc.gov/2016039948

British Library Cataloging-in-Publication Data is available

This book has been composed in Miller

Printed on acid-free paper. ∞

Printed in the United States of America

10 9 8 7 6 5 4 3 2 1

I DEDICATE THIS BOOK to the many social scientists whose resourcefulness and industry in digging out the facts bearing on hard issues make works of synthesis like this one possible

CONTENTS

ACKNOWLEDGMENTS

I UNDERTOOK THIS PROJECT for two reasons—to deepen my own understanding of some of the central social policy issues of the day and to communicate what I have learned to other conscientious citizens who want to dig into them more deeply and need a balanced, objective synthesis to do so.

Along the way, a number of distinguished experts in these fields were kind and patient enough to answer my questions, refer me to relevant sources, and in some cases offer detailed comments on draft chapters in their areas of specialization. They include Hank Aaron, Steve Ansolabehere, Adam Cox, Bob Doar, Nicole Garnett, Rick Garnett, Ron Haskins, Steve Heyman, Sandy Jencks, Ray LaRaja, Chip Lupu, David Martin, Larry Mead, Shep Melnick, Michael Olivas, Nate Persily, Jon Rauch, Cristina Rodriguez, Marc Rosenblum, Rick Sander, Belle Sawhill, David Shapiro, Laura Tach, Jack Weinstein, and Robin Wilson. I am greatly indebted to these wise, generous, busy, and exceedingly well-informed scholars. Their colleagueship inspires my own.

Four law students provided excellent research assistance, especially during the early stages of my work: David Barillari (Yale Law School class of 2016), Rachel Hecht (Yale Law School class of 2017),

Marissa Roy (Yale Law School class of 2017), and Tony Cheng (NYU Law School class of 2018), who also prepared the index. I presented an early version of the introductory chapter to the Berkeley Law School faculty. NYU Law School has provided me an institutional home away from my Yale home in New York City for more than fifteen years through the deanships of John Sexton, Ricky Revesz, and now Trevor Morrison. Their generosity, and that of their fine faculty, have been remarkable and invaluable.

Parts of chapters 5 and 6 are adapted from my article, "Affirmative Action: Past, Present, and Future," originally published in the *Yale Law & Policy Review*, volume 20, issue 1, 2002. Much of the material on religious diversity was published in 2003 by Harvard University Press's Belknap Press in my book *Diversity in America: Keeping Government at a Safe Distance* and is reproduced here, with some updates, and with the permission of the original publishers. Specific page numbers can be found in the endnotes to these discussions.

Peter Dougherty, the visionary director of Princeton University Press, his senior editor Eric Crahan, and others on the Press's staff provided discerning intelligence and other valuable support during the book's gestation period. My thanks as well to the anonymous outside readers whose comments made this a better book. Alas, I alone am responsible for any errors.

Finally, I thank Marcy, my beloved wife of fifty years. Without her, as the quip goes, I would have written this book much more quickly.

November 2016

ONE NATION UNDECIDED

CHAPTER 1

INTRODUCTION

YOU ARE A SERIOUS, well-educated voter. You read print and online media, listen to the views of opinion leaders and organizations that you trust, discuss current events informally with interested friends, and generally try to keep up with current events. You want to participate responsibly in the democratic process through which the policies that govern us are formed, but you find this difficult. Busy with your family, work, and other private commitments, you don't have much spare time to navigate the daunting complexity of the substantive policy issues. Social groups and peer pressure urge you to take clear positions on these issues. You might feel more comfortable if you could conscientiously do so. But you feel uneasy in taking firm positions on these important issues because, in all honesty, you know that you haven't given them all that much thought or done your homework. So what is a conscientious but understandably distracted citizen like you to do?

I wrote this book for you. It is about hard public issues and how Americans should think about them before deciding where they stand. The success of our deliberative democracy—in which We the People and our representatives really do decide how such issues are resolved—depends on citizens' knowing what they are talking and voting about.

1

What makes an issue hard? Why are some issues getting even harder, while others seem to become easier?* Is more public debate on hard issues needed? What do I mean by clear thinking about issues? What is the quality of today's debates? How much must citizens know about the issues in order to think clearly about them, and how realistic is this? What can this book hope to contribute to these debates?

This chapter answers these questions in general, and the chapters that follow get down to specifics. But which ones? The list of domestic policy† decisions on which Americans sharply disagree with one another—in the voting booth and in conversations—is very long. No single person could explicate most of them. To do so would require far more knowledge, technical skill, time, and patience than any individual (certainly *this* one) possesses.

The reader's patience is short, so I focus my analysis on five domestic policy issues: poverty; immigration; campaign finance; affirmative action; and conflicts between religious and secular values. Why these? Reasonable people will disagree about the most important issues facing the nation. The first—poverty—is an enduring challenge to the American dream. The next two—immigration and campaign finance—are perennially controversial, especially during election campaigns. The debate over affirmative action remains as robust as ever, even after the U.S. Supreme Court upheld its constitutionality in 2016. (The Court did not endorse its policy merits and the decision was a narrow one, limited—as the majority emphasized—to Texas's "sui generis" plan.) The final issue, which I shall call "religious accommodation" as a shorthand, has always been controversial in our public life, and its prominence today is especially high in light of two recent Supreme Court decisions, discussed in chapter 6.

Each of the five is a very hard issue according to the criteria I present immediately below—although some of them are more hotly de-

---

* An example is wage supplements for the working poor, which are now widely accepted as a better way to increase their incomes than raising the minimum wage. I discuss this issue in chapter 2.

† A policy is a statement of goals; a program is an instrument for implementing a policy. Generally, I shall use the terms interchangeably.

bated, affect more people, are more politically sensitive, and raise more basic constitutional issues than others. And some issues that I do not analyze here are even harder and arguably more consequential—for example, climate change and the financing and delivery of health care—are more complicated. But trying to compare the hardness of different public issues (rather than of, say, different minerals) is a fool's errand. Each of the five vitally affects our democracy and society. We have argued about all of them for so long that their contours are relatively well defined and thus amenable to the kind of close analysis presented in this book. And the analytical structure that I use to dissect each of them invites the reader to apply it to other issues not considered here.

WHAT MAKES AN ISSUE HARD?

In my usage, an issue is hard to the extent that the following characteristics are *inherent* to it: Hard issues also have *external or contingent* aspects (e.g., political conditions, timing, leadership, unexpected events, international developments).

- It is a *public and federal* issue. Government institutions, especially at the federal level, play an important role in resolving it through the political process and in embodying it in public law. In contrast, most issues never make it on to the public agenda at all.[1]
- It is *highly salient to a large number of people*. This means that they care deeply, passionately, and perhaps even militantly about it. People tend to have at least provisional opinions or intuitions about where they stand on it when it enters their world.
- It constitutes an *ensemble of interrelated disputed questions*. We may try to treat the issue as if it were analytically discrete or self-contained, but in reality its knot of questions interact in complicated, opaque, and hard-to-disentangle ways.
- It is *historically inflected*, bearing the strong imprint of earlier struggles that continue to haunt current debates, affect the

terms of discussion, and perhaps limit the menu of future options.

- It consists in part of *complex empirical disputes* that our existing knowledge cannot authoritatively resolve and on which even the experts are usually divided. Hard issues, moreover, often are subject to a "meta" empirical issue—i.e., whether the empirical disputes have in fact been settled or are instead still open to dispute. Efforts to persuade the public that a given issue is or is not still open to serious, responsible debate is a high-stakes game played by competing interests. Climate change is probably the clearest current example.* Reformers typically cite a looming crisis that must be addressed immediately, while those who favor the status quo or emphasize our ignorance or uncertainty usually favor delay, urging more deliberation, better information, and thus a more durable public consensus.

- It is embedded in *normative disputes*. The contested values are usually widely held and deeply felt by their proponents. Depending on the nature and content of these values, they may be more or less sensitive or tractable to empirical facts that might (or might not) seem relevant to them. Thus, people who employ a utilitarian framework that values a particular policy according to its consequences (often measured by its costs and benefits) will want to know which conditions cause which effects (among other empirical facts) before they choose a preferred policy or action. In contrast, others may assess the desirability of a policy or action deontologically—i.e., in light of whether it conforms to preexisting rules or precepts while according less (or no) significance to such empirical contingencies.

The complexity and passion surrounding normative disputes often make them seem intractable. In a democratic society, they can be re-

* Although climate change is a highly divisive issue, research suggests that people become *more* polarized, not less, as their capacity for understanding scientific evidence and their open-mindedness increases. Dan Kahan and Jonathan Corbin, "A Note on the Perverse Effects of Actively Open-Minded Thinking on Climate-Change Polarization," *Research and Politics* (in press).

solved, if at all, only through compromise in which the competing values are traded off against one another, or by decentralizing disputes so that different jurisdictions may reach different results without the need for any overarching national solution. Values may compete with one another in at least two ways. Most commonly, pursuing goal A in fact entails some sacrifice of goal B (and vice versa). Such value conflicts, moreover, often reflect quite different worldviews so that those who hold them will tend to disagree about many other important issues, including the factual claims that underlie the values.

Occasionally, however, a normative dispute is so basic that it essentially forecloses any reasoned debate on empirical issues or even on value trade-offs. Abortion, I believe, is an example, which is one reason why I do not include it here. If one strongly believes that life begins at conception (or alternatively, that a woman's control of her body and right to choose how it is used are absolute), then abortion is murder (or alternatively, a basic right of personal autonomy), and there really isn't much more to talk about, except perhaps at the edges of the issue-space (e.g., narrow exceptions, or differentiating among trimesters). Similarly, many if not most opponents of capital punishment believe that it is simply immoral for the state to take life, although many opponents also object on other, more empirical grounds (e.g., uncertainty and arbitrariness).

Issues of this kind often implicate not merely differences in perspective but competing worldviews. Those who hold them may be especially unwilling, or even epistemologically unable, to yield or compromise on them because too much of their sense of reality or morality seems to be at stake. Indeed, such issues cause such people to perceive and interpret factual evidence in ways that conform to or reinforce that worldview. Scholars have approached this interpretive phenomenon in different ways.*

---

* Dan Kahan calls it "cultural cognition." He posits two cultures: "hierarchical" and "egalitarian," and with co-authors has tested it empirically on a wide range of policy issues with important factual components—from gun control to vaccine use to date rape. E.g., Dan Kahan, "Fixing the Communications Failure," 463 *Nature* 296–97 (2010). For a meth-

Some issues are normatively divisive for a particular reason that makes them even harder to resolve. This occurs when people harbor strong views but either conceal or sanitize them out of fear that they will be stigmatized as socially abhorrent. People with racist or homophobic views, for example, are often reluctant to acknowledge them. Opponents of affirmative action often fear being accused of racism by its advocates. Conservatives may depict critics of aggressive foreign policies as unpatriotic, critics of Israel as anti-Semitic, and critics of tough police practices as soft-on-crime apologists for social disorder. Such tactics are part and parcel of robust, sharp-elbowed debate in a society deeply committed to free speech. There really is no good remedy for this other than greater self-restraint and tolerance.[2] But when such fears cause the timorous (who probably include all of us at times) to pull their punches, retreat from public fora, or misrepresent their views when asked for them, the public debate is deformed and people's true positions on issues become more difficult to gauge.

- Analyzing a hard issue requires drawing *relatively fine distinctions*, which the general public may find difficult to understand or accept. As we shall see, legal doctrine tends to multiply such distinctions over time in response to new, often unanticipated factual situations that arise. These new situations might be covered by existing rule A but might (as some will plausibly argue) be covered better by existing or new rule B. Policy makers and judges, like other people, must decide which distinctions to make and how to formulate them. In the policy process, new distinctions are often added to earlier ones, which makes the policy ever more technical and complex but also, hopefully, more responsive to emerging social needs.

---

odological critique of his work, see Mary Douglas, "Being Fair to Hierarchists," 151 *University of Pennsylvania Law Review* 1349 (2003). Two decades earlier, Mary Douglas and Aaron Wildavsky identified four different worldviews, "hierarchical," "individualistic," "radical communitarian," and "fatalistic," which they thought explained one's orientations to issues involving risk. Mary Douglas and Aaron Wildavsky, *Risk and Culture* (1982). Jonathan Haidt, a social psychologist, posits six "moral foundations"—care/harm; fairness/cheating; liberty/oppression; loyalty/betrayal; authority/subversion; and sanctity/degradation—that he thinks shape worldviews and help account for attitudinal and hence sociopolitical polarization. Haidt, *The Righteous Mind: Why Good People Are Divided by Politics and Religion* (2012).

- *Institutional density* makes it harder to both understand and solve issues.* By this, I mean the number of agencies, levels of government, civil society groups, and private markets interacting in a particular issue-space.
- Hard issues confront *particularly severe constraints on policy solutions*. Any genuine solutions (not mere patches or temporary fixes) are likely to be very costly. Sometimes, these costs are not only large (for example, Medicare and Social Security reforms) but cannot be easily concealed from the likely cost-bearers, hard as politicians may try.† Knowing who will ultimately pay affects political conflict, particularly where the conflict seems zero-sum. Budgetary issues are often of this type, but so are policies that may trigger status conflicts that cause one group to feel diminished in social esteem by the rise of another. Immigration, affirmative action, and demands for religious accommodation can trigger feelings of this kind. But for most hard issues, the constraints are not only fiscal or even political. Sometimes they are moral (as with antipoverty policies). Legal rules, including constitutional ones, may foreclose certain solutions, as we shall see in several of the chapters that follow—especially campaign finance, religious accommodation, and affirmative action.

WHY ARE SOME HARD ISSUES GETTING EVEN HARDER?

Public policy disputes seem to be getting more protracted, more impervious to reasoned debate, and their solutions more elusive. This impression is difficult to prove definitively because we lack clear gauges: The characteristics that make issues hard are largely quali-

---

* Eric Biber reminds us that a *dearth* of institutions can also make complex problems that much harder to solve. But his example, climate change, suggests that what he has in mind is a dearth of *authoritative* institutions capable of negotiating and resolving conflicts among governments and countless private actors throughout the world.

† In an earlier book, I identified six political techniques for concealing or obscuring such costs: ignoring them, disguising them, deferring them, shifting them, treating a resource as if it were free, and delegating key decisions to agencies. *Why Government Fails So Often, and How It Can Do Better* (2014), pp. 137–38.

tative and resist measurement. We must also bridle our tendency to imagine a past "golden age" of consensus and high-toned debate, just as we should not assume that today's policy struggles are nastier, more politicized, more irrational, and more polarized than in earlier times. The belief in such a harmonious past betrays more ignorance about our history than insight about our current challenges. The sharp, sometimes violent divisions documented by American historians throughout our history belie such a fantasy.[3] Abraham Lincoln, long sainted in our collective national memory, was in his own time vilified in the most intemperate, despicable terms.[4] Although the period between World War II and the Vietnam War now seems unusually harmonious (except for the McCarthy era), that was abnormal. Arguably, the 1800 presidential election was uglier than 2016's.[5]

Still, some features of our contemporary policy-making context do make many issues harder to understand and resolve. In one sense, today's hard issues are harder almost by definition: We have already picked some of the lower-hanging fruit—policy changes that over time came to be widely seen as morally compelled—leaving us twenty-first-century Americans to debate issues that have not yet achieved that consensus (if they ever will). My point, emphatically, is *not* that universal suffrage, safety net entitlements, antidiscrimination laws, environmental and consumer protection programs, and labor rights came easily. Far from it; they were extraordinarily hard issues at the time, resolved only after protracted political and cultural struggle— and, in some cases, widespread violence. Even today when these policies' basic parameters seem fairly well settled, bitter conflict continues over their precise contours. Efforts to roll them back continue, albeit nonviolently.

Perhaps as time passes, many of the hard issues that roil today's Americans will seem more tractable than now appears possible—for example, the cultural conflicts over same-sex marriage and transgender rights, discussed in chapter 6—but powerful arguments exist on all sides of hard issues. By some measures, our politics really *is* more polarized than at any time since the post–Civil War era, at least in the

U.S. Congress.[6] Even issues not now on the political agenda seem more contested today than since World War II.[7] Even though today's policy makers can access much better social data and analytical tools for answering the underlying factual and normative questions, a wider gap exists between what we know* and what we now realize we *need* to know in order to frame sound policy. Poverty is perhaps the clearest example of this "policy-knowledge gap." As chapter 2 shows, we now know far more about how to measure it and about its causes, effects, types, remedies, lessons from other developed societies, and much else, but we also know more about what we *don't* know—but *need* to learn—in order to remedy it wisely. For the hard issues discussed in this book, some of the most basic, policy-relevant facts are elusive and difficult to grasp for epistemological reasons that confound even the most scrupulous, well-intentioned efforts.

Today's hard issues are also harder than before because institutional density (discussed above) has increased dramatically. The vast profusion of laws and regulations has clotted the veins of decision and action in almost every field,[8] and the courts are more active in reviewing and shaping policy than ever before. Consider just two examples of this greater institutional/legal density. Infrastructure projects that created our present way of life are almost impossible to execute today within any reasonable parameters of cost and time.† And more than six years after Dodd-Frank was enacted, many statutorily required regulations had not yet been issued, while some of those that were issued were fiercely contested and in some cases rolled back for imposing crushing regulatory costs on smaller institutions. The higher stakes in such decisions have multiplied the cost of negotiating political bargains among the more numerous and diverse Washington-based interest groups, lobbyists, and stakeholders—some with veto

---

* As Mark Twain put it, "What gets us into trouble is not what we don't know, it's what we know for sure that just ain't so."

† The George Washington Bridge, built in a relatively short time, would take much longer today (if it could be approved at all) despite enormous technical advances. Ernst Frankel, *Saving American from Itself: American Revival Opportunities* (2011), p. 53; Philip K. Howard, "Why It Takes So Long to Build a Bridge in America," *Wall Street Journal*, November 22, 2013.

power but all prepared to weigh in on how issues should be framed and resolved.

The post-1960 proliferation of rights—social welfare entitlements and antidiscrimination remedies, for example—has also "hardened" issues. By rights, I mean claims that explicitly trump competing views and interests, with legally enforceable sanctions. But in practice, they do more than this, also rendering the competing claims illegitimate in a sense. De-legitimating the opposition tends to impoverish political discourse, in several ways: suppressing deeply felt meanings that society needs to apprehend (even if it rejects them), blocking social pressures that seek release and respect, and forcing them underground, as it were, where mutual understanding and accommodation are more difficult to achieve and may now even be illegal. And because this density of rights fills in so much more of the issue-space where interests and social accommodations were once debated, it reduces the leeway that a diverse society needs to navigate such politically-contested terrain.

Our society has become more difficult to govern in other ways. A better-educated, more sophisticated, and cosmopolitan citizenry tends to be more opinionated and less deferential to all forms of authority, including political leadership. Their confidence and self-assertion may cause resentment by their less elite compatriots who increasingly retreat from voting and other political activity that could defend their interests and perhaps improve policy outcomes. Trust in non-military institutions—Congress, the Supreme Court, the presidency, candidates for high office, religious entities, and markets—has declined markedly, creating additional barriers to issue resolution. This disaffection saps public confidence in the very possibility of viable solutions. After all, the thinking goes, if none of those institutions can solve problems, there is little hope for effectively addressing them. Mistrust also reduces politicians' ability to assemble and legitimate the power necessary to overcome the inertia that is probably the most decisive force in politics. As chapter 5 explains, the parties traditionally performed this function by framing issues, organizing alternative remedies, taking a more long-term view, and appealing to the median voter, but they have been systematically weakened. This has left us with a more chaotic, free-wheeling, volatile, and polarized politics. And with much of the public's energy siphoned off by cultural and technological distractions, the remaining energy is that much harder to concentrate and mobilize in order to resolve hard issues and change policy.

Many other factors make hard issues even harder today. Globalization and increased foreign competition, for example, constrain policy choice in the fields of immigration (chapter 3) and to a lesser extent poverty (chapter 2), as well as in many other important issue-areas such as taxation, financial regulation, trade, and antitrust.* A perpetual news cycle and ubiquitous social media inhibit deliberation, confidentiality, compromise, and deal-making. Likewise, some "good government" measures—for example, the elimination of congressional earmarks, the decentralization of power within Congress, "sunshine laws," and term limits—have made it harder to strike enduring political bargains. And a strong case can be made (as we shall see in chapter 4) that the often well-intended campaign finance reforms enacted since the 1970s have contributed to the same rigidifying, polarizing effects on our politics.

DO WE NEED MORE PUBLIC DEBATE ON HARD ISSUES?

People hoping to stimulate more discussion of some issue (or who want to see it resolved in a particular way) often call for a "public debate" on it. (Indeed, I just used the term!) Presidents Clinton and Obama, for example, each advocated a public debate on race relations following some notable incident or development. Similarly, many have urged that a public debate on inequality is long overdue. As I write, many editorialists call for more public debate on reducing sexual assaults on campus and elsewhere. What do they mean by the term?

In truth, all the issues discussed in this book are debated by the public all the time. These debates occur in countless forms and ven-

---

* As Richard Buxbaum has noted, globalization has also multiplied the number and types of international fora in which policy issues in the United States may be shaped, making them that much harder to resolve in most cases.

ues, many of them opaque to outsiders: conversations within families and among neighbors, friends, colleagues, and strangers; traditional media (TV, radio, newspapers, magazines, books) and Internet postings on countless websites; school and college classrooms; church sermons; hearings and interactions among legislators at all levels of government; civic and trade associations; and within people's minds, as they ponder what they have heard, imagined, seen, thought, and remembered. These remarkably diffuse viewpoints on such issues bubble up, down, and across through osmotic, low-visibility processes of information, communication, and influence. Those who assert that we lack a genuine public debate evidently entertain a very crabbed conception of what such a debate is and of how it shapes citizens' consciousness. (Often, the real anxiety prompting such assertions is that too many other Americans disagree with them about these issues, and that further instruction and persuasion are therefore needed.) It is in the nature of hard issues that they seldom can be resolved finally and conclusively. This is true even of Supreme Court decisions such as *Roe v. Wade* which purport to settle an issue once and for all but instead intensify the debate over it.

The fact that hard policy issues like those discussed in this book are continually being debated says nothing, of course, about the *quality* of these debates—and specifically, about how well they meet our democracy's need to resolve these issues wisely. Daniel Yankelovich, a leading expert on public opinion, has usefully distinguished between *mass opinion* (the poor-quality, volatile public opinion often captured in polls), and *public judgment* (a more mature public opinion marked by citizens' reflection and responsibility).[9] Now surfeited with mass opinion, we desperately need more public judgment.

WHAT DO I MEAN BY CLEAR THINKING ABOUT HARD ISSUES?

My main purpose in this book is to help Americans *think* more clearly about hard public issues. My method is to present my analyses of the five hard issues I have selected, analyses that I hope exemplify clear thinking.

What do I mean by this? Clear thinking about policy issues entails five elements or criteria:

- It rests upon *factual information* that is accurate, timely, and relevant to each important aspect of the question under consideration.
- It identifies the relevant *values* held by the public.
- It analyzes the likely *consequences* of various policy alternatives that might improve the conditions in question.
- It identifies the *trade-offs* implicated by the relevant facts, values, and options.
- It prefers the policy that is (a) most *cost-effective* (i.e., that achieves a social good at the lowest cost, or achieves the most good at a given cost); and (b) most *implementable* in light of the institutional, administrative, political, legal, and social obstacles to achieving that goal in the real world.[10]

Some readers may object to these criteria as excessively and unrealistically technocratic for all but the relative handful of Americans who spend their lives in universities and think tanks and who have the time, training, information, and inclination to analyze public issues in this way. I call this the *intellectual capacity objection* to this kind of means-end rationality. It is a serious objection, which I shall take up shortly.

Some readers may also entertain what amounts to a *moral objection* to this kind of reasoning; they doubt whether it is right to think about complex human issues in this way. I believe that this moral critique is quite wrong. Obviously, one cannot think clearly about a hard issue without considering the values affected by it. No value is served by ignoring the facts about how different courses of action will affect it. Ignorance about the actual relation between means and ends is more likely to undermine those ends—whatever they may be—than to advance them. Yet taking values seriously enough to analyze the trade-offs that pursuing them entails is essential to truly understanding those values: knowing what they are, how they interact with other values, and thus how much we truly care about them. If one truly wills an end, it has been said, then one must will the necessary means to that end. Morally speaking, then, one should ascertain what those means are—which costs and trade-offs they necessarily entail—before embracing the end or value to which the means is instrumental.

As we shall see in the chapters that follow, it is precisely this means-end relationship that clear thinking can help us see. Indeed, as Paul Krugman observes, "a commitment to facing hard choices as opposed to taking the easy way out [is] an important value in itself."[11] Means-end rationality is desirable even when we concede the intellectual capacity objection and our need to "muddle through"* with a more limited form of rationality given the real-world constraints of limited analytical resources and politics. Decisions about hard issues cannot be perfectly rational, but clear thinking can improve them.

Clear thinking focuses not only on means-end rationality but also on the *processes* for deciding which policies to adopt. A democratically effective process must be broadly participatory from the grassroots up; be likely to yield correct answers to the questions put to it and thus approach the truth of the matter; facilitate compromise among affected groups; be considered legitimate even by those who don't get their way;[12] and reveal the necessary trade-offs. Federal policy making—generally and comparatively speaking—scores quite well on the process values of participation, truth-seeking, compromise, and legitimacy, while often scoring poorly on the decisions' substantive merits.[13]

Process also matters because we live not in a pure democracy but in a representative one where accountability to "We the People" is paramount and where a constantly evolving public debate moves seamlessly, almost invisibly, back and forth between officials and the rest of us. In reality, officials enjoy some "political slack" or leeway and do not always follow public opinion.[14] They know that most voters are ill-informed about public issues and that many citizens do not even vote. Political parties and legislative voting rules also can be used to increase political slack for officials, and policies almost always give

---

* This is the term used by Charles Lindblom in his seminal model of complex decision making, "The Science of Muddling Through," 19 *Public Administration Review* 79 (1959).

them hard-to-control discretion. This slack is desirable to an extent. We should neither want nor expect our officials to act as mere automatons, simply registering citizen preferences. The hope is that we elect them because we think that they have superior judgment in political and policy matters, know more about how government actually works, are embedded in institutions designed to encourage deliberation, and are skilled at negotiation and compromise under conditions that voters cannot easily monitor and anticipate. Edmund Burke famously told his Bristol constituents that he would "betray" them if he sacrificed his "judgment" to their "opinion"—a much-needed antidote to the pandering that is all too common among today's politicians.[15]

WHAT IS THE QUALITY OF TODAY'S PUBLIC DEBATE ON HARD ISSUES?

Public debate on hard issues today is woefully deficient, which is why I have gone to the trouble to write this book. This deficiency largely reflects the public's ignorance about such issues and the obstacles they would have to overcome in order to dispel that ignorance. Studies of what voters know about the important issues of the day invariably find egregious levels of ignorance about the most basic facts.* Having found that only 50 percent of citizens correctly answer seven out of ten questions on the citizenship exam compared with 97.5 percent of those seeking naturalization, the Foss Institute has convinced a growing number of states to make passage of a test of such knowledge a prerequisite for high school graduation.[16]

Some analysts, while conceding this inattention and ignorance, dismiss these findings on various grounds: that voters' ignorance is actually rational because they use "information shortcuts" such as party identification, endorsements by opinion leaders, and other cues to decide whom to vote for; that the most ignorant citizens don't

---

* This ignorance is by no means limited to policy issues. Even more remarkable is the fact that most Americans profess strong religious convictions but appear to know little about the most basic religious ideas and facts. For examples, see Peter H. Schuck, *Diversity in America: Keeping Government at a Safe Distance* (2003), pp. 269-70.

bother to vote at all; that aggregating large numbers of voters substitutes the "wisdom of crowds" for widespread ignorance; that they vote the same way they would vote if they were better informed; that they are well enough informed about how well they are doing to vote rationally; and that even if none of these explanations produces rational voting, this irrationality does not affect electoral outcomes. Political scientist Larry Bartels refutes each of these "rationalizations" of irrational voting behavior, showing that such behavior indeed affects many important electoral and policy outcomes.[17]

Another reason for citizens' ignorance is that they get much of their information about public issues directly or indirectly from government officials, yet Americans increasingly lack trust in these officials to tell the truth, do the right thing, or faithfully represent their interests. Opinion polls show that a large share of the population accepts conspiracy theories based on a belief that the government has intentionally lied or covered up the truth—for example, with regard to the Kennedy and Martin Luther King assassinations, the Oklahoma City and 9/11 bombings, WMDs in Iraq, President Obama's birthplace, and many others.[18] (The 2016 presidential election campaign is probably deepening this belief in conspiracies.) Convinced that officials fabricate the facts, such voters would have to go to great lengths to inform themselves independently of the government—a costly expedition that few of them seem likely to undertake.

But it is not only conspiracy theorists who doubt the government's versions of the facts. In reality, our government sometimes *does* lie to us, and engages in what comedian Stephen Colbert terms "truthiness"—and not just in national security matters where obfuscation is sometimes necessary.

The populist belief that ordinary people are more trustworthy than elites is another important source of mistrust. Rooted in our history and social practice,* populism tends to flatter ordinary citizens' intuitions—their "commonsense" beliefs—about public issues

---

* Suspicion of elites seems to be growing elsewhere as well. See Neil Irwin, "Scotland's Independence Vote Shows a Global Crisis of the Elites," *New York Times*, September 18, 2014.

that are in fact highly complex and can only be understood through careful study and analysis. Politicians often pander to this populist strain: "The people against the interests" is a prominent trope in almost all political campaigns, and both the Republican and Democratic candidates for the presidency in 2016 used this trope constantly even though both are themselves wealthy elites. Moreover, candidates often use populist demonology to focus voters' attention on a policy proposal's provenance rather than on its merits. This tactic encourages the use of *ad hominem* arguments which assume that all one really needs to know to assess a fact or position is who is advancing it on behalf of which group. The idea that we are known by the company we keep is better advice to our children than to those wishing to assess policy proposals. Such mental shortcuts are tempting—like any simplistic process, they reduce our decision costs—but clear thinking requires more rigor and effort.

Adding to people's ignorance about public issues are certain patterns of irrationality in the face of facts. Four sources of this irrationality are well established in the experimental psychology and behavioral law-and-economics literatures. These sources are: (1) cognitive biases and logical errors; (2) predictably incoherent judgments; (3) a propensity to assess objective evidence so as to maintain consistency with preexisting cultural or ideological commitments; and (4) deeply rooted moral schema that have this same distorting effect.[19] These systematic distortions have a radical and quite disturbing implication revealed by many tests of "cultural cognition" on many policy issues: The more people know about the facts bearing on an issue, the more polarized and unyielding both sides may become.[20]

This discussion by no means exhausts the reasons for the public's ignorance about hard policy issues. For example, I have not discussed here the problem of information costs,[21] the role of interest groups in strategically deploying often misleading information and influence,[22] unequal access to information,[23] or changing patterns of communication and consumption of information on public affairs.[24] Chapter 5 will note the declining deference by ignorant voters to better-informed political professionals. But the main points should by now be clear:

Citizens do not yet know what they need to know in order to make informed decisions about hard issues. This ignorance significantly affects outcomes, it cannot easily be overcome, and it places the quality of government decisions at grave risk. Indeed, the wonder is that public policy is not even worse than it is.

HOW MUCH MUST CITIZENS KNOW IN ORDER TO THINK CLEARLY, AND HOW REALISTIC IS THIS?

This brings us to a difficult question that I foreshadowed earlier: What can we realistically expect people to know or learn about hard issues? The health of a liberal polity like ours—indeed, its very survival—depends on a large body of citizens actively engaging with public questions, deliberating about them, selecting representatives to resolve them, and then holding those representatives accountable. This need for constant civic engagement is perhaps greater in America than in other liberal democracies where governing elites tend to enjoy greater insulation and deference from public opinion and thus enjoy a freer rein.

The obstacles to attaining this civic engagement are immense. Despite many reformers' efforts to promote more deliberation and genteel debate, American politics is more like a gigantic, endless wrestling match with few if any rules—war without the violence. Americans are busy with other activities in the market and civil society, and their minds are occupied by many matters other than policy and politics; in this sense, at least, their ignorance may well be rational. They are not policy wonks—and judging by how they spend their time, they do not want to be. People who have studied the so-called policy sciences (economics, politics, public administration, law, sociology, etc.) in any depth are a minority of even the well-educated. Much issue-relevant information is inevitably technical and boring. Unfamiliar, difficult concepts may be needed to understand and deliberate about the issue. Not only is there no clear remedy for the public's ignorance, inattention, and insouciance; as we saw, many would deny that this is even a problem.

If one believes, as I and many others do, that public ignorance about hard issues poses a genuine and growing dilemma for our democracy, then our condition is unquestionably grave. Many thoughtful commentators have recognized this challenge,[25] but no solution seems fully adequate to it. One approach, discussed in chapter 5, is to encourage more structured, carefully designed deliberations by citizens before elections.[26] Another is for citizens and officials to rely more on experts who possess specialized training in the relevant policy areas, yet, as noted earlier, the experts often disagree and the public tends to mistrust them anyway. A third, technological approach is the proliferation of websites that can better inform the public about these issues—but of course citizens need to be interested and conversant enough to search the Web for them in the first place. A fourth—a hardy perennial with many conservatives—is to shrink government's responsibilities and thus the number of hard issues that must be resolved publicly. But as I have explained elsewhere, conservative administrations have actually presided over a steady expansion of government, a pattern that for structural reasons seems likely to continue.[27] Finally, we can continue a status quo in which voters defer to politicians and parties that specialize in such issues and over time have built reputations for identifying and representing the public interest. But the deep disillusionment of voters with the parties and politicians so evident in the 2016 election campaign suggests that even this familiar approach is losing ground.

WHAT CAN THIS BOOK HOPE TO CONTRIBUTE?

In the end, there simply is no substitute for a well-informed electorate concerning public affairs. My goal here is to encourage clear thinking about the five hard issues analyzed in this book and, by extension, about other issues not discussed here. I must emphasize that *clear thinking about policy issues is not the same as support for specific outcomes.* In truth, I do not much care where readers come out on these issues so long as they approach them with what I have called clear thinking. Precisely because these *are* all hard issues, plausible arguments can be mustered on various sides, arguments that we should want our fellow citizens to ponder before reaching their own conclusions.

This distinction between how we should think about issues and where we should come out on them might seem disingenuous. After all, I do not write on a blank slate but rather have opinions on these issues (many published elsewhere) that I have reached only after careful study. In the case of affirmative action (chapter 4), for example, my own analyses have brought me to firm conclusions on the issue not only about how people should think about it but also on how I think they should come out in the end.* At the same time, I also believe that reasonable people can—and manifestly do—take a different view. As we have seen, this is part of what makes an issue hard in the first place.

My views on the merits of the four other issues considered here, however, are far less firm. Indeed, it was partly a desire to learn more about them that prompted me to undertake this project. Even though I have taught and written about immigration (chapter 3) for more than thirty years, I am less tendentious about it. Immigration, as I shall explain, raises a complex, vexing, and multifaceted set of policy issues. Although my previous work on immigration informs those issues, it leaves some of them unresolved for me.[28] The other issues considered here—poverty (chapter 2), campaign finance (chapter 5), and religious accommodation (chapter 6)—are relatively unexplored territory for me. But while I am more agnostic about policy outcomes in these areas, I am convinced—and shall try to persuade the reader— that some ways of thinking about them and their policy implications are more coherent, rigorous, and persuasive than others.

Our democracy is an ongoing experiment—about citizens' ability and willingness to inform themselves and to think clearly and carefully enough to govern themselves wisely. Certainly, there are reasons

---

* I shall not keep the reader in suspense. I conclude that affirmative action on behalf of blacks is constitutional—but poor public policy. Preferences for other groups are even less justified. See chapter 5.

to despair. Winston Churchill, although a committed democrat, used his signature puckishness to mock our civic ignorance: "The greatest argument against democracy is a five-minute conversation with the average voter." Another danger signal is a World Values Survey indicating that young Americans are less and less committed to the most basic liberal democratic values. Yet there are also reasons, both theoretical and practical, to think that America's experiment in self-government has succeeded well enough to justify my optimism that we can improve its performance, citizen by conscientious citizen.[29] This book's raison d'être is that there is no good alternative to such an effort.

THE STRUCTURE OF EACH CHAPTER

Each chapter is designed to help the reader understand the hard issue featured there by mapping and then analyzing it. Each begins by presenting the issue's *context*—the relevant history, law, institutions, politics, and public opinion. Next, it disaggregates the issue into its main components. Beginning with key definitional and measurement questions (as in the case of poverty), it then elaborates the competing norms invoked by different groups and identifies the key factual claims and uncertainties. (Those who dominate public debates on these issues often suppress or ignore these uncertainties, either deliberately or because of their own ignorance.) Finally, each chapter discusses and assesses the main *policy proposals* on the table in that area. Be forewarned: As a self-styled "militant moderate,"[30] I am more inclined toward incremental policy changes than radical ones. This is particularly so in areas where constitutional issues may well be implicated—for example, campaign finance, religious accommodation, and affirmative action. But all five issues are sufficiently complex that, the more radical the change is, the more we can assume that unforeseen and possibly irreversible consequences will ensue.

* * *

To analyze hard issues is, well, hard work. It demands a lot from readers and will likely challenge their intuitions and assumptions about these problems. But the potential payoff is great: a deeper understanding of our complex social reality and some of our knottiest domestic policy problems. I hope that this will help my readers to become more enlightened, engaged citizens.

CHAPTER 2

POVERTY

POVERTY HAS BLIGHTED EVERY society in every era. Deuteronomy tells us: "There will always be poor people in the land. Therefore I command you to be open-handed toward your brothers and toward the poor and needy in your land."[1] Likewise, Jesus said, "For you always have the poor with you." (He immediately added "and whenever you wish you can do good to them.")[2]

Before the Industrial Revolution, almost everyone was poor by today's standards. Elites and most of the poor themselves took pervasive poverty as a simple, inevitable, and lamentable fact of social life like illness, early death, deep anxieties, and other forms of human suffering. Until then, economic growth was minimal so few could hope to escape poverty's grasp, at least in this world. Religion often provided solace along with hope for a better life in the hereafter (leading Marx to deride it as "the opium of the people"—though only after calling it "the heart of a heartless world"). The state's role was mainly to press the poor to work (often as its own cannon fodder, slaves, and taxpayers), minimize and isolate their vagrancy and violence, prevent them from threatening property, and repress threats to the powerful.[3]

Popular revolutions, the spread of democracy and suffrage, economic growth, and the gradual development of welfare states in the

West transformed poverty into a social issue, an object of meliorative public policy. In the United States, federal solicitude for the poor focused first on veterans' pensions after the Civil War, and then in the New Deal era, on the elderly, the unemployed, and needy mothers of dependent children. (Some states had already established programs directed toward the poor.) Even then, concern focused mostly on the jobless, not poor people generally.

Antipoverty policy entered a new era when President Lyndon B. Johnson launched what he called a "War on Poverty" in his 1964 State of the Union address. This campaign led to the immediate creation of an Office of Equal Opportunity, establishing community action agencies at the local level,* and instituting over time a wide variety of antipoverty programs. Such programs were adopted at all levels of government. For centuries, of course, religious and other voluntary organizations had sought to alleviate poverty at the local level. Today, even putting aside the political motives, the humane impulses that favor antipoverty programs are obvious: a moral revulsion against persistent destitution in a society as wealthy as ours; a desire to reduce the suffering, and improve the future prospects, of helpless children; and a conviction that poverty lies at the root of many of our most disturbing social problems, including family disintegration, crime, drug addiction, ill health, domestic violence, communal breakdown, and reduced social mobility.

Some fifty years—two or three generations later—tax professor Edward Kleinbard assesses where we stand despite those efforts. "The United States has the highest poverty rate, the greatest income inequality, and the greatest wealth inequality of any major developed economy in the world. Our parents' incomes play a larger role in our personal economic fortunes than is true for other peer countries."[4]

---

* Christopher Jencks, a leading scholar on poverty policy, rightly states: "The community action programs that challenged the authority of elected local officials . . . might have been a fine idea if they had been privately funded, but using federal money to pay for attacks on elected officials was a political disaster." http://www.nybooks.com/articles /archives/2015/apr/01/war-poverty-was-it-lost/. They have little anti-poverty significance today, and I shall say no more about them.

Future progress depends, among other things, on understanding the nature, magnitude, sources, and consequences of poverty and of limited mobility in America.* At the same time, synthesizing the relevant social science research, policy design, and program implementation should also deepen our appreciation of how hard it is to define poverty in a rigorous way, how complex its diagnosis remains, how resistant it has been in the face of a half-century of diverse policy approaches, but also how much progress has been made in reducing it.

I do not review either the history of poverty or the moral issues that surround it. Large literatures exist on both of these topics—especially the moral issues that have long preoccupied many religious writers, novelists, social philosophers, and other commentators.[5] Instead, I proceed on two assumptions: Alleviating poverty is an urgent social imperative, and the social science that I synthesize here provides the best basis for understanding poverty and thus the soundest foundation for remedying this ancient scourge.

This is the longest chapter in the book, as befits its importance, its complexity, and the enormous amount of social science research devoted to it. Accordingly, I hope to help the reader by identifying its major themes in advance. The measure of poverty is highly controversial, but by all accounts it has declined significantly since 1965 (and sharply in 2015). The standard of living of the poor has improved substantially, but certain subgroups—particularly jobless black men and mothers and children in female-headed households—are worse off in some important respects. Poverty has many causes—bad luck, bad choices, family breakdown, educational deficits, dysfunctional and self-reinforcing cultural patterns, social and neighborhood isolation, immigration, discrimination, mass incarceration, and economic dislocations among them—and most of those causes are also its effects, producing complex, tragic feedback loops. (One cause, immigration, can cut both ways.) Antipoverty programs vary in their ef-

---

* Outside the United States, progress in eliminating the most abject poverty has been dramatic in some areas, particularly China, but the levels of absolute deprivation remain high. Rakesh Kochhar, "A Global Middle Class Is More Promise Than Reality," *Pew Research Center*, July 8, 2015.

fectiveness, with the elderly benefiting most and being affected least by the work disincentives built into many of the programs. Remedies for poverty do exist, but they all entail difficult trade-offs that must be seriously considered.

The chapter proceeds in four parts, beginning with the context of antipoverty policy. This includes the distinction between poverty and inequality; the definitions of poverty; its measures; its incidence among certain subgroups; intergenerational mobility; and poverty trends over time. A second part analyzes its many complex causes. The third part discusses existing antipoverty programs—their nature, size, and effectiveness. The final part discusses how policy makers can best seek to reduce poverty going forward.

CONTEXT

Although the chapter focuses on poverty, I begin by briefly discussing inequality in America. Because poverty and inequality are closely correlated as a factual matter, people often use these terms interchangeably, as if they are essentially the same conditions, pose the same problems, and yield to the same approaches. In truth, however, they are distinct phenomena. Treating them as if they were the same engenders confusion and can lead to incoherent policy. The rest of the chapter, then, analyzes poverty as such.

Inequality

Rigorous historical and empirical study of inequality only became possible in the second half of the twentieth century when economists Simon Kuznets (in the United States) and Anthony Atkinson (in the UK) developed the necessary databases, analytical tools, and methodology.[6] Although researchers have had access to aggregate federal income tax data for about a century, household survey data did not become available until after 1960 and more refined data until even more recently. Today, public debate about inequality is more intense, partly spurred by a long, highly technical, even abstruse, economic analysis of inequality by Thomas Piketty, a French economist previously known only to the professional cognoscenti. Improbably, Piketty's tome became a best-selling book in the United States when an English translation was published in 2014.[7]

Social concern about inequality is widespread—more among liberals, who point to its unfairness and social corrosiveness, than among conservatives, who stress its inevitability in a competitive economic system and oppose many proposals for combating it (often because they think those policies will increase it). Today's concern reflects recent evidence that inequality has grown significantly since the 1970s. A 2015 analysis by Emmanuel Saez, a frequent Piketty collaborator, finds that pretax family market income* inequality rose during the Clinton-era (1993–2000), Bush-era (2002–7), and Obama-era (2009–14) expansions. In these three periods, Saez argues, real *average* income grew 20.6, 16.1, and 8.4 percent, respectively, yet the income of the top 1 percent (those with incomes above $423,000 in 2014) grew much more, capturing 45 percent of the total gains during the Clinton expansion, 65 percent during the Bush expansion, and 58 percent during the Obama expansion.[8] Saez claims that this spread continued to grow even in 2013–14, as real recovery from the Great Recession progressed, when average family income rose 4.8 percent (the highest annual increase since 1999). In 2014, he finds, the bottom 99 percent's income grew substantially (3.3 percent), but the top 1 percent's incomes grew even faster (10.8 percent). The spread also widened a bit further down the income distribution: The share of the top 10 percent (incomes above $121,400), driven mainly by the top 1 percent, was the highest ever except for 2012.[9] More recent analyses find that this tax data overstates inequality by not including nontaxable income received by lower-quintile groups.[10] Inequality is also much lower when measured on an after-tax basis and taking government transfers into account, which neither Saez nor the official poverty statistics do. Inequality, thus measured, has actually narrowed

---

* Saez defines family market income to include salaries and realized capital gains but not government transfers. As we shall see, these transfers are a very important component of overall income for poor families.

since 2007 even though income grew at a negligible rate until very recently.[11] And in 2015, income gains were much larger—in percentage terms—for households in the tenth percentile of income than for those in the ninetieth.[12]

Inequality (whether it is widening or not) has many causes, and economists and other social scientists are by no means agreed about their relative importance, policy remedies, and future trends.[13] Political scientists Martin Gilens and Benjamin Page emphasize what they term "economic-elite domination" and "biased pluralism" that stack the political decks against the poor.[14] For economists, the usual suspects include: a growing gap between the share of national income going to labor and capital; wage pressures from global competition; technological change; higher returns to college education and advanced skills; the growing fraction of single-parent-headed households and rising divorce levels; the wage gap between high- and low-profit employers;[15] alcohol and drug abuse; the effects of residential segregation; weaker labor unions; and more assortative mating (reversing a pattern of nonwork by the wives of high-earning men).[16] Before the 2015 figures came out, these mating changes alone accounted for an estimated 26 percent increase in household income inequality;[17] if marriage patterns remained the same as in 1960, today's inequality would be much lower.[18] The 2015 Economic Report of the President finds that if income was shared in the same proportion as in 1973, and if productivity gains and female workforce participation stayed at 1995 levels, middle-class households' mean income would have doubled in the last twenty years (up $51,000).[19]

Since the 2011 Occupy Wall Street protests, politicians and other opinion leaders have used election campaigns and mass media to make inequality reduction a higher priority.[20] A 2015 poll finds that a strong majority of Americans want the government to do more to reduce income and wealth inequality, a view that crosses income and partisan lines, but not uniformly.[21] Yet, a number of studies show that Americans, a highly competitive people, favor some level of economic inequality, reflecting economist Richard Easterlin's finding that happiness depends on being wealthier than one's reference group (and H. L. Mencken's quip defining wealth as "any income that is at least $100 more a year than the income of one's wife's sister's husband").[22] Relative mobility, after all, is a zero-sum game.[23]

Americans tend to oppose explicit redistribution, believing that better education is the answer.[24] The parties differ sharply on the priority of reducing inequality: 90 percent of Democrats, but only 36 percent of Republicans, want their presidential candidate to focus on it.[25] Compared with Europeans, Americans find given levels of inequality less objectionable, partly because we are much more likely than they are to believe that individual effort is more important than luck in causing people's economic fates.[26] Americans also disagree about how much deprivation and suffering actually exist,* a question analyzed later in the chapter.

President Obama calls inequality reduction "the defining challenge of our time."[27] Left-populist politicians like Senators Elizabeth Warren and Bernie Sanders argue that government policies have increased inequality, especially tax, regulatory, and other advantages enjoyed by wealthy business interests. They argue that policy changes could reduce or eliminate these unwarranted advantages.[28] Some conservatives also blame the government for the level of inequality. *Wall Street Journal* editorials often denounce "crony capitalism" (e.g., the Export-Import Bank and subsidies to agribusiness) and "corporate welfare" (e.g., many inefficient and poorly targeted tax breaks). Conservatives also contest some liberals' claims about inequality as well as many of their specific proposals for reducing it. Ben Bernanke, the former Federal Reserve Board chairman (and no populist), also laments current levels of inequality, but ascribes them less to public policy than to "deep structural economic reasons including globalization, technological progress, demographic trends, and institutional change in the labor market and elsewhere."[29] As Bernanke's list implies, liberals and conservatives disagree sharply about how unjust

---

* It is not clear which way this would cut. Some psychological studies suggest that smaller differences in well-being may only make the remaining ones more objectionable.

these inequalities are and how much they are needed to enhance economic efficiency.

Poverty and inequality overlap significantly but, as noted earlier, they are not the same. Poverty is a condition of deprivation that causes suffering among those who endure it (and among many of us who observe it), and it is conventionally assessed against some measure of well-being. In contrast, inequality is measured by the amount of dispersion within a relevant population with respect to income, wealth, or some other aspect of well-being. Both poverty and inequality exist in even the wealthiest societies; in this sense, both are matters of degree.

We also distinguish between inequality and inequity. In ordinary discourse, we often characterize inequalities as inequitable or unfair—and they often are, by almost all accounts. In principle, however, they are distinct ideas. Inequality is an *empirical fact* whose conventional measures are discussed below; even Piketty says that it is "not necessarily bad in itself." By contrast, inequity is not a fact but a *moral judgment* about the fairness or justness of a particular level of inequality. Almost everyone, of course, agrees that certain inequalities are unjust, but *which* ones remains a morally contested claim—although less contested where children and some other groups are concerned. In judging the fairness of any particular inequality, most people want to know which choices, behaviors, or factors contributed to it.[30] Even if we could answer such questions empirically, reasonable people would surely disagree about how to assess and weigh the normative factors. Notably, Americans view some inequalities as more acceptable than others, countenancing economic inequalities more than political ones.[31] Even so, many Americans deplore our current levels of economic inequality.

Complicating analyses of inequality is a separate, intensely empirical dispute about the effectiveness of various approaches to reducing it. Policies meant to redistribute wealth *could* end up reducing the total wealth created by society and thus available (in principle) for redistribution. Economist Arthur Okun called this "the big tradeoff" between equity and economic efficiency. He likened it to a leaky bucket used to carry wealth from the rich to the poor, with some leaks caused by incentive effects reducing productive effort by both rich and poor, and other leaks due to the administrative costs of taxing and transferring wealth from one group to another.[32] Whether these leaks could be offset through well-crafted antipoverty policies is a hard question that I address at length later in the chapter.

Not surprisingly, analysts disagree about the magnitude and location of these incentive effects and tax-and-transfer costs, about the factors that create them, about how various policies aimed at reducing inequality would actually work, and even about how such policies have worked in the past! After all, an extraordinarily complex mélange of factors affects economic outcomes, so even the most careful analysis cannot isolate each factor's causal contribution to inequality. Another factor contributing to this causal uncertainty is "rational expectations": one's propensity to anticipate policy changes (most of which will take effect in the future) and adjust one's own behavior to reduce the new policy's costs to oneself (e.g., estate taxes on the wealthy, which they can minimize or avoid through astute tax and estate planning).

The key point is that efforts to reduce inequality to help the "99 percent" might possibly make them worse off, depending on these incentive and cost effects.[33] Another hard policy choice is whether to reduce inequality by raising the incomes of the worst off, lowering those of the well-off, or both.[34] A recent simulation by Brookings tax experts found that raising the top individual tax bracket to 50 percent and redistributing all the proceeds to the bottom 20 percent of households would reduce the Gini coefficient (discussed just below) by only a trivial amount—*even assuming no behavioral changes.*[35] I explore some of these issues later in the chapter.

Different dimensions of inequality produce different results. For example, consumption is more equally distributed than income, and income is more equally distributed than wealth (net worth). The incomes of families are also more equal than those of individuals, and pretax market income is more unequal than post-tax income. Including fringe benefits in income makes it more unequal, while including means-tested noncash benefits to the poor makes incomes more equal.[36] For inequality trends over time, use of particular inflation adjustments and other methodological choices will affect the conclusions.[37] Definitional and methodological choices also affect conclusions concerning the trajectory of the "middle class" or any other class. This is evident in varying interpretations of Census Bureau and Pew data released in December 2015.[38]

Analyses of economic inequality usually focus on the "Gini coefficient," which measures the dispersion of incomes across society; it ranges from zero (all people have equal income) to 1 (all national income goes to only one person).* By this measure (there are several others),[39] the United States is an outlier among the world's rich nations. Among the thirty-four relatively wealthy nations in the Organization for Economic Cooperation and Development (OECD), the United States has the second highest Gini coefficient (the highest is Mexico; in some comparisons, Chile is also higher than the United States).[40] When other non-Gini measures mentioned in the previous paragraph are used instead, inequality in the United States is somewhat lower and less of an outlier—but it is still large in comparative terms.

These comparisons, however, mask a very significant, underappreciated fact about inequality: It has been increasing in almost all OECD countries, including many like Sweden and Norway with strong traditions and policies of social democracy. Today, the average income of the richest 10 percent in OECD countries is almost ten times that of the poorest 10 percent, up from seven times in the 1980s.[41] In the United States, this ratio rose from 15.1 in 2007 to 18.8 in 2014.[42] These OECD trends strongly suggest that many causes of inequality are endemic to post-industrial economies. (Of course, some of them, like the United States, are more unequal than others.) The international differences that remain largely reflect differences in our public policy preferences.

---

* In the United States and most if not all other societies, wealth is distributed much more unequally than income, while consumption is distributed much less unequally.

Philosopher Harry Frankfurt recently published a provocative, clarifying essay on the moral status of economic inequality and its relationship to poverty.[43] He distinguishes sharply between *equality* (i.e., whether everyone has the goods that others have, especially money that can be converted to so many other things of value) and *sufficiency* (i.e., whether they have enough to lead a life that will reasonably satisfy them). He personally favors more equality, believing that more equality will promote various social and political ideals, but he insists that economic equality, unlike sufficiency, is not a *moral* imperative (i.e., a goal whose goodness is intrinsic, not derived from other things). Morally, he maintains, what matters most is whether we have good lives, not how our lives compare with others' lives.[44] Morality is not treating people equally but treating them with *respect*, which means impartially, not arbitrarily: seeking "outcomes matched specifically to the particularities of the individual," whether or not those outcomes seem equal.[45] I might question Frankfurt's dismissal of comparison in moral analysis, but his goal of sufficiency seems to be the proper goal of antipoverty efforts. If such efforts succeed, equality would probably increase, yet it is sufficiency—assuring that all of us have enough to lead reasonably satisfying lives—that should be the main measure of our success.

Poverty

Definitions. Poverty, as noted earlier, is best understood as a state of deprivation or suffering. It can take many forms: hunger, homelessness, inadequate medical care, emotional stress, social isolation, limited opportunities, the "digital divide," ignorance, stigma, spiritual emptiness, and other life-limiting conditions. For perfectly understandable reasons, however, officials and the public have sought a specific, numerical definition of poverty that could be calculated each year to determine how poverty is trending. After clarifying these definitions, the rest of the chapter will use the terms "poverty" and the "poor" more loosely not only to include those who meet such definitions but also to include the broader population toward whom antipoverty programs are typically directed. That the terms are often used in ill-defined and even circular ways is no accident. Indeed, such usage—sometimes careless but often self-conscious and tactical—constitutes an important feature of the poverty debate.

The federal government's poverty definition was originally devised in 1963–65 by Mollie Orshansky, a Social Security Administration statistician-economist.[46] Liberal and conservative analysts criticized it from the very beginning on many grounds, and no one today defends its accuracy.[47] (Partly to meet these criticisms, and following a National Academy of Sciences report on the subject, the Census Bureau in 2011 introduced a "Supplemental Poverty Measure" (SPM), which among other changes incorporated new family composition patterns and deducted out-of-pocket medical and child care expenses from family income. Leading poverty experts, however, still find it inadequate in many ways.)[48] Reviewing these critiques brings some of poverty's measurement difficulties into clear view.

A number of important social changes since 1965 seriously distort—and vastly overstate—the official overall poverty rate, which in 2015 had declined to 13.5 percent. (The SPM rate was 14.3 percent.)[49] A refined understanding of the poverty rate requires a number of adjustments to the official one. Here are some of the most important:

- Noncash government benefits are excluded. Including food and housing benefits would reduce the poverty rate by about 3 percentage points. But even those adjustments do not take account of the valuable services that Medicare and Medicaid provide to the poor, services that they would otherwise under-consume.
- The refundable Earned Income Tax Credit (EITC) is excluded; including it would lower the poverty rate by another 3 percent.
- The standard consumer price index (CPI) to compare poverty rates over time overstates the cost of maintaining a constant standard of living; correcting for this would have reduced the 2013 poverty rate by 3.7 percent. These first three adjustments alone would have yielded a poverty rate of 4.8 percent, far below the official rate. (That rate declined further in 2015.)

- The official rate treats cohabiting couples (an estimated 11 percent of opposite-sex couples living together) differently than married ones; treating them the same would lower the poverty rate even more.[50]
- The official rate does not consider either regional differences in the cost of living or the episodic nature of much poverty during a given year.
- Today's households are smaller, reducing their living costs correspondingly relative to earlier periods.[51] Some measures take this into account, some do not.[52]
- Many poor people who work at least part of the year can tap into other "work-based safety net" benefits such as unemployment insurance and the refundable child tax credit.[53]

When the Congressional Budget Office (CBO) made some (not all) of these adjustments, it found that real median household income actually increased between 1980 and 2010—and not by 15 percent (as in the non-adjusted calculation) but by 53 percent.[54] (Median income increased significantly in 2015.) If consumption of new products and improved goods and services during that period is included, the increase would be about 2.5 percent a year over the thirty years—a substantial gain.[55]

The official poverty rate is also exaggerated because of vast under-reporting of income and government transfers, and over-reliance on Current Population Survey data. An important 2015 study compared Census Bureau data based on responses to its CPS with records of what was *actually disbursed* to those same respondents. CPS data, it found, sharply understates poor households' income: "the poverty reducing effect of all programs together is nearly doubled while the effect of housing assistance is tripled," and "the share of single mothers falling through the safety net [falls] by one-half or more."[56] Another leading study on under-reporting finds that "as many as half of the dollars received through Food Stamps, Temporary Assistance for Needy Families (TANF) and Workers' Compensation [a state program] has not been reported in the [CPS]. High rates of understatement are found for many other government transfer programs and in datasets such as the Survey of Income and Program Participation (SIPP) and the Panel Study of Income Dynamics (PSID). These datasets are among our most important for analyzing incomes and their distribution as well as transfer receipt. Thus, this understatement has major implications for our understanding of the economic circumstances of the population and the working of government programs."[57] Finally, studies of low-income urban communities find that residents receive substantial off-the-books income.[58]

Experts on poverty measures agree that the official poverty measure casts little useful light on either current poverty or poverty trends. Strong arguments exist for focusing not on income levels but instead on *consumption* levels, which more closely reflect both permanent income and well-being. Bruce Meyer and James Sullivan show that it better identifies those who are less likely to have health insurance and have less education, smaller and cheaper cars, and fewer household appliances and amenities; that it can overcome four biases in the CPI (not factoring in big-box store discounts, substitutions of cheaper products, product quality improvements, and new products); and that mainly for these reasons, a consumption measure substantially reduces the poverty rate, especially for single-parent families and the elderly.[59]

Indeed, studies show large *consumption* gains by the poor. "Low-income and poverty-level households today," demographer Nicholas Eberstadt finds, "are better-fed and less threatened by undernourishment than they were a generation ago. Their homes are larger, better equipped with plumbing and kitchen facilities, and more capaciously furnished with modern conveniences. They are more likely to own a car (or a light truck, or another type of motor vehicle) now than thirty years earlier. By most every indicator apart from obesity, their health care status is considerably more favorable today than at the start of the War on Poverty. Their utilization of health and medical services has steadily increased over recent decades."[60] Greatly improved living conditions are also reflected in declining crime rates in many low-income neighborhoods.[61] (In 2015, however, homicides in the fifty largest cities rose by almost 70 percent, despite a substantial decline in gun violence.)[62] In 2014, the federal government reported that homelessness (which is likely undercounted) had declined by almost a third since 2007.[63]

Most Americans do not consider these conditions to constitute abject poverty, particularly if informed that the typical poor American has considerably more living space than the average European does.[64] Consumption-wise, then, today's poverty problem is not so much absolute material deprivation (Frankfurt's "sufficiency") as it is *relative* poverty—relative both to other Americans and to people in other wealthy countries. Note, however, that while relative poverty may seem an appropriate focus, it means that the poverty rate rises as society becomes wealthier, a logic that may seem counterintuitive.

Subgroups. More fine-grained analyses of subgroups and poverty dynamics provide additional insight into the nature of poverty in America. I first compare child and elder poverty, and then discuss the special case of immigrants. Another subgroup, households with children headed by single women, is central to so many aspects of American poverty that I analyze it extensively below, primarily in connection with family breakdown.

The federal government spends vastly more per capita on the elderly than on children, who are supported mainly by state and local programs: "Whereas aged Americans receive $5.72 in federal spending for each $1.00 received by someone under 19, those under 19 receive $10.11 in state and local spending for each $1.00 received by someone who is 65 or older. To be sure, total federal spending is considerably greater than that of state and local governments, but the imbalance of public spending on the young and the old is less extreme than federal budget statistics suggest."[65] Although the official poverty rates for children and the elderly in 2015 were 19.7 and 8.8 percent, respectively, those rates do not include government transfers and tax credits. Common adjustments to the official rates lowered child and elder poverty to about 15 and 2.6 percent, respectively.[66] (In 2015, these rates presumably declined even further.) Despite seniors' inflation-indexed Social Security benefits, those with low earnings histories, especially women, remain poor due to lower benefits.

Many immigrants who are poor have nevertheless achieved high, sometimes dramatic, income mobility: they left much poorer countries and earned much more here than they did there. Our poverty index defines them as poor by our standards* even if their income here would make them solidly middle-class in their home countries— presumably their main socioeconomic reference point. Writing almost twenty years ago, economist Robert Lerman explained that our poverty statistics obscure this important fact, analogizing to Germany's experience after its 1989 reunification when it in effect absorbed a large low-wage country: "The U.S. did not absorb a country equal to 20% of its initial population, but the high levels of immigration to the U.S. in the 1980s and 1990s raise a similar compositional issue. Immigrants who settled in the U.S. since 1980 made up about 7% of the 1996 U.S. work force and over 17% of the work force without a high school degree. Moreover, over 90% of these recent immigrants came from low wage countries."[67]

Intergenerational Mobility. The most damning fact about American society today is the high correlation between the social status of parents and that of their grown children. The likelihood that children born into poverty will escape it, so celebrated in our self-congratulatory Horatio Alger mythology, is not particularly high, casting doubt on our ability to fulfill the American dream. Intergenerational mobility is among the most crucial of all social indicators— more so than inequality and more so than national poverty measures at any given point in time.

As the earlier quotation from Edward Kleinbard indicates, the United States has lagged badly on this measure. By the most common measure of income mobility (the extent to which a father's income can predict his son's income) or indeed by any measure, we are less mobile

---

* They also increase the number of poor people to the extent that they depress wages for low-income American workers. As discussed in chapter 3 labor economists intensely debate this question.

than most other OECD countries. One study finds that 40 percent of grown sons born here to fathers in the lowest quintile remain in the lowest quintile. (Christopher Jencks, a leading poverty researcher whose work is discussed below, notes that even with perfect mobility, the figure would be 20 percent; the Scandinavian figure is about 30 percent.)[68] This low mobility is consistent across all income groups, applies to education level, and has changed little in the last fifty years, a period when our economy vastly expanded. As we shall see, research can readily identify which factors *correlate* with poverty, but determining causality is much harder.

Trends. The difference between the poverty rate in 1965 and today matters not just to the poor. It also is central to the debate over what the War on Poverty actually accomplished. As the previous discussion showed, this question remains controversial for at least three reasons.

- Good faith disagreements exist among poverty experts about how poverty should be measured, and the different methods produce quite different results. What is clear, however, is that the poverty rate has declined substantially during this period according to the official measure (19.5 percent in 1964 and 13.5 percent in 2015, a decline of about 30 percent).[69] As we have seen, the decline in poverty is much more impressive if one includes government transfers and measures it according to actual standard of living.
- Despite this progress in reducing poverty (however measured), those households with children who live in *extreme* poverty (defined as less than $2 a day for at least one month per year) were arguably worse off in 2012 than they were in 1996 when TANF was enacted.[70] However, a 2016 analysis of child poverty rejects this claim[71] and the USDA announced a significant decline in food insecurity in 2015, the first such decline since 2010.[72] Presumably, the 2015 decline in the child poverty rate further reduced extreme child poverty.
- Determining precisely which factors *caused* how much decline in

poverty is even more controversial than how to measure it. The combined effects of immense global changes—many poverty-reducing, some not—probably dwarf the causal significance of particular U.S. government policies, yet the sheer size and diffusion of global effects obscure the relative contributions of each. The same multiplicity of factors makes the causal effects of domestic policy changes hard to determine. That said, federal (and some state) transfer and tax credit programs clearly helped to reduce poverty significantly.[73] I discuss this further below. Three groups have benefited most. The elderly (particularly "young" ones under the age of seventy-five) have enjoyed substantial increases in Social Security payments while also benefiting from traditional defined-benefit pensions and real estate and stock market gains.[74] Working-poor parents' income has been boosted by the EITC. And food stamps and child care, energy, and housing subsidies have also lifted many recipients out of poverty. (Medicare, Medicaid, and other low-income health-care benefits clearly enable them to lower their out-of-pocket expenses, but quantifying this cost avoidance is difficult.)

• Assessing the second-order effects of antipoverty policies—how they affected recipients' work effort, independence, family life, and other behaviors—is as difficult as it is important. Virtually all analysts acknowledge the possibility that these perverse incentives can blunt poverty-reduction efforts to some degree. Studies of programs like unemployment compensation and disability insurance have detected such effects.[75] The size of work disincentives is debatable but they clearly contribute to both programs' looming insolvencies.[76]

In the following analysis of poverty's causes, the discussion and data will often focus on blacks. (I explain elsewhere why I say "blacks" instead of "African Americans"; any such term is unsatisfactory in some respects).[77] The focus on blacks is emphatically *not* because they account for most of America's poor. In fact, whites constitute the largest group of poor people (about 19 million). Blacks do not have the highest poverty rate (the rate for Native Americans and Alaskan natives, 27 percent, is slightly higher). Nor are most blacks poor (indeed, more than 75 percent of them were *not* poor in 2015). And black African immigrants do well here; 35 percent of those aged twenty-five and older had a college degree or better in 2013; 15 percent have advanced degrees;[78] and their income is sharply higher than for U.S.-born blacks.[79] Blacks have reduced the education gap more than have poor people generally, leaving the gap between poor and rich children nearly double that between black and white children.[80] But this is a mixed blessing, as it also reflects the growing plight of working-class (and nonworking) whites: worsening marital stability, household structure, substance abuse, morbidity and mortality, children's school readiness, incarceration rates, and employability.[81] Their decline means that while the racial gap in these measures remains deeply troubling, the class gap is even wider. Although the categories significantly overlap, of course, *class is now a stronger predictor of disadvantage in many important areas of social well-being.*[82] *An even stronger predictor is being born to an unmarried mother and an absent father.*

Blacks' prominence in poverty analysis, then, has many causes. Slavery, Jim Crow, racial hatred, and other forms of oppression—what Gunnar Myrdal famously called "An American Dilemma"[83]—have isolated them, impeding their climb out of poverty more than probably any others. Also, their share of the poverty population (25.8 percent according to the 2007–2011 Census) is more disproportionate than that of any other large, well-defined group.[84] (Native Americans are a small group, with much higher out-marriage rates. Hispanics, as explained in chapter 5, are a far less discrete, identifiable group.) Blacks are the largest single component of the long-term poor and of long-term welfare dependents.[85] That poverty tends to be equated with blacks may also reflect their vastly disproportionate presence in public housing, the iconic image of poverty. Indeed, blacks constitute 48 percent of public housing residents nationwide, almost quadruple their share of the population. In many large cities, the percentage exceeds 90 percent.[86] They also commit a vastly disproportionate share of violent crimes, disproportionately against other poor blacks. For all these reasons, any analysis of poverty and of possible remedies for it must place blacks at the center, while recognizing that other groups, including whites, are well-represented there.

POVERTY'S CAUSES

This too is an ancient question and one on which strong disagreement persists, even in recent decades when a great deal of social science research has been devoted to answering it. Indeed, the more we have learned about poverty, the more analysts seem to disagree about the mix of poverty's causes, the effectiveness of various antipoverty policies, or both. One might call some of this disagreement political or ideological in the sense that one can usually predict how people with particular worldviews will explain poverty's causes and cures.

Liberals tend to emphasize the social structures, inequalities, and discrimination that cause and entrench poverty, as well as the bad luck (discussed below), job loss, or divorce that casts many people into poverty and helps keep them there. Conservatives tend to assign more explanatory weight to moral, cultural, and familial decay—"the breakdown of social order and authority," in poverty scholar Lawrence Mead's phrase—and to the perverse incentives created by many existing policies and institutions. Each side denounces special interests but focuses on different ones: Liberals blame corporate rapacity and influence over government, while conservatives blame labor unions, self-aggrandizing government bureaucracies, and individuals' bad choices. Restrictionists like the Federation for American Immigration Reform blame undocumented and even some legal immigrants. These and other conflicting explanations are hardly surprising: The data are often ambiguous about causes, and people exhibit a strong propensity to interpret it in ways that render it consistent with their preexisting social and moral frames, a process of cultural cognition discussed earlier.[87]

Some research has found IQ and other standardized test differences among subpopulations due to some combination of genetic and environmental causes which together could help account for poverty. These findings remain highly speculative as to both the relative contributions of each cause and the quality and significance of the underlying data. These questions, however, are anything but academic: They arouse the deepest concerns about the potentially toxic effects of such findings on our social, moral, and political arrangements. Indeed, those who have dared to present them are invariably pilloried as racists.[88] Researchers today seem to believe that both environment and genes probably play some role in cognitive differences and thus in poverty, but there agreement ends.[89]

The main *proximate* cause of poverty is under- and unemployment by working-age, non-disabled family heads. (This presumes the same hourly wage they now earn or could earn given their work-relevant credentials.) Poor families with children work far fewer hours (less than half as many) than non-poor families with children. If the poor (or their partners) worked full-time, holding all else constant, the poverty rate would drop about 40 percent. [90]

In the rest of this section, I present nine factors— we might call them more ultimate causes—whose effects on work effort and thus on poverty are fairly well substantiated by social science studies. They are (1) bad luck; (2) family and community breakdown; (3) disappearing jobs; (4) educational deficits; (5) isolation; (6) discrimination; (7) bad choices; (8) incarceration; and (9) the culture of poverty. Tragically— for it makes finding effective remedies much more difficult—they overlap considerably, so I discuss them in no particular order. The discussion contains a blizzard of empirical findings and statistics drawn from published studies, yet some key concepts cannot be defined with precision and the evidence is often weak, conflicting, dated, and context-specific. Interactions among key variables are often difficult to identify and interpret, and we cannot rule out the possibility that another, unidentified variable is doing some of the causal work. Indeed, even causality's *direction* is often uncertain: We cannot always tell what is cause, what is effect, and under what conditions each is true. (One example is the relation between family breakdown and poverty, discussed just below. Another is poor people's legal problems.[91]) Randomized controlled trials (RCTs), common in hard science research, are usually (not always, as we shall see) impossible to design and conduct by social scientists, but they are considered the gold standard.

These preliminary considerations help explain why poverty's causes are complex—but they also suggest why much of what we think we know may be wrong. Those with political or ideological axes to grind contest these causes, but so do leading social scientists who use rigorous, objective data to study poverty. Their disagreements should chasten any claims of certainty about poverty's causes.[92]

Bad Luck. Some people are much luckier than others. It is not simply that some of us are born with better parents, greater intelligence, happier dispositions, stronger constitutions, and in a favorable birth order.[93] It is also that what happens to us later on may have little or nothing to do with those initial endowments or with the kinds of bad choices that I shall discuss below. Impoverishing misfortunes can come in many forms—debilitating illness, depression, job loss, uninsured disaster—and can overtake anyone at almost any moment, rendering them poor for a considerable period of time. Divorce often impoverishes women. A 1996 study of such women found that in the first year after divorce, the average wife's standard of living decreased by 27 percent; the husband's *improved* by 10 percent![94] Even if these differences have narrowed since then, poverty can still be just a bad divorce (or divorce lawyer) away, especially for women.*

Family and Community Breakdown. As the family is the essential core of any society, the steady decline of two-parent family households in the United States is probably the single most important social trend of the last half-century. In 1965, Daniel Patrick Moynihan famously predicted that this decline would be most precipitous in black families,[95] but even he under-estimated the trend: 72 percent

---

* On the other side, economist Robert Frank explains that recognizing one's own good luck seems to increase one's generosity to others with less of it. http://www.theatlantic .com/magazine/archive/2016/05/why-luck-matters-more-than-you-might-think /476394/

of black babies are now born out of wedlock, *triple* the 1965 rate. Regardless of race, children with no father at home are now four to five times more likely to be poor than children of married parents.[96] (Many of their unmarried mothers do have live-in partners for certain periods.) Children in female-headed households account for well over half of all poor children.[97] Indeed, Harvard's Equality of Opportunity Project finds that the single best predictor of low upward mobility in an area is the fraction of children with single parents.[98]

In a tragic convergence, moreover, family decline now also blights the white working class (a hard-to-define group, often described as blue-collar workers). The rates of divorce, non-marital births,[99] and single-parent households among working-class whites now are equal to or exceed those of black families five decades ago. For instance, the percentage of white children living with a single parent in 2014 was 25 percent—greater than the 22 percent of black children in the same predicament in 1960.[100] And, contrary to conventional wisdom, family breakdown is worse in some red, more religiously observant states, particularly in the South, than in many blue, relatively secular ones.[101] (The correlation is muddy, with some striking exceptions and uncertain causal patterns.)[102] Strikingly, this weakening of families has coincided with enormous economic growth and much greater antipoverty spending at all governmental levels. Some other wealthy societies (e.g., Sweden, Switzerland) also have high divorce rates,[103] but the effect on poverty there is less extreme, perhaps because of more generous child subsidies.

Fortunately, the poverty-related news isn't *all* bad. As noted earlier, the poverty rate declined sharply in 2015 among all demographic groups. Teenage pregnancy has declined by more than 50 percent since 1991, including in 2015. High school completion is up, with the black-white gap closing and stabilizing over the last twenty-five years at around 85 percent. The uptick in divorce rates seems to have stabilized, albeit at a high level. Crime has dropped in low-income communities as well as wealthier ones. The crime rate in 2015 was about half of what it was in 1991, with violent crime falling by 51 percent and property crime by 43 percent.

A related but distinct aspect of family and community breakdown is the phenomenon sometimes referred to as "disappearing black men." (Before discussing this problem, it is worth nothing that most African American men are not poor, out of work, destined to spend time in prison, or unmarriageable.)[104] A *New York Times* analysis published in April 2015 found that "more than one out of every six black men who should be between 25 and 54 years old has disappeared from daily life"; incarceration and early deaths overwhelmingly cause this gap. Higher incarceration rates account for almost 600,000 of the 1.5 million missing black men from ages 25 to 54 (demographically the prime-age years)—almost 1 in 12 black men compared with 1 in 60 nonblack men in that age group. But as we shall see, these disappearances began well before the big rise in incarceration rates. The other main cause of the disappearance is higher mortality. The Census counts about 900,000 fewer working-age black men than black women. Homicide, the leading cause of death for young black men, plays a large role, but men in this group also die more often from heart disease, respiratory disease, and accidents than other demographic groups do, including black women. There are only eighty-three non-jailed black men for every one hundred black women in this age group. (For whites, the comparable number is ninety-nine non-jailed men for every one hundred women.)[105]

Such "disappearances" and demographic disparities distort social dynamics in these communities, entrenching emotional as well as economic poverty. Orlando Patterson, a leading scholar of black Americans, finds these patterns rooted in the culture of slavery, which severely deformed male behavior, relationships between men and women, and thus those between parents. Writing almost twenty years ago, Patterson noted that "Afro-American men are not only far behind their Euro-American counterparts but also significantly worse off than Afro-American women" with respect to life expectancy, suicide rates, crime, and education and skill levels, including in the professions and hard sciences.[106] (Black women, however, suffer a particularly appalling disadvantage: Their maternal mortality rate is more than *triple* the rate for whites and Hispanics, probably due to worse health conditions and worse care.)[107]

These disparities corrode family relations in many ways. Black men, who are less likely to marry in the first place, experience more divorce and separation, which in turn harms their children in many ways, including future economic mobility.[108] And when black men's marriages dissolve, they are also far less likely to remarry. In fact, black women typically spend only 22 percent of their lives being married; white women are married about twice as long.[109] Andrew Cherlin, a prominent sociologist of marriage, describes it as "just a temporary stage of life for blacks, preceded by a lengthening period of singlehood and followed by a long period of living without a spouse." Many unmarried mothers cohabit with men,[110] but these relationships, Cherlin shows, tend to be relatively short.[111] Black couples are far more likely than other groups to have very different educational attainments—another potential source of marital discord—and this mismatch has even worsened over time with the increase in black college graduates. Indeed, 45 percent of black women with a college degree had a current sexual partner whose education amounted to a high school diploma or less. (Black men with college degrees also had less well-educated partners.)[112] Given black women's severely constrained choices, then, we should not be surprised to learn that those with advanced degrees are about as likely to be single mothers as are white women with high school diplomas.[113] (Although the definition of "marriageable men" has changed due to women's growing economic independence, black women still face the greatest shortage of such men.)[114]

Patterson shows that educated, prosperous black men are no more likely to marry than their poorer counterparts; indeed, they are *less* likely than poor blacks to have ever married.[115] (But foreign-born blacks are different; 52 percent are married, compared with only 28 percent for U.S.-born blacks.)[116] Contributing to this reluctance to marry, Patterson finds, are very different expectations about marriage, fidelity, sexual morality, and sexual practices between black men and women. For example, 44 percent of black husbands say they have been unfaithful to their wives, far higher than the rates for white and Latino men and for all groups of women. Black families experience much higher levels of child neglect and abuse than other families, and the quality of conjugal relationships is worse in other ways.* Nor are these dysfunctional family and cultural patterns outliers: According to Patterson's estimates, about 35 percent of blacks experience them.

This distorted marital bargain encourages the abandonment of wives, sexual partners, and children. Not surprisingly, the effects on children are devastating. The Fragile Families and Child Wellbeing Study, a decades-long research project run by Princeton University and Columbia University, studies five thousand children born to unmarried parents in large U.S. cities between 1998 and 2000. Although most unmarried fathers express good intentions at and shortly after the time of birth, only 35 percent of these couples are still together five years later and less than half of these are married. Fathers' involvement with the children declines over time; by age five, only half the fathers have seen their child in the previous month. By age five, 30 percent of the children have had two or more "father figures" in their home.[117] Growing up in such chaotic family settings is bound to affect the school performance of many of these children. This may help to explain why, after controlling for the usual socioeconomic variables, Harvard economist Roland Fryer found that a black-white gap in performance, non-existent in kindergarten, appears by the third grade, when blacks are 20 percent less likely than white children to do multiplication and other standard functions. He has also confirmed the importance of peer group ("acting white") effects: The popularity of black and Hispanic pupils drops as their GPAs rise; for whites, it is the opposite.[118]

All of these factors—economic and physical "disappearances" of black men, low marriage rates, family and custodial chaos—contribute to the persistence of disproportionate black child poverty, even as

---

* For law professor Robin Lenhardt, the dire conditions of black subordination deprived marriage of the dignitary value that white America—and the Supreme Court, most recently in its *Obergefell* decision upholding same-sex marriage—celebrates, and help explain why blacks are the least-married group in America. For blacks, she argues, nonmarriage is more dignity-enhancing and should be supported by social policy. Lenhardt, "Race, Dignity, and the Right to Marry," 84 *Fordham Law Review* 53 (2015).

a recovering economy lowers child poverty rates. Among female-headed families generally, the child poverty rate was 45.8 percent in 2013 compared with 55.4 percent in 1991, before welfare reform.[119] A Pew analysis of Census data finds that while the child poverty rate for other ethnic groups has declined since 2010, the rate for black children has remained high and disproportionate at 38 percent. Indeed, the number of them in poverty (4.2 million in 2013) may now be larger than for white children—even though there are three times as many white children as black children.[120] Robert Rector of the Heritage Foundation, among others, has probed how marriage affects child poverty, especially among blacks. Analyzing how the child poverty level would have changed if marriage rates among parents had simply continued at the 1960s rates, Rector pairs single mothers with the single men of similar age, race, and education whom they might have married (but also might have divorced at some point). Had they done so, he finds, child poverty in these hypothetical families would have plummeted 82 percent, from 37.1 percent to 6.8 percent. Since single mothers tend to be less educated than married ones, he controls for their education level and finds that marriage would still lower the poverty rate 75 percent—and even more for black children. (Births to teens are not a large part of this problem: Only 7.7 percent of unmarried mothers are younger than age 18.)[121]

Most of the other drivers of poverty that I shall discuss here correlate strongly with, and are likely caused by, children growing up in single-parent, fatherless homes, and the correlation is larger here than in most other countries.[122] Indeed, Raj Chetty's research on locational factors, discussed below, confirms other studies' findings: Growing up in such families is the single best predictor of later poverty.[123]

Disappearing Jobs. Jobs, particularly full-time ones, are the single most important route out of poverty. Only 2.9 percent of full-time workers were poor in 2014, compared with 14.3 percent working part-time, and 24.2 percent of those who did not work at all during the year.[124] Yet even with a very low unemployment rate (5.1 percent in September 2015), the labor force participation rate in the United States, at 62.4 percent, was the lowest in almost forty years. Our aging demographics can explain only some of this non-work. In 2000 and 2007, years when the unemployment rate was also this low, prime working-age people were more likely to work. Wage growth has also been sluggish.[125] Even in a tight labor market, it seems harder for poorly educated people to find steady work and family-sustaining wages.

The sociologist William Julius Wilson is a leading proponent of the idea that social ills and unemployment among the poor (especially blacks) is the result of "deindustrialization"—the disappearance of traditionally well-paid, often unionized blue-collar manufacturing jobs caused by permanent structural changes in the economy since the 1970s. Indeed, Wilson suggests that the disappearance of such jobs and the "disappearance" of so many black men from family and community life and into prisons are intimately connected. Particularly affected were rust belt cities. Long-term unemployment has increased since the 1970s: In 1979, 8.6 percent of the unemployed had been out of work for more than six months; in August 2015, this figure was 26.1 percent despite a much larger economy.[126]

In Wilson's book, *The Declining Significance of Race: Blacks and Changing American Institutions*, and in more recent work,[127] he finds that the main reason for joblessness is not racial discrimination (although it still exists) but the mismatch between employers' needs for workers with skills (now including teamwork, flexibility, and other social skills that computers lack)[128] and proximity (low-income workers now live even farther from metropolitan-area jobs than in the past).[129]

Wilson's diagnosis, however, is challenged (or augmented) from several directions. Some analysts emphasize structural social practices—family wealth, social and neighborhood networks, and institutional selection—that "lock in white advantage" even without racial bias.[130] Law professor Joseph Fishkin finds the greatest barriers to equal opportunity ("bottlenecks") in assumed but discredited notions of merit, talent, luck, and human development—notions he claims compound one another, entrenching and institutionalizing existing advantages of the more privileged.[131] Decades ago, sociologist Roger Waldinger pointed out that although many low-skill and unionized jobs have indeed disappeared, many more (non-unionized) jobs have been created, noting that black immigrants and other minorities have still managed to find work, with those who can't find work presumably return home for not working.[132] As discussed later in the chapter, a surprisingly small percentage of working-age unemployed men cite lack of jobs as the reason. Immigrants' higher employment might reflect greater docility, wariness of unions, acceptance of poor work conditions, or better social networks (discussed below). But it could also reflect deeper cultural differences. Indeed, sociologists find that fellow workers including immigrant blacks also criticize many U.S.-born blacks for their job habits.[133]

Patterson insists that the community and cultural breakdown and behavioral pathologies discussed above—the lack of a stable, co-parenting family environment for children—explain black male workers' marginality better than Wilson's factors.[134] As we saw, many low-skill mothers who were on welfare before TANF pushed (and the EITC helped pull) them into the workforce have found jobs even through multiple recessions.[135] Gender also complicates the unemployment analysis: Growing up poor predicts adult joblessness more for men than for women.[136] Finally, Mead argues that the decline in well-paid jobs for the low-skilled matters less than their lack of self-discipline, which impedes their getting and holding the available low-paid jobs, and explains employers' doubts about hiring them.[137]

Educational Deficits. Years of formal education and skills training ("human capital") strongly predict wealth and income. In 2014, almost 30 percent of people aged 25 and older without a high school degree, but only 10 percent of those with some college but no degree, were poor.[138] Although high school graduation rates have risen, reaching a record 81 percent in 2013,* more than a third of those

---

* This increased high school completion rate may help to explain why the National Assessment of Educational Progress, the leading measure of student performance, has

graduates do not get further education.[139] Many of them remain poor, confirming that today's economy demands more education and training to lift people out of poverty, that schools' standards have fallen, or both.

The average wage premium for having a college degree rather than only a high school degree is huge—74 percent and slowly rising, nearly the highest in the OECD. Yet educational mobility in the United States is low: Only 30 percent of Americans today have achieved more education than their parents did, one of the OECD's lowest levels. (This low educational mobility between generations, moreover, sharply reverses past trends when the United States led the world in graduation rates and mobility.)[140] Moreover, global competition and technological advance increasingly require job competencies that neither high schools nor most college programs provide. Since 2010, the ManPower Group's annual survey of hiring managers has found that the hardest segment of the workforce to fill is not web developers, engineers, or nurses, but rather skilled trade workers such as electricians and machinists.[141] On both the national and state levels, today's skilled trade workers are typically 45 years of age or older, which suggests an even larger impending skills gap as baby boomers retire.[142] Even if business owners' confidence in the economy strengthens, their inability to locate qualified candidates may leave many good jobs unfulfilled.[143] Much of the public blames these educational deficits on inadequate schools, but *the deficits exist before U.S. children even begin school*. International comparisons support the view that poverty is the main factor[144]—although defining and then controlling for poverty makes such comparisons difficult.

Isolation. Poor people are isolated in a number of ways that can hold them in poverty.* The digital divide deprives them of information and connections of all sorts.[145] A related but even more important form

---

remained fairly flat in recent years, as many relatively marginal students remain in school longer and take the tests.

* High-income Americans are also isolated from the mainstream culture, according to Charles Murray's "bubble quiz." http://www.aei.org/publication/lessons-from-the

of isolation is geographic: They tend to live in areas of low economic growth, modest wage levels, and high unemployment. (As one expert puts it, "those with get up and go have already gotten up and gone.") Recent research by economists led by Raj Chetty has confirmed what an earlier experiment, Moving to Opportunity (MTO), had seemed to deny—that the quality of one's neighborhood (controlling for other factors) independently and significantly affects one's economic prospects. The MTO study had found that lower-class families given vouchers enabling them to move to better neighborhoods did no better in most respects (including employment) and in some ways did worse after the move (particularly young men). But when Chetty's group controlled for the age at which they moved to the new neighborhoods, and hence the amount of time they had lived there and gained its advantages, the results were much more encouraging—although they took many years to materialize. As one commentator put it, "the net present value of the extra earnings that will eventually accrue to a child who moved at age 8 is $99,000, meaning that for a family with two children, the program yields $198,000 in extra earnings."[146] Reinforcing and extending this "neighborhood matters a lot" finding is another study by the group that tracked five million movers over seventeen years. It showed that the earlier a family moved to a better neighborhood, the better the children's long-term outcome (up to age twenty-three).[147]* Conversely, researchers also find that the

-bubble-quiz-1/?utm_source=paramount&utm_medium=email&utm_content=AEITO DAY&utm_campaign=040516

* Less encouraging is research on the effects of the Harlem Children's Zone, the most celebrated effort to flood a low-income neighborhood with improved social services and targeted programs. A Brookings Institution analysis of the research found that the charter schools in the Zone significantly improved student performance but that the other community programs in the Zone had no effect. http://www.brookings.edu/research/reports /2010/07/20-hcz-whitehurst

Other neighborhood effects can cause or entrench poverty. Children growing up in poor neighborhoods are more likely to ingest toxic levels of lead. http://www.cdc.gov/nceh/lead /acclpp/final_document_010412.pdf. A Dutch study finds suggestive evidence that even after controlling for the usual socioeconomic and individual factors, living in an undesirable neighborhood causes cellular changes that accelerate aging, illness, and death. Nicholas Bakalar, "Neighborhood May Age You," *New York Times*, June 30, 2014, D4.

negative effects of staying in bad areas persist beyond the children's generation.[148] And a new study, which controls for the likelihood that those who entered the MTO voucher lottery were *already* more highly motivated parents, finds that the observed positive effects of moving are actually understated.[149]

The social isolation of many poor people is not limited to geography, and it severely restricts their mobility and opportunity. Consider a recent summary of the research findings:

> Friends and relatives can lend money, pool risk, mind children and bring news of job openings. Researchers from the London School of Economics found that when a group of Bangladeshi women were given business training and free livestock, not only did they move up the income ladder, but their friends' lot improved too. A year later the friends' consumption had risen by almost 20%, and they claimed to have become savvier about business as well. The downside is that not having the right friends can cement hardship. The more concentrated the poverty, the less helpful social networks tend to be. In Atlanta, living in a poor neighborhood decreases the chance of having a friend with a job by almost 60%, and [the chances] of having a friend who had been to university by over a third. A global survey conducted in 2014 by Gallup . . . found that 30% of people in the poorest fifth of their country's population had nobody to rely on in times of need, compared to 16% of the richest fifth. . . . [O]ne American study found that in poor neighborhoods, three-quarters of jobholders found work through friends.[150]

Upward mobility, then, depends on a complex social process consisting of relationships, networks, and institutions that can help one gain human capital by earning trust, acquiring experience, and then using it to advantage. One's "embeddedness" is measured by "density," the extent to which individuals in one's group of contacts also know each other. Network sociologist Mark Granovetter has shown how this density can be both an advantage and a disadvantage, a conclusion confirmed by an ethnographic study.[151] A very dense network, he shows, may provide emotional support and friendship, but can make it harder to find a job or other kinds of opportunity because this very density tends to limit access to information from outside the group. In a paradox he calls "the strength of weak ties," people seeking to rise may benefit more (at least economically) from mere acquaintances than from friends because the former can pass on information from other networks of which they are members.[152] Granovetter also shows that information generated by weak ties is often crucial to finding a job.[153]

Orlando Patterson's work on social networks provides additional, and dismaying, insight into the role of social isolation in perpetuating poverty among blacks—even as a large black middle class has emerged against great odds.[154] In work published in 1998, Patterson took on what he called "the Myth of the 'Hood." He found that blacks' social networks were smaller, denser, and included remarkably few kinsmen; indeed, almost half of them had no kinsmen in their networks. In a "truly startling finding," no relationship whatsoever existed between network density and education level; Patterson inferred that more education did not expand their ties much. Unlike other groups for whom employed people had much less dense ties than retired people, blacks' networks were about as dense among retirees as among those still working. In other groups, lower-class people had much denser networks than higher-class ones. Among blacks, network density had little relationship to class. And while marriage for other groups was strongly related to the proportion of kinsmen in other groups' core networks, black marriages had little or no effect on network composition. Indeed, blacks had many fewer kinsmen in their networks than any other group; 91 percent reported *none* in their closest circle of contacts.

These patterns, Patterson concluded, put blacks in the "worst possible position. Their networks are smaller than those of nearly all other groups, and they are denser and hence their range of contacts narrower than those of other Americans. What is more, they do not enjoy the main benefits that usually come with dense networks—the trust, security, and support of kinsmen. For, contrary to conventional wisdom and ideology, their networks have the smallest proportion of kinsmen of all native-born Americans."[155] As if this were not isolation enough, Patterson adds another dimension—marital and familial—that reinforces the opportunity-limiting density of black networks: The odds that a black woman will marry a black man are 27,444 times greater than that a non-black woman will marry a black man![156]

Discrimination. Being an ethno-racial minority correlates strongly with being poor. Discrimination against minorities and poor people surely contributes to their poverty. But the meaning of discrimination depends on context. When we condemn discrimination, we usually mean treating people differently for reasons that should be socially and morally irrelevant, that can harm them in unacceptable ways, and that should thus be presumptively illegal. For clarity, I call this "invidious" discrimination.

What actions constitute invidious discrimination? Conceptually, I distinguish three types of discrimination. In *intentional discrimination*, the decision maker (say, an employer) treats A differently than B *because of* a characteristic of A's that the law (or society, usually both) holds should be irrelevant to the decision. Antidiscrimination law terms this invidious discrimination "disparate treatment." It identifies a number of such characteristics—race, religion, national origin, disability, illegitimacy, gender, age, (increasingly) sexual preference, and others—and protects them from such discriminatory decisions in employment and some other settings. Depending on the characteristic at issue, the law protects it by subjecting such decisions to different levels of judicial review, with the highest level ("strict scrutiny") applying to race and the lowest ("rationality") applying to age. Intentional discrimination based on these characteristics is difficult to prove; people are loath to recognize it in themselves, much less admit it, in a society that professes egalitarian ideals.

In *statistical discrimination*, decision makers treat A and B differently because they predict, based on what they think is a statistically justified generalization about the racial (or other) groups to which A and B belong, that they will behave or perform differently.

The accuracy of this generalization depends on the quality of the information on which it is based and how many exceptions to the generalization there are. Condemnation of such generalizations as "stereotypes" raises three important questions: How accurate is it as a general proposition; how accurate is it as applied to the individual in question (e.g., a job applicant); and how legitimate is using such a stereotype? Here, too, context is crucial. Stereotypes are inescapable and valuable because they economize on information in the countless daily situations when we need to predict how one will behave but cannot easily find out whether one fits the relevant stereotype or is an exception to it. But because stereotypes are sometimes false and unjustly harm individuals in certain situations, the law weighs various factors to decide when they may and may not be used.[157]

Unintentional discrimination occurs when government and private actors act in ways that are facially neutral and not motivated by bias. But in a society as unequal and diverse as ours, innocent decisions and actions that fall most heavily on protected minorities may reflect and reinforce existing inequalities. Antidiscrimination law terms this "disparate impact," punishing it even though the actor lacked invidious intent. Much rides on this distinction between treatment and impact. Title VII of the 1964 Civil Rights Act, which bars employment discrimination, punishes both, and the U.S. Supreme Court, after decades of uncertainty, recently held that Title VIII's ban on discrimination in housing also punishes both.[158] But although the distinction is crucial in most other legal areas, the Court has left it quite muddy.[159]

For present purposes, the key point is this: *Poverty is not a protected characteristic in any of these three discrimination situations.* Americans (and, I suspect, all other societies) feel great sympathy toward the poor but view exclusion on the basis of poverty ("classism") as normatively and legally acceptable in most contexts (exceptions to this include imposing a fee on divorce petitioners unable to pay,[160] and poll taxes[161]), while viewing racial discrimination of any kind as normatively and legally unacceptable, even in many private realms.[162]

This difference also makes it harder to prove racial bias legally. Neighborhoods, for example, are almost always class-identified. The non-poor regard this class differentiation in neighborhoods (strongly reinforced by public housing location policies) as desirable and natural, and evidence from the MTO study shows that many poor people agree with them. Because race and income are so highly correlated, classists may behave much as racists do, seeking to avoid the same people. These same decisions may have been motivated by classism rather than racism. Racists can easily invoke a classist rationale for their decisions, thus escaping both the moral censure and the illegality that racism would arouse. Another complication arising from this overlap is the problem of asymmetric information between whites who already live there and minorities who want to do so. When government subsidizes low-income people to move into middle-class communities, both classists and racists may assume that the newcomers are lower-class unless they can somehow signal a higher status and residents can easily ascertain the truth of the matter.

Whatever the precise mix of causes for class and racial isolation in neighborhoods, it surely contributes to the concentration of poverty. This concentration has grown significantly since the Great Recession, with more people living in "extremely poor neighborhoods (i.e., census tracts where 40 percent or more of the population lives below the federal poverty line)."[163] So entrenched is this isolation that typical middle-income blacks (with some geographic variations) actually live in lower-income neighborhoods than poorer whites do![164] As I discuss further below, such neighborhood effects practically ensure the projection of inequalities into education, employment, culture, personal networks, freedom from crime, and the many other opportunities, amenities, and freedoms that are so closely related to location. (Locational effects on future mobility are smaller for better-off children.) All these inequalities can perpetuate poverty. But again, conflating prohibited racism and normatively approved classism makes these issues harder to disentangle and thus to resolve.

The relationship between discrimination and poverty is further complicated by the experience of immigrant groups, some of which have been resilient enough to weather even the harshest forms of discrimination. Thomas Sowell, an economist who has written widely about the relative progress of various groups, reports that although the interment of the Japanese in the United States reduced the internees' income in the immediate postwar years, they achieved economic parity with Americans by 1959; in Canada, where the internments were even more damaging economically, their rebound was "spectacular." In 1959, only sixteen years after the repeal of the virulently racist Chinese Exclusion Act, Chinese family income in the United States (some of which reflected previously affluent refugees from the Communist takeover) approximated the national average.[165] Sowell documents many other examples of groups—Jews and Indians, notably—succeeding here and in other destinations where they faced severe discrimination.[166]

The remarkable advances of so many immigrant groups in so many unwelcoming (to say the least) societies complicates any simple explanation of poverty. Could it be that anti-immigrant animus, which so cruelly and perversely disadvantaged these groups in the short run, actually strengthened their economic and other social positions in the long run? In some paradoxical way, might hostility and discrimination promote the survival and prosperity of the very group (if not always of each member) that the destination societies hope to exclude? These are intriguing questions suggested, but certainly not answered, by this cross-cultural evidence. To ask them, of course, is certainly *not* to countenance discrimination against the poor, which inflicts undeserved suffering on many innocent, hardworking people. But such questions do suggest that discrimination cannot fully explain persistent poverty.

Indeed, it is impossible to know how much of today's poverty is due to racial discrimination. Black poverty is "over-determined," a product of many different, powerful causes whose separate contributions cannot be disentangled. (Ironically, as Wilson points out, the same decline in discrimination that enabled many blacks to move to middle-class neighborhoods and jobs also deprived those left behind in the ghettoes of their salutary influence.) Further confounding our understanding are public attitudes about race relations. On the one hand, Americans—surely influenced by intense coverage of white-on-black violence and Ferguson-type conflagrations—believe that race relations are worsening despite much evidence (not just the election and reelection of a black president) that racism has declined dramatically, that a majority of blacks think there has been a lot of progress, and that two out of three blacks (in a CBS/*New York Times* poll conducted after these violent events) consider race relations in their own communities generally good.[167] Perhaps this is akin to the frequent finding that the public has a very low opinion of Congress but a much higher opinion of their own representative, especially if they know the representative's name. (This gap has declined in recent years as disaffection with Congress has reached record levels.)[168]

Bad Choices. Many people are poor for a reason that they sometimes acknowledge to themselves and others: They have made bad choices in the past that continue to harm them. Those who make this point are often accused of "blaming the victim," lacking compassion, and ignoring structural causes of behavior. But any analysis that fails to take the role of bad choices seriously misses an important clue to what causes some poverty and what might reduce it.[169] By "bad choices," I mean decisions that squander or foreclose opportunities to better one's socioeconomic prospects in the future. Some bad decisions, such as narcotics or alcohol abuse, are self-destructive. Many are not only antisocial but illegal; if detected and punished, they will foreclose many paths out of poverty. Most bad choices, however, are simply shortsighted; they sacrifice the real possibility of future, durable gains for more immediate but transitory ones. Common examples include chronic truancy, dropping out of high school, alcohol abuse, gambling, habitual indiscipline, ignoring schoolwork in favor of TV or video games, excessive borrowing and spending, domestic violence, parenting children whom one cannot afford or do not know how to care for, cultivating self-destructive habits and hanging out with antisocial people; and quitting jobs or training programs from which one could acquire useful skills or experience.

People are drawn to bad choices for various reasons. It may be difficult to envision alternative courses of action. Alternatives may be imaginable but seem too distant, hard, or downright unattractive. One may hope to avoid hard choices, thinking that one can enjoy short-term pleasures without actually sacrificing longer-term opportunities. One may make bad choices because one is too present-oriented, discounting future possibilities very heavily.* Their deeper causes—impulsivity, low intelligence, limited imagination, lack of empathy, habituation, and emotional or neurological conditions—surely apply differently to different people and in different combinations. The stresses of living with severe scarcity, according to recent research, can affect brain function in ways that lead to bad choices.[170]

Incarceration. A June 2015 report by the *Economist* magazine presents the now-familiar but disturbing contours of this problem:

> No country in the world imprisons as many people as America does, or for so long. Across the array of state and federal prisons, local jails and immigration detention centres, some 2.3m people are locked up at any one time. America, with less than 5% of the world's population, accounts for around 25% of the world's prisoners. The system is particularly punishing towards black people and Hispanics, who are imprisoned at six times and twice the rates of whites respectively. A third of young black men can expect to be incarcerated at some point in their lives. The system is riddled with drugs, abuse and violence.[171]

The report goes on to note both the recent reductions in incarceration and the severe constraints on achieving further declines. The popular nostrum of releasing or diverting those convicted of minor offenses or those above a certain age, while desirable, will actually have little impact on incarceration.[172] Those imprisoned for mere drug possession, the low-hanging fruit for de-incarceration efforts, now account for

* Unfortunately, new research suggests that self-control may also accelerate the aging process, especially for the poor. "No good deed goes unpunished," *The Economist*, July 18, 2015, p. 67.

about 3 percent of state prisoners, who constitute 87 percent of U.S. prisoners. And even the imprisoned drug offenders were usually plea-bargained down from more serious trafficking offenses. People whose only offense is using drugs almost never go to prison and rarely spend much time there.[173] The core problem is far more daunting: Almost half of prisoners are violent offenders; another 12 percent are sex offenders. An Urban Institute study confirms that even limiting incarceration to these serious criminals would hardly make a dent in the problem.[174] U.S. incarceration rates are much higher than in Europe partly because our incidence of violent crime and recidivism is so much higher.

Prisoners, especially for long periods, rupture their ties to legitimate sources of upward mobility, perhaps permanently. Their access to good jobs is severely limited—hence the "ban the box" movement to limit employers' information about applicants' criminal records,* and President Obama's proposals to ease their reentry.[175] Convicts' family and communal relationships are severed or strained, their friendships attenuated, their trustworthiness cast in doubt, their skills atrophied, and their emotional lives blighted. Recidivism and a continuing life of crime are strong possibilities—and magnify and extend these poverty-inducing effects. Indeed, more than half of those released from prison are arrested for a new crime within three years of release. Even if they were not poor before imprisonment, they are likely to be poor thereafter. Still, the timing and trajectories of family dissolution and poverty suggest that incarceration is not a leading driver of poverty. Even when black non-marital births soared in the 1960s and early '70s, black incarceration remained quite stable—at about *one-tenth of today's rate!* Much of the damage to black families and communities, then, had already been done before black incarceration rates began their rapid rise.[176] Still, the historical relationship between incarceration and poverty remains uncertain. For present purposes, then, the crucial points are that (1) that incarceration is

---

* New research finds that this policy actually *reduces* their job prospects. Jennifer R. Doleac and Benjamin Harrison, NBER Working Paper No. 22469, July 2016.

a cause of poverty, not just a consequence of it, but (2) it is not a principal cause, and (3) release of minor offenders would not affect poverty much.

Culture of Poverty. I have been discussing factors that are known to contribute to poverty. Some of them, like bad luck and invidious discrimination, are ultimate causes in the sense that if we could somehow eliminate them, we could end the amount of poverty attributable to those particular factors. But, welcome as that would be, ending such discrimination would have a relatively minor impact on poverty because it contributes far less to it than the other causal factors I have discussed: family and community breakdown, disappearing jobs, educational deficits, isolation, bad choices, and mass incarceration. Those factors are themselves symptoms or manifestations of the more fundamental ("root") causes—both social and individual—that drive them.*

Many poverty researchers maintain that what causes, compounds, and perpetuates most or all of the factors discussed above (except invidious discrimination) is an underlying "culture of poverty."† Culture (of any kind) is notoriously difficult to define, but in this case it usually denotes widespread, entrenched, self-reinforcing patterns of despair, present-orientation, inability to grasp what limited opportunity there is, and self-destructive behavior. The Moynihan Report imbroglio made this phrase highly controversial in the United States, yet the post-1965 proliferation of cultural studies programs in lead-

---

* It is quite wrong to argue that we cannot reduce poverty without first eliminating these root causes. More commonly, as with crime control and health care, policy can *only* deal with symptoms unless and until it is able to understand and solve (if possible) the root causes. Indeed, root causes are themselves products of other, even more fundamental and more elusive ones. This is why insisting that we address root causes rather than symptoms, while understandable, can produce misguided policies, inaction, and lost opportunities for reform.

† Mass incarceration is an important example of this phenomenon. It both causes poverty, as discussed above, and fosters its own distinctive culture inside prison walls, which cultivates norms and behaviors that replicate and deepen poverty. See Loic Wacquant, "Deadly Symbiosis: When Ghetto and Prison Meet and Mesh," 3 *Punishment & Society* 95 (2001).

ing universities signaled its growing legitimacy, while more systematic studies of poor communities provided empirical support. Even so, antipoverty activists often resist this because they see it as "blaming the victim," and an excuse for society to throw up its hands and do nothing. Although they are wrong to dismiss culture, its conceptual blurriness can breed misunderstanding.[177] Culture does resist change and usually changes slowly, although examples of fairly rapid change do exist (as with attitudes toward same-sex marriage). And it is shaped by even more stable factors: geography and climate, natural resources, entrenched institutions, history, and others.[178] Interestingly, however, opinion surveys indicate that poor and non-poor Americans view poverty, welfare, and future progress in much the same way, views that have not changed much in the last thirty years.[179]

Culture's salience in explaining much of what goes on in poor communities is widely accepted today. As William Julius Wilson puts it, "it's more than just race."[180] The culture of poverty posits a milieu in which the causes of poverty and dependency discussed above are widespread and entrenched. In particular, the bad choices described above have a kind of coherence to participants in this culture; in that sense, these perverse choices seem rational. These choices, reinforced and validated by other aspects of the culture, create a "poverty trap" from which escape is especially difficult.[181] Changing the culture and removing the trap pose the single greatest challenge to government, policy makers, and to the poor themselves.

CURRENT ANTIPOVERTY PROGRAMS

According to the Congressional Research Service, the federal government spent $848 billion in fiscal 2015 on programs with an explicit focus on low-income people or communities, a very large increase over the fiscal 2008 (just before the Great Recession) level of $561 billion. (These numbers *exclude* three spending program categories: (1) social insurance programs such as Social Security, Medicare, and Unemployment Insurance; (2) tax provisions other than the refundable portions of the EITC and the Child Tax Credit; and (3) state and local spending on such programs.)[182] The common assertion that the federal government's social welfare spending lags far behind that in OECD welfare states is false. It ignores the fact that a far greater share of that spending occurs through off-budget, tax-expenditure modalities—what political scientist Christopher Howard calls the "hidden welfare state."[183] Taking this into account, a recent comparison of social welfare spending in the OECD states as a share of their GDPs shows that "only the French spend more than Americans, while the alleged welfare-addicted Scandinavians and Europeans spend less on average." Our approach has some advantages but seems to produce worse outcomes in alleviating poverty.[184]

For this reason, Christopher Jencks's exhortation "to come clean about which parts of the War on Poverty worked and which ones do not appear to have worked, and stop supporting the parts that appear ineffective" is particularly wise and welcome.[185] But as Jencks well knows, this is easier said than done; rigorous studies are hard to come by.[186] In the rest of this section, I marshal the best evidence on how effective antipoverty programs are. To set the stage, I must clarify some terms, distinctions, techniques, and constraints.

Terminology, Distinctions, Techniques, and Constraints. Broadly speaking, antipoverty programs are financed in three ways. *Entitlement* programs are those in which a statute confers eligibility on various groups of people based on specific criteria. They may be universal or means-tested. People who satisfy the statutory criteria are entitled to claim the benefits specified in the law, and Congress is morally if not legally obliged to appropriate the funds necessary to satisfy those claims. It always does so. Social Security and Medicare, the two largest, are universal programs in the sense that they cover virtually everyone above a specified age. These two programs contribute enormously to poverty prevention and alleviation, but as noted earlier, they are not counted as antipoverty programs. Indeed, their political popularity depends on the widespread belief that their beneficiaries have financed their own benefits by contributing to a centrally administered "trust fund," a self-financed social insurance fund. In fact, this is untrue. Most of those who die before retirement age get far less than they paid into the system through their payroll taxes, while today's beneficiaries receive far more in benefits than they paid in.[187] Other important entitlements include unemployment compensation (though many unemployed do not qualify for it) and veteran's benefits. The most important means-tested ones are Medicaid, a joint state-federal program providing health care to the poor; the Food Stamp program (now Supplemental Nutrition Assistance Program, or SNAP); Supplemental Security Income (SSI), which provides income support for the aged, blind, and disabled; the refundable portions of the EITC and Child Tax Credit; and the low-income subsidy for Medicare Part D.

Discretionary programs constitute the largest group of antipoverty programs, including almost all of those to be discussed below. Congress must reauthorize them periodically, and their funding requires periodic (often annual) appropriations. These programs are means-tested. Section 8 housing vouchers ($17.9 billion in 2013) and Head Start ($8 billion) are the largest examples—and enjoy more political support than other such programs.

Some *tax* programs are designed to reduce poverty. Authorized in the Internal Revenue Code, they are created by two powerful congressional committees (House Ways and Means; Senate Finance). They do not need appropriations and once enacted are more or less permanent. Most of them are targeted at either businesses (e.g., depreciation allowances) or middle- and upper-class people (e.g., deductions for medical insurance and home mortgage interest), but some target the poor. The EITC is means-tested and targets parent-earners and some noncustodial workers (Congress is considering expanding eligibility for this second group) on a sliding income scale; in 2014, it phased out at incomes around $52,000 for a married couple with three or more children. The Child Tax Credit is also means-tested but does not begin to phase out until the income level reaches $110,000, so relatively little of the benefit ($21.6 billion in 2013) goes to the poor. (Most of them are exempt from federal income taxes anyway but must still pay federal payroll tax, which takes a large bite out of any on-the-books wages they earn.)

Some other programmatic distinctions merit brief mention. One is between programs that affirmatively confer benefits on the poor (the traditional form of antipoverty programs) and policies that instead incentivize self-help by the poor—for example, by exempting low-wage workers from requirements. Another distinction concerns the specific form that benefits take. Some antipoverty programs provide cash. The main examples are the EITC and TANF (which replaced traditional welfare in 1996). Others provide "near-cash" for the purchase of approved categories of goods. The major examples here are SNAP and Section 8 housing vouchers.

Few other antipoverty programs give benefits directly to the poor. The vast majority of programs instead pay middle- and upper-class intermediaries, many of them professionals, to provide their services to the poor. Providing services rather than cash (or near-cash, as with SNAP)—what Moynihan mocked as "feeding the horses to feed the sparrows"—is by far the dominant approach to our way of fighting poverty—and a dubious one at that. Indeed, "of the $800 billion spent on poverty programs in 2012, less than $150 billion was distributed in cash income, if one includes as cash benefit the tax rebate under the EITC. That is a grand total of 18 percent of the whole. The rest was . . . money paid to providers of various kinds, most of whom have incomes well above the poverty line."[188]

Antipoverty programs also differ in their relationships to various levels of government and the private sector. Federal programs are almost never operated solely by Washington. (Social Security is a rare exception.) Instead, the federal government usually funnels money to states (and through the states sometimes to localities), which then operate the programs under regulations issued by the federal and state governments. Implementation of federal programs is almost entirely a state and local responsibility, a fact that usually reshapes programs in important ways not always envisioned by Washington.[189]

States also have their own antipoverty programs in policy areas where they traditionally bear primary responsibility: public health, labor standards (including minimum wage regulation), housing, and so forth.

A final distinction concerns the identity of the beneficiary groups. As noted earlier, and despite the effusive rhetoric about children being our future, programs for the elderly are much better funded than those targeted at poor families with children. Those favoring the working poor are much better funded than those for the nonworking poor. (In this context, "working" usually includes those who are in job training or educational programs.) Notably, the 2016 presidential campaign paid little attention to the nonworking poor.[190]

Studying the effectiveness of a policy is replete with methodological difficulties.[191] What does it mean to say that a policy is effective or ineffective? In a previous book, I devoted a long chapter to analyzing this very question, which of course is essential to any such discussion.[192] Readers who want the more complex, nuanced, and qualified analysis will find it there. Here, I present a much shorter and conclusory summary of that analysis.

All policies succeed in some respects (after all, the money benefits *someone*) and fail in others. Program advocates' promises may bear little resemblance to actual performance. Mere common sense or inferences drawn from a program's intentions or political support are poor guides to program evaluation; only systematic analysis and evidence can do that. A policy may fail for many reasons—a flawed theory or design, costs that exceed benefits, muddled implementation, erratic enforcement, or political compromises that undermine its efficacy either at its inception or as it plays out in the real world. Another common reason for program failure is unforeseen behavioral responses to its incentives—as when many people with private health insurance dropped it once Medicaid expansion make them eligible, or when public pensions reduce private retirement savings. Moral hazard—greater risk-taking when a program insures against loss—is a common effect that increased the huge mortgage losses that helped cause the Great Recession.[193]

Public policies should not be held to impossible standards. Instead, they should be assessed according to four obvious and minimal criteria, as well as some other factors.

- *Its benefits should exceed its costs.* The standard tool for determining this is cost-benefit analysis. CBA does not demand that policies be perfect, only that they be more beneficial on net than alternative policies, including the status quo. This is simple rationality, which is why every president from Ronald Reagan to Barack Obama has mandated its use to analyze proposed government regulations. Some critics oppose the very idea of using CBA to analyze programs designed to protect values such as human life and health, biological diversity, and environmental purity that are difficult to measure, much less price; some argue that the very efforts to do so are immoral. Some criticisms of CBA are more technical or methodological in nature; many of these do not object in principle to using CBA but rather to particular applications of it. Such disagreement is desirable and will improve the method. In the end, CBA—when conscientiously conducted and attentive to its own potential flaws—is probably the best that we can do to assess the efficiency merits of policies. What other decision modes are better? Good intentions, intuition, caprice, political power, abstract philosophical theories, or coin flips are not acceptable ways to make sound decisions. As environmental economist Bjorn Lonborg has put it, CBA "is a for more effective and moral approach than basing decisions on the media's roving gaze or the loudness of competing interest groups." Adapting Winston Churchill's quip about democracy, CBA is the worst decision tool except for all the others that have been proposed so far. A proper CBA should at least shift the burden of proof to those who would challenge its verdict on effectiveness.
- The *cost-effectiveness* criterion (or the "most bang for the buck" principle) means that whatever a program's purposes are and whatever level of benefits it actually produces, those purposes and this level should be attained at the lowest possible cost. The flip

side of this principle is that at any given level of cost, the program should produce as many benefits as possible. One reason that a program may not be cost-effective is that it uses the wrong tool. The government has many in its tool shed: subsidies, taxation, regulation, tort law, market incentives, competition, and many others. The best choice for a given policy goal will usually depend on a number of factors, so answering this question can be difficult. For example, if the policy seeks to raise the income of the working poor, almost all economists believe that the EITC is ordinarily a far more effective tool for doing that than raising the minimum wage. I discuss this below.

- *Target efficiency* means that a program should target its benefits on those who will benefit most from the policy.[194]* Although this is just common sense, policy makers often fail this test, even when they want to reduce poverty. They may lack information about key facts, such as how much program resources will produce desired policy outcomes. Political factors often sacrifice targeting to other legitimate goals such as greater universality (e.g., Social Security retirement) or a desire to keep higher-income people in the program mix (e.g., public housing in New York City where more than 10,000 over-income families remain despite a waiting list of more than 300,000 income-eligible ones).[195]

Disputed normative judgments may also compromise targeting. We do not *always* want antipoverty programs to target the most disadvantaged of the eligibles. We may predict that the neediest people will not use the benefits wisely or effectively, or that they can be independent without the government's help, or are needy only because of some sort of self-destructiveness or other personal failing. The once-colloquial, morally loaded terms "deserving" and "undeserving" poor are now derided in much public discourse. President Obama, visiting a federal prison in July 2015, observed, "There but for the grace of God [go I]" but also strongly

---

* In my view, an antipoverty program's costs should also be borne progressively through a progressive tax system. The classic debate on this is Walter J. Blum & Harry Kalven, Jr., *The Uneasy Case for Progressive Taxation* (1953).

condemned violent criminals.[196] He surely recognized that this distinction was fundamental to Americans' thinking about which low-income groups most merit society's solicitude. Indeed, those who live in close proximity to the culture of poverty (and perhaps narrowly escaped from it) probably draw this distinction more easily than the rest of us. But however one comes out on this moral debate, the key point about target efficiency is this: Many of our costly programs fail its test. The huge federal student loan program whose benefits flow largely to the better off is but one example;[197] indeed, Hillary Clinton's proposed fix to the program may exacerbate this.[198]

- *"Invisible" or "silent" victims.* A program may make people worse off who are unaware of this fact. Policy makers will not attend to the interests of these cost-bearers unless they make a special effort to anticipate and assess the program's impacts on them. These costs ordinarily gain little recognition because they are small at the individual level and because the causal link between the policy and these costs is difficult to trace, even or especially by its victims; they often cannot organize politically to protect their interests even though the benefits of doing so may be quite large when aggregated across all of them. They include, for example, those who will not get a job opportunity or benefit, or retain one, because a new regulation, higher minimum wage, or litigation-averse employer chills job creation, causes layoffs, or affects firms' locations.[199] Many poor people do not receive their Medicaid benefits because its rigid, inadequate reimbursement rates induce doctors not to participate. And many restaurants respond to minimum wage increases by prohibiting tips for servers.[200]

Inherent, Severe Constraints on Designing Effective Programs. The first constraint is political, by which I mean the difficulty of gaining Congress's support for antipoverty programs. The poor are but a small minority with little in common other than their poverty. Many are dispirited, do not vote even if they are U.S. citizens, and are notoriously difficult to organize, especially at the national level. Accordingly, they exert relatively little pressure on Congress.[201] They are heavily concentrated in urban centers and Appalachia, which dilutes their voting power nationally.* As noted earlier, most Americans still believe that self-help (including disciplined frugality) can achieve the American dream and thus that many of the poor are largely responsible for their low condition. The upward mobility of so many immigrants, ostensibly with little or no government assistance, fortifies this view. Antipoverty programs' reputation as inefficient and fraud-prone reinforces political resistance to creating or expanding them.

One kind of trade-off that invariably constrains antipoverty programs arises out of the intersection of market forces and the public's distinction between the deserving and the undeserving poor, one that Americans commonly make, at least implicitly, but that may apply differently in specific cases. Consider the EITC, discussed below. Most economists favor it for the working poor and agree that some "benefit reduction rate" must be imposed as income rises in order to phase out the subsidy. They recognize the trade-off that this entails between work incentives, target efficiency, the cost of the subsidy, and income supplementation for low-wage workers. Another example of this trade-off was President Nixon's proposal of a negative income tax (NIT) in the early 1970s, which took the form of a family assistance plan that coupled a guaranteed minimum income with work and training requirements for the employable. The government funded rigorous experimental research in various cities to see what an NIT's effects would be under different program designs. Key researchers in these experiments explain some of the trade-offs they found:

> Economic theory unambiguously predicts that extending welfare to a new group will reduce their work effort. But the effect of different tax rates is ambiguous. In particular, lower tax rates are something of a two-edged sword: they clearly encourage people

---

* Indeed, the Food Stamp (SNAP) program could not survive without the support of more powerful agricultural interests eager to expand consumption of their products—an old political fact dramatized most recently in 2014.

who are not working to take a job; but they also keep working families, who would have become ineligible under a higher tax rate, on welfare longer and thereby extend all the negative work incentives to those families. Which effect would predominate—more work by those currently on welfare or less work by those newly affected by it? Economic theory could not say, and no reliable evidence existed to answer the question. . . . The bottom line from the studies was that the NIT reduced rather than increased overall work effort.[202]

The NIT had another important effect: It increased marital breakups, probably by enabling unhappily married women to get by on their own. Upon learning of this effect, Senator Moynihan immediately dropped his support for the proposal, which doomed it.[203]

Particular Antipoverty Programs. The fact that the actual poverty rate, properly measured, has declined substantially over the last fifty years does not tell us how effective specific antipoverty programs have been. After all, Christopher Jencks notes, the rate "could have declined despite the War on Poverty, not because of it."[204] In assessing the most important programs explicitly targeted at poverty (in no particular order), I draw on his recent review of a collection of War on Poverty assessments[205] and on other systematic evaluations.

Temporary Assistance for Needy Families (TANF)

Probably no social policy faces greater implementation obstacles than programs seeking to move unmarried, unemployed, poorly educated, welfare-dependent mothers to self-supporting work while assuring decent care for their children. TANF, which spent $17.3 billion in 2016, is no exception. But due to a combination of an unusual bipartisan coalition, encouraging state-level experimentation with various approaches, a robust economy, and state creation of work-readiness and childcare supports, TANF swiftly produced a rapid decline in the welfare caseload as welfare mothers entered the work force. But even TANF's supporters worried about what would happen when a recession occurred, which it did beginning late in 2000 and again in 2008.

As it turned out, the former welfare recipients who TANF helped have held on to most of their gains, even after years of the Great Recession.[206] A former head of New York City's Human Resources agency and long-time administrator of TANF and other welfare-to-work programs summarized the data: "labor force participation among never-married mothers in the U.S. increased from 59.9 percent in 1995 (the year before [TANF] was passed) to a peak of 73.8 percent in 2001.... [L]abor force participation among this group was still 69.9 percent in 2013. This increase in labor force participation led to substantial declines in the official measure of poverty among never-married mothers. In 1995, the poverty rate among this group was 51 percent. By 2001 it declined to 38.5 percent and even after the Great Recession, the poverty rate among never-married mothers remains below that of 1995 (43 percent in 2013)."[207]

Against these successes are some shortcomings.

- Although TANF's provisions significantly raised child support payments by fathers from $12 billion to $32 billion between 1995 and 2012, that situation, Sawhill notes, "remains dismal. In 2011, only 35 percent of all single mothers received any child support, and among single mothers living in poverty, the proportion was lower: only 29 percent. Payments to these mothers are typically small; even excluding mothers who get no payments, the average benefit to an unmarried mother is around $4,500 per year . . ., and the average payment for low-income mothers is even smaller. Obviously, this is a drop in the bucket of what it takes to raise a family."[208] Brookings researchers propose that delinquent fathers care for their children while the mothers work, in lieu of cash payments.[209] The practical obstacles to this seem insuperable.

- The take-up rate for TANF-eligible families is far below those for SNAP, EITC, and AFDC (before its replacement by TANF); indeed, almost twenty years after its enactment, their participation

rate is less than 33 percent. Finding out why should be a top priority. TANF did seek to substitute work income for AFDC benefits
and has made some progress; female-headed families' poverty rate
is lower under TANF than it was under AFDC.[210] More troubling,
some states may have made it hard to apply and diverted some of
their TANF block grants (more than $11 billion of the $16.5 billion, by one account)[211] to other uses.[212] If so, federal policy makers should rectify this.

- So-called disconnected mothers—those who receive neither work-
  related income nor TANF benefits—are very poor, have few job
  prospects, and are growing in number and as a share of the low-
  income population.[213] And as noted earlier, "extreme poverty"
  (less than $2 per day cash income for at least a month) may be
  higher now than in 1996 when TANF was enacted.
- TANF's cash benefits are not indexed to inflation, so their value
  and adequacy have eroded substantially. In the median state, according to a congressional study, the maximum benefit for a family
  of three was 42 percent below the median state's maximum AFDC
  benefit for such a family in 1988 in real terms.[214]

Food Stamps (SNAP)

SNAP, which is administered by the U.S. Department of Agriculture
(USDA), had 46.5 million recipients (in about half that number of
households) in 2014, at a cost of $74.1 billion. The program expanded
greatly during the Great Recession, but that crisis explains only about
half of SNAP's growth; the rest seems to reflect eased federal standards and states' more aggressive enrollment (they bear few of the
costs). Along with unemployment insurance, SNAP is our main coun-
tercyclical entitlement program, and it is well targeted on the nutri-
tional and income needs of households that include children, seniors,
or people with disabilities. Studies confirm its positive effects on the
maternal and child health of recipients.[215] It made more than $2 bil-
lion in improper payments in 2014, but its error rate was actually
lower than that of most other large antipoverty programs.[216]

As a result of SNAP's rapid expansion and relatively weak enforcement of work rules, Congress ordered the USDA in 2014 to seek to increase participants' employment, earnings, and work incentives. In response, the USDA plans to commission research on the SNAP Employment and Training Program's effectiveness, noting that research has been "relatively scarce."[217] An older study found that this employment program failed on all measures of employment, earnings, and general welfare cash assistance, and had a minute effect on reducing food stamp use.[218]

Earned Income Tax Credit

The EITC was not part of the original War on Poverty. It was enacted in 1975 after Congress failed to enact a family income maintenance plan. In 2014, it provided more than $65 billion in refunds to 26.7 million low-income working families (an average of $2,400 per family). It is generally regarded as one of the most successful social policies for low-income families, and many other countries have now adopted it. Because the EITC is designed to increase work effort, it is politically popular. (Some of the benefit goes to employers, but the greatest benefit by far goes to the workers.)[219] Indeed, Congress has expanded eligibility and benefits several times since the Great Recession, and more than half the states now provide EITC supplements.[220] The EITC draws many single mothers into the work force, and is also far better targeted at low-income workers with children than are minimum wage increases (discussed later) because the EITC is tied to household income, not a worker's wage, and it varies with family size, so almost all benefits go to parents. It exemplifies what Mead approvingly calls "help and hassle" programs, providing new benefits but only alongside work requirements. He does question, however, whether the EITC in fact raises work effort rather than simply raising the incomes of those who are already working at a given level.[221] A July 2015 analysis has a less skeptical view than Mead's; it predicts that expanding the EITC by $1,000 per recipient would increase employment of single mothers by 7.3 percent, substantially reducing family poverty.[222]

For all of its advantages, the EITC has some major flaws. Its effective marginal tax rate at the benefit phase-out level is high, sharply reducing work incentives as that point. It made $17 billion in improper payments in 2014 (exceeded only by Medicare), an error rate of more than 27 percent due to some combination of governmental errors, honest beneficiary errors, and outright fraud.[223] The program provides little support to other single workers or single non-custodial parents; increasing it would be quite costly.[224] Due to its complexity, many eligible families do not apply for the program, and the form of the benefit—a lump-sum payment once a year—helps beneficiaries less than a monthly wage supplement would (although many recipients have preferred the former).[225] Some also question whether expanding the EITC would be cost-justified in terms of how much work effort it might engender in a period of historically low labor participation.[226]

Head Start

Head Start, which began in 1965, is a very popular, politically well-connected program that serves almost one million preschoolers, costing about $8 billion a year. The evidence on its effects is disputed. Supporters usually cite the Perry Preschool in Ypsilanti, Michigan, which opened in the early 1960s. For many years, researchers followed a pool of poor black three-year-olds who were divided into those randomly selected into the program and those not admitted. Studies found that any difference in test scores between the two groups vanished over time. A 2010 federal government study of Head Start found, similarly, that participation has no significant impact on measureable outcomes (e.g., academic, social-emotional, or health status at the end of the first grade). When the government then extended the study to third graders, it found the same "fadeout" of benefits. (Nobel economist James Heckman's research may help to explain why; it suggests that even Head Start begins years too late to help disadvantaged children in school.) Preschool programs in other countries have also had mixed results, with no clear patterns explaining why some succeed more than others.

Nor is Head Start alone in these disappointing results. The Even Start Family Literacy Program failed to improve child and parent reading, at a cost exceeding $1 billion before it was finally defunded; the Scared Straight programs that bring at-risk youngsters into prison to learn about what might await them actually seem to increase their criminal behavior; and 21st Century Community Leaning Centers fail to improve academic outcomes but increase various forms of disciplinary problems, yet receive more than $1 billion a year in federal funds. A July 2013 Brookings research report on pre-K programs using random assignments finds little or no success,[227] and an RCT of Tennessee's statewide voluntary pre-K programs in 2015 found negative effects by the end of first grade.[228] (In Canada, a study of Quebec's universal child care program in 2015 found a large increase in its use but a deterioration in a host of measures of child well-being.)[229]

Still, pre-K education has strong advocates among liberal groups, citing the success of the Chicago Child-Parent Center Program[230] and long-term positive effects of Perry and Head Start. A follow-up of Perry pupils at age twenty-seven found that they were less likely to have been arrested for any crime, had higher incomes, were less likely to smoke, and had other better outcomes. Several studies found that those who attended Head Start did better on high school completion and some other social indicia compared with siblings who did not enroll. Heckman has also found long-term positive effects on adult behavior and income. One skeptic, noting that these studies lack the methodological rigor of the RCTs that found that any positive effects soon dissipate, asks a sensible question about the studies finding delayed effects: "If Head Start has little to no effect when participants are children, how can the program suddenly become effective in adulthood?"[231] Jencks's answer to this question is that Head Start may somehow help youths develop character traits that only affect outcomes later in life.[232] After thirty years of skepticism about Head

Start, he "more or less became a convert: no persistent test score effects but non-trivial positive effects on social and economic outcomes in adulthood."[233]

Title I

The program was a core element of the original War on Poverty and has been periodically reauthorized ever since. Under Title I, Washington distributes more than $14 billion annually to about 66,000 local education agencies (LEAs) serving 33 million students. Its purpose is to reduce inequalities in the resources available to LEAs, inequalities that arise because public education in the United States is almost entirely a local responsibility funded mostly by each local community through local taxes that reflect that community's wealth.

Jencks summarizes the evidence on Title I's effectiveness: The funding "helped reduce spending disparities between rich and poor districts in the 1960s and 1970s but not after 1990. Nor does Title I seem to have reduced expenditure differences between schools servicing rich and poor children in the same district. Finally there is no solid evidence that Title I reduced differences between rich and poor school districts on reading or math tests. If there was any such impact, it was small." He also notes that Title I did give the federal government more leverage over LEAs when it came to desegregation and, more recently, to increasing accountability for test results. A November 2015 review by the Brookings Institution of Title I is quite critical:[234]

> [I]ts funding per student is quite low, averaging about $500 to $600 a year. And there is little evidence that the overall program is effective or that its funds are used for effective services and activities. Large proportions of school principals report using Title I funds for teacher professional development, which many studies have shown to be ineffective and which teachers do not find valuable. Other services on which principals spent Title I funds include after-school and summer programs, technology purchases, and supplemental services, which also have been shown to be inef-

fective, and class-size reductions, which are unlikely to be of the size needed to generate effects found in previous research.

Upward Bound

This relatively small program ($265 million in 2014) was created in 1965 as part of the War on Poverty. It provides supplemental academic and support services and activities to help about 61,000 low-income high school students, disproportionately females and blacks, become college-ready. The final evaluation, which used RCTs, found that two years after they were scheduled to graduate from high school, the program had no effect on any of the twenty-one effectiveness measures, except for the high school dropout rate, which, surprisingly, was slightly higher for those who, prior to random assignment, indicated a "high expectation" of attending college. A follow-up study seven to nine years after scheduled high school graduation found that the program had no effect on the likelihood that the high-expectations students would attain a bachelor's degree, certificate, or license, and it lowered their probability of attaining an associate's degree. Unexpectedly, the program appears to have given a small boost to students with lower expectations, though it was unclear which post-secondary credential they obtained.[235]

Other Family-Centered Services

After a very detailed review of the formal assessments of many other federal programs intended to improve the prospects for poor families and children, Heritage Foundation analyst David Muhlhausen delivers a grim report: "Federal social programs largely fail at improving the academic and cognitive abilities of infants, toddlers, and other children. Overall, these programs do little to move people out of poverty. And forget about becoming economically self-sufficient."[236] The studies also found that these programs "fail to stop kids from having sex, get couples married, or keep marriages together."* The most no-

---

* This last refers to two George W. Bush administration programs. Building Strong Families provided counseling in relationship skills, emotional support, and other social

table exception, he found, was welfare-to-work programs, and even there the positive effects were small. Some special services were beneficial but none succeeded in moving participants into full-time employment beyond what TANF's work and job search requirements (and, to a lesser extent, the time limits) did after 1996.[237]

College Financial Aid

Federal grants and loans to college students mushroomed from $800 million in 1963–64 to $157 billion in 2010–11 (in constant dollars). The Pell Grant program, targeted at low-income students, cost $31.9 billion in 2013. Most federal financial aid, however, goes to the nonpoor; 57 percent of college students now receive federal aid, up from 47 percent only four years ago. In July 2013, the Consumer Financial Protection Bureau estimated that outstanding student loans, almost all guaranteed by the federal government, had reached $1.2 trillion—a 20 percent rise since the end of 2011 and almost twice the 2008 level.

Although these programs are supposed to close the opportunity gap by enabling more children from low-income families to attend and complete college, Jencks reports, "[t]hat has not happened. In the mid-1990s Congress broadened federal financial aid to include middle-income families, reducing low-income students' share of the pot. But the college attendance gap had been widening even before that." The gap between college dropout rates of high- and low-income freshmen also increased between 1979 and 2001.[238] Two-thirds of low-income freshmen and about half of middle-income freshmen in four-year colleges drop out. Poor targeting—a major failing of Title I at the pre-college level as well, as we just saw—is not the only serious flaw in student financial aid programs. Others include little marginal

---

services to encourage marriage by low-income unmarried couples with or expecting a child. Supporting Healthy Marriage used counseling and other services to keep married parents of low-income families together. Unsurprisingly both failed to show any significant results; marrying the father of her child may only magnify her problems. Muhlhausen did not review findings about Head Start's impact on adults, discussed above, because he finds these studies to lack the same scientific rigor as evaluations based on random assignment.

effect on the decision to attend college; much fraud; growing student debt; high and rising loan delinquency; encouraging tuition and fee increases; and little internal assessment of program effectiveness.[239] "As an experiment in social policy," Jencks concludes, "college loans may not have been a complete failure, but they cannot be counted as a success."[240] On the other hand, the efforts by the University of California system to attract lower-income students have been unusually effective and surely can provide lessons for other states and institutions.[241]

Job Training

The GAO studied forty-seven programs designed to improve job information, training, and the hiring of unemployed or underemployed workers. The programs were spread across nine agencies and spent $18 billion in 2009. Only five of them had assessed their impacts and only some of these demonstrated positive effects; these effects tended to be small or short-term.[242] The United States is far behind OECD countries in assessing such programs, and the results on cost-effectiveness, such as they are, are underwhelming.[243]

According to Robert La Londe, a leading expert on these policies, job search assistance programs are more likely than other employment programs to yield positive short-term impacts. The mixed results for other programs depend on the targeted groups. Classroom training consistently generates modest short- and medium-term benefits for economically disadvantaged adult women, but just as consistently fails to produce gains for youths. For adult males, the results vary greatly across studies, partly because of methodological differences and sample sizes that are too small to measure program impacts with the same precision. On-the-job training programs have received less study. Some researchers find short-term benefits but with some doubt as to how long they persist. For reasons that are not altogether clear, private employers seldom participate in these programs, even though they might obtain substantial wage subsidies for hiring disadvantaged workers. A study of the Dayton Target Jobs tax credit during the 1980s suggested that these economically disadvantaged workers cannot overcome the labor market stigma of being classified as such.[244] An exhaustive analysis of the studies on the fifty-year-old, $1.8 billion annually, Job Corps program finds few, if any, positive effects.[245]

Social Security Retirement

Jencks echoes other poverty analysts in saying that Social Security was "the simplest, least controversial, and most effective anti-poverty program of the past half-century"—even though, strictly speaking, it is not targeted toward the poor. In 1964, about 30 percent of the elderly were poor. Today, the poverty rate for the elderly is only two-thirds of the rate for eighteen- to sixty-four-year-olds and half the rate for children. Its administrative costs and error rates are low. Social Security has many critics among small-government conservatives, but the main functional critiques—that it displaces private savings for old age, pays too low a return, is vulnerable to both political meddling and long-term insolvency, and has become less progressive due to life expectancy differences and rising retirement ages—have had little resonance with the public.[246]

Social Security Disability (SSDI)

This program, part of the Social Security system, has alleviated much poverty by providing income replacement during periods when workers cannot work due to disability. But at the same time, it contributes to poverty through incentives to reduce work effort, in effect operating as a parallel unemployment insurance scheme—although one with badly backlogged claiming and payment processes. SSDI recipients have tripled since 1990 despite a much healthier working-age population. Much of this expansion occurred among young people, and little was caused by the Great Recession. The workers-to-disability recipient ratio has plummeted from 134:1 to only about 16:1 (or, by another measure, 11:1). Recipients are now much younger: In 1960, only 6 percent were in their thirties or early forties; by 2011, more than 15 percent were that young. More than 15 percent are now granted disability for "mood disorders" and another 29 percent for musculoskeletal and connective tissue conditions—both of which, being almost impossible to disprove, encourage fraud. A recent analysis of the program finds that although the expansion is mainly due to demographic changes (more baby boomers in their disability-prone years, more women in the work force), it is also driven by program changes that invited more fraud-prone claims, and by business cycle factors.[247] Poor work incentives and program controls, a dysfunctional appeals process, and eased eligibility also play a role, with 58 percent of recipients now qualifying because of non-medical impairments.[248]

Supplemental Security Income (SSI)

This program, established in 1974, provides monthly cash payments to low-income people who are elderly, blind, or disabled. Although the asset criterion for eligibility has been restricted over time, more than 8 million people receive SSI benefits totaling in excess of $54.8 billion in 2013; 86 percent have disabilities, mostly mental. It constitutes the only source of income for almost 60 percent of the recipients, and substantially reduces the poverty gap for many recipients.[249] Like other antipoverty programs, improper payments are large: Totaling more than $5.1 billion, with an error rate of 9.2 percent, it is the sixth largest among federal programs.[250]

Housing

According to a comprehensive 2015 analysis on which this part is largely based,[251] the federal government spends around $40 billion annually for means-tested housing programs, plus another $6 billion or so annually in tax expenditures on the Low Income Housing Tax Credit (LIHTC).* (This is well over twice the level of federal spending

---

* The same analysis notes that most federal spending on housing (roughly $195 billion of an estimated $270 billion) subsidizes homeowners through the tax code. The non-

on either cash welfare or the Title I compensatory program in education and five times what it spends on Head Start.) These programs seek to make decent housing more affordable for the poor. In-kind housing programs, the theory goes, generate more housing consumption than would similarly costly cash transfers. That is, if the poor were given an equivalent value in cash, they would (except in the highest rent cities) probably spend less of it on housing than the government wants, and more of it on other things.

Public housing tends to be occupied by very poor people. Half of the households in public housing earn less than $10,000 a year, and only 4 percent are two-parent families with children. Much the same is true of those receiving housing vouchers, which subsidize rents in private apartments: Almost half of tenants earn less than $10,000 a year, and single parents rent some 900,000 units. Unlike recipients of TANF, who are subject to time limits on benefits, public-housing residents can remain indefinitely—and many do. The median "tenure" for both public-housing and voucher units is more than nine years; in New York City, the nation's largest public-housing system, it is seventeen years.[252] (For comparison, the median renter had lived in his home for 2.2 years.)

Two features of housing subsidies differentiate them from the other major antipoverty programs.

- Public housing is located in particular neighborhoods rather than being attached to beneficiaries wherever located. Voucher recipients can use them most anywhere and do improve their housing conditions, but most still remain in low-income neighborhoods.
- Targeting is crucial since only a small percentage of poor people receive these valuable benefits. Fewer than one-quarter of income-eligible households receive HUD benefits, but those who do can receive subsidies worth roughly $8,000 per year; in more expensive cities, they can be worth $12,000 per year or even more. More

---

taxation of imputed rent also subsidizes them by roughly $600 billion. The vast majority of these subsidies go to non-poor households.

than 6.5 million households were on wait lists for these benefits in 2012.

The 2015 study summarizes the limited evidence on how these subsidies affect the poor:

> [T]here is surprisingly little good evidence about the effects of existing programs on the behavior and well-being of participating families. We say "surprisingly" both because these programs consume significant amounts of government resources each year (and so are important), and because the excess demand for these program services (fewer than one out of four income-eligible families in the U.S. participates in such a program) would seem to offer numerous opportunities to carry out studies with truly comparable comparison groups.
>
> The best available evidence suggests that increasing housing consumption without improving neighborhood conditions may have little detectable impact on conventional measures of human capital accumulation of children and may reduce labor supply of working-age adults. But these questions are hardly settled; there is considerable room for further evidence on the effects of housing subsidy receipt on families and children. Indeed there is virtually no evidence about the effects of what is currently our largest low-income housing subsidy program, the Low Income Housing Tax Credit program. There is more robust evidence about the importance of neighborhoods, which suggests that exposure to less-distressed neighborhood conditions can improve health outcomes, and, as may be suggested by more recent research, among young children to boost their long-term labor market success as adults.

POLICY REFORMS

The poverty rate in the United States, correctly defined, is much lower than it was fifty years ago, and antipoverty programs have played an important role in that progress. This is a great achievement but leaves us with a kind of paradox. The reduction was in the low-hanging fruit that could most easily be picked off the hard-to-reach branches of poverty. Cash, near-cash, and social services of various kinds could be dispensed to those poor people who were in the best position to take advantage of them. These benefits helped to lift many of them (or their children) into the safer though still-fragile precincts of the working class or, in some cases, beyond.

But the millions who remain behind must rest their hopes for better living conditions and social advancement elsewhere. For some, especially immigrants who come here in middle age or later without much opportunity to employ their old skills, to acquire new marketable ones, or to learn English well enough to enter the wider market economy, aspirations may focus on the next generation, which has a better chance of doing so. Indeed, for the vast majority of low-skill immigrants, full integration into American life has always been a multigenerational process. This may help explain the somewhat surprising finding that Latinos (and blacks) are more optimistic about the future than whites generally.[253] Many other poor people, including some single and childless individuals, noncustodial parents, and the homeless, live mostly hand-to-mouth. They survive on food from soup kitchens and clothing from local social service agencies. More than 5 percent of households average seven months a year of hunger.[254] The poorest depend on begging, petty crime, or SSI for cash, on nocturnal trips to shelters and brief stays with family and friends. Many of the elderly barely get by on Social Security, SSI, food stamps, and help from children. They do not expect upward mobility, only a dignified sustenance.

Other poor people need more, and perhaps different, help if they are to escape poverty. They include adolescents who do poorly in school, have little interest in it, and are unlikely to find relief in an unwelcoming job market; other young people neither in school nor in the job market;[255] those with little or no family support and no useful networks outside their family. They are often dropouts from high school, community college, or vocational programs; mothers trying to raise small children alone with little or no child support (especially those who are also disconnected from both TANF and the job market); other young working-age individuals who can barely survive on their SSI checks and may not qualify for other benefits; criminals recently released from prison with no place to go; and others with poor prospects.

One source of help to the poor in America is private charity—on a scale that dwarfs such contributions in other wealthy societies where antipoverty efforts are almost entirely government-funded.[256] Alexis de Tocqueville emphasized this distinctive feature of American society in the Jacksonian era, but it goes back much earlier to colonial times and our religious roots.[257] In 2015, Americans donated an estimated $373 billion to more than one million charities, with 80 percent of the total given by individuals and bequests. This was the largest amount on record and an increase of 4 percent over 2014.[258] The categories in which contributions are reported obscures how much goes directly or indirectly to the poor, but it is surely immense.* Perhaps surprisingly, poor people, who tend to be more religious, contribute more of their household incomes than rich people do; both groups give away much more than middle-class people do.[259] For all the poverty alleviation that private charity on such a vast scale may do, however, no one should imagine that it could solve the problem of poverty in America, so the question remains: What should the federal government do about it?

In the remainder of this chapter, I canvass possible *government strategies and policies* for managing and ameliorating poverty. I think of strategies here as general, somewhat theorized approaches to either reducing poverty or minimizing its adverse effects on both the poor and the non-poor. Policies are the specific instruments for implementing strategies. (Many policies, of course, are already in place.) The strategies are not pure types—they merely serve as rubrics for the more specific policy discussion—and are less discrete and more eclec-

---

* The largest category by far is religion, though it is a steadily declining share of the total. Second largest is education, with presumably most of that going to elite institutions. Human services is third, with more than 15 percent of the total. Aid to the poor is probably a goal of other categories, including health, foundations, and religion.

tic than they appear to be. Indeed, because the strategies mirror our social diversity and complexity, they propel antipoverty policy in directions that sometimes seem inconsistent, even incoherent.* Three preliminary cautions are in order.

- As already noted, policy makers do distinguish between the "deserving" and "undeserving" poor, although seldom explicitly. Rather, the distinction is implicit in how they define the policy problem and which policies they favor. (When using these terms below, then, I shall not enclose them in scare quotes.) But to target benefits on those most likely to use them to escape poverty is not nearly as straightforward as it sounds. In practice, it is hard to define, apply, and publicly justify the idea of deservingness. As is often the case, the most needy may not be the most deserving, and vice versa. Only 14 percent of Americans support giving cash to poor, able-bodied adults without dependent children. The *least deserving* group, in the public's view, is a family with no adults who are continuously working (or, presumably, in training or school), and with no elderly or disabled member.[260] According to journalist Eduardo Porter, these judgments about deservingness help explain why the very poorest families receive a much smaller percentage of government antipoverty support than they did in the early 1980s.[261]
- Serious policy proposals must be analyzed far more systematically than is possible here. Ideally (but probably seldom in practice), the analysis would clarify the proposal's often conflicting goals; marshal and scrutinize the relevant facts; predict its downstream political and policy effects; consider all trade-offs that the proposal entails; compare its benefits and costs to alternatives including the status quo, with special attention to costs borne by invisible victims (especially likely with poor people); and be rigorously tested

---

* Such pragmatism and opportunism are endemic to American culture, institutions, and politics. As the political scientist Nelson Polsby warned, "The complexity of the American political system may as well be directly acknowledged. . . . [It] stymies proposed reforms based on false analogies with simpler systems."

for effectiveness on a pilot basis. (A promising development in this last respect is the growing interest of for-profit companies in "social impact bonds" through which they can invest in research-tested pilot programs that may yield monetizable cost savings from promising innovative approaches to old problems.)[262] All of this requires deep immersion in a program's operational details and political context by analysts with no axe to grind. My goal here is to identify and clarify such choices rather than to firmly advocate solutions—except those that are most compelling.

- Good policy requires good data, which is exceedingly hard to come by. RCTs and other high-quality studies often find that hopeful-sounding policy innovations—like the NIT discussed earlier—are unsuccessful (or worse), wasting the government's time, money, and credibility.[263]

Any antipoverty approach that involves spending (i.e., almost all of them) must address how it can compete with other budgetary demands. The 800-pound gorilla in this room is the sizeable, demographically driven increase in the future costs of Social Security and Medicare, as well as more interest on a larger national debt.[264] Those two programs are far more popular than antipoverty programs, and the debt interest is implacable. Any funding mechanism also raises a set of design issues: Who will bear the burden initially and then after the cost is passed on to others; the behavioral incentives and changes it might elicit; the government entity and level that imposes it; how difficult is it to administer; and other factors. No program can succeed without good answers to these questions, of course, and by saying little about them I in no way minimize their importance.

My purpose here is to discuss plausible strategies and policies, not how to pay for them. (Significantly, the sequestration provisions enacted in 2011, implemented starting in 2013, and relaxed only slightly for domestic programs in 2016, have seriously constrained the budgets of many domestic and defense programs, but they exempt almost all programs targeting the poor.)[265] Nevertheless, a few points about the revenue side deserve brief mention.

- Tax reform is both possible and desirable, though politically difficult. Eliminating or better targeting some of the hugely inefficient, poorly targeted tax expenditures that mainly benefit the better-off could raise substantial revenue.[266] For example, about 70 percent of the benefits of the popular 529 College Savings program go to households making more than $200,000 a year, costing the government $1 billion in foregone revenue over the next decade.[267] Congress could raise tax rates on the "1 percent" and give the proceeds to the poor through one of the approaches discussed here. Liberals often propose returning these rates to their much higher 1970s levels. Economists, however, note that the effective rates for that elite then were actually far lower than the nominal rates were, and indeed not so much higher than today's.[268] They also disagree sharply about the details of such a change and its effects. The top 1 percent (average income $1.3 million; more than a third comes from capital gains) already pay more in federal income taxes than the bottom 90 percent, and its share, now more than 35 percent of tax revenues, has grown significantly (even after the Bush tax cuts that favored the rich relative to other groups and relative to prior law).[269]
- A 2015 Brookings study finds that even a large tax increase on the top 1 or even 5 percent would have only an "exceedingly modest effect on overall inequality"—an important reality check on optimistic predictions about how much redistribution this popular proposal would actually yield.[270]
- Some key tax policy questions are: How high can the rates be raised without adversely affecting work and investment incentives and perhaps even lowering tax revenues? How much new legal tax avoidance would the super-rich undertake? How much of the new revenue would end up being redistributed to the poor rather than, say, be used for a perennially popular "middle-class tax cut"? Spread out over the entire poverty population, how much difference would it make? And how desirable would it be to reduce high-end inequality even if it does not raise all that much revenue?

Several other sources of funding are less controversial, at least in principle. The amount of fraud, waste, and abuse in federal programs is vast. If rectified—more enforcement could be highly cost-effective—the savings alone would be enough to substantially reduce or eliminate poverty. To cite just one egregious example: In 2012, the Treasury Department failed to collect either the $780 billion that Americans already owed in delinquent loans, fines, and penalties, or the additional $300 billion they already owed in back taxes. (This included $1 billion owed by federal employees and $757 million owed by federal contractors!) Improper payments under Medicare and Medicaid alone exceeded $77 billion in 2014.[271] And "simply" ending clearly ineffective programs and redirecting their funds to poverty reduction would eliminate poverty, at least from a purely fiscal perspective (and not taking into account any adverse work incentives).

With all these clarifications in mind—and leaving the question of political feasibility to the pundits—I now present nine antipoverty strategies, along with some policy proposals that might be used to implement them. (I do not discuss separately here the numerous specific proposals to improve existing antipoverty programs, but I have mentioned some of them already [for example, TANF].)[272] They are: (1) encourage macroeconomic growth; (2) redistribute wealth directly to the poor; (3) help "disconnected mothers"; (4) supplement or insure wages; (5) enhance human capital; (6) strengthen families; (7) dismantle existing barriers to economic opportunity; (8) facilitate residential mobility; and (9) improve health.

Two omissions are worth noting here. First, I do not include a strategy to combat class bias, discussed earlier. Classism does indeed harm some poor people, but, as explained there, almost everyone finds it acceptable, including (or especially) the working poor whom classism often targets. Indeed, as they live closest to underclass dysfunction, they probably fear it the most. Second, I do not separately discuss *Opportunity, Responsibility, Security*, an admirable, ideologically broad-based report issued in December 2015 by a joint

AEI/Brookings working group. My analysis draws heavily, often explicitly, on some of the scholars and analysts who produced it, and I am guided by the same three values underscored in the title of their report.

Macroeconomic Growth

Although poverty experts seldom discuss macroeconomic policy, most of them recognize that balanced economic growth* is the single best strategy for reducing poverty. For that reason, it is worth a brief mention.

By increasing demand for goods and services, economic growth expands the supply of jobs at decent wages that rise with productivity, strengthens poor people's incentives to develop their human capital, and does not require convincing voters to support special programs aimed at the poor—programs that are hard to enact, fund, and (as we just saw) implement effectively. No economist doubts this. They also agree that economic growth is driven primarily by demand, investment, productivity, and innovation, and that the government has some role to play in fostering it—for example, by regulating pollution and other externalities, producing public goods that the market will not adequately supply, running an efficient tax system, and maintaining competitive markets through antitrust law, freer trade, disclosure, and other policies. They also agree that all levels of government erect too many barriers to starting new businesses, and that such barriers seem to be increasing.[273] Even so, the United States is rated the most competitive large economy in the world.[274]

Economists famously disagree, however, about which regulatory techniques, deregulatory measures, public goods, competition policies, and tax regimes are most conducive to such growth. These debates reflect differences over what the government's role should be,

---

* By "balanced growth," economists generally mean growth that produces solid job and wage growth in all economic sectors at a low rate of inflation and without unsustainable asset bubbles or other distortions.

over what causes economic phenomena,* and over the likely effects of particular interventions. To vastly over-simplify long-standing, highly technical debates: Keynesians (or neo-Keynesians) believe that government spending should be used to maintain the demand that will produce such growth, and that the Federal Reserve should provide the liquidity to sustain it. In contrast, monetarists argue that the Fed's chief role should be to maintain a rate of monetary growth that is stable and predictable, so that the "real" (non-financial) economy can function efficiently without monetary distortions. Conservative and liberal economists differ sharply about how efficient markets are, which types of regulation will improve that efficiency, and which policies—particularly tax law[275]—will strike the right balance between promoting efficient growth and ensuring fairness. There is no consensus on these issues, and little point for present purposes in further analyzing the competing arguments.

Redistributing Wealth Directly

One might think that the most straightforward way to reduce poverty is to have the government write checks to the poor. Alaska, Texas, and Wyoming have long practiced what one proponent calls "conservative socialism," distributing proceeds from state-controlled mineral extraction.[276] As we shall see in a moment, many of our foremost analysts—both liberal and conservative—have advocated this policy in some form. I shall describe the most plausible approaches and then explain why they would be very difficult, perhaps impossible, to sell politically. Another approach is to increase benefits and participation rates under existing antipoverty programs.

One way to achieve redistribution directly through the Treasury is to reduce federal taxes on the poor. Although few poor households now pay federal income tax (43 percent of all households do not pay it), the vast majority of poor workers do pay a federal payroll tax of

---

* For example, they agree that productivity has stalled since the late 1990s but disagree about why.

12.4 percent of covered earnings for Social Security.[277] Making the tax even more regressive, it exempts earnings above $126,000 (in 2017). The Medicare tax is 2.9 percent of wages, and has no wage cap.* These payroll taxes are actually twice as high for workers as they seem: Although the employer nominally pays half the tax, standard economics teaches us that the actual incidence of the employer's half comes out of wages, effectively reducing the worker's pay by that amount, so the worker bears the full tax in the end. A strong case can be made for reducing the resulting fiscal hit on low-income workers, but the best way to do that is probably through a refundable tax credit like the EITS or an NIT discussed earlier and next.†

A much more ambitious approach would be some form of a universal basic income (UBI) grant to all Americans. Prominent policy analysts and scholars—including leading libertarian conservatives—have proposed such a grant, which could take the form of a guaranteed income. In 1962, Milton Friedman, a Nobel laureate in economics and conservative guru, proposed an NIT,[278] an idea also supported by Friedrich von Hayek, another Nobel Prize winner in economics:

> The assurance of a certain minimum income for everyone, or a sort of floor below which nobody need fall even when he is unable to provide for himself, appears not only to be a wholly legitimate protection against a risk common to all, but a necessary part of the Great Society in which the individual no longer has specific claims on the members of the particular small group into which he was born.

Hayek added, however, that such a scheme must be designed so as to "not destroy the market order or infringe on the basic principles of individual liberty." Because he would apply it "only to those who

* The *benefit* side of both programs is *progressive*, flowing disproportionately to low-income people—so these payments, conventionally viewed as taxes, might instead be viewed as prices for a deferred benefit. On the other hand, such people tend to die much earlier, roughly offsetting this benefit.

† This would require many low-income workers who need not file tax returns now to begin doing so.

themselves obey liberal principles," it probably would not include the undeserving poor. [279] Many liberals have advocated a guaranteed income for the poor—most notably George McGovern, who proposed a "demogrant" in his 1972 presidential campaign. Legal scholars Bruce Ackerman and Anne Alstott proposed a scheme in which the government would pay $80,000 to every qualifying American at the verge of adulthood.[280] Even the prominent conservative Charles Murray has endorsed a guaranteed income of $10,000, which would wholly replace all income-support programs.[281]

Under most such proposals, the payments would be virtually universal, extending to all citizens, and would replace current federal means-tested programs. In 2012, Robert Rector listed seventy-nine such programs, costing $927 billion. About half of this sum goes for medical care. Another 40 percent is allocated for cash, food, and housing, and the remaining 10–12 percent is for programs that seek to help the poor become more self-sufficient. "If converted to cash," Rector told the House Budget Committee, "means-tested welfare spending is more than sufficient to bring the income of every lower-income American to 200 percent of the federal poverty level, roughly $44,000 per year for a family of four."[282] This fact, together with the fact that many poor people do not now receive benefits from these programs and all are beholden to the legions of bureaucrats who now regulate and dispense them, constitutes a powerful argument for cashing out these programs and using some or all of the proceeds to fund a guaranteed income that will eliminate poverty (at least as officially defined).

In the United States, direct redistribution schemes of this sort are political non-starters.* As we have seen, even a minimal guaranteed

---

* Finland, with the agreement of all major political parties, plans to inaugurate a guaranteed income in 2016, providing every adult citizen about $900 a month with few if any strings attached—while largely eliminating its social welfare bureaucracy. In June 2016, on the other hand, 77 percent of voters in Switzerland rejected a proposal to provide a basic monthly income of 2,500 Swiss francs (US $2560) to adults and 625 francs to children under 18 regardless of employment status (http://www.nytimes.com/2016/06/06/world /europe/switzerland-swiss-vote-basic-income.html).

family income plan could not pass Congress in the early 1970s, and it would be no more palatable today. Indeed, the elderly, a crucial voting bloc, increasingly oppose such redistribution.[283] Congress has not enacted a new low-income entitlement since the Child Tax Credit (CTC) in 1997. The only programs that provide cash (or near-cash) directly to the poor are those that claim to be insurance programs to which recipients contributed (Social Security retirement); provide basic nutrition (SNAP); assist the putatively deserving poor (SSI and EITC); are time- and amount-limited, and hedged with eligibility restrictions (TANF); and provide a refundable tax credit to poor working families with children (CTC). Henry Aaron, a senior Brookings analyst, sees most Americans as "commodity egalitarians"—they will support programs that prevent poor people from going hungry, living in decrepit housing, or going untreated—but only a tiny minority are "cash egalitarians" who support providing money to those without cash. Thus, "we far more willingly vote refundable tax credits to pay for health care than we do refundable tax credits for low incomes—besides, troublesome though administration of the health credits may be, it is child's play next to administering large transfers of cash."[284] Past experience supports this assessment.

A UBI would require some tough policy choices—for example, which conditions should be imposed (e.g., work or training effort), whether higher-income people should be included, whether the payment itself should be taxable, the scheme's effects on state programs, what happens to recipients who still run out of money, and especially how it affects work incentives. (Americans work many more hours per year than Europeans do.) Even if a UBI were limited to the working poor, work effort would likely decline. The many whose work is repetitious, boring, physically demanding, dirty, dangerous, or poorly paid would need ever more subsidies just to be sustained at any given income level. Finally, as the *Economist* points out in a broad review of such proposals, a UBI would wreak havoc on immigration policy: "The right to an income would encourage rich-world governments either to shut the doors to immigrants, or to create second-class citizenries without access to state support."[285]

A more politically viable approach to redistribution would be to increase benefits under *existing* antipoverty programs. There are at least four ways to do this.

- Congress could raise benefit levels under programs like EITC, CTC, TANF, and SSI. Grants or larger tax subsidies for *children*, as the Century Foundation proposes, might be more attractive politically.[286]
- It could index cash and near-cash benefits to inflation (or some portion of it), just as it did for Social Security decades ago.
- Using a conditional cash transfer (CCT) approach, it could grant additional cash benefits conditional on improved behaviors regarding preventive health measures, children's school attendance, and other desirable conduct. A controlled trial of CCT in several cities reported in September 2016 that it had few significant effects even with the addition of proactive guidance of the families, and it reduced work effort somewhat.[287]
- The programs themselves could surely increase participation rates among eligible poor people, which are often surprisingly low. A recent congressional study of take-up rates in 2012 found that only 70 percent participated in SNAP, 65 percent in WIC, and a mere 28 percent in TANF.[288] Take-up rates respond to bureaucratic efforts, as large state-to-state variations and some studies of policy changes show.[289] Even so, many who know they are eligible still fail to apply because they don't want to depend on government.[290] This is not true of Medicare and Social Security. TANF is long overdue for reauthorization (it has been on continuing resolutions since 2010), which should be the occasion for its reform.

A final approach to redistribution is to create *new* entitlements to social provision or social insurance that relieve the poor of having to spend what little money they have on such goods, shifting those costs to non-poor taxpayers. The recent expansion of Medicaid did this, and proposals for more universal child care support and free community colleges would do so as well. More flexible work arrangements that enable more poor people to both work and care for their children would also enhance income. And eliminating the digital divide is a relatively cheap and uncontroversial way to enhance opportunity.[291] As always, however, much turns on the policy details.

Disconnected Mothers

As noted previously, a large and growing number of single mothers are disconnected from TANF work (they may be unemployable), EITC (the same reason), child support (the fathers are too poor or elude enforcement), or simply fall through the safety net for other reasons. A surprising—and encouraging—finding, however, is that "most" of the $2-a-day poor (not including government transfers) "have a recent history of work"[292] and so may be less disconnected than one might assume. Poverty analysts like Rebecca Blank have proposed ways to help these disconnected adults and their children, usually by temporarily waiving TANF and SNAP work requirements while conducting case-by-case reviews of whether and how they can be made employable, and if not, designing arrangements that will support them without undermining the work rules.[293] In addition, programs to increase paternal child support, which has declined significantly in the last decade, can be strengthened by linking them to benefits under other antipoverty programs, including job training for non-custodial parents.[294]

Wage Supplements and Insurance

There are three main ways to augment earnings from work: raise the minimum wage; increase EITC benefits; and insure against wage losses.

Minimum Wage. The federal minimum wage (as well as state and local ones) can be raised. This approach has galvanized public support in recent years, as unions and other advocates for low-income workers mounted successful campaigns in various cities and states to raise it (sometimes across the board, sometimes for particular groups such as fast-food workers or chains of a particular size) to $15 an hour, while pressing Congress to raise the national minimum to that level. Minimum wage increases, however, are not well targeted on the working poor, as noted earlier. A 2010 study found that less than 25 percent of those who receive the minimum wage are poor or near-poor, while 63 percent live in households with incomes above twice the poverty line; 42 percent are in households above three times the poverty line.[295]

Numerous studies of the income and employment effects of minimum wage increases, including recent reviews,[296] find negative employment effects on low-skill worker employment (especially entry-level; teen employment declined sharply between 2000 and 2014);[297] on consumers of the products and services they produce; and on small businesses. Such increases also encourage employers to substitute machines for labor. David Card and Alan Krueger's 1994 study, the major exception,[298] was strongly criticized for its data and methodology.[299] In 2014, the CBO reviewed the many studies on the minimum wage, analyzing two options. The largest was a raise to $10.10 an hour (much lower than jurisdictions have been enacting since then). The CBO found that this would move 900,000 workers above the (officially defined) poverty line while reducing employment by at least 500,000 jobs.[300] The job losers, only 0.3 percent of the workforce, are a highly vulnerable group, disproportionately minorities and high school dropouts.[301] Small minimum wage increases may have less adverse effects on jobs, but those as large as some jurisdictions are now adopting, especially if focused on specific sectors and firm sizes, may lead to larger long-term effects. Although harder to predict, they are also likely to have a net negative effect on low-skill workers.[302] A recent research summary predicts much larger longer-term (if the increase is inflation indexed) job losses: in the restaurant industry, one hundred times more than in the short term, and much lower future job growth for young, unskilled workers.[303] (President Obama has also ordered an increase in overtime pay under the Fair Labor Standards Act, a step that, like minimum wage increases, will likely have mixed effects on the poor.)[304] Finally, a 2015 review finds that the minimum wage reduces inequality somewhat at the lower end of the wage distribution, but the impact is "almost negligible for males" and "the net effects on inequality are less than half as large as previously claimed."[305]

EITC. Several proposed reforms have considerable bipartisan support.[306] Including noncustodial single workers (Mead would condition this on their working full time and paying child support, if any)[307] would create few, if any, of the job-displacement or relocation risks of a higher minimum wage. In addition, government could subsidize employers to pay higher wages or make it easier for unions to organize workers—but both approaches have a number of efficiency and other disadvantages that cannot be analyzed here.

Wage Insurance. Some leading economists propose adding protection against wage loss to existing safety net programs. Existing protections are limited to the disabled (SSDI) and to older workers displaced by foreign competition and earning less than $50,000. Thus, ample room for expansion of such protection exists—probably through a progressive form of payroll tax, together with some restrictions for limiting moral hazard.[308]

Enhancing Human Capital. Permanent escape from poverty means, at a minimum, that one must possess the knowledge, analytical ability, and training to be a productive citizen who can earn an adequate income in the market. Our educational system is supposed to provide this. Traditionally, it led the world but that day is long past, except in post-secondary education, where the United States is peerless. Interested readers will find a vast body of research on our system presented in a recent book by leading educational policy experts, on which I shall draw here.[309] My limited purpose is to summarize some findings on the education of low-income children, and to describe some programmatic approaches that reformers are now investigating.

- Only seven of the seventy-seven educational interventions evaluated by RCTs (without major study limitations) commissioned by the Institute for Education Sciences (IES) since 2002 were found to produce positive effects—despite the fact that most of them had shown promising results in earlier research. And statistics like these likely overstate the fraction of interventions found to be successful due to publication bias—i.e., the tendency for researchers and journals to dismiss or reject studies that find no effect.[310]

- The public has a low opinion of our public schools: "They know that only somewhat more than 70 percent of students graduate from high school within four years after entering ninth grade. Only about one-fifth of the public gives the nation's schools an A or a B on the five-letter scale traditionally used to grade students [but grade their own children's schools higher]."[311]

- Our failures in educating children have continued despite enormous increases in per-pupil expenditures and reductions in class size. Results are so consistently negative that a broad scholarly consensus has emerged that simple increases in financial resources or reductions in class size across the board, without more fundamental changes, yield few benefits for student performance. Of course, perhaps more compelling than the academic debates is the fact that the United States has tried these policies over the past half century with little to no obvious results; the country has dramatically increased expenditures and reduced pupil-teacher ratios, yet [National Assessment of Educational Progress] scores of U.S. seventeen-year-olds have been constant. . . . Just about as many high-spending states showed relatively small gains as showed large ones. . . . [The research does not hold that money never matters]. . . . How money is spent is much more important than how much is spent.[312]

- Although low-income children enter school with many disadvantages in terms of vocabulary, reading skills, home stability, health, stress, and parental support, these factors do not fully explain their low academic outcomes. What goes on *within* the schools is also crucial.

- "[P]erformance differences between the United States and other countries [cannot] be attributed simply to ethnic heterogeneity or poverty. The United States is not the only country with a diverse population. . . . [T]he proficiency rates of white students and of the most advantaged socioeconomic subgroup of children of college-educated parents in the United States fail to keep pace with the proficiency rates of all students in many countries across the globe."[313]

- The quality of teachers can make a difference to academic and later-life outcomes for students, especially low-income ones: "One study, focusing entirely on a disadvantaged group of students in Gary, Indiana, finds that the difference in student performance gains with a highly effective teacher compared to an ineffective teacher was one full year of learning for each academic year: the top teachers produced gains of 1.5 grade levels, while the bottom teachers produced gains of 0.5 grade level in an academic year. Again, these impacts of teachers were recorded for precisely the group of students that are the focus of those emphasizing the centrality of socioeconomic issues. Furthermore, the well-documented differences in teacher effectiveness indicate that three to five years in a class with a top teacher versus an average teacher is sufficient to erase the average achievement gap between poor and better-off children. That is, regardless of the source of any preexisting achievement differences, effective teachers can eliminate them. Family background is not fate."[314]

- These facts are widely appreciated by educational reformers, who have devised many programs to address them. Earlier, I discussed some of them, such as Head Start and other early childhood, pre-K programs. The most promising approaches for elementary and secondary education, such as KIPP, grow out of the alternative (often charter) schools and parental choice movements that have gained considerable traction. In a multiyear study of 41 urban areas in 22 states, a Stanford research center found that compared with matched peers, charter school students experienced greater growth in math and reading.[315] These gains were particularly pronounced among blacks, Hispanics, low-income, and special education students, as charter students typically receive 25-plus days of extra learning.[316] A RAND Corporation study even found that charter high schools outpaced regular district schools in graduation rates (by 15 percent) and college attendance rates (by 8 percent).[317] On the other hand, recent studies of statewide programs in Louisiana and Indiana providing vouchers for private schools found lower academic performance compared with similar students that remained in public schools.[318]

- Despite the demonstrated effectiveness of some of these alternative school programs, they still account for a tiny fraction of the nation's students. Another study ascribes the limited reach of such reforms to the fierce campaigns waged against them by the teachers' unions: "Opposition to change is not the result of intense conflict among the public at large. Differences of opinion do not loom large between parents and nonparents, old and young, affluent and those of more moderate means, renters and homeowners, those from different religious and cultural backgrounds or among groups of varying ethnic background, or even between Democrats and Republicans. By far the deepest cleavage over education policy is between the members of the teaching profession and the general public."[319]

More low-income students who manage to complete high school go on to college than ever before (45 percent in 2012, up from 28 percent in 1970). But this good news is subject to some important caveats.

- Many of those who are qualified for admission to high-ranked private universities do not apply (this is also true, to a lesser extent, of more affluent ones) and end up enrolling in lower-ranked public ones, even though the former (because of financial aid packages) would have cost them less than the latter. (Research shows that they could be better informed about this choice at trivial cost.)[320]
- The vast majority of them do not graduate—only 20 percent, about the same as in 1970.[321] (This includes those who enrolled in

two-year colleges.) Indeed, only 55 percent of *all* students who matriculate in U.S. colleges graduate[322]—the highest dropout rate in the developed world.[323] Also troubling, a prominent study finds that college students actually don't learn much there.[324] The problem is not just affordability. Consider a Kalamazoo, Michigan, program that makes college tuition-free for the city's high school graduates, of whom nearly 90 percent from the classes of 2006–08 were eligible. Even so, only 40 percent of the program recipients earned a post-secondary credential within six years of high school graduation, and only 21 percent of those who enrolled in community colleges earned a post-secondary credential.[325] This suggests that President Obama's plan to make community college free for two years[326] may help low-income students get to campus, but keeping them there is another thing altogether. Indeed, studies suggest that comparable students are more likely to graduate from four-year colleges than from community colleges.[327]

• The immense for-profit college-and-vocational training industry enrolls primarily older, female, low-income job-seekers. Typically, these schools get the vast majority of their revenue from federal student loans, and they account for nearly half of the defaults. When Corinthian Colleges, one of the largest, filed for bankruptcy in 2015 after repeated criticism for maladministration and poor teaching, the government decided to forgive loans to their students, estimating that if all 350,000 of them over the last five years received forgiveness, it could cost $3.5 billion.[328] Under pressure, some other private companies may forgive some loans as well.[329] Corinthian's failure may be just the tip of the iceberg of for-profit educational fraud.[330] Far more extensive loan forgiveness will place even more political pressure on the federal loan system on which so many low-income people depend. More and better information to applicants about these schools and the economic payoffs to their students is essential, but designing and enforcing such disclosure systems is difficult.[331] A more radical approach would bar government loans to students attending schools with very low graduation rates, but this would deny many low-income students access. Making grants for only the first year and thereafter providing loans based on continued performance should also be tried.

Some private initiatives to train unskilled youngsters for good jobs show more promise. Working with high schools, some major corporations, hospitals, and other entities have instituted a program, known as P-Tech, that is designed to transform the idea of vocational education. It is a six-year program, based on a company-developed curriculum combining conventional high school subjects with science, technology, and math training that leads students to an associate's degree at no cost to them, with mentoring and paid internships along the way. According to the *Economist*, more than seventy small and large companies have already adopted, or are working with schools to adopt, this model—so far with considerable success.[332] Such employer-led approaches should be expanded.[333] Some classroom-linked, specific-field certificate programs do fairly well on job-readiness preparation with weak students; cities vary considerably in their use of them.[334] Finally, reformers are showing much more interest in apprenticeship programs, drawing on the experience of other countries that have used them more extensively than the United States to prepare academically limited poor people for jobs.[335]

Other approaches to human capital focus on altering the behavioral patterns of at-risk youngsters, including their decisions to drop out of high school, get involved with drugs or gangs, and get into confrontations that can escalate to violence. In three large RCTs, researchers found that certain techniques designed to reduce the tendency of poor young men to respond unthinkingly to dangerous social stimuli in high-stakes situations did succeed in reducing their criminality and dangerous choices.[336]

Strengthening Families. Of all antipoverty strategies, this is surely the most important. As noted earlier, the single best predictor of low economic mobility is the fraction of children with single parents. Research also finds that "Children of married parents also have higher rates of upward mobility if they live in communities with fewer single parents."[337]* But this strategy is also the most challenging. Although family is the basic unit of any society, its dynamics differs among cultures, resists outside intervention, seems impervious to conventional policy tools, and for all its ubiquity and "familiarity" remains poorly understood.

In this discussion, I consider three different approaches to strengthening families: delay their formation through better choices, encourage marriage, and provide services to at-risk families. (Needless to say, much of the earlier analysis of poverty's causes and possible remedies is highly relevant to the flourishing of families, so I shall try to avoid repetition.)

Delaying family formation means not having children until after completion of what Sawhill and Ron Haskins call the "success sequence" consisting of three key choices that, singly and especially together, would greatly reduce the poverty rate.

- Work effort is clearly the most important. This was discussed earlier.
- Having children only when married and after age twenty-one.
- If every household head at least completed high school, the rate would drop even further. (GED holders do not do as well.)[338]

Newer simulations using 2013 data yielded similar findings.[339] Even among those who follow the success sequence, whites tend to do better across a broad range of poverty- and middle-level incomes.[340]

Poor people obviously have more control over some of these choices than others. High school completion and delaying children are more clearly matters of choice. Marital stability is some combination of rational choice (whether, when, and whom to marry) and unpredictable developments. Sawhill and Haskins know, of course, that full-time work is not always simply a matter of choice, but they note three facts relevant to this point:

---

* This last conclusion about communities is not robust because the Chetty et al. study relied on IRS data lacking a number of potentially important uncontrolled variables. Email to author from Christopher Jencks, December 5, 2015.

- Lack of available jobs is *not* the main reason why the poor work so much less than the non-poor do. An update of their analysis based on 2014 data yields a remarkable finding: for nonworking heads of households *who do not receive disability income*, a surprisingly small fraction (only 11 percent of females and 20 percent of males) gave as the reason for not working that they were "unable to find work." The most important reason women gave for not working was "taking care of home or family," while for men it was being "ill or disabled." (Note, again, that the study *excluded* those who said that they received SSDI or SSI, as well as adults younger than age twenty-five, or older than fifty-four.)[341]
- Given how antipoverty programs are structured, "disincentives to work are large. As incomes rise, various forms of assistance are scaled back and payroll and other taxes begin to take a larger bite out of people's earnings."[342]
- Choices about work affect the other three choices (and probably additional ones as well): "Young people who know that they are going to have to work would be more likely to finish school. Those who aspire to be stay-at-home mothers for an extended period would be more likely to delay having children until they are married since the government would no longer subsidize them to be full-time mothers. And those required to work would have less time to care for additional children and might plan their families accordingly. Indeed, serious work requirements may be more of an incentive to finish school, delay childbearing until marriage, and limit the size of one's family than all the combined government programs directly aimed at these objectives.[343]

The "success sequence"—*if young low-income people could somehow be induced to follow it*—would enable many or most of them to avoid or escape poverty. Of course, altering behavior shaped by youthful impulsiveness and poor judgment, sexual and maternal urges, inter-personal power struggles, and cultural signals is exceedingly difficult, as many social reformers have found.* Our society has a huge

---

* Their Brookings colleague, economist and poverty analyst Henry Aaron, is skeptical about their success sequence claims: "So, the bottom line is that a) we don't know how to

stake in propagating the importance of the success sequence to one's prospects in life, while designing policies to encourage people to make those choices—certainly the three that are wholly within their control. And we have made great progress on one of these choices. "Teen pregnancy rates," Haskins reports, "have declined every year except two since 1991; over that period the rate has declined more than 50 percent, saving billions of dollars in taxpayer spending and improving other serious problems including school failure and poverty."[344] The cause(s) of the decline are not certain, but the abstinence education that Congress mandated in 1996 clearly was *not* one of them. [345] Even so, Haskins notes, we still have the highest rate among advanced economies.

Sawhill's 2014 book, *Generation Unbound: Drifting into Sex and Parenthood without Marriage*, establishes a powerful nexus between poverty reduction and carefully planned and deferred parenthood. Echoing the American College of Obstetricians and Gynecologists,[346] she urges that at-risk teens and women be educated about sexuality, contraception, abortion and its alternatives, and the dire consequences of premature family formation. Indeed, even after a decades-long drop in teenage births and the lowest number of unwanted pregnancies (defined as unwanted now or within the next two years) since the 1980s,[347] nearly half of each year's 6.6 million pregnancies are still unintended. The abortion rate for poor women has risen nearly 20 percent in the last twenty years, while dropping nearly 30 percent for well-off ones.[348] Yet a simple remedy for unwanted births exists: delaying childbearing through long-acting reversible contraceptives (LARCs), in the form of IUDs and hormonal implants, which are twenty times more effective than the pill and other common methods, and are safe. Indeed, in only five years, Colorado has used LARCs to

---

change the relevant behaviors; and b) even if we could get the people being studied to have acted differently from the way they did the results would *not* be as they were for the people who actually did behave differently. [Sawhill and Haskins'] response would be: 'look we tried everything we could to control for individual differences and this is what came out; you are really saying that the sort of thing we are attempting can't be done.' Which *is* just what I am saying.'" Email to author dated November 8, 2015. Jencks agrees: "We've tried this for decades. It has helped a little, not a lot." Written comment to author dated November 30, 2015.

raise the median age of first births to women in its poorest areas from before age 21 to after age 24, thus helping young women to finish school and gain a foothold in the job market.[349] Even so, fewer than 10 percent of sexually active women use the devices—partly because many doctors fail to recommend them[350] and partly, one presumes, because many women are reluctant to make a long-term commitment to not getting pregnant.[351]

A second way to strengthen families—encouraging marriage—is less tractable to public policy. Indeed, it runs counter to one of our (and Europe's) strongest and most troubling trends: non-marital childbearing, discussed earlier. The second Bush administration's Health Marriage Initiative designed to encourage and sustain marriage was evidently ineffective.[352] And while Robert Rector, Sawhill, and others note the substantial "marriage penalties" in our tax code and welfare programs, these appear to have little effect on marriage one way or the other. (They would also be fiscally very costly to eliminate.)[353]

The third approach is to provide discrete support services to low-income households. Public and private programs of this kind have existed for generations; they are numerous and remarkably diverse. Taken together, they seek to address every cause of poverty discussed above—and then some (e.g., religious approaches). One private-sector success, celebrated by management guru Peter Drucker, is the Salvation Army's ability to discourage bad choices.[354] A governmental success, the Nurse-Family Partnership program sends nurses to visit poor women with first pregnancies, counseling them on nutrition, avoidance of risky behavior, breast-feeding, conversational teaching, and affection—and continues their visits until the child reaches age 2. According to three RCTs, the program improves many social outcomes and is cost-effective.[355] But relatively few other service programs have been rigorously evaluated.

Dismantle Barriers to Opportunity. Perversely, the same governments that claim to fight poverty—including through civil rights law mandating equal opportunity in employment, credit, and other areas—often help to entrench it by erecting ill-advised barriers to self-help and small-scale entrepreneurship. (The United States ranks forty-sixth in the world in ease of starting a business!)[356] One area in which this occurs is occupational licensing rules, which often serve little or no purpose except to protect existing businesses from competition and innovation by new, low-income entrants. The portion of the U.S. workforce covered by state licensing grew from less than 5 percent in the early 1950s to 25 percent in 2008—largely because of the number of occupations requiring a license, rather than due to employment growth within certain heavily licensed fields such as health care and education.[357] The Institute of Justice, a conservative public-interest organization, has challenged many of them—laws requiring hair braiders to first obtain a cosmetology license requiring 1600 hours at a private cosmetology school, laws limiting vending or car service opportunities to a monopoly firm, laws barring the sale of caskets, laws requiring florists and interior designers to pass a licensing exam, and many others.[358] President Obama's Council of Economic Advisers recently expressed alarm about the growth of these restrictions. Today, it found, they cost millions of jobs nationwide and cost consumers over $100 billion annually. The Council proposes more efforts to dismantle them.[359]

Several other kinds of barriers raise closer policy questions where legitimate competing interests exist on both sides—unlike the absurd anti-competitive licensing mandates that have no plausible public-interest justification just discussed. One example is employer rules requiring job applicants to agree to credit checks or to disclose any criminal record (discussed earlier). Like many other progressives, Joseph Fishkin strongly opposes such practices, viewing them as "opportunity bottlenecks."[360] But past criminal activity or chronic credit problems sometimes helps predict an applicant's character and likely job performance, information that reasonable employers might legitimately consider relevant. Another example of a close question is the use by some institutions of standardized tests on which poor people, especially blacks, do worse on average. The merits of such tests can certainly be debated (some institutions have abandoned them while others find them essential) and Fishkin's distinctions based on a practice's arbitrariness, legitimacy, and strictness are helpful in assessing its use. But policy makers must consider the possibility that banning them may induce employers and institutions to make worse decisions by resorting to cruder proxies (address, for example) that turn out to be more unfair to the poor.

Residential Mobility. In the earlier discussion on isolation as a cause of poverty, we saw the importance of the geographical enclave factor in entrenching poverty, now confirmed by the Chetty group's research. So convincing are these findings that efforts are under way in some low-income neighborhoods to implement the Chetty strategy of subsidized out-migration through more tenant- and landlord-friendly Section 8 vouchers and other affordable housing programs.[361] Like previous efforts,[362] these will surely encounter fiscal, zoning, classist, environmental, political, and other barriers that exemplify the competing interests at stake.[363] In July 2015, the Obama administration adopted a new remedy in the form of a HUD rule designed to induce, if not force, local communities to integrate housing economically, not just racially.[364] Whether the next administration continues this rule and how it implements it, of course, remains to be seen. On the other hand, some evidence suggests that even poor people who are mobile usually move to neighborhoods that are little better than the ones that they left.[365] A New York study suggests that improving the neighborhoods where they already live (often criticized as gentrification) may be a better approach than trying to move them.[366] Finally, programs could encourage the jobless in declining regions to move to job-growth areas in other states—what Henry Olson proposes as a "new Homestead Act."[367]

Improve Health. Poor people are much less healthy than better-off Americans, whether the index is acute and chronic diseases, mental health, or longevity.[368] Unsurprisingly, poor health correlates with (and presumably causes and is caused by) joblessness, family chaos, parental neglect, and other conditions associated with poverty. A par-

tial list of reasons for this would include higher rates of smoking, dia-
betes, obesity, substance abuse, high blood pressure, inactivity, accidents, and violence. Indeed, the Health Inequality Project reported in
2016 that these behaviors are far more detrimental to life expectancy
among the poor than either levels of income inequality or access to
health care.[369] (Poor people use fewer health services even when they
have insured access!)[370]

This is why public and private programs have long focused on
improving poor people's health. Changing entrenched behaviors,
however, is notoriously difficult. Solutions—other than expanding access to health care (which of course addresses symptoms more than
causes)—are far from clear. Unless effectiveness seems very likely on
the program's face, the most promising approaches should at a minimum be rigorously evaluated and resources targeted accordingly.

CONCLUSION

Poverty is an immensely complex, tangled, and recalcitrant problem.
Among the wealthiest societies in the world, America is also uniquely
charitable, innovative, and animated by a can-do spirit, yet we have
failed to solve the poverty issue. This does not mean that we have not
made significant progress. Properly measured, the poverty rate is far
below what it was when the War on Poverty began a half-century ago,
especially for the elderly. Moreover, the standard of living of most
people who still live in poverty is much higher than it was then.
Through a combination of government transfer programs and economic growth, the United States has managed to abolish the worst
forms of material deprivation for the vast majority of the poor.

But the hardest-core poverty has proved (by definition) resistant
to our best efforts—and to the trillions of dollars that we have devoted
to the task. The evidence casts serious doubt on the hope that more
money for more programs would cure it. Yes, better teachers could
make a big difference for poor children and higher pay might attract
more of them, but they cannot remedy the domestic chaos that brings
so many already severely disadvantaged students into the nation's

classrooms. Tragically, many of the reinforcing causes of this chaos— family breakdown, incarceration, educational deficits, and bad choices—have worsened, especially for poor black men. Their disadvantages will surely be deepened by the many forces transforming America: global competition; mechanization; robotics; fewer decent-paying unskilled jobs, with highly motivated immigrants competing for them; more children raised in non-marital households; the decline of many urban cores (and the rise of others that the poor can no longer afford); waning religiosity; and less confidence that government can solve these problems.

Americans should take some comfort in the real progress that has been made in reducing poverty. But just as the costs and difficulties of solving the last 10 percent of almost any social problem far exceed those necessary to reach that point, eliminating the poverty that remains will be much, much harder to accomplish.

CHAPTER 3

IMMIGRATION

MORE THAN 78 MILLION people in the United States are either immigrants (legal and undocumented) or their children—about one in four of us.[1] The stakes for America's future in admitting the right ones and integrating them into our society could not be higher. More than fifty years after the landmark Hart-Celler Act of 1965, which established the basic structure of our immigration system, and more than twenty-five years after the Immigration Act of 1990, which updated that system, the issue (really a set of issues) remains stalemated.

Indeed, pundits consider immigration reform (like Social Security reform) a "third rail" of politics likely to inflict serious harm on those bold or foolish enough to touch it. As I write (a few days after the 2016 elections) President Obama and a Republican-controlled Congress are so deeply divided about how to deal with the 11 million undocumented immigrants living in the United States that the Supreme Court will have to rule on it—and a divided, now-truncated Court probably cannot do so. Especially with the election of Donal Trump, a political resolution seems unlikely, even with respect to legal immigrants, for several years,

Why is immigration so hard to address constructively? The answer lies in the uniquely vexed historical, ethno-racial, political, cultural,

and economic conditions (including the always-potent force of inertia) in which any immigration policy must be forged. The chapter
analyzes those conditions. It first sets out the broad *context* for understanding these conditions, focusing on five elements (history, current
immigration levels, administration, politics, and economic impact).
It then analyzes the central immigration *policy issues*, concluding
with my own reform suggestions, subject to my now-familiar caveats
about the importance of policy specifics.

CONTEXT

A Thumbnail History

In an old joke, an Indian chieftain explains why his tribe was forced
to follow the Trail of Tears: "We should have paid more attention to
our immigration policy." Centuries before the Indian wars, however,
America had already experienced extraordinary ethnic and religious
diversity, producing a complex pattern of both peaceful coexistence
and bitter, sometimes violent conflict. Aristide Zolberg's magisterial
history of American immigration, pointedly titled "A Nation by Design," begins with his master theme: "A nation of immigrants, to be
sure, but not just any immigrants. From the moment they managed
their own affairs, well before political independence, Americans were
determined to select who might join them, and they have remained
so ever since."[2]

The principal subthemes of our rich immigration history, all too
briefly and simply put, are as follows. The Founders clearly understood that immigration and naturalization would together constitute
a central pillar in the construction of the American nation, and we
waged many battles (literally, in some cases) over this issue with Great
Britain and other countries. For a century, immigration policy was
essentially unregulated, save for state and local public health measures generally directed at poor migrants. State laws also helped to
shape immigration patterns and population development, particularly in the western territories.[3] This early period, Zolberg empha-

sizes, was marked by "*inclusiveness*, indicated by the absence of religious or national origins qualifications [which] constituted an obvious invitation to non-British nationals and, on the religious side, to Roman Catholics and Jews."[4] But discrimination against immigrants, particularly non-whites and religious minorities, was rife from the beginning.[5]

Direct federal regulation began in 1875, focusing on prostitutes, the destitute, and other categories of "undesirables," and was followed by treaties and laws limiting non-merchant migrants from Asia, notably the Chinese and Japanese, and regulating "contract labor" from abroad—restrictions that were often evaded by resourceful migrants, employers, and families. But even well before these federal restrictions were adopted, bitter controversies about migration to the United States precipitated political crises over race, slavery, religion, and access to cheap labor. These crises transformed the American party system, contributed to the Civil War, roiled politics in California and other destination states, and fueled violent divisions over worker rights in an era of industrialism and globalization of trade and migration.

During this entire period (except for the Civil War), the number of immigrants to the United States from Europe (and, to a much lesser degree, Asia and Latin America) soared. By 1890, 32.7 percent of the almost 63 million residents were either immigrants or the children of at least one immigrant; for each ethnic group, moreover, immigrants exceeded the native-born by a considerable margin. And by 1890, Catholicism—reviled by nativist Protestants as theologically heterodox, disloyal, authoritarian, conspiratorial, morally depraved, and un-American—was the largest Christian denomination in the country, and this antagonism generated constant political struggles over the Sabbatarian, temperance, and common school reform movements, as well as over naturalization, public funds for parochial schools, and indeed the very nature of democratic politics.

Historians often view the decade of the 1890s, which perhaps not coincidentally also saw the closing of the western frontier, as a watershed separating the "old" immigration from the "new." More than 18.2

million newcomers entered the country between 1890 and 1920, a total almost double that in the 1860–90 period and quadruple that in the 1830–60 period. This migration, which other receiving countries in the Americas, Australia, and New Zealand also experienced, was as striking for its ethno-racial and source-country diversity as for its size. Most new immigrants were unskilled laborers, farm workers, or servants; Jews were a notable exception, as many were tailors, tradesmen, and merchants; very few were farm workers. Many of these groups returned home at very high rates.

Deploring these changes, immigration restrictionists mobilized politically. In 1907, President Theodore Roosevelt responded to anti-Japanese pressure in California by negotiating limits to their migration, and in 1911 the Dillingham Commission reported to Congress on immigrants' criminality, physical and intellectual inferiority relative to the native stock, and impacts on the economy. This report, and the fact that the foreign-born share of the population was approaching 15 percent, fed the long-standing demand for an English literacy requirement for admission, not just for naturalization. This demand, which had been stymied by presidential vetoes, was finally enacted in 1917 over Woodrow Wilson's veto (though it required only fluency in a language of the applicant's choice for those age sixteen or older), along with a blatantly racist ban on immigration from Asia, which would not be fully repealed until 1965. Immigration declined sharply during World War I and its aftermath. Anti-German recriminations were widespread, and an "Americanization" movement led by business and civic organizations pressed for various forms of acculturation to efface ethnic identities.

The postwar years witnessed assimilation by earlier immigrants whose ranks were no longer being replenished. After an economic slump, a resurgence of Protestant fundamentalism and the Ku Klux Klan, organized labor hostility to immigration, and militant anticommunism, Congress in 1921 and more comprehensively in 1924 enacted a popular system of restrictions. Most significant was the national origins quota system, designed to mimic the ethno-racial composition that had existed back in 1890. A reluctant President

Hoover put the system into effect in 1929 and it largely remained in effect until 1965. During the 1930s, only 500,000 immigrants came to the United States, just more than 10 percent of those who came in the 1920s, and many of these did not remain; in 1932, almost three times as many immigrants left the country as entered it. Despite the growing refugee crisis, the nation's response was too little too late; in what may be the cruelest single action in our immigration history, Congress defeated a bill in 1939 to rescue 20,000 children from Nazi Germany despite American families' eagerness to sponsor them—on the ground that the children would exceed Germany's quota!

In the twenty years after World War II, four portentous developments shaped the current immigration policy landscape. Immediately after the war, the United States negotiated with Mexico a large-scale program that eventually brought in 4.5 million temporary farmworkers known as *braceros*, in order to fill labor needs in the South and Southwest. Its termination in 1964 continues to have enormous significance today because the seasonal rhythms of labor migration encouraged by the program became embedded in ways that institutionalized the large-scale illegal migration from Central America that continues today. Second, the United States admitted hundreds of thousands of refugees under Cold War legislation aimed at Communist regimes—an ad hoc pattern later institutionalized in the Refugee Act of 1980, which now governs refugee and asylum admissions.* Third, the McCarran-Walters Act of 1952, enacted over President Truman's veto, continued the national origins quotas but also established the basic structure of our current immigration system with preferences favoring family ties and labor skills. (It also ended the Japanese exclusion and created a small quota for the Asia-Pacific region.) Finally, the 1965 law, reflecting the concurrent civil rights ferment,[6] abolished the national origins quotas, replacing it with a per-country limit on every country outside the Western Hemisphere, and for the first time imposed an overall ceiling on immigrants from this hemi-

---

* The legal standard for asylum is "persecution or a well-founded fear of persecution on account of race, religion, nationality, membership in a particular social group, or political opinion."

sphere. (Later laws modified some of its provisions and raised the admission numbers.) For reasons I have explained elsewhere, few laws on any subject have had a more profound effect on American society than the 1965 law,[7] yet some commentators insist that these effects were unintended at the time.[8]

Since 1980, immigration legislation has been directed mostly at particular problems of administration and enforcement, especially with respect to undocumented and criminal immigrants.* In 1986, Congress enacted an amnesty for 2.7 million undocumented workers, while authorizing sanctions against employers who hire undocumented workers and against sham marriages for purposes of evading immigration restrictions. In 1996, Congress made it much easier to exclude and remove those who committed crimes in the United States as well as asylum-seekers with weak claims, and it mandated the detention of both groups pending their removal—a mandate whose rigor has been eased somewhat by Supreme Court decisions and administrative limitations on detention space and budget. In the late 1990s, Congress extended additional amnesties for certain Central American and Caribbean groups, as well as authorizing "temporary protected status" to others. This nominally short-term relief has often become in effect permanent residence.

Many notable developments have occurred since 2001, which I shall mention in the specific issues analyses that follow. They include (1) enactment of the USA Patriot Act, which strengthened the government's authority to detain, deport,† and prosecute suspected terrorists; (2) the transfer of immigration regulation to a new Department of Homeland Security; (3) Congress's failure—during both the Bush

---

* "Lest this fact be misunderstood, immigrants are less likely to commit serious crimes or be behind bars than the native-born, and high rates of immigration are associated with lower rates of violent crime and property crime. This holds true for both legal immigrants and the unauthorized, regardless of their country of origin or level of education." http://immigrationpolicy.org/special-reports/criminalization-immigration-united-states; http://www.nytimes.com/2016/01/14/world/europe/research-doesnt-back-a-link-between-migrants-and-crime-in-us.html?_r=0. The 2015 NAS report, discussed below, confirms this finding.

† In 1996, the term "remove" supplanted "deport" in the law, but in common usage they are interchangeable, and I shall ordinarily use the more familiar term "deport."

and Obama administrations—to enact so-called comprehensive immigration reform; (4) a sharp increase in enforcement budget and manpower, especially at the southern border; (5) a recession-driven ebb in illegal migration after 2008, which reversed somewhat by 2016;[9] (6) a peak number of deportations in 2012, followed by declines that in 2015 produced the lowest level since 2006 and a decline of over 25 percent from 2014;[10] (7) rising Hispanic voting and political influence;* (8) a related emergence of a "Dreamer" movement leading to President Obama's creation in 2012 of a Deferred Action for Childhood Arrival (DACA) program providing relief from deportation for potentially millions of young immigrants, a program he tried to substantially expand in 2014, so far unsuccessfully; (9) presidential candidate Donald Trump's proposals to bar Muslims from the country and to build a higher, impregnable wall on the Mexican border; and (10) bold terrorist actions (including attacks in Paris, Brussels, and Orlando), and many foiled attempts. These attacks sparked public demands for more controls over those entering (a) on refugee or other visas (including laws in several states, so far rejected by the federal courts, seeking to bar refugees from the Syrian conflict); and (b) through the visa waiver program (under which nationals of thirty-eight countries can enter for up to ninety days without a visa). Even so, the Obama administration proposed to admit 110,000 refugees in 2017, a 60 percent increase over 2015. Presumably, many of them will be Syrians.

Another important trend is the steady growth of remittances from foreign workers in the United States to their families abroad: an estimated $68.3 billion to Latin America and the Caribbean in 2015 alone, which often constitutes recipient countries' largest source of foreign currency.[11] (A proposed law would tax remittances and use them to identify illegal immigrants, who account for a substantial fraction of the funds.) The economic, social, and foreign relations

---

* In 2016, the Supreme Court cemented this influence by ruling that states may continue their traditional practice of including non-citizens in population counts for redistricting purposes. *Evenwel v. Abbott*, 136 S. Ct. 1120.

effects of remittances are immense, but I shall not discuss them further.[12]

Current Immigration Levels

Legal immigration consists of two major categories: permanent resident admissions (LPRs), and temporary admissions of people who must show that they do not intend to remain ("non-immigrants"). In addition, the law recognizes dozens of other categories of immigrants who are "lawfully present" under a variety of conditions, most of whom have authorization to work.[13]

LPRs. The United States admits by far the largest number of LPRs of any country in the world.* In 2014, 1,016,518 LPRs were admitted; the number has remained a bit over 1 million in recent years, offset slightly by permanent departures. Most LPRs already lived in the United States when they received their green cards; they adjusted their status from a non-immigrant category because they were present in the United States and met the requirements for a permanent visa. LPRs consist of four main streams. The largest is family-based (63.5 percent of the total), with about two-thirds of them entering— without numerical limitations and fairly automatically—as "immediate relatives": spouses of, children of, and parents of adult children of U.S. citizens. The other categories are employment-based (14.9 percent); humanitarian, divided into refugees and asylees (13.2 percent); and so-called diversity admissions (5.3 percent). Two small subcategories within the employment-based category are for job-creating investors (1.1 percent) and a grab bag of "special" immigrants (0.8 percent). Accompanying family members get roughly two-thirds of the total visas in all categories; these "derivative" visas count against the total for each LPR category.[14]

---

* Canada, with 35.7 million people, admitted 258,953 immigrants in 2013—many more on a per capita basis than the United States, which is in the middle of the OECD pack. Of Canadian admissions, 9.3 percent were refugees, also a higher share than here.

The countries of origin of new LPRs are very diverse. By far the largest cohort comes from Mexico (13.6 percent in 2014). Next are China and India (7.2 and 6.9 percent), followed by the Philippines, Cuba, Dominican Republic, Vietnam, Iraq, El Salvador, Pakistan, and South Korea.[15]

Non-immigrants. In 2014, the United States admitted 180.5 million non-immigrants under a variety of specific categories: foreign government and international organization officials, business travelers, tourists, treaty traders and investors, students and exchange visitors, humanitarian cases, fiancées of U.S. citizens, intracompany transferees, temporary workers (business, agricultural, cultural, religious), foreign journalists, and so forth.[16] Some people are temporarily "paroled" into the country for health or other reasons, though they may end up staying indefinitely. The main controversy on non-immigrant visas concerns the limits on high-skilled and technical workers and on farmworkers—an issue in which businesses, agricultural groups, and unions have an outsize interest and play a major role.

Illegal (or "undocumented" or "unauthorized") immigrants[17] raise a very different set of issues. Their precise number in the United States is unknown, of course, but the best estimates are 11.1 million in 2014[18] with the total, especially Mexicans, declining about 200,000 each year since 2007 and with new arrivals from Mexico now at their lowest level since the early 1980s.[19] Accordingly, illegals' length of stay in the country has grown dramatically; in 2013, 60 percent had been in the United States for ten or more years, compared with 26 percent in 2000.[20] About half of them are Mexicans (a recent estimate is only a third[21]), and 60 percent live in only six states (California, Texas, Florida, New York, New Jersey, and Illinois).[22] The net inflow (new entries minus departures) has been negative since the Great Recession, but the decline's trend line began before then.[23] An October 2014 Census report suggests a resurgence, especially among Asians.[24] An estimated 40 percent of these are out of status because they overstayed or otherwise violated the terms of their non-immigrant visas,[25] so they must be apprehended, if at all, through interior enforcement, not at the border. The rest entered illegally in the first place.[26]

Three other features of the undocumented population profoundly affect their incentives to remain or depart, as well as government enforcement policy. First, according to a 2011 study, at least 9 million people live in mixed-status families that include at least one unauthorized adult and one U.S. citizen child, constituting at least 54 percent of the 16.6 million people in families with at least one unauthorized immigrant. An estimated 400,000 unauthorized immigrant children live in such families with U.S. citizen siblings.[27] A more recent study found that between 2009 and 2013, 5.1 million children younger than age 18 were living with an unauthorized immigrant parent—representing 7 percent of the total U.S. child population.[28] While 79 percent of these children were citizens, 19 percent were themselves unauthorized.[29] Second, the legal status of many undocumented immigrants changes over time; they become eligible for legal status under certain conditions—for example, by returning to their home countries, applying for a visa, and staying there during the mandated waiting periods, often many years. By the same token, many LPRs spend some time in illegal status before receiving their green cards.[30] Third, undocumented males of working age constitute a disproportionately large share of the workforce, being considerably more likely than citizen and legal immigrant males to be part of the workforce; the shares are 91, 79, and 84 percent, respectively. And these undocumented workers work predominantly in three sectors: services (22 percent), leisure and hospitality (18 percent), and construction (16 percent). They are also prominent in manufacturing (13 percent) and agriculture (5 percent).[31]

Administration

Bureaucracy. The Immigration and Nationality Act (INA) is administered (since 2003) by the Department of Homeland Security (DHS). The INA is a very long, complex, and frequently amended statute that confusingly combines close congressional control over DHS officials and broad delegations of discretion to those same officials. Clear, binding statutory rules are often qualified by a grant of power, usually in very general terms, to allow waivers and exceptions to those rules. DHS, like most administrative agencies, has fleshed out these rules with detailed regulations, but these regulations often provide little real guidance on how the agency would decide particular cases. In certain provisions in the far-reaching 1996 legislation revamping immigration enforcement, the statute is very specific, expansive, punitive, and mandatory, leaving officials relatively little discretion to soften their application in individual cases that warrant equitable relief.*

Another important aspect of the administrative context is the relatively low quality of the immigration bureaucracy. Few if any other federal agencies have been so long and so often rebuked by the courts for illegality, and by congressional committees and other government watchdog agencies for administrative failure and incompetence. This pattern has persisted even when the agency has had high-quality leadership determined to improve its rogue bureaucratic culture. Unsurprisingly, then, the public and the courts have little confidence in the immigration bureaucracy's commitment to the rule of law or in its ability to implement policy. Indeed, the federal government's own employees seem to agree; in 2015, as in previous years, they ranked DHS at or near the bottom of all federal agencies.[32]

The administrative implementation of immigration policy is organizationally complex. While focused in DHS, responsibilities are also spread out over a number of different government departments and agencies, including the Departments of Justice (immigration judges who adjudicate, and U.S. attorneys who prosecute crimes); State (visa processing and refugee quotas); Labor (employment-related visa processing); Agriculture (farmworkers); and Health and Human Services (public health and some refugee services and child welfare aspects). This diffusion of administrative authority and implementation

---

* Examples include the provisions defining "aggravated felony" and the penalties for immigrants who commit them; and the lengthy bars to legal admission for those who have previously lived in the United States illegally.

demands coordination among (and within, as we shall see) agencies with very different missions, regulatory apparatuses, and politics. Recent decades have seen a growing intersection between immigration law and criminal law (what specialists call crimmigration). This raises new administrative, enforcement, and policy problems for this "immigration-industrial complex."[33] And again, the immigration bureaucracy has a long-standing reputation for fecklessness.

Budget. Since 9/11, Congress has substantially increased appropriations for DHS's immigration-related functions—customs and border protection (CBP), immigration and customs enforcement (ICE), and citizenship and immigration services (USCIS)—during a period of budgetary and staffing restraint, even retrenchment, in much of the federal government generally. For 2016, Congress appropriated approximately $22.4 billion for these functions,[34] a 71 percent increase since 2006, compared with a growth of only 51 percent in the federal budget overall during that decade. Congress especially favors the Border Patrol; its budget increased roughly *tenfold* between 1993 and 2015.[35] But ICE's interior enforcement budget has also grown apace (although it declined slightly in 2016). (USCIS is funded almost entirely by fees.) Authorized positions in these two DHS agencies increased dramatically in the last decade. From 2003 to 2015, Border Patrol staff nearly doubled from 10,717 to 20,273.[36] Over the same period, the number of ICE officers assigned to Enforcement and Removal Operations more than doubled from 2,710 to 5,900.[37]

Backlogs. Delays in visa processing by the departments of State (DOS) and Labor (DLS) and DHS, in adjudications by the front-line immigration judges and Board of Immigration Appeals (BIA) tribunals within DOJ, and in federal appellate court review of these agency decisions, are also persistent problems, creating chronic impediments to effective deterrence and enforcement. For example, the 250-odd immigration judges (a corps to be expanded under the 2016 omnibus appropriation law) faces a record, rising backlog exceeding 500,000 cases.[38] These delays aggravate another serious problem: unnecessary

detention of immigrants pending decisions in their cases. This detention (discussed below) is costly to the government, deprives immigrants of their freedom, and impairs their ability to assemble a legal
defense where, against the odds, they may have one. Yet some detention is essential to the effectiveness of enforcement, as discussed below.

Politics

The political environment surrounding immigration makes it extraordinarily hard to implement existing immigration policies, much
less produce genuine reforms. The problem is not only that immigration lies at the epicenter of numerous conflicting interest groups—
warring interests, after all, characterize almost any important policy
area—but also that it arouses unusually intense passions: patriotism,
security, control of borders, morality, ethno-racial identities, family
nostalgia, partisanship, demographic destiny, economic futures, and
other potent feelings. These passions combine to produce an often
unsavory brew, as the 2016 campaigns have demonstrated.

Public attitudes about immigration are not at all straightforward,
especially during the 2016 presidential campaign. A recent study
finds that immigration, especially by Latinos, is pushing Americans'
voting and partisanship to the right where they support a conservative political agenda including restrictions on public spending for social services.[39] This account, which uses media coverage of immigration and state-by-state immigration populations to explain growing
white conservatism, is not wholly convincing. Substantial Latino
growth, for example, has not prevented New York, California, and
Colorado from becoming more liberal, nor has it produced restrictive
immigration policies at the federal level where most immigration
policy is made.[40] Other factors also affect policy outcomes. Still, the
study is further evidence of how complex immigration politics is. For
example, a Pew survey in mid-2015 found that 72 percent of Americans thought that illegal immigrants should be allowed to remain
here if they meet certain conditions.[41] (*Which* conditions remains
unclear.) And, according to a large 2016 survey, only 19 percent (only

30 percent of Republicans) want to identify and deport those living here illegally.[42]

Americans like immigrants more than they like immigration. They favor past immigration more than recent immigration, prefer legal immigrants to illegal ones, prefer refugees to other immigrants (this was before ISIS attacks on Paris kindled fear about jihadists coming to the United States as Syrian war refugees,[43] and before the chairman of the Senate immigration subcommittee released a long list of refugees who were found in 2015 to have engaged in terrorism[44]). The public also supports immigrants' access to educational and health benefits but not to welfare or Social Security, and feels that immigrants' distinctive cultures have contributed positively to American life and that diversity continues to strengthen American society today. At the same time, Americans overwhelmingly resist any conception of multiculturalism that discourages immigrants from learning and using the English language.[45]

They tend to admire the groups, widely reviled when they came in the nineteenth and early twentieth centuries, for their largely successful struggles to gain acceptance in a hostile society under difficult conditions, yet they also view more recent groups with greater misgivings and concerns about their assimilability. Sociologist Rita Simon has captured this ambivalence in an arresting metaphor: "We view immigrants with rose-colored glasses turned backwards." Yet negative attitudes toward current immigrants are common—in 2015, 45 percent of all Americans thought that the impact of immigration on society was positive on net, while 37 percent thought it was a net negative—but views on such questions vary by race, income, age, education level, ethnicity, and partisanship,[46] with white working-class people especially concerned.[47]

While cherishing their immigrant roots, Americans think that current immigration levels are too high. Indeed, the public has *always* thought that the immigration levels of their day were too high—although I doubt that they know what those levels actually are!* News

---

* Three examples among many of voters' ignorance about such magnitudes: they vastly overestimate the share of the federal budget that is spent on foreign aid (http://kff

developments can intensify this view at the margin, but the pattern is fairly stable. In January 2015, however, a Gallup poll found a substantial increase in the number of Americans expressing dissatisfaction with current levels of immigration, rising in one year from 54 percent to 60 percent (although even this was well below the 72 percent who were dissatisfied seven years earlier). Of the dissatisfied, the vast majority wanted immigration either to decrease or stay the same; only 14 percent wanted more of it.* Those wanting less immigration reached 22 percent after the Border Patrol picked up almost 70,000 unaccompanied minors (presumably undocumented), generating much media coverage and White House disarray.[48] Public concern surely grew in 2016 with (1) campaign-stoked fears about terrorists exploiting the border control, refugee, asylum, and visa waiver programs to gain entry;[49] (2) strong opposition to President Obama's November 2014 non-enforcement policy (discussed below); and (3) a press report that the government released some 80 percent of these unaccompanied minors into the hands of people lacking legal status.[50]

Republicans tend to be more restrictionist than Democrats are, but many conservatives—business groups, libertarians, and the influential *Wall Street Journal*—strongly advocate more immigration, and as noted below, many Democrats prefer less, or no more, immigration than we now have. Traditionally, most respondents placed it relatively low on their priority issue list, but now both Democrats and Republicans (82 and 85 percent, respectively) want their candidates to focus on it.[51]

Americans' attitudes toward immigration are further complicated by ignorance about how the system actually works. Abstract opinions

---

.org/global-health-policy/poll-finding/data-note-americans-views-on-the-u-s-role-in -global-health/); the risks of crime, war, and terrorism (Jonathan Rauch, "Be Not Afraid," *The Atlantic*, March 2015, p. 19); and corporate profits (Mark Perry, "The Public Thinks the Average Company Makes a 36% Profit Margin, Which Is About 5X Too High," *American Enterprise Institute*, April 2, 2015).

* These results can seem inconsistent, as with a recent Gallup poll finding that 33 percent favored current levels and 22 percent wanted *more* of them. http://www.gallup .com/poll/1660/Immigration.aspx

about immigration may not translate straightforwardly into opinions about specific immigration policies and preferences, where the public's views are much more favorable but probably less informed.[52]

On legal admissions, they do not realize how long it takes for even fully eligible petitioners to get a green card and be able to come here. Although the waiting time on the queue varies by immigration category, it can take decades for those from high-immigration countries, especially Mexico (discussed below). The public is also confused about the intersection between legal and illegal immigration. (Indeed, some opinion surveys do not distinguish between them.) Many people think of legal immigrants as good and illegal ones as bad,[53] probably not realizing that these are often the very same people, but at different points in time. For example, many who enter illegally would be eligible for a green card to join their families, but it will take years for their number to come up so that they can actually get one. As noted above, about half of illegal immigrants entered legally and then fell out of status. In a reverse pattern, most asylum claimants arrive without papers but may later succeed in proving their claims and gaining full legal status; about 25,000 did so in 2013.[54]

Many Americans, moreover, probably sympathize with at least some undocumented migrants who took great risks, braved physical hardships, struggled through dangerous desert terrain or perilous voyages, were abused, robbed, and tricked by smugglers, and endured long separation from loved ones in a desperate effort to work, feed their families, and perhaps share in the American dream—which Latinos (and blacks) seem to embrace more than the white population does![55] (Illegal immigrants themselves often exploit this moral ambiguity.)[56] "There but for the grace of God go I" is surely a common response to their plight by many law-abiding Americans. Indeed, as discussed below, many cities and religious communities have extended sanctuary and sympathy to illegal border crossers. Widespread recognition of these moral complexities probably helps explain why ordinary illegal entry is a misdemeanor, not a felony, and carries relatively light penalties that traditionally were seldom imposed absent some aggravating factor.[57] Today, prosecutions along the southern

border are more common. Indeed, almost all Mexicans, once apprehended, received expedited removal, reinstatement of earlier removal
orders, or criminal prosecution.

Which more general beliefs lie behind these survey responses? I
believe that neither nativism nor xenophobia accounts for much of
the restrictionist sentiment among Americans today.* A large minority of Americans categorically oppose "amnesty" for illegal immigrants regardless of their attributes simply out of the public's concern
for law-abidingness.[58]

Most Republican voters in 2016 probably do support Trump's
proposals to wall out Mexicans and to bar Muslims,[59] but their true
motivation is uncertain. After all, few Americans favor illegal border
crossing (which mostly comes from Mexico), and Trump's "until we
figure out what's going on" qualifier on a Muslim ban may have made
sense to many non-xenophobes upset about recent Islamic terrorism
in Europe. (Indeed, a Brookings poll conducted *after* the June 2016
Orlando shootings actually showed *more* favorable attitudes toward
Muslims [62 percent] and even toward the Muslim religion [44 per-
cent].)[60] On the other hand, Americans apparently prefer Christian
and "non-religious" immigrants to Muslims even when individual
attributes pertaining to skills and cultural integration are held
constant.[61]

---

* Aristide Zolberg expresses skepticism about John Higham's canonical account of
immigration restriction in the 1880–1925 period, *Strangers in the Land*, which Higham
attributed to nativism. Zolberg not only offers methodological objection to Higham's nativist explanation but also points out that many restrictionist fears were based on rational
grounds, not just cultural ones. Zolberg, *A Nation by Design*, at 6–8.

Nativism, however, did play an important role earlier in our history, most prominently
with the American Republican Party (often called Know-Nothings because of their secret
practices). This group won municipal elections in New York City and Philadelphia in 1844
and then a large national following a decade later, sending seventy-five members to Congress, taking control of several state governments in the Northeast, and also doing well in
other regions. The Know-Nothings failed, however, to enact its proposals, which politicians
had promoted unsuccessfully since the 1830s, to impose twenty-one-year waiting periods
for naturalization and to make aliens ineligible for political office. With the sharp decline
in immigration after 1854 due to the end of the Irish famine and the Panic of 1857 in the
United States, the party quickly faded. And as noted earlier, anti-Catholic hatred, much of
which probably coincided with nativism, ran deep during much of our history.

My guess is that the vast majority of Americans favoring lower immigration rates are either what I call *principled* or *pragmatic* restrictionists. The main difference is that principled restrictionists, exemplified by the groups Federation for American Immigration Reform (FAIR) and NumbersUSA,[62] believe that immigration's threat to their goals or values is inherent in the nature and fact of immigration, while pragmatic restrictionists view such threats not as inevitable but as contingent on various factual conditions, including numbers and skills, that may change.

Pragmatic restrictionists tend to think, for example, that the actual effects of immigration on population, the environment, national unity, cultural consensus, and so forth are all empirical questions whose answers depend on the interaction of a variety of factors. They do not oppose immigration in principle or in general. They may even be prepared to support it if they can be persuaded, for instance, that immigrants actually create jobs rather than take them away from native workers, that they are mastering the English language without undue delay, and that they do not exploit the welfare system, commit too many serious crimes, or otherwise threaten social cohesion. Although some Americans and interest groups may have closed their minds on these factual questions, the pragmatist remains, at least in theory, open to persuasion by contrary evidence. Most Americans, I suspect, are pragmatic restrictionists—although again one cannot be certain. That is, they favor lower levels but are open to argument and evidence about what those levels should be and about what immigration's actual effects are.*

Another wrinkle in public attitudes toward immigration surely contributes to the Janus-like quality of these attitudes. When illegal migration brings willing workers and employers together to yield

---

* As noted earlier, restrictionist sentiment had declined a bit before the 2016 campaign. Even attitudes toward hot-button, stereotype-driven policy issues about race appear to be notably responsive to counterargument. See Paul Sniderman & Thomas Piazza, *The Scar of Race* (1993). Even more rapid and dramatic changes in public attitudes have occurred with respect to gay marriage, women in the military, and—most recently—transgender identities.

shared productivity and no clearly identifiable losers, many Americans see this as a victimless crime. This is so even though (1) employers can be legally sanctioned for hiring unauthorized workers,[63] (2) some labor economists find adverse effects on low-income Americans' wages and job opportunities, and (3) the public fears that illegal migration is out of control. These facts are simply aspects of the ambivalent attitudes described earlier that complicate how the public perceives both the illegal migration problem and immigration enforcement. These attitudes also affect how enforcement officials view their own role, which in turn may help to explain some of the agency's deep pathologies—its scattershot enforcement,* low morale, arbitrariness, inconsistency, incompetence,† illegality, and political vulnerability.[64] Just a few of many examples are illustrative. In September 2016, it was revealed that because of its flawed fingerprint system, DHS granted citizenship to hundreds of people previously ordered deported.[65] Even the Border Patrol, its supposedly elite unit, sometimes commits abuse, violence, and concealment,[66] and also accepts bribes.[67] Perhaps most damning, a survey of 392,000 federal employees conducted by the Partnership for Public Service in 2014 ranked ICE the next-to-worst federal agency (314 out of 315),[68] and a 2015 survey of employee job satisfaction by the federal government's own personnel agency found DHS to be the worst department of all.[69]

---

* "Scattershot" has an especially ominous meaning in the immigration enforcement context. Between 2005 and 2013, CBP officers killed at least forty-six people, including many U.S. citizens and minors, and most of them unarmed, yet not one officer was disciplined, much less indicted. http://www.newrepublic.com/article/120687/border-patrol-officers-get-impunity-anonymity-immigrant-killings?utm_source=Sailthru&utm_medium=email&utm_term=TNR%20Daily%20Newsletter&utm_campaign=Daily%20Newsletter%20Template%20-%20Jan%205. In 2015, CBP issued rules and expanded training to limit excessive use of force. See https://www.cbp.gov/sites/default/files/documents/cbp-teds-policy-20151005.pdf

† Other agencies that work closely with ICE on tracking dangerous immigrants appear no better. The State Department unit that issues and revokes visas recently disclosed that it had revoked 121,000 visas since 2001—9,500 for terrorism reasons!—but did not know where those people were. http://www.newsmax.com/Newsfront/revoked-visas-terrorism-concerns/2015/12/17/id/706296/

This attitudinal mix also helps explain a striking feature of modern immigration politics: It yields laws that are far more expansionist than the public says it wants. The Immigration Act of 1990, the most recent overhaul of the legal admissions system,* raised the total number and allowable categories of admissions, defeating advocates for either restriction or the status quo. Immigration expansion in 1990 was doubly impressive because it occurred during an economic recession (traditionally conducive to restriction) and at a time when even limited immigration was strongly opposed in virtually all other democratic nations.

The interest groups that pressed in the late 1980s both for more legal immigration and for amnesties or other barriers to removing illegal immigrants continue to do so today. Growers are perhaps the most important of these groups; their demand for field labor seems inexhaustible and their prosperity is vital to the economies and political establishments in many states, including the largest ones (e.g., California, Texas, Florida, and New York). Grower interests were behind the large (and fraud-ridden) legalization program for undocumented "special agricultural workers" (SAWs) adopted in the Immigration Reform and Control Act of 1986 (IRCA), and they continue to be among the strongest supporters of proposals for new amnesty and guestworker programs, especially those targeting Mexican labor.

Many other business- and university-related groups depend increasingly (sometimes almost entirely) on immigration for their workforces. At the high-skill end is the computer software industry and a large number of other high-tech employers who look abroad for programmers, engineers, researchers, and other specialists to augment the domestic workforce through the H-1B and other "temporary" visa programs, which in fact provide a majority of those who later qualify for green cards. (As noted previously, most new LPRs were already in the United States when they obtained green cards.)

---

* In contrast, the Illegal Immigration Reform and Immigrant Responsibility Act of 1996 (IIRIRA) dealt largely with the system for removing illegal entrants, out-of-status immigrants, and criminals, the Patriotic Act of 2001 focused on terrorism threats, and other legislation has dealt with non-immigrants.

American hospitals chronically depend on foreign doctors and nurses to staff their wards, and many universities look to foreign students (more than 1.1 million in 2014)[70] to pay tuition; at graduate levels, they conduct research and teach undergraduates. At the lower end, foreign nannies help free up mothers to gain outside jobs, and hotels and restaurants rely heavily on (often undocumented) immigrants to do work that U.S. workers are often said (controversially, as we shall see) to reject.

Ethnic groups are also major, and often effective, proponents of immigration expansion. In the case of the 1990 Immigration Act, the Irish were particularly important advocates, possessing some uniquely valuable political allies and succeeding in getting the adoption of an Irish-friendly lottery awarding a large number of "diversity" visas (also discussed below). But other groups, including Jewish, Hispanic, and Asian organizations, also lobbied effectively for more visas and lower admission barriers. Today, with immigrants filling the pews of Catholic, evangelical, and other churches and synagogues and reinvigorating religious communities in many urban areas, the ethnic coalition seeking to expand immigration has grown more powerful.

Given this politically potent array of expansionist interests, where are the restrictionists? As noted earlier, explicitly nativist and xenophobic organizations are few and far between in the United States today. Hate groups, many monitored by the FBI, presumably operate largely underground. (This contrasts sharply with the EU bloc where avowedly anti-immigration and racist parties are prominent and gaining ground.)[71] But some more mainstream groups favor restriction. Environmentalists, concerned about migrants' relatively high fertility rates, sometimes lament the effect of immigration on natural resources, wildlife, and human ecology in the United States (and globally). Environmentalists, however, tend to be ideologically liberal and inclusive, which tends to neutralize whatever anti-immigration feelings they might otherwise entertain. Exemplifying this ambivalence are the periodic debates within the Sierra Club, the oldest and most iconic environmental group, over what its position on immigration should be. So far, the restrictionists have lost, thus limiting the organization's potential as a political counterforce to the dominant expansionists.

Until recently, the most important group opposing immigration was organized labor. Like black groups, unions traditionally viewed immigrants as low-wage competitors for members' jobs and a brake on wage growth. But the gradual weakening of unions' organizing strength and their need to look to immigrants as new members led to a seismic political shift, voting to push legalization of the undocumented in hopes of making them easier to organize, improving their economic well-being, and strengthening the government's enforcement of labor standards. Black civil rights organizations, another traditional opponent of immigration out of concerns about its effects on black jobs and wages, have also been neutralized by their liberal positions on other issues and by their tactical alliances with Hispanic and other pro-immigration groups to secure their cooperation.

Immigrant-receiving states and localities, which now include most parts of the country due to the increasingly diffuse migration patterns and distribution of immigrants, bear a disproportionate share of the costs of the social services that immigrants, especially low-skilled ones, require and whatever disruptions their presence may cause. (These jurisdictions, of course, also reap many of the benefits flowing from immigrants' work and presence.) For these reasons, their officials have sometimes called for restrictions on immigration, although their loudest complaints have tended to be about criminals, not immigrants generally. This anger has usually focused on Washington's failure both to control the borders and to defray the local costs incurred by this failure. Even so, politicians are mindful of the difficulty of opposing immigration—even of the undocumented—without offending a significant number of voters in high-immigration states or localities who may resist strict enforcement of the immigration law.* Indeed, California goes so far as to bar the term "alien" in its labor

---

* Racial minorities account for almost all of our population growth, with most of that coming from immigrants, not U.S.-born blacks. http://www.brookings.edu/blogs/the-avenue/posts/2015/08/03-voting-rights-minority-turnout-next-election-frey#.VcDd7iU5lGg.email

laws, for being insulting—even though Congress uses the term in all immigration statutes.[72]

These varying attitudes of voters and officials toward immigration enforcement produce quite different policies across jurisdictions. Many states, citing inadequate federal policies and enforcement, have enacted a variety of restrictions designed to make life harder for immigrants and enable ICE to remove them more easily, hoping that they will "self-deport" or remain in the shadows or *at least* move to other states—but the political viability of such laws is not entirely clear.[73] The courts have struck down some (or some parts) of these laws, usually on the constitutional ground that federal authority in this area preempts state and local regulation.[74] At the other pole, by 2015 some 360 localities, many with large immigrant populations, had moved to stymie ICE enforcement by adopting "sanctuary" policies to shield illegals.[75] Some jurisdictions have gone even further, instructing their officials to ignore ICE detainers seeking to hold immigrants in local jails until ICE can take custody of them. This state and local refusal to cooperate with ICE grew steadily; more than 18,000 ICE detainers were declined from January 2014 to September 2015;[76] in early 2016, Philadelphia adopted this policy.[77] The most important example of this resistance, California's Trust Act, has sharply reduced deportations from California since its enactment in 2013.[78] In some states, however, a political backlash against non-cooperation has reversed that policy,[79] some through legislation.[80]

The upshot of all these political forces is that immigration policy is much more expansive than most Americans seem to want—although their ignorance about the baseline, as well as the imprecise phrasing of survey questions, leaves some doubts about what they *really* want. Even the IIRIRA, which aimed almost entirely at undocumented and criminal immigrants and contained some misguided and unfair provisions, left the levels of legal immigration set in the 1990 law (quite high by post-1924 historical standards) as they were. And efforts by Jeff Sessions, the Senate's most powerful voice for restriction,[81] have failed to reduce legal immigration levels despite high levels of legal and illegal migration, numerous immigrants in our overcrowded prisons and jails,[82] chronically weak enforcement, and high public anxiety and anger about these trends. Indeed, as we shall see, only the Great Recession managed to stem the illegal flow—and even that perhaps only temporarily.

Probably the most important cause and consequence of this political inertia has been the struggle within the Republican Party to reach a policy consensus on immigration, a struggle that has roiled the 2016 elections. Desperately seeking independent, Hispanic, Asian, and other Democrat-leaning voters, many Republican leaders like John McCain, George W. and Jeb Bush, Marco Rubio, Paul Ryan, Rand Paul, and Karl Rove are proposing more overtures to immigrants given demographic trends and in the wake of the political death of comprehensive immigration reform measures in Congress during the Bush and Obama administrations. Many conservative business groups, religious leaders, and conservative publications (the *Wall Street Journal*, most notably) are doing the same.* But Republican candidate Donald Trump makes restrictionist claims that resonate with many conservative voters and party activists who fear immigration's economic, demographic, and electoral effects.[83] The Speaker of the House, Paul Ryan, has refused to take up immigration legislation during the Obama presidency. In truth, almost all Americans favor stronger border control.[84]

Economic Impact

A useful way to think about immigration policy is to consider the nature of the implicit contract between desirable migrants and the United States. The government must offer beneficial "terms" (e.g., opportunity, low risk of deportation, occupational mobility, social benefits if things go wrong for eligibles) to induce them to invest in the United States economically, socially, and emotionally rather than

---

* In the 2014 midterm elections, the victorious Republicans did reduce somewhat the Democratic advantage with Hispanic voters in some important states. Julia Preston, "GOP's Inroads with Latinos Hint at a Path for 2016," *New York Times*, November 5, 2014.

go elsewhere.[85] (Even the undocumented live and work here under conditions that entail certain well-understood trade-offs.) A key question, then, is: What economic benefits does the United States get in return?

Immigration's economic impact is hotly contested—partly because it is methodologically difficult to measure and assess, and partly because it varies depending on the immigrant's legal status, location, industry, skill level, English fluency, and other factors. In September 2016, the National Academy of Sciences (NAS) issued a comprehensive review of the research on immigration's economic and fiscal effects, replete with cautions that firm conclusions on most issues are hard to reach.[86] Still, the evidence identifies some general patterns. Immigrants' human capital is distributed bimodally, with large numbers at the high-skill end but many more at the low education levels. Immigrants, with just over 16 percent of the labor force, account for a much higher share of those with low literacy and numeracy skills. Another study found that even those with college educations are far less literate in English than natives are.[87] According to George Borjas, a leading labor economist and skeptic about the desirability of low-skill immigrants, recent immigrant cohorts come with less human capital (relative to the U.S. population) than earlier cohorts, mainly due to the large influx of low-skill undocumented migrants since the 1980s.[88] (Recall that working-age males in this group are more likely to be employed than either their citizen or legal immigrant counterparts.)

These very low education levels help to explain why the NAS, which published an earlier review in 1997,[89] continues to find only modest net economic benefits from immigration—on the order of $80,000 over each immigrant's lifetime (in the 1997 report). In some industries, immigrant workers may increase American workers' efficiency by enabling skill and production complementarities. A recent study suggests that this is true of skilled (H-1B) workers.[90] Certain economic sectors—agriculture, hospitality, construction, health services, child and elderly care, and some manufacturing—benefit disproportionately from immigrant labor, much of it unauthorized.[91] Consumers—especially middle- and upper-class ones—pay lower prices for some goods and services as a result, and also benefit from ethnically diverse cuisines, music, and so forth.

Immigrants' relatively high fertility rates, which gradually converge with that of the native-born, also aid our social dynamism, economic growth, and future fiscal solvency. Now accounting for 95 percent of our population growth, they largely explain why our population is much younger than that of our developed-world competitors.[92] Because most of them arrive as young adults, they tend to impose fewer burdens on education and child-oriented social services (a difference that of course vanishes in the second generation). Undocumented migrants who work on the books pay Social Security and income taxes; all of them, of course, pay sales taxes.

Finally, immigrants contribute disproportionately to the nation's innovation (at the high-skill end) and entrepreneurship (at all skill levels). Here is a summary based on 2013 data:[93]

> Immigrants' role in Main Street businesses is striking. While accounting for 16 percent of the labor force nationally and 18 percent of business owners, immigrants make up 28 percent of Main Street business owners. And, immigrants play an even bigger role in certain Main Street businesses. [I]n the U.S. as a whole immigrants make up 61 percent of all gas station owners, 58 percent of dry cleaners owners, 53 percent of grocery store owners, 45 percent of nail salon owners, 43 percent of liquor store owners, 38 percent of restaurant owners, and 32 percent of both jewelry and clothing store owners. And, immigrants make up a bigger proportion of Main Street business owners in metropolitan areas with large immigrant populations. Immigrants make up fully 64 percent of all Main Street business owners in the Los Angeles metro area, 61 percent in metro San Jose, 56 percent in metro Washington, DC, and 54 percent in metro Miami. Main Street businesses make a direct contribution to the economy, but they also leverage

that contribution by playing a critical role in making neighbor-hoods attractive places to live and work.

How does immigration affect wages and working conditions? The NAS reports detail the many reasons why studying wage effects is so hard. The infusion of a large number of undocumented workers, most of them low-skilled, surely creates downward pressure on wages and conditions. But as just noted, immigrants also can facilitate "comple-mentarities" that increase the efficiency of other workers, and their own consumption of goods and services creates jobs. The debate, then, is over how large these effects are, which groups bear the nega-tive ones, how they net out, and how they are altered by changes in immigrants' skills mix (which, as noted above, Borjas finds are declin-ing). Some studies conclude that such downward pressure primarily harms the wages of other immigrants, not American workers.[94] But others, including a new analysis on the effects of the 1980 Cuban Marielito influx on Miami-area American workers,[95] find that low-skill immigrants significantly and adversely affect Americans who are high school dropouts, minorities, non-unionized, and low-skill work-ers, as well as those seeking their first, entry-level jobs.[96] This compe-tition at the bottom is particularly acute because many employers ap-parently prefer immigrants, including blacks, over African American workers.[97] Immigrants' net fiscal impacts on government are also very hard to gauge, partly because of what I call a "fiscal mismatch": Their use of public services, especially education and hospitals, mainly bur-den state and local budgets, sometimes severely, while the revenues that their work generates go disproportionately to Washington—a long-standing intergovernmental inequity that should be rectified.[98]

Another important economic—and broadly social—question is how immigration affects intergenerational mobility. The United States traditionally prided itself on its leadership among other eco-nomically developed societies on this important social factor. Today, however, almost all commentary on mobility stresses that we have fallen to the middle of the OECD, especially after taking taxes and transfers into account.[99] But significantly, this comparison fails to include the dramatic economic and social gains of the approximately 90 percent of immigrants who come to the United States from relatively low-wage countries. As economist Robert Lerman has shown, including them would dramatically improve our absolute and comparative performance on both mobility and wage inequality.* He analogizes to assessing Germany's performance on mobility and inequality without including the effects of incorporating the former East Germany in 1990.[100] In both instances, absorbing a large population of low-income individuals increased inequality but produced the economic gains that migrants to the United States experienced by moving from a poor to a wealthy society, as the East Germans did. In the same way, millions of U.S. residents who are at the lower end of today's income distribution actually experienced substantial income mobility, thus reducing inequality. Because LPRs and most undocumented immigrants are in effect part of our society and will remain so, they should be included in the mobility analysis.

POLICY ISSUES

Commentators on immigration policy almost always begin with the same cliché—the current system is "broken"—but they disagree fundamentally about which parts are broken, what has caused this, and how it can best be repaired. I shall now discuss thirteen issues roiling current immigration policy debates. (Space limitations affect my selection.) They are: "comprehensive" immigration reform; high-skill workers; agricultural workers; LPR admissions; the Mexican quota; legalization; immigration federalism; welfare benefits; citizenship; population growth; enforcement; legal representation; and social integration. (Asylum and detention policies are mainly discussed under legalization and enforcement.) These analyses include my own policy recommendations.

---

* A recent summary of the evidence suggests that economic mobility for low-skill immigrants in Europe is relatively low. http://www.city-journal.org/2014/24_4_achievement-gap.html

"Comprehensive" Immigration Reform

All legislative efforts to enact immigration reform have had to deal with what can be viewed as an initial framing issue: how comprehensive should reform be? Most proponents of "comprehensive immigration reform" (CIR) include at least the following sets of programs in the broad reform package: amnesty or "earned legalization" (the term advocates prefer) for many of the undocumented; agricultural guestworkers; high-skill immigrants; and enhanced enforcement at both the border and the interior. Some CIR advocates also want the package to include changes in the preference system for LPRs (e.g., the numerical limits for different categories, per-country ceilings, "diversity" visas), but view them as less urgent for inclusion in a CIR compromise.

For both substantive and political reasons, almost all liberal expansionists advocate CIR, but some conservatives do so as well. In substantive programmatic terms, each of the CIR package's elements is linked to the others, particularly as applied to the undocumented. But because liberal and conservative groups know that each bloc can defeat the other's reforms in Congress, they see CIR as the only politically practical way to forge the compromises needed to achieve their legislative goals. For example, businesses eager to expand the availability of technical worker visas may be willing to support another reform such as legalization that they may care less about or even oppose, in order to win support for gaining more technical visas. The same is true of the business groups forming the Essential Worker Immigration Coalition. By expanding the number of issues in play, a CIR package can facilitate these trades.

Like all logrolling efforts, however, CIR may fail if some of the quid pro quos being demanded by all sides are unacceptable, the threats are too hard to enforce, and the trading becomes too complex, causing the political package to fall of its own weight. And if that happens, some measures like technical visas that were probably popular enough to pass on their own but got caught up in the competing threats that the CIR approach entails may not pass either. This is essentially what happened in the failed attempts by presidents George W. Bush and Barack Obama to achieve *either* CIR *or* the more popular reforms—leading two former chairs of the immigration committees in Congress to urge adoption of a single reform (mandating E-Verify, a computer-based identity system used by employers to check the work-authorized status of new hires, while tying it closely to a new government process as a mechanism for case-by-case legalization of workers), leaving the rest for later.[101] In sum, CIR may seem like a neater, more rational approach to policy change than narrower, piecemeal efforts, but choosing between them entails complex political tactics and trade-offs. Where one comes out on this framing issue of comprehensiveness, then, is not at all obvious—even to the politicians.

Still, some immigration reform does get enacted. In its 2016 omnibus appropriations law, Congress abruptly, unceremoniously, and with little notice adopted some important policy changes. These included expanding and liberalizing the H-2B visa program for non-agricultural temporary workers in certain fields; raising employers' fees for H-1B (discussed below) and L-1 (intracompany transfer) visas for high-skill temporary workers; adopting stricter visa waiver program rules; providing development funding for Central American source countries; extending certain special visa programs; and funding more immigration judges. Indeed, the political advantages of including immigration policy changes in must-pass omnibus laws, which are increasingly common,[102] may make them, not CIR, Congress's vehicle of choice for future reforms.[103]

High-Skill Workers

The goal of attracting high-skill workers to the United States is widely considered a policy no-brainer—so much so that many members of Congress from both parties favor the idea of stapling a green card to the diplomas of foreign students who graduate from American institutions in the science, technology, engineering, and mathematics (STEM) fields. Policy makers also emphasize that Canada and some other countries are now competing effectively for these same workers. An important part of this picture are student visas, for which there is rising demand and which are often converted to a work visa after the student graduates and finds a U.S. job.[104] In March 2016, the DHS issued a final rule extending the time period in which STEM students can pursue practical training in the United States after their academic studies.[105]

Some American STEM workers, of course, disagree with this goal. Shortages, they say, are exaggerated and are caused by inadequate compensation, and importing workers will reduce American workers' wages and discourage others from entering these fields.[106] Other analysts, however, generally support expanding STEM and other skilled worker visas. U.S. taxpayers, they note, are already subsidizing much of their educations here, and it is shortsighted to force them to move to foreign economies that compete with ours for talent, technology, and trade. American firms and universities are desperate to hire them to fill vacant positions that can add to the nation's innovation and productivity. Foreign STEM workers account for a vastly disproportionate share of patents, new technologies, and entrepreneurial start-ups in these fields—and not just in America's proliferating Silicon Valleys. Their work generates valuable knowledge and many new jobs.[107] Their stock of human capital—general intelligence, education, work skills and experience, and English facility—makes it relatively easy for them to assimilate and succeed in American society, enriching not only our economy but our culture.

Unfortunately, our existing policies limit many of these advantages. The annual quota for employment-based *permanent* visas for skilled workers (variously defined) is relatively small (140,000 in 2015,[108] less than 15 percent of all legal admissions), and roughly two-thirds of these visas are used up by derivative visas (for accompanying family members), not the skilled workers themselves. The number of *temporary* high-skill workers (H-1Bs) who may be admitted each year is capped at 65,000 (another 20,000 visas are granted in certain circumstances), a number so low relative to the demand for slots that the cap was reached within six days after the date when petitions could be filed for 2017,[109] a regular occurrence. (The cap was raised to 195,000 in 2000–2003, but was then reduced to its current level due to an economic slowdown.) These and other obstacles help explain why presidents from ninety top American universities jointly sent a letter to President Obama calling for immigration reform ensuring the retention of top graduates.[110] In fact, foreign-origin applicants now account for half of all patent applications and grants.[111] On the other hand, employers have sometimes tried to use H-1Bs to replace their existing workers,[112] and even to train foreign workers to move U.S. jobs overseas;[113] an extensive *New York Times* analysis shows how they use outsourcing firms to game the system.[114] Another approach was included in the Obama administration's November 2014 policy change (discussed below) but received less attention at the time amid the bitter controversy unleashed by the order's other non-enforcement provisions. The policy grants protection on a case-by-case ("parole") basis to inventors, researchers, and entrepreneurs who can show that they received substantial financing from U.S. investors or are otherwise likely to innovate or create jobs.[115]

There are better ways to address this problem. The most straightforward is for Congress to simply increase the quotas for permanent skilled worker visas. But the most interested groups know that Congress has not increased the total number of these visas since 1990, is not poised to do so now, and sees the competition between the family and employment categories as zero-sum, with correspondingly high stakes. (Were Congress to raise the total number of available visas, these categories would still compete for the additional ones.) Like some other analysts, I favor adjusting the balance between these two categories: Skilled workers should get a larger share than the current 16 percent, while the share for family members[116] should be correspondingly lower. The main reason is that skilled workers add to our national wealth in many ways. Many family-based immigrants often do as well (especially if one takes into account family network effects), have a built-in advantage in becoming socially integrated, and are job-mobile.[117] Still, the more extended family members tend to have lower skills and can already visit and communicate with their U.S.-based relatives far more easily than ever before. A less conflictual way to increase skilled LPRs—and indeed the other LPR categories as well—would be to not count their family members' derivative visas against the quotas.[118] This change, which probably requires new legislation, would greatly reduce the skilled visa backlog. But assuming that we still want LPRs to bring their closest family members with them for humanitarian, economic, and assimilation reasons, we would have to correspondingly increase those quotas, raising the same political objections discussed earlier and below.

A very different approach to increasing high-skilled workers is to adopt a point system. Used by Canada, Australia, and some other countries, such systems assign a number of points to applicants according to the characteristics that the society wants to favor, including attracting immigrants with desired skills and credentials. Observing that the United States failed to adopt such a system in 2007 and ever since, the MPI has canvassed point systems operating elsewhere and summarized those countries' experiences:

> [G]overnment administrators cannot match abstract sets of skills to the always dynamic and specific labor needs of employers. Evidence on outcomes for immigrants entering through points systems also suggests that the selection process needs constant fine-tuning. Yet points systems serve a useful purpose in expanding a country's human-capital base and advancing important priorities (such as local language proficiency and broader immigrant-integration goals)—even if employers may at times value such attributes less than policymakers and the broader society. Furthermore, evidence on long-term outcomes indicates that by monitoring which characteristics are more highly correlated with success, policymakers can perform the adjustments that define the most agile—and successful—points systems. Finally, points sys-

tems also provide transparency and greater governmental control over a key component of any immigration system, an essential element of winning over skeptical publics.[119]

The United States (and some other countries, including Sweden and Norway) has rejected point systems in favor of what MPI terms "demand-driven and private-sector-led" systems, mainly out of concerns about how responsive a point system would be to the rapidly shifting needs of employers. Moreover, any particular assignment of points to different factors would certainly arouse political conflict. A point system, of course, can be adjusted in any number of ways to reflect the relative importance any particular country wishes to assign to different factors (e.g., skills, language, family relations). Accordingly, nations with point systems, concerned that some immigrants have not found suitable work, are increasingly moving to hybrid systems that assign more weight, as in the United States, to employer demand.[120]

Agricultural Workers

Farming is a concentrated sector and many jobs are seasonal. In 2012, fewer than a quarter of the 2.1 million U.S. farms reported using hired labor at all, yet 2.5 million people earn wages on farms. About 70 percent of those employed on crop farms were born in Mexico, almost half are undocumented, and almost all new workers on these farms are undocumented Mexicans.[121] Half are under age thirty-five, two-thirds have less than ten years of schooling, and two-thirds speak little or no English.[122] In recent years, this group has become older, worked more days, and has become more inclined to remain as farmworkers.

Assuring an adequate supply of farm labor at affordable cost is difficult, although farm labor wages account for only 30 percent of retail food costs.[123] Because migration from Mexico has slowed in recent years and the SAWs who were legalized under IRCA today comprise less than 10 percent of farm workers, wages have risen and are now well above the federal minimum wage, so poverty rates among these workers have fallen.[124] Wages may have to increase further to attract enough domestic workers.

The main way to import farm guestworkers legally is through the H-2A program, created in 1986 as a successor to the bracero program that had been repealed in 1964. Under the program, foreign farmworkers (about 100,000 a year recently, although there is no cap) can be admitted to fill seasonal farm jobs once the DOL certifies that U.S. workers are not available. Employers must provide free housing to their guestworkers. If the program does not assure an adequate flow of workers, or if it becomes too costly for employers, mechanization will accelerate and imports of fruits and vegetables will likely increase.[125] This may be a good thing for consumers.

The demand for agricultural workers raises a number of difficult policy issues. What is the actual extent of the farm labor shortage? How many Americans could be induced to do farm work if wages and conditions were better? (The conventional wisdom is not many, but this likely depends on how much better the package would be.) Growers, of course, insist that severe labor shortages exist, leaving crops to rot in the fields, but a recent review of data on H-2A levels and wage trends suggests only localized shortages.[126] How fast would mechanization spread in response to rising labor costs? Would greater use of E-Verify, which CIR would surely expand, affect these variables?[127] How might a legalization program in the agricultural sector (discussed below) work, and how would it affect the cost and availability of farm labor? These are key issues.

LPR Admissions

Policy issues concerning LPRs tend to focus on what the numbers and proportions in the various categories should be (including whether adult siblings should still receive preferential treatment and whether the diversity visa category should be reduced or eliminated altogether); whether these categories should be replaced by some sort of point system; and what to do about the massive backlogs for Mexico, China, India, the Philippines, and other major source countries due to the per-country ceiling (about 26,000 in 2014).[128]

The two principal policy issues regarding LPR admissions concern *numbers* and *preference categories*.

Numbers. As noted earlier, the 1990 Act set numerical limits and other qualifications that produce approximately 1 million new LPRs annually, and the politics since then have not yielded a larger (or smaller) number of slots—despite the U.S. economy having tripled in size.[129] For the majority of Americans who think that we already admit more LPRs than we should, this stasis is a good thing—and fewer would be even better. (As noted below with regard to enforcement strategy, however, their support for more legal admissions would be greater if they thought that the borders and interior were under tighter control.) But if we are to increase admissions, as I propose, the employment-based category could be enlarged most readily as both a political and policy matter, as business interests' desire for a larger labor supply dovetails with the demands of a more skills-based economy and with the expansionist agendas of many other groups. Also, unions, which had a strong hand in drafting the INA, have some assurance that new workers admitted in this category will not compete unduly with their existing members.* The law requires employers (not the workers) to first file petitions with the DOL for particular positions, and the position cannot be filled unless the DOL certifies that hiring the worker would neither displace nor otherwise disadvantage U.S. workers. Critics perennially condemn this certification process as sluggish, cumbersome, and unresponsive to changing

---

* Only "some" assurance for two reasons. First, much depends on how strictly the DOL administers these provisions, but as already noted, the frequent delays in DOL certification are more likely to keep needed workers out than to admit those who could adversely affect existing workers. Second, increasing the supply of workers is bound to reduce upward wage pressures for those jobs at the margin.

labor market conditions. Congress should change it, perhaps by relying more on employer certification while at the same time finding
ways to minimize the fraud that certification can facilitate.

The easiest way to increase both the number and quality of admissions is to end the current diversity lottery and use those 50,000 visas
in other ways.* It makes no sense for the most diverse advanced society on earth to distribute scarce, precious visas randomly. No other
country does this, and there is no evidence that lottery winners (sometimes called "new seeds") will flourish as well as qualified immigrants
do. Indeed, there are good reasons to suppose the opposite: the minimal education, job skills, English fluency, and work experience required to participate in the lottery, and the widespread fraud that it
promotes by many of the over 11 million applicants in 2014 (and more
in some years[130]). In contrast, family and work ties to the United
States make successful integration much more likely. A program that
favors lottery winners over individuals who have waited in line, often
for many years, for family- and employment-based visas seems patently unfair. Favoring them also magnifies others' existing temptation to jump the queue and take their chances as undocumented migrants and lottery applicants, a calculation prompting most of our
existing illegal immigrants.[131]

Preference Categories. The present LPR preference categories have
existed for a long time and are most unlikely to be altered—although
their specific numerical quotas might well be changed. Instead, reform proposals center on two subcategories. One is the investor program (EB-5), created in 1990 to foster job creation. It authorizes
10,000 visas per year but only reached this cap in 2014.[132] (Many
other countries have similar programs crafted to attract the rich and
raise revenues through hefty fees.)[133] The program has been plagued
by fraud, favoritism, maladministration (especially in the largely unregulated regional centers where most of the investors' money goes),

---

* As discussed in the conclusion, those 50,000 visas would still not be enough to meet
our current needs.

national security risks, and other failures. Reform proposals abound and are urgent, given the "buying visas" critique of the program.[134]

Another vulnerable subcategory under the family preference quota is adult siblings of U.S. citizens. Arguably, this subcategory could be reduced or eliminated without serious hardship to citizens given the unlimited admission of their "immediate relatives" and the large quotas for other, closer family categories. After all, changes in technology and travel make it much easier for siblings abroad to visit on temporary visas and to stay in constant touch with their U.S. relatives.

Most policy proposals focus on skills, as noted earlier. We could assess employers' needs for skilled workers by market demand, an administrative point system (as Canada does), Bureau of Labor Statistics data, or some combination of these indicia. Another reform, a kind of legalization (see below), would create a new visa for long-resident, noncriminal undocumented workers who must pay an annual fee for the option of going to the end of the queue and waiting their turn, while enjoying some protection from deportation in the interim.[135] Finally, some economists urge the government to auction off some green cards to the highest bidders, who would tend to be high-skill people. Indeed, I have long proposed to auction off some visas now allocated by lottery (see below). The fraud-ridden EB-5 program is a ripe candidate for the lottery approach.

Mexican Quota

Mexico dominates U.S. immigration flows. In 2014, more than 11.7 million Mexican immigrants resided in the United States, accounting for 28 percent of the 42.4 million foreign-born population—by far the largest immigrant origin group in the country. (Of *new* LPRs, Mexico is no longer the top source; China and India overtook it in 2014.) The vast majority of Mexican LPRs enter as "immediate relatives" (63 percent) or under other family preferences (26 percent). Their prominence in the illegal migration flow is even more pronounced. In 2013, they constituted 56 percent of the undocumented population in the United States, by far the largest share.[136] Even in

New York City, so far from the southern border, Mexicans may soon become the largest Hispanic cohort (replacing Puerto Ricans and Dominicans).[137]

Geography, of course, is the main reason. Mexico and the United States share an almost 2,000-mile border, which separates the world's wealthiest society from the "Third World" of Central and South America. The two economies are increasingly integrated through the North American Free Trade Agreement (NAFTA), with Mexico being the United States' second largest goods export market and third largest agricultural export market.[138] Culturally and historically, the two countries have been closely linked for hundreds of years, particularly in the southwestern United States, which was part of Mexico until the 1848 Treaty of Guadalupe Hidalgo, which granted citizenship to those Mexicans who chose to remain. Traditionally, the United States did not impose any numerical limits on Mexican immigration; they were exempted from the national origins quota laws. Indeed, limits were imposed only in the 1970s, prompting the large illegal flow that has ensued.

Yet despite the outsized importance of Mexican migration, its annual per-country cap is the same (26,337 in 2014) as for all countries regardless of their relationship to the U.S. society and economy. Thus, the waiting list of Mexican immigrants for fiscal year 2016 was 1,344,429 applicants—exponentially higher than the per-country cap—and the waiting time for green cards is very long: In May 2016, it was twenty-one years even for (unmarried) sons and daughters of U.S citizens.[139]

These excruciatingly long waits create a strong incentive for even Mexicans who might qualify for a visa to jump the queue and enter or remain in the United States illegally. A larger quota would not eliminate this incentive but would surely reduce it. Some recent changes in Mexico—declining fertility rates, improved education, and domestic economic growth—along with slower job growth in the United States suggest that pressures to migrate here may be easing, but the durability of this development depends on many factors, especially economic conditions, largely beyond our control. The argument for a larger quota can also be seen as a concession to reality: if more Mexicans are going to come here anyway, it may be better to have them come with legal status. (This is akin to one argument in favor of a legalization program, discussed in the next section.)

Arguments against a larger Mexican quota include claims that immigration levels should not be increased, that the notion of a special relationship with Mexico is overblown, and that some of the additional migrants would inevitably bring with them more of the drugs, gang violence, and other problems so rife there. A more controversial claim advanced by the late Harvard political scientist Samuel Huntington argues that Latino culture is less compatible with democratic values and American ways.[140] Although many dispute his claim, Mexican migration does have several worrisome aspects. One is that eligible Mexican LPRs naturalize at low rates—only 36 percent, or half that of the eligible LPRs from all other countries combined, and lower than among immigrants from Latin America and the Caribbean (61 percent). Another is that only 30 percent of Hispanic LPRs report that they speak English "very well" or "pretty well"[141]—which partly reflects lack of access by the undocumented to English-language classes.

These facts are troubling, particularly to those like me who believe that culture can significantly affect social values and behavior.[142] Nevertheless, I resist Huntington's argument for several reasons: its cultural reductionism;[143] the historical refutation of similar claims made about almost every new immigrant group; the exceptional power of American life to integrate migrants from the most disparate cultures; and the self-selection aspect of migration that tends to attract the most enterprising, adaptable, and motivated individuals.[144] As discussed below, real assimilation typically occurs only in the second or third generations.

Cuban Migration

The Cuban Adjustment Act of 1966, a Cold War policy deeply embedded in politics as well as law, has become particularly controversial since President Obama established diplomatic relations with Cuba in

January 2015, arguing that the embargo on travel to and trade with Cuba has been ineffective and should be scrapped. Unless Congress reverses this major policy shift, it must decide whether the act is justified today, whether or not it was earlier.[145]

Under the 1966 law, Cuban migrants can qualify for legal status, and eventually citizenship, in the United States far more easily than other migrants can. They also enjoy other advantages: a generous annual permanent admissions quota, very permissive tourist visas, and much easier access to political asylum with a lower standard of proof of persecution. Indeed, the "wet feet, dry feet" interpretation of the act enables those who manage to reach American shores to gain legal status almost automatically, whereas those intercepted at sea by U.S. vessels are turned back. The act gives Cubans vastly preferential treatment compared not only with other undocumented migrants but also with their Caribbean neighbors from Haiti.[146] Many critics of the act ascribe this difference to racial favoritism, but it also reflects Cubans' political influence, especially in Florida where so many have settled and prospered both socially and economically, often voting Republican. Varying attitudes toward the act also reflect generational differences due to the aging of the cohorts of fiercely anticommunist Cubans who fled Cuba shortly after Fidel Castro's takeover, the Marielito group in the early 1980s, and the rafters in 1994. Their second- and third-generation descendants tend to be less reflexively anti-Castro, more likely to vote Democratic, and more open to détente than the earlier cohorts.

The patent favoritism that the act accords to Cubans was always hard to justify under an immigration system that claims to be even-handed as to countries of origin, but it is especially anomalous now that normal relations with Cuba are being established. (This is why Cubans' migration to the United States spiked 77 percent in 2015 after President Obama's demarche, as they fear losing their special access.)[147] Politics aside, its migrants should not be treated so much more favorably than those from other countries, even assuming (contrary to much evidence) that the current regime oppresses its people less than Fidel's did. In principle, the act should be jettisoned, but in some other situations—for example, for Iraqis who aided the United

States at considerable risk to themselves[148]—our foreign policy goals may and should dictate special treatment. That is no longer the case with today's Cubans.

Legalization*

At the end of 2014, the number of undocumented people living in the United States was 11.1 million, down from the 12.2 million peak in 2007 reached just as the Great Recession was beginning. This included declines in illegal Mexican migration.[149] The undocumented contribute to the U.S. economy and perhaps in other ways, but their continuing illegal status while here is objectionable for many reasons in addition to the fact of their having broken U.S. immigration law. First, it means that they must live in the shadows (as the cliché has it). This is demoralizing and also renders them more vulnerable to many afflictions: blackmail and other crimes, fear of the police and of using other public services, untreated illness, and other ills resulting from social isolation. Second, as noted earlier, many live in mixed-status families that include U.S. citizen children entitled to be here and thus have important ties to the United States and its institutions despite their outlaw status. Third, their relations with American citizens and LPRs may be deeply compromised and prone to social and economic exploitation. Fourth, their liminal status reduces their stake or desire to assimilate more fully into American life despite their possibly permanent presence here.

For these and other reasons, the U.S. Congress has periodically enacted programs to confer legal status of one kind or another—usually a path to LPR status under specified conditions—on certain groups of the undocumented.† These legalizations have taken various

* The term "amnesty" is often used interchangeably, but some proponents object to the term because legalization imposes certain preconditions before the new status can be acquired. However, since amnesties also impose such preconditions, the distinction strikes me as more cosmetic than meaningful.

† The statute authorizes relief from deportation for particular individuals, which is granted more commonly and can result in their gaining legal status. This discussion, however, is not concerned with such case-by-case adjudications.

forms. One provision enabled spouses and other immediate relatives of U.S. citizens in illegal status to apply for legal status under certain conditions, including a fee. This provision, which expired in 1998 and protected citizens' family lives, should be reenacted but with strong anti-fraud controls.

Another form of legalization ("registry") authorizes giving LPR status to those who can show that they have continuously resided in the United States since a certain date, are not within the most serious inadmissibility categories, and meet a good moral character standard.[150] Congress periodically advanced the registry date but not since IRCA—enacted three decades ago!—set the date at 1972. Even with the slowdown in new illegal migration during the Great Recession, the size of the *long-term* undocumented resident population has risen substantially: The median time of U.S. residence for undocumented adults is now about thirteen years (a five-year increase since 2003), while only 15 percent (DHS estimates are even lower) have been here for fewer than five years.[151] Congress should advance the registry date to at least 2000 and perhaps later, a continuous residency period analogous to that which it adopted in IRCA. I can think of no reasonable objection to this unless one opposes even this most plausible, long-sanctioned form of legalization of a group of individuals whom the government will not conceivably seek to remove.

Four other types of legalization programs have been far more central to the immigration debate than registry. Varying in breadth, they are directed at (1) the general undocumented population; (2) agricultural workers, (3) young people who have grown up here; and (4) other family members.

General Legalization. The main precedent for very broad relief is IRCA, which legalized almost 2.7 million people. These included 1.6 million general workers, 1.1 million agricultural workers (SAWs), and 38,000 Haitians and Cubans. Congress subsequently enacted smaller amnesties for those from particular countries: Nicaragua and Cuba in 1997, Haiti in 1998.

Depending on how the program is designed (largely determined by legislative bargaining and administrative needs), it may impose a number of eligibility requirements: a defined period of residence and of illegal status in the country; absence of criminal conduct (variously defined); payment of penalties, back taxes, and fees; documentary evidence of illegal residence; a "touch back" requirement that the applicant first return to the home country; a waiting period on the queue; transitional legal status for a certain period, perhaps leading to a path to a green card and eventually citizenship; access to work permits pending approval of their applications; limits on job mobility and access to public benefits for certain periods; provisions for certain family members; and many other provisions.

Several aspects of IRCA's broad amnesties should be noted. Because they purported to require case-by-case assessment for eligibility, they generated high administrative costs and lengthy litigation. Fraud and error were rampant, especially in the SAW program. Documentary evidence of eligibility was often hard to come by. With a long path to citizenship, "family fairness" adjustments were necessary for humanitarian reasons. NGOs played a major role in mobilizing applicants fearful of deportation. Eligibility for welfare, Medicaid, and other benefits for the legalized was a hot political issue at all levels of government.

These design issues are not only difficult in themselves; they also entail hard practical and moral trade-offs. The more generous and inclusive the program, the more the public may feel that illegality is being rewarded. Yet if the conditions are too onerous, the undocumented may decide to take their chances by remaining in the shadows rather than apply. Allowing the newly legalized to jump the queue for green cards will be unfair to those who have been waiting in it for years. The easier it is for them to change jobs during the process or once legalized, the less likely employers will be to support the program. No legalization program is likely to pass unless eligibles are barred from accessing federally funded welfare benefits (discussed below) for some years, as they proceed through various provisional statuses to green cards and then citizenship. The list of issues and trade-offs like these is very long indeed.

Regardless of how these design issues are resolved, deterrence is an important concern about any amnesty program, and perhaps the strongest argument against it. Fear that this amnesty might encourage more illegal migrants to come in hopes that new ones will be granted in the future is not an idle concern. After all, Congress enacted IRCA in 1986 and additional country-specific ones in the late 1990s, and President Obama ordered even larger ones (but granting more limited rights) in 2012 and 2014, now under legal challenge. Any new one would likely erode further the credibility of the government's enforcement stance. At the margin, people carefully weighing the benefits and risks of coming to the United States illegally may be more likely to take the chance, hoping for yet another amnesty or an extension of the new one. Those who are already here and hoping to stay would have less reason to return home.

On balance, however, I strongly favor some such program for the long-resident, noncriminal undocumented, especially if it is coupled with serious enforcement efforts directed at new undocumented arrivals. For one thing, no government, regardless of which party controls it, will deport most of them anyway—especially the so-called Dreamers. Since they will remain indefinitely, it is better for them, their families, and American society that they gain legal status and get on with their lives and their connections to the rest of us—however inconsistent with rule-of-law rhetoric this may be. Simply stated, the alternative—maintaining the status quo for an ever-increasing undocumented population—is worse. As so many Americans already recognize, a rule of law so patently, even hypocritically, unenforceable mocks itself.

A starting point for any new legalization policy debate would be S. 744, a comprehensive immigration reform bill that passed the Senate in 2013 but was not taken up by the House. Its Registered Provisional Immigrant (RPI) program had three discrete components—for Dreamers, farmworkers, and others in the United States since December 31, 2011—and specified the kinds of eligibility requirements and other limitations discussed above.

Agricultural Workers. As just noted, IRCA legalized 1.1 million SAWs in 1986; the administrative and litigation processes stretched out for many years thereafter. The three decades since IRCA have attracted new cohorts of undocumented farmworkers. During this period, a number of proposals for a new legalization program have been advanced, including the Agricultural Jobs, Opportunity, Benefits and Security Act (AgJOBS). Various versions contain certain features: undocumented immigrants who have worked in agriculture for a certain period of time could apply for probationary status, which would allow them to work and travel within the United States and enter and leave it. If they continued such work for a certain number of years (their employers would be required to furnish documentation of their work), they and certain family members would gain a path to LPR and ultimately citizenship. AgJOBS would make it easier for farms to recruit and employ H-2A guestworkers, while revising housing and minimum wage rules. But labor economist Philip Martin points to another trade-off: AgJOBS might favor current unauthorized workers over future guestworkers, since those who are now working illegally in U.S. agriculture could later become U.S. citizens, while future guestworkers under such a program will have lower wages and fewer protections.

Young People. This type of legalization is represented by the June 2012 DACA program. DACA benefits the Dreamers, who present the most compelling equitable case for not being deported because they are young people who were brought to the United States as children at an age when they bore no conceivable responsibility for their parents' actions in migrating here unlawfully and who have been raised and educated in the United States and have stayed out of trouble with the law. Starting in 2001, Congress considered various versions of bipartisan legislation to accord the Dreamers conditional legal status, but it became embroiled in political disputes over immigration and other issues, and never passed Congress. Hoping to finesse this log-jam, President Obama established DACA unilaterally in 2012, invoking the executive branch's prosecutorial discretion, which he sought to distinguish from amnesty. This precipitated lawsuits challenging his legal authority to do so without congressional approval.[152]

Under the 2012 version of DACA, eligibles must be between fifteen and thirty years of age, have arrived in the United States before age sixteen, resided here continuously for five years, be enrolled in or graduated from high school or be veterans, and have not been convicted of a serious crime. Provided they continue to meet the requirements, they are not subject to removal, can get benefits described below, and can renew this status every two years. About 1.2 million Dreamers were immediately DACA-eligible, plus 400,000 would become eligible later when they reached age fifteen and satisfied the education requirement.[153]

In November 2014, President Obama—again invoking prosecutorial discretion—further extended DACA eligibility by easing some DACA eligibility requirements and establishing a new program granting relief and similar benefits to the parents of U.S. citizen children (Deferred Action for Parental Accountability, "DAPA"), and shortly thereafter DHS announced that it was offering a similar status to Central Americans who are parents and children of those qualifying under these programs.[154] An estimated 3.9 million are eligible under DAPA and another 1.5 million under DACA.[155] In June 2016, an equally divided, truncated Supreme Court left in place an appellate panel's ruling that upheld a district judge's injunction against both DAPA and the government's extension of the DACA period for exceeding presidential authority.[156] (The district judge has excoriated DHS for extending relief to many more of the undocumented than its own rules permit.)[157] DHS also reported that a dragnet operation against serious noncitizen criminals had arrested twenty-three DACA-eligibles,[158] one of whom was a known gang member scheduled to stand trial for the murder of four people.[159] The Pentagon has proposed allowing DACA-eligibles to enlist in the military.[160] DAPA and DACA will lapse with the end of the Obama administration unless a new president revives them; a new Republican Congress would seek to eliminate the program altogether.

Quite apart from the legality of DACA and DAPA, strong policy arguments cut against deporting noncriminal Dreamers and parents of birthright citizens. Given ICE's priorities and limited enforcement resources, and the Dreamers' equitable claims to remain here with their parents and contribute to American society, ICE is far less likely to actually deport this group than it would other undocumented people. The main issues surrounding relief for Dreamers and parents of citizens, then, are whether Congress should authorize such relief, what the precise eligibility criteria should be, and which benefits those eligible under the programs can receive.

The first issue is easily resolved. Even if the president had the legal power to authorize the programs unilaterally—which I and some other immigration scholars doubt[161] but which the Supreme Court may eventually decide[162]—Congress is the better institution to establish it and design its general parameters. As the chief policy maker in the immigration area, only Congress can forge the political compromises and funding that are necessary to its political support and successful implementation. (Obama's November 2014 programs could be funded without congressional appropriations only because of revenue from fees charged by the agency, an unusual source that an angry Congress may decide to limit in the future.) The second and third issues—eligibility criteria and benefits to participants—were resolved by the new policy. Together, the programs granted eligible undocumenteds work authorization, Social Security cards, substantial tax benefits, and even income supplements under the child and Earned Income Tax credits.[163] One analyst estimates the cost of these benefits at $7.8 billion a year,[164] with the agency also incurring large implementation costs.[165] The administration argues that these benefits are already authorized under statute-based "deferred action" policy, but critics disagree.

Family Members. Congress has sometimes authorized "family fairness" programs to confer legal status on close family members of those whom it has already legalized in order to protect such relatives from deportation pending administrative implementation of the legalization. As noted above, President Obama's DACA and DAPA programs, created just before the 2014 midterm elections in which his party did very poorly, could potentially give more than 5 million undocumented people relief from deportation, work permits, and a legal status—although he was careful not to call it legalization. The order does not expressly extend welfare benefits to this large group, but a large number of the undocumented are receiving these benefits nonetheless.[166] It aroused furious opposition by the incoming Republican congressional majority and even some Democratic members. Many commentators predicted that the order, lacking congressional approval, would kill any chance to gain congressional approval of broader immigration reforms in the new Congress.[167] Indeed, it has fueled resistance to even clearly authorized actions such as increasing the number of Syrian refugees in view of the refugee crisis in Europe.[168]

Immigration Federalism

In 1994, California adopted Proposition 187 limiting social benefits to the undocumented; a federal court enjoined most of it. Ever since, some states and localities have tried to augment what they rightly perceived as weak federal enforcement—in part by impeding access by the undocumented to jobs, housing, schools, and other amenities in hopes of encouraging them to "self-deport." At the same time, and partly in response, many other states—especially those with liberal governments and large immigration-friendly voting blocs—have adopted policies designed to make life easier for immigrants, often including the undocumented. Roberto Suro captures this patchwork pattern well:

> At the start of 2015 in California home to a quarter of all foreign-born in the United States including some 2.5 million unauthorized immigrants, an individual regarded as out-of-status by federal

standards can get a driver's license, apply for a number of health and welfare programs, go to a state university and pay in-state tuition, and practice law. Meanwhile, across the state line in Arizona the same person would be subject to the "show-me-your-papers" provision of SB 1070 which the Supreme Court let stand. They would also be subject to state regulations that could turn any contact with a state agency into an encounter with a federal agent, and any prospective employer would be obliged to check the individual's identity against a federal database.[169]

These state law actions and differences raise a complex legal issue under the Supremacy Clause of the U.S. Constitution. The clause invalidates state laws that are inconsistent with federal policy, especially where Congress has "occupied the field." Immigration policy is one of the areas subject to this "field preemption." The clause, however, allows states to regulate its inhabitants, including immigrants, in a host of ways. The line between "immigration" policy (preempted) and "immigrant" policy (not preempted) is blurry, and the Supreme Court has failed to clarify it very much in its recent decisions, including *Arizona v. United States*,[170] which struck down some of the state's enforcement provisions while upholding others.[171] Although this legal uncertainty does cast a cloud over state laws targeting the undocumented, California and some other states have sought to protect them—especially the Dreamers—in various ways. In 2015, ten states plus the District of Columbia and Puerto Rico permitted the undocumented to obtain drivers' licenses; in California most new licenses are reportedly issued to them;[172] and in 2016, New York made them eligible for a wide range of professional and occupational licenses.[173] (New political leadership in some states seeks to reverse this.)[174] In 2016, New Mexico,[175] Massachusetts,[176] and some other states extended driving "privileges" to undocumented residents.

Within this preemption constraint, two policy issues remain. First, how much authority should Congress devolve to the states (as the clause allows it to do) to shape immigration policy? In other words, how much diversity in states' treatment of immigrants should Congress permit? In an article, "Taking Immigration Federalism Seriously," I proposed a larger role for the states in certain areas—for example, in making employment-based visas more sensitive to local economic conditions[177]—and some others have also urged this approach.[178] But as with other federalism questions, there will be difficult trade-offs between the advantages of national uniformity (e.g., avoiding interstate externalities and "races to the bottom") and the disadvantages (e.g., a confusing patchwork sending conflicting signals; lack of experimentation with diverse regimes). Since states and their localities bear most of the fiscal costs imposed by immigrants but enjoy only some of the benefits, this is an even more difficult call. The second issue is: within the zone of discretion that federal law leaves to the states, which policies should they adopt with respect to immigrants who reside there? There is no general answer to this question, but the following section and those on economic impact and social integration suggest how one might think about good answers.

Welfare Benefits

Americans' attitudes toward immigration are affected by their values and perceptions about whether, to what extent, in which categories, and under what conditions immigrants are eligible for and actually use welfare benefits, especially those that are means-tested. Voters who oppose a more expansive welfare state—which is to say, most Americans—fear that extending benefits to immigrants would not only be costly and weaken work incentives but would socialize our newest residents into a culture of excessive dependency on government. Strong egalitarians reject any distinction between citizens and legal immigrants, including (or especially) access to benefits.

Many voters would favor higher levels of immigration if they felt assured that immigrants would be self-supporting and ineligible for benefits, at least for a significant period of time after arrival. Congress institutionalized this widespread sentiment in1996 in two ways: conditioning new immigrant visas on a sponsor's affidavit of support to assure that the immigrant will not become a "public charge" (an exclusion ground going back to 1875); and barring most new LPRs from federally funded benefits for five years. Indeed, a leading pro-immigration scholar has proposed that new immigrants must insure against their use of such benefits.[179] Any legalization proposal will surely regulate applicants' access to benefits.

For many reasons, it is hard to measure immigrants' actual use of public benefits, especially the more controversial means-tested programs like SNAP (formerly food stamps), Temporary Assistance for Needy Families (formerly welfare), Medicaid, public housing, and the Earned Income Tax Credit (EITC). The programs are complex, with each having its own eligibility rules and administrative structure. The rules of many programs (e.g., Medicaid) vary from state to state, and as Roberto Suro notes above, some states extend important benefits even to the undocumented. People cycle on and off programs as their circumstances change. Data are based largely on responses to government surveys, in which utilization tends to be under-reported. In addition, immigrants' use depends on their specific status (e.g., LPRs, refugees, various non-immigrant categories, undocumented), household composition (all foreign-born vs. mixed-status families), members in the labor force, household size, and other variables. And immigrant take-up rates also vary with economic conditions.

Several immigrant utilization patterns are notable. A review by the restrictionist Center for Immigration Studies (CIS) in 2011 found that all-immigrant households with children used welfare programs at higher levels than similar American households do, even controlling for the number of children. Refugee families tend to have relatively high utilization rates. (A 2015 CIS study found that caring for a Middle Eastern refugee in the United States is twelve times more costly than doing so in her home region.)[180] Usage by families with children tends to grow with years in the United States, peaking at about fifteen years. Higher usage by immigrant households with children, of course, reflects the lower education levels of immigrants generally, but remains true even among the better-educated. Households with children headed by a legal immigrant with no more than a high school education had the highest rates (71.8 percent). The highest usage by households with children is for those from Dominican Republic, Mexico, Guatemala, and Ecuador.[181] Lawfully present immigrants are major Affordable Care Act beneficiaries.[182] Some other surveys find lower utilization levels in some of these categories.[183]

Limiting immigrants' access to benefits is legally and practically difficult. U.S.-born children, like all other citizens, are entitled to benefits even if their undocumented parents are not. The 1996 welfare reform barred most new LPRs from many federally subsidized programs for their first five years, but most LPRs have been here longer than that. Federal benefit programs already bar the undocumented, but the 1996 law lets states use their own funds, which California, New York, and some other large immigrant-receiving states do.

Citizenship

United States citizenship policies are well-established and seldom change. Citizenship can be acquired in three ways: by being born here (birthright or *jus soli* citizenship), by having one or more U.S. citizen parents (*jus sanguinis*), and by naturalization. The main citizenship issues today are (1) whether birthright citizenship should be denied to U.S.-born children of parents who are here illegally; (2) whether the standards for naturalization should change with respect to cultural knowledge and plural citizenships; (3) whether the incentives to naturalize are sufficient; and (4) how difficult it should be for the government to take away the citizenship of Americans whose loyalty is doubtful or divided (denationalization). Although these issues raise interesting, difficult theoretical and legal questions, there is little political support for altering the current rules. Accordingly, my discussion of them will be brief.

Birthright Citizenship. Birthright citizenship for the U.S.-born children of illegal immigrants is perhaps the most controversial of these because on its face it seems to encourage this illegality, rewarding law-breaking parents or "maternity tourists"[184] by enabling their children to gain a precious privilege simply by being born here, which also can eventually give the parents a legal foothold. Under the traditional practice and understanding, assumed but not squarely decided by the Supreme Court, birthright citizenship for these children is mandated by the Fourteenth Amendment's Citizenship Clause: "All persons born or naturalized in the United States, and subject to the jurisdiction thereof, are citizens of the United States. . . ."

In a 1985 book, Rogers Smith and I reviewed the philosophical, legal, and constitutional history of birthright citizenship from its origins in the seventeenth-century English common law to the present day.[185] Briefly stated, we concluded that a citizenship automatically ascribed at birth was in fundamental tension with the liberal idea of mutual consent to political membership that the clause's authors embraced; that its purpose was to confer citizenship at birth on the recently emancipated blacks but to exclude from this status Native Americans and others ruled by other sovereignties; that the Framers' consensual principles would have excluded from birthright citizenship the children of illegal immigrants, had such a category then existed (which it did not); and therefore that Congress remained free to decide this question for itself. We then canvassed the arguments for and against the birthright citizenship rule.

Public concern about illegal immigration has not led to a call to change the traditional rule. Some in Congress want to jettison it, arguing that it encourages illegal migrants to have "anchor babies" (and those on tourist and other temporary visas to have "tourism babies") here who can then use these children to gain legal status for the parents—although, significantly, the child cannot do this until age twenty-one. No one knows how many such children are born in the United States; the CIS estimates that undocumented parents and temporary visa holders annually give birth to 350,000 and 35,000 birthright citizens, respectively; the former number would approximate 10 percent of annual U.S. births.[186]

Congress, however, has shown no inclination to eliminate the traditional rule, nor has it shown interest in my compromise proposal to give these children birthright citizenship once they live and attend school here for a certain number of years.[187] In April 2015, a House Judiciary subcommittee held a hearing on the issue, the first in ten years.[188] This inaction probably reflects the advantages of the traditional rule, which is clear, easily administered, inclusive, and avoids illegal status for the future generations of long-term residents. Repealing it retroactively would also increase the undocumented population by an estimated 3 million people.[189]

Naturalization. The Constitution empowers Congress to enact a "uniform rule of naturalization," and eligibility requirements were controversial from the very beginning. The Naturalization Act of 1790 limited naturalization to free whites who had resided in the United States for at least two years and were of "good moral character." The five-year residency period has been required since 1802. Some racial exclusions continued until 1943 when the bar to Asian naturalization was lifted due to our alliance with Chiang Kai-shek during World War II. The statute still bars communists, anarchists, totalitarians, and others who advocate overthrow of the government from naturalizing—even after a 1990 law dropped most of these ideological exclusions as applied to visa eligibility. In 2015, approximately 730,000 naturalizations occurred—an increase over 2014 but far below the record 1.04 million set in the 2008 election year, which represented a 60 percent increase over the previous year.[190] In the run-up to the 2016 elections, the Obama administration launched a naturalization drive,[191] just as the Clinton administration did (controversially) in the 1990s,[192] and Trump's anti-Mexican speeches are spurring many more applications.[193]

Today, the main naturalization policy issues concern (1) the level of knowledge of American culture that applicants should have to demonstrate on the naturalization test, (2) the period of time required to petition for naturalization, and (3) access to dual or plural citizenship. The public, it seems, does not regard any of these naturalization issues as urgent.

The naturalization test—a bit of a misnomer; the answers are provided in advance—was long criticized for being too easy, focusing on rote memorization of facts; the passage rate was 84 percent.* On the redesigned test, introduced in 2008, 91 percent pass. Even so, some immigrant advocates consider it too subjective and demanding, while other critics emphasize that it still does not test for meaningful understanding of American civic values, instead asking questions like "the location of the Statue of Liberty."[194] The debate on testing is far more intense in Europe, where many countries use it to control migration by demanding much cultural knowledge and linguistic mastery. A leading comparative law scholar finds this strategy "illiberal" in means and purpose, in contrast to the much easier U.S. test.[195]

How active should the government be in encouraging naturalization? This is partly a question of one's conception of the appropriate relation between state and individual in a liberal polity. In contrast to Canada, which actively promotes naturalization in a number of ways, the United States is more passive, leaving it to LPRs to take the initiative on citizenship if they wish. This more laissez-faire stance with respect to citizenship, which is simply one aspect of our hands-off approach to immigrant integration generally, is consistent with many other American practices—for example, relying on the political parties to mobilize voters.[196] Even so, a variety of Canadian-type policy changes might well encourage LPRs to naturalize. This in turn would consolidate, if not accelerate, their social and political integration.

The American debate over plural citizenships has been contentious in the past, but today it is not particularly intense. The history of dual citizenship in the United States and elsewhere is complex,[197] and the normative issues are interesting.[198] The United States long

---

* Most Americans would fail a similar civics test, a situation that many states are trying to rectify. http://www.aei.org/publication/person-born-already-love-country-ap-poll-agrees/?utm_source=today&utm_medium=paramount&utm_campaign=123114. For example, only 40 percent of voters can name all three branches of the federal government, and 65 percent do not know that Congress is empowered to declare war. Rick Shenkman, *Just How Stupid Are We? Facing the Truth about the American Voter* (2008).

opposed it but now accepts it in recognition of the plurality of citizenships that result from international marriages, parentage, mobility, and the interaction of *jus soli* and *jus sanguinis* regimes.[199] One traditional barrier was the statutory naturalization oath in which new citizens must renounce loyalty to any other state of which they were citizens. This oath, however, no longer impedes plural citizenship. The State Department holds that this renunciation will not subject dual citizens to any risk of denaturalization, even if their nations of prior citizenship do not recognize their renunciation. They, like any other citizen, may acquire additional citizenships by naturalizing elsewhere. In 2015, a record 4,279 individuals renounced their U.S. citizenship or long-term residency, many of them for tax reasons in the wake of new legally required reporting by foreign financial institutions of their customers' nationality.[200] Presumably, these individuals held another nationality.

Incentives to Naturalize. Approximately 8.8 million LPRs were eligible to naturalize in 2013.[201] Their propensity to naturalize varies by country of origin, and their naturalization rates are affected by whether the undocumented from a country are included in the denominator, which has been the practice and lowers their reported naturalization rates.[202] The naturalization rate for eligible Mexican LPRs, who constitute the largest group of LPRs (about a third) is only 36 percent, compared with 68 percent for all non-Mexican groups and 61 percent for all other Latin American and Caribbean eligibles.[203] The predominance of Mexican LPRs among those eligible for naturalization helps to explain why our naturalization rate is only about 50 percent overall, well below many European countries, and far lower than other traditional receiving countries like Australia and Canada.[204]

Most eligibles report that they would like to naturalize but fail to do so because of poor command of the English language, administrative barriers, and the cost, which has increased substantially, scheduled to rise in late 2016 to $725. The median period spent in LPR status before naturalizing is seven years, but many take much longer, especially Mexicans. More than twenty years after the 1986 IRCA legalization, only 40 percent of those eligible for naturalization had done so, mostly Mexicans.[205] This is all the more striking because Mexicans since 1998 have been able to naturalize here without losing their Mexican nationality or right to vote there.

Why might a foreign national *want* to become an American citizen?* In a 1989 article, I argued that the United States had pursued a liberal public philosophy by expanding the equality and due process principles in ways that "reduced almost to the vanishing point the marginal value of becoming a citizen compared with remaining an LPR. These changes have minimized an LPR's incentive to naturalize, but have also altered the social significance of citizenship."[206] Today, the principal difference is that LPRs cannot vote, serve on juries, receive certain welfare benefits, get top priority in securing visas for family members, or be a government employee (in some jurisdictions). Some also point to shorter waits for citizens at ports of entry. Indeed, even these differences are eroding; some municipalities allow LPRs to vote in local elections (as is common in Europe) and others propose doing so. Some jurisdictions make LPRs eligible for certain welfare benefits, and even grant some important and valuable benefits to the undocumented, as noted earlier. (In 1996, however, Congress denied *federal* welfare benefits to the undocumented and even to some LPRs—partly to "revalue" American citizenship.)[207]

These developments raise a difficult policy question: Should we expand or limit the differential treatment of citizens and LPRs, and if so, how? This is only partly a question of incentives; at the margin, equalization of status does discourage LPRs from going to the trouble to naturalize. But beyond incentives, why should we care which choice LPRs make? After all, they must obey laws and pay taxes, may serve in the military (which may qualify them for a faster path to citizenship

---

* Wealthy individuals often seek plural citizenships or passports under programs created by countries seeking to attract investment. Such "economic citizens" spend an estimated $2 billion a year on additional passports or visas. Robert Frank, "Some of the Rich Collect Art. Others Collect Passports," *New York Times*, December 14, 2014, BU 4.

under a recently expanded program),[208] and do nearly everything else that citizens do—except vote.* (Noncitizens can even be counted for redistricting purposes.)[209] Some argue that any differences between citizens and LPRs in rights and duties are anachronistic in a globalizing world. A cosmopolitan society, they insist, should recognize universal human rights that attach to individuals *qua* human beings, not limit those rights to national members. In this view, voting and thus influencing the government that exercises power over them in the name of democracy is one such right.[210]

The counterargument, which I favor, contends that allowing LPRs to vote in national elections would further weaken their incentives to become citizens and aggravate voters' deplorable ignorance, discussed earlier, about the United States. (Local school board elections may raise other considerations.) Nationally, they should be allowed to vote only when they demonstrate a commitment to the United States by undergoing a naturalization process assuring minimal familiarity with American society, government, institutions, and values.

Denationalization. Loss of one's citizenship (denationalization) without one's consent is as harsh a sanction as there is, comparable in some ways to capital punishment. It may render an individual stateless, depriving him of the precious right to have rights (as Hannah Arendt put it), but even if it does not, loss of citizenship may cut him off from the polity and society that he has inhabited all his life. In addition, governments may be tempted to use this powerful weapon to silence and punish their critics or to seek revenge against unpopular minorities.[211] Indeed, this sanction is so severe and so vulnerable to political abuse that it must be reserved, in my view, for only the most extreme cases in which the citizen's disloyalty and threat to national security are imminent and crystal clear.[212] Some commentators believe that it cannot be justified even then.[213]

---

* A recent political science study finds that despite this bar, many noncitizens actually *do* vote in federal elections—enough to affect important outcomes. http://www.science direct.com/science/article/pii/S0261379414000973

The United States has succumbed in the past to the temptation to denationalize some of its citizens,[214] and might do so again as it prosecutes its war on terror.* The statute contains a list of actions by citizens that, if voluntary and taken with the specific intent to relinquish citizenship, will divest individuals of U.S. citizenship. The actions are (generally speaking) naturalizing in a foreign state; taking an oath or other formal declaration of allegiance to a foreign state; serving in a foreign military as an officer or if it is engaged in hostilities with the United States; being employed by a foreign state of which one is a citizen; doing so under an oath of allegiance to that state; formally renouncing U.S. citizenship; and engaging in treason against the United States, or attempting to overthrow or bearing arms against it.† In a 1967 decision, however, the Supreme Court greatly narrowed the denationalization sanction, holding that the government could not invoke it against a citizen who voted in a foreign election (a denationalizing act then listed in the statute) unless the government could prove that he *consented* to losing his U.S. citizenship.[215] In 1980, the Court made it easier to denationalize a citizen, upholding a statutory provision allowing the State Department to prove its claim by merely a preponderance of the evidence (the standard used in ordinary civil cases), and with a presumption that a citizen who performed one of the listed denationalizing acts did so voluntarily, unless the citizen can prove otherwise.[216] Even so, the government still bears the burden of proving the citizen's specific intent to renounce, which is hard to do. Accordingly, in 1990 the State Department adopted a self-denying, retroactive policy that made it much harder to take away citizenship unless the citizen expressly renounces it, which at that

---

* The United States has targeted and sometimes killed Americans, notably Anwar al-Awlaki, whom the president found to be engaged in military conflict against the United States through the direction of terrorist acts. In my view, this ultimate form of denationalization is not barred by the Supreme Court decisions discussed immediately following. Peter H. Schuck, "Citizen Terrorist," *Policy Review*, December 2010.

† Living abroad even for a protracted period is *not* a ground; an estimated 7.6 million Americans do so. http://www.migrationpolicy.org/article/americans-abroad-disillusioned-diaspora

time occurred in only about two hundred cases annually.[217] In 2015, 4,279 did so. And there the matter rests.

Enforcement Strategy

Immigration enforcement—at the borders and in the interior through use of exclusion, deportation, and various other civil and criminal sanctions—is a perennially difficult issue for many reasons. First, enforcement is an inherently problematic task, especially in a system like ours that heavily relies on it as a post-admissions screening system to back up prior, often categorical admissions choices.[218] Undocumented workers may be indistinguishable in appearance from legal ones, take great pains to avoid interactions with police or ICE officials, can easily and cheaply obtain false documents, and may successfully elude detection for decades, often with the help of sympathetic employers and neighbors. As noted earlier, enforcement decisions are vexed because so many immigrants go in and out of legal status themselves while often acquiring new "equities" based on family (spouses and children with legal status) and employment relationships—equities that can defeat deportation efforts.

In addition, a growing public acceptance of human rights principles makes it harder for liberal democratic states to remove (or even detain) migrants. This is especially true with respect to women, children, and asylum-seekers, whose circumstances may arouse widespread media attention, public sympathy, or even solidarity expressed through civil disobedience and sanctuary movements. Compared with these compelling political and humanitarian claims, the legalistic arguments advanced by immigration officials often seem petty, hollow, even immoral. Confronted by a courageous, hard-working migrant's well-publicized human drama, liberal societies are strongly tempted to make room for one more, ignoring (or repressing) the reality that one more may actually mean many more. Defense of the larger, inevitably anonymous "system" against such heart-rending claims falls largely to the beleaguered, often justly-criticized immigration bureaucracy. Even today, of course, most undocumented immigrants who are apprehended do not arouse this kind of public support, but are unceremoniously detained and removed. Still, constant criticism of the immigration agency for obtuse heartlessness inevitably weakens its enforcement incentives in future cases.

And then there is the insistent question of the *cost-effectiveness* of enforcement at the margin. In truth, much illegal migration confers significant benefits on many Americans and legal immigrants, while the costs of eliminating it in terms of enforcement resources, opportunity costs, civil liberties, foreign policy interests, needed workers, and so forth would be manifestly prohibitive.[219] On the cost side, mass deportation of illegal immigrants would be very expensive and require a massive increase in enforcement officials. Likewise, building impregnable walls on our borders, as Republican presidential candidate Donald Trump proposed, is impractical for many reasons.[220] Unsurprisingly, most Americans, including most Republicans (and especially young ones),[221] do not favor such measures.[222] The optimal level of enforcement, then, is far below 100 percent—even if that were attainable, which it certainly is not.[223]

The U.S. asylum system, which until the European refugee crisis of 2015 usually attracted the most claims of any industrialized country, makes swift enforcement difficult. Those who have colorable asylum claims—that is, a "credible fear" of the kinds of persecution covered by the Refugee Act—can thereby get a full hearing on their asylum claims, which in turn may enable them to delay removal proceedings for years and perhaps even prevail and gain asylum or other legal status. (The government is not obliged to provide free lawyers to asylum-seekers or other immigrants in civil enforcement proceedings, but many still manage to obtain lawyers privately or through legal services groups.) And if they can somehow avoid being detained (discussed below) during their removal proceedings, they have strong incentives to try to reach the U.S. border, apply for asylum, delay removal as long as possible, perhaps marry citizens or LPRs or find employers willing to sponsor them—and hope for the best. Indeed, in 2015, the asylum hearing officers found credible fear in almost

34,000 cases, many of them children. This was more than triple the 2012 level and represented a credible fear finding rate of 70 percent.[224] Would-be migrants, with good "grapevine" information about their prospects in the United States, tend to take notice. Another popular route to asylum is the "well-founded fear of persecution on account of . . . membership in a social group" claim, an elastic category that lawyers increasingly use to seek relief for sympathetic clients. As of late 2015, the asylum adjudication system was so gridlocked that the resulting long delays before resolution of claims gave applicants some assurance that any deportation hearings would occur far in the future. These factors, taken together, have driven yet another large increase in asylum claims. In a December 2015 report, the GAO criticized the agency for having "limited capabilities to detect asylum fraud."[225]

Politics is another major obstacle to immigration enforcement. As noted earlier, various powerful interest groups favor more immigrants, depict undocumented work as a victimless crime, oppose effective enforcement, and use their influence to thwart it. ICE's workplace inspections (raids) are particularly unpopular precisely when they are most effective, and its sanctions on employers are usually too lenient and sporadic to deter them from hiring the undocumented willing to work at lower wages and resist union organizers. Members of Congress receive angry complaints from employers when raids cut off companies' access to pliable low-cost labor, threaten them with sanctions, interrupt their businesses, and harass their citizen employees. Unions complain that raids impede their organizing efforts, especially with illegal workers who are a growing target of opportunity, especially if legalization occurs. Except for the private prison industry and the enforcement worker unions, immigration enforcement is largely supported by weak and diffuse interests but opposed by strong, concentrated ones.[226]

Needless to say, this undermines the coherence and effectiveness of ICE enforcement. A review of the Criminal Alien Program (CAP), responsible for more than two-thirds of all removals, finds that it is poorly targeted, deporting mainly those without criminal records or who have committed non-serious crimes.[227] The fate of the much-heralded Secure Communities program is also instructive.[228] Seeking to integrate federal databases on immigrants' legal and criminal status with local law enforcement, the program was a valuable tool in the immigration enforcement kit bag. (It did not reduce the crime rate.)[229] The program's promise explains why President Obama spent five years extending it nationwide, with the DHS secretary endorsing it as recently as 2014.[230] But immigrant advocates (and some local police departments that resent its burdens on them) strongly oppose it for picking up not just serious criminals but also many traffic and other minor offenders, which divided and disrupted mixed-status families. They also claim that it reduced community cooperation with the police. (Empirical studies, however, cast doubt on this claim.)[231] In November 2014, the president, acting at the insistence of immigrant advocacy groups, suddenly abandoned Secure Communities, he replaced it with a Priority Enforcement Program (PEP), which the House Judiciary Committee chairman, echoing pro-enforcement groups, criticized (perhaps unfairly) as being toothless and facilitating the release of criminal aliens.[232] Even more far-reaching, DHS also issued new policy guidance in 2015 setting deportation priorities: those convicted of serious crimes, threats to public safety, recent illegal entrants, and violators of recent deportation orders. The Migration Policy Institute predicts that only 13 percent of all undocumented immigrants are in these categories, in effect giving a degree of protection from deportation to 87 percent, or 9.6 million, of them![233]

This last charge gained force in mid-2015 when a snafu between ICE and the San Francisco police—a proud sanctuary city that refuses to honor ICE requests unless accompanied by a court-ordered arrest warrant—enabled a criminal with seven felony convictions, recent jail time for illegal border-crossing, and five deportation orders to murder a woman walking with her family on the Embarcadero—using a federal agent's weapon![234] Mutual recriminations and finger-pointing by the city and ICE followed,[235] and Congress considered a law to punish sanctuary cities.[236] In another high-profile case only a month later, an illegal alien whom ICE decided not to hold was arrested for murder and attempted rape.[237] The politics emerging from such events are pushing Los Angeles and perhaps other communities to support immigration enforcement more energetically.[238]

Two other obstacles to effective enforcement are the agency's constrained enforcement budget, and its limited (though increased) detention capacity. Congress, to be sure, has made immigration enforcement a high priority during the last twenty-five years by funding it (especially the Border Patrol) very generously compared with most other agencies. This largesse places great political pressure on the agency to deliver. Yet its budget is still insufficient to remove all of the undocumented, much less to also invoke formal criminal and civil sanctions against violations by immigrants, their employers, document fraudsters, smugglers, drug gangs, and others subject to those sanctions. Pressure for stricter enforcement from Congress and restrictionist groups is met with counterpressures from immigrant advocates. Although part of President Obama's political base, they bitterly denounce him as "deporter-in-chief" for removing a record 2,750,00 immigrants during his time in office.[239] His political goal, however, was to convince Republicans and the public that he could be trusted to secure the borders and negotiate and administer a version of CIR that does not tilt too much in favor of the undocumented.

Detention capacity has expanded but remains an important constraint on enforcement. Congress has funded about 34,000 beds (Obama's 2017 budget reduces this figure to 30,913 beds)[240] and ordered the agency to keep them filled every night, yet bed shortages remain in some high-load localities.* In June 2015, the government opened its newest and largest detention center in south Texas.[241] Detention, while costly to the government and hard on the detainees, is nevertheless crucial to effective enforcement, and the government

* A Center for Migration Studies profile on detention found that in September 2012, more than 35,000 were in custody in 189 facilities; most were located in border states and a large majority were privately owned or operated. About 40 percent of detainees were under removal orders, more than 50 percent were in pending removal proceedings, and 61 percent had criminal convictions. Fewer than 10 percent had committed violent crimes. The vast majority were from Mexico and Central America. http://jmhs.cmsny.org/index.php /jmhs/article/view/55

boasts of its detention efforts.[242] The reason is that unless ICE can detain those undocumented who have only weak or no legal defenses to removal (i.e., most of those who do not have a credible asylum claim), a large fraction of them—based on past experience—will abscond rather than appear for their removal hearings.

This enforcement apparatus is "built to fail," according to a former immigration judge. Detailing ICE's chronic failure to find absconders or enforce final deportation orders, he notes that immigration judges have no independent enforcement authority, and that the DOJ under-reports the true, stratospheric level of non-enforcement.[243] (Tellingly, ICE letters ordering deportable immigrants to report for actual removal are known in the trade as "run" letters; most targets abscond immediately with little or no ICE follow-through, perhaps at the behest of higher-ups.) And DHS's own inspector general reported in 2015 that ICE's Intensive Supervision Appearance Program (ISAP), aimed at assuring the prompt removal of those already found to be dangerous and to pose a high risk of absconding, is so poorly administered that many of those targets abscond and commit other crimes, and the agency has no measure of ISAP's effectiveness.[244] This ignorance about ISAP is surprising in light of a House Judiciary Committee report that ICE has released many convicted criminals pending their often long-delayed removal hearings, some of them murderers and other "Threat Level 1" offenders.[245] ICE also admitted to a Senate inquiry in May 2015 that it had released from custody 121 criminal aliens while they were in removal proceedings who were later charged with homicide-related offenses.[246] ICE's explanation of these released-criminal statistics is strongly disputed by FAIR, the restrictionist group.[247] All of this amply justified criticism, of course, only increases ICE's defensiveness and low morale—especially when coupled with a federal judge's harsh criticism and hard-to-meet orders for the release of undocumented families with children.[248]

ICE does possess some prosecutorial discretion concerning how to allocate its limited resources, and often exercises it.* This is all the

---

* This discretion, while broad, is not boundless. A number of immigration scholars who mostly favor the policy merits of the DACA and DAPA programs (indeed, I favor a

more reason why ICE must make hard decisions about how to allocate its funds and personnel in countless enforcement choices—for example, the border versus the interior, workplace raids versus other kinds of measures, informal removals versus formal adjudications, civil sanctions versus criminal prosecutions. Even at the southern border, the agency must decide whether the congressionally mandated fence along the southern border should be further extended—and if so, how quickly (the cost is estimated at about $10 billion) and with how many layers of fencing—versus other cheaper but arguably less effective enforcement strategies. (Drones raise new tactical and resource issues.) Yet, while ICE bases controversial policies like DACA on prosecutorial discretion, the Office of Inspector General finds that ICE does not know how often the agency uses it or in what circumstances.[249]*

Enforcement policy must confront an even more difficult set of constraints and trade-offs between humanitarian values and effective deterrence. This tension is particularly acute at the southern border, where some 4,000 to 6,000 migrants have reportedly died between 1994 and 2009 trying to enter the United States illegally,[250] and others have suffered grave physical harms from the harsh desert conditions in the Southwest, as well as exploitation, violence, and abuse at the hands of smugglers. In 2014, the Border Patrol picked up more than 68,000 unaccompanied minors at the southwestern border, keeping many of them in makeshift or improper facilities pending disposition.[251] This alarming situation resumed in 2015,[252] where some 10,000 unaccompanied minors were apprehended in just two months.[253] (It was made worse by the disclosure that the Department of Health and Human Services, which works with DHS to protect these children, had released a dozen or more of them into the custody

---

broader, more permanent legalization program) have argued that the president's (and hence ICE's) prosecutorial discretion is not broad enough to legally justify the programs protecting a large proportion of the undocumented population by administrative fiat. See sources cited at notes 152 and 161. The court challenges are discussed above.

    * According to David Martin, whose legal and policy expertise is discussed below, "operating agencies get charged with setting up an underfunded program in a hurry and then get blamed by an office (OIG) that is well-funded, has no direct operational responsibilities, and is tightly focused on metrics."

of human traffickers!)[254] In 2016, almost 60,000 unaccompanied minors were apprehended.[255] Presumably, the generous DACA program, together with rumors of eased enforcement against children presenting especially sympathetic cases, helped to cause the new surge. On the other hand—and there are many hands in this complex policy mix—beefed-up border patrol may have altered what one scholar calls "the industrial organization of human smuggling" in favor of larger, better-financed, and perhaps more effective criminal syndicates.[256]

As these patterns suggest, laxer and more humane policies tend—at the margin where desperate migrants make such momentous choices—to attract more of them, just as it has with the homeless.[257] After all, they are rational, highly motivated people; if we are honest, we recognize that in their situation we might well do the same. On the other side, interdiction and return of Haitian migrants by the Coast Guard, a harsh policy upheld by the Supreme Court in 1993,[258] did sharply reduce their numbers—at least for a while. This same humanitarian-deterrence trade-off haunts the legalization debate discussed above, given that any relief from enforcement will attract others hoping to benefit from future concessions. And because such effects always vary over time, this difficult choice has yet another dimension—between a given policy's short-term and long-term effects. A different kind of trade-off pits the desire to deport the many serious criminal aliens in American prisons as soon as they have exhausted their appeals, against the diplomatic obstacles to getting their countries of origin to accept and incarcerate them.[259]

To responsibly assess these trade-offs, then, the agency—and the Congress and larger society for which it is an agent—must make very painful value choices: for example, how should our moral calculus be affected by the fact that the migrants are children, or are seeking to escape pervasive poverty, corruption, and violence? How cruel is detention, even if it is legally permissible? How unjust is it to divide families and fates according to their members' legal status? How should we weigh the adverse economic effects of illegal migration on struggling Americans and LPRs? More generally, how committed are we to our existing immigration restrictions?

These daunting normative questions, moreover, cannot be answered in isolation. They also pose a host of empirical ones about the likely costs, benefits, and other hard-to-measure effects of various policy alternatives. These questions may be impossible to answer with certainty given a lack of good data, difficulty in defining relevant consequences, and many other methodological challenges. But our immigration policy makers often do not even ask them, much less enable the agency to search through methodical analysis for the best answers. The Pew Center, MPI, the Center for Immigration Studies, and other private research groups generate more useful data and policy analysis than does DHS, which mainly compiles standard statistical information.[260] Empirically informed policy analysis by Congress (through CBO) and DHS should be a much higher priority than it is now. In September 2016, its Office of Immigration Statistics published a strategic plan to do so.

For those like me who favor admitting more *legal* immigrants than we do now, another hard question looms large: More effective enforcement against the undocumented is a *political precondition* for public willingness to support more generous policies. David Martin, probably the country's leading immigration scholar, one with high-level agency experience, and a liberal immigration reform advocate, emphasizes this crucial but often-ignored political link between a more expansive immigration policy and public perception of enforcement effectiveness. In his aptly titled article "Resolute Enforcement Is Not Just for Restrictionists," Martin shows how weak enforcement has almost always led the public to demand harsh, often ill-advised restrictions that actually magnify enforcement failures, stymie more useful reforms, and make expanding legal immigration politically impossible.[261] (Fallout from the San Francisco murder mentioned above, which postdated Martin's article, will surely vindicate his point.)

Martin goes on to propose strategies to enhance enforcement success, proposals that I support. Correctly noting that interior enforcement is the "weakest part" of our system, he urges shifting some resources from the Border Patrol to identifying and apprehending overstays and those who enter without inspection (EWIs), emphasizing that collecting biometric information for exit verification is insufficient without other enforcement changes.* He also proposes that DHS strengthen and mandate the E-Verify program, which in principle provides real-time online information to potential employers and local enforcement agencies on the legal status of those who seek work authorization or other benefits. Immigrant advocates criticize the program's unreliable database, confusion of common Hispanic names, false positive hits, and vulnerability to identity theft. But recent changes, Martin shows, have reduced these problems, increased E-Verify's reliability, and can be further strengthened—for example, by including digitized state driver's license photos. He also proposes streamlined removal procedures for the most straightforward overstay cases.[262]

Population Growth

As noted in the discussion of immigration politics, many on both sides point to immigrants' higher fertility rates. Immigration advocates view population growth as a social and economic advantage, particularly compared with the birth dearth in most of Europe. Opponents maintain that the U.S. is already overcrowded and that immigration adversely affects the environment and other social conditions.

In 2013, the United States experienced its lowest-ever general birthrate, although it has risen since then.[263] A 2015 Census Bureau population projection, its first in fourteen years, predicted that the foreign-born share, now almost 14 percent, will by 2025 exceed the previous record (14.8 percent, set in the second decade of the twenti-

---

* Indeed, it took DHS *almost 20 years* to comply with a statutory requirement to report on visa overstays, and did so only after Congress threatened it with budgetary sanctions. In early 2016, a top DHS official admitted that the agency did not know the magnitude of the overstay problem and had not met a statutory requirement to develop exit verification. http://www.nytimes.com/2016/01/02/us/politics/us-doesnt-know-how -many-foreign-visitors-overstay-visas.html?smid=nytcore-iphone-share&smprod=nytcore -iphone. Later that month, DHS finally issued its report, which noted that "only" 1 percent of work and tourist visa holders overstayed—half a million people, not counting other visa categories. http://www.nytimes.com/2016/01/21/us/few-foreign-visitors-to-us-overstay -visa-federal-report-says.html

eth century) and by 2060 will reach almost 19 percent.[264] Such projections, of course, depend on many uncertain assumptions which the Bureau often changes.[265] One variable is the birthrates of the native and immigrant (both legal and illegal) populations. Immigrant women's birthrates are nearly 50 percent higher than those of native-born women, but have been declining faster than native birthrates in recent years.[266] Indeed, the longer they are in the United States, the more their fertility tends to converge with that of the native-born.[267] I believe that a modest increase in fertility, especially within strong families, would benefit American society; expanded legal immigration poses no demographic threat.

Legal Representation

Although immigrants have a right to retain lawyers to protect their rights in removal and other enforcement proceedings against them, for the INA any such representation must be at their own expense. As a result, immigrants who cannot pay for counsel themselves or are not fortunate enough to be represented by legal aid lawyers, law school immigration rights clinics, or other pro bono assistance must endure these proceedings alone, without full knowledge of how to protect their interests. To address this problem, a federal appeals court judge began the Immigrant Justice Corps in New York City: Cohorts of inexperienced lawyers are hired, paid, and trained by veteran immigration lawyers, and are then placed in community organizations where they can provide representation. Programs like the Immigrant Justice Corps increase legal representation but also face common challenges in securing reliable funding streams; justifying the selection and rejection of cases; obtaining cooperation from existing institutions, especially DHS; and procuring trained support staff such as translators, social workers, investigators, and expert witnesses. Because demands for such public services typically rise to meet any increases in their supply,[268] pro bono immigrant services risk being engulfed by the demand for services that they can never fully satisfy. Still, some representation is certainly better than nothing.

Social Integration

The peaceful, respectful integration* of immigrants into the receiving society is among the most vital challenges facing all receiving nations, and few of them—even including liberal democratic ones—have been very successful at it. Among large polyglot nations, the United States is the greatest exception. (Canada, despite severe linguistic divisions, has also managed integration well.) This was not always the case, as my brief sketch of our immigration history already suggested. Rogers Smith puts it starkly: "For over 80% of U.S. history, American laws declared most people in the world legally ineligible to become full U.S. citizens solely because of the race, original nationality, or gender. For at least two-thirds of American history, most of the domestic adult population was also ineligible for full citizenship for the same reasons. Those racial, ethnic, and gender restrictions were blatant, not 'latent.'"[269]

Today, the integration of *legal* immigrants, at least, is remarkably well advanced.[270]† Most easily integrated are high-skill immigrants and those who arrive with extensive family networks here; many have become U.S. citizens. But groups from different places advance at different rates; gender roles in the source country affect behavior in the United States, particularly among women.[271] Real integration seldom occurs in the first (immigrant) generation, although that generation, as we have seen, experiences dramatic wage mobility compared with their countries of origin.[272] It is only in the second generation—when immigrants' children attend American schools, speak English as their

---

* "Integration" and "incorporation" are widely used today instead of the more politically incorrect "assimilation." Assimilation offends many who believe, correctly, that the receiving society adjusts to immigrants so that the assimilation goes both ways, but who also believe, incorrectly, that our society continues to demand the oppressive, often racist, "Anglo-conformity" that was a motif of the Americanization movement a century ago.

† This contrasts sharply with Europe, where nativist parties are rapidly gaining ground. One index that focuses on *government integration programs*, however, ranks the United States ninth of thirty-one countries, well behind not only Canada and Sweden but Portugal! http://www.mipex.eu/countries. One suspects that relatively few immigrants would agree. This modest ranking may be because in the United States, the government's role is modest relative both to its domestic market and civil society processes, and to other countries with more interventionist states.

first language, and then marry Americans or well-integrated LPRs—
that integration is consolidated.[273] By the third generation (the immigrants' grandchildren), the individual prefers English and knows
little or nothing of the grandparents' first language.[274] As this discussion implies, the two most important markers of integration are substantial English fluency and, to a lesser extent, out-group marriage—
and the main engines driving it are the public schools and libraries,[275]
as well as immigrants' participation in the market, churches, popular
culture, and other civil society institutions.

English proficiency, so essential to full integration, poses a major
challenge. Over 61 million people, more than a fifth of the population, speak a language other than English at home. More than 25
million of them self-report that they are what the Census Bureau
terms Limited English Proficient (LEP)—an 80 percent increase
just since 1990.[276] This problem is especially severe for Mexican
immigrants. In 2014, about 69 percent of them (age five and older)
claimed to be LEP, compared with 50 percent of all immigrants. The
LEP problem is especially great for undocumented children, who
are constitutionally entitled to public education.[277] Approximately
4 percent of Mexican immigrants speak only English at home, versus 16 percent of all immigrants.[278] At the same time, the United
States is almost entirely monolingual in all of its governmental and
major social institutions, even as it is the world's most diverse industrialized nation and attracts immigrants speaking more than 325
languages. (This monolingual culture contrasts sharply with bilingual Canada and multilingual India, Indonesia, Russia, and the European Union.) In the 1960s, many called this monolingual tradition
into question, demanding recognition of minority language rights,
primarily through bilingual education and multilingual ballots. The
ballots now cause little conflict,[279] but bilingual education remains
highly controversial. (California voters largely banned it in 1998 but
some state legislators hope to reverse the ban by putting it on the
2016 ballot.) Opposition to it mainly reflects widespread rejection
of multiculturalism even among many minority voters, as well as
evidence that some types of bilingual programs—several variants

compete, each with its proponents—in fact retards students' mastery of English.[280]

Despite this language challenge, integration of legal immigrants today appears to be no slower or more problematic than it has ever been, according to an authoritative 2015 report of the National Academy of Sciences, Engineering, and Medicine.[281] Indeed, the high rate of Asian out-group marriage suggests that integration may be occurring even faster than before. And a recent study of immigrants' integration, as evidenced by their own attitudes, finds:

> [T]he heaviest waves of Mexican immigration have come too recently to have reached any stable equilibrium level of assimilation as yet. Nevertheless, we find numerous indications of integration among southern California Latinos already. Nativity matters, as the assimilation model assumes. . . . U.S.-born Latinos are considerably more patriotic than are the foreign-born. They are more likely to identify as "just American" or as both American and ethnic than as purely ethnic. They show less group consciousness. They are less likely to see value in remaining separate as opposed to blending into the broader society. . . . (xxv) [Still, the empirical evidence shows] that today's immigrants, including Hispanics, are following the same trajectory of incorporation taken by their European predecessors.[282]

(Indeed, demographer Nick Eberstadt shows that Hispanic, Asian, and Pacific Islander residents in the United States [not just citizens] live longer than whites.)[283]

Becoming a citizen through naturalization, discussed earlier, is less a cause of integration than a sign that it is already achieved or well advanced. One does not ordinarily seek to naturalize unless and until one already feels a part of American society in some important sense. The decision to seek naturalization after having lived here for the requisite number of years, coupled with the process of preparing for the citizenship test, surely consolidates and furthers that integration, especially voting. But for better *and* for worse, many LPRs live most of their lives in the United States integrated into American society in most other respects without ever having become a citizen.

Integration of the undocumented, of course, is far more problematic and, from a purely enforcement perspective, undesirable. As discussed above, they have reason to fear that more contact with Americans and legal immigrants could increase the risk of detection and removal, although the Obama administration's announced easing of enforcement against 87 percent of them may reduce this fear somewhat—at the cost of swelling their numbers. For them, as for legal immigrants, integration largely occurs through their U.S.-born children—but for the undocumented perhaps not even then. Only legalization can remedy their isolation and fear.

CONCLUSION

Thinking clearly about immigration, we have seen, is challenging for a number of reasons. Its deep emotional resonance goes to the very definition of what America has been, is, and may become. Our personal identification with our ancestors' immigrant experience and their social mobility here predisposes us, more than other peoples, toward a complex view of immigration and immigrants, both legal and undocumented. For most of us, the questions are: how many, which ones, and under what conditions, and how are the resulting policies going to be enforced? As we attempt to answer these questions, the facts presented in this chapter are essential—but they do not always speak for themselves or lead us to unambiguous answers.

For me, these facts argue in favor of far-reaching legislative and administrative policy changes. As noted above, the U.S. economy has tripled in size since 1990 when Congress established the current LPR quotas, and its demand for well-trained workers has grown accordingly. For complicated reasons, American workers cannot fully meet these needs, and equipping them for today's economy must be among our highest social priorities. But until this happens, Congress should increase the number of legal admissions for high-skill individuals, both LPRs and non-immigrants. (Reasonable people can certainly differ about the optimal size of the increase and the requisite credentials.) It should also repeal the diversity lottery, using those visas to experiment with auctions that will attract more skilled workers and potential employers, yielding revenues that can be put to good social use.

Congress should enact a legalization program that is fair to those already in the green card queue and generous enough to induce the undocumented to apply for it rather than remain in the shadows. It should update the registry provision. It should craft an expanded guestworker program that achieves several goals: protecting farmhands from exploitation, ensuring that they will depart at season's end, and being timely enough to meet growers' planning needs. Another reform priority is to ease some of the simplistic restrictions on necessary agency enforcement discretion that Congress imposed in the 1996 law.

As noted earlier, the public will not support these reforms until it becomes convinced that enforcement—in the interior as well as at the border—is more effective than it was in the past. The agency, for its part, should eliminate the bugs from E-Verify, mandate it nationally, and link it to prioritized legalization of otherwise eligible undocumented workers. It should rationalize its enforcement programs—for example, by focusing the recently established Priority Enforcement Program (the successor to Secure Communities) on more serious crimes and immigration violations while using the new legalization program to decide which minor offenses should disqualify applicants.[284] Strengthening E-Verify, it should pursue employer sanctions much more aggressively than it has, with more meaningful penalties. It should monitor overstays more closely, deport removable criminals as soon as their appeals are exhausted, and consider using bounties to enforce "run letters" more effectively.[285] It should carefully review how immigration judges make bond decisions, an important but understudied part of the enforcement system.[286] It should follow up on earlier experiments with alternatives to detention, including better monitoring technology and more liberal bonding decisions using newly-developed algorithms to reduce errors[287]—alternatives that can still reduce the high pre-removal absconding rate.[288] It should study why immigrants' naturalization rates (especially among Mexicans) are so low for eligibles, and how to increase them. New York State, for example, is experimenting with a lottery that would pay the naturalization fees for thousands of low-income green card holders.[289] And, working with other departments, local education agencies, and the private sector, it should increase the resources needed to accelerate English-language acquisition, which is so vital to the high priority of fully integrating immigrants into American life.[290]

CHAPTER 4

CAMPAIGN FINANCE

IN OUR POLITICAL SYSTEM, election campaigns are perpetual. In contrast, some other democracies—no less committed to political representation than we Americans are—try to keep electoral politics in its place: They limit campaigns to a certain period before Election Day, schedule national elections irregularly, and limit campaigning further through informal traditions.[1]

I begin with this mundane fact simply to highlight how different—and, in many ways, unique—U.S. campaigns, parties, financing, and electoral arrangements are. Here, such limits on campaigning are not only unfeasible; they might be *unconstitutional*! Our political system, the most complex in the world, establishes a national government operating over an immense land mass but sharing political authority with fifty state—and countless local—polities. In each state (and in "home rule" localities, where permitted), the campaign finance laws and electoral arrangements are largely autonomous and uncoordinated with the federal government. Further insulating these elections from federal regulation is the U.S. Constitution, whose protection of freedom of speech applies most robustly to political speech about elections and other public issues. All state constitutions do so as well.

Indeed, the heart of our political system is located at the state level. As political scientist Nelson Polsby put it, "party structures are based primarily on local authority, and nominations to public office are locally made and sustained. Thus the American political system [is] close to a one-hundred-party system."[2] Although this is perhaps less true now than when he wrote it in 2008, it remains a loose coalition of state parties that convene every four years to nominate presidential candidates. This chapter's focus on federal campaign finance should not obscure a fundamental point: These state systems are where almost all of our national politicians come from—and where promising reforms are most likely to originate. The common focus on the federal campaign finance system, which this chapter shares, is in this sense a bit off target.

Our campaign finance arrangements at all governmental levels are likewise remarkably complex and exceedingly legalistic, pervaded (as we shall see) by issues of constitutional law, especially the First Amendment. Indeed, I exaggerate only slightly in saying that only politicians and their special teams of campaign finance lawyers, consultants, and accountants have managed to master them.* The leading treatise on the subject explains why:

> Campaign finance is an extremely complicated area of legal doctrine because of the competing claims of First Amendment rights of speech and association and the rights of citizens, through legislation, to create a democratic regime that is widely accepted as legitimate, fair, and responsive. It is also an extremely complicated area of regulatory policy; each regulatory intervention spawns further efforts to circumvent the intervention by various actors who seek to influence the outcomes of elections. The intersection between legal doctrine and policy effectiveness makes the problem all the more daunting.[3]

For this reason, any sophisticated discussion of campaign finance issues must take due account of these technicalities—although I mean to keep them to a minimum here.

---

* Even so, candidates often violate the rules, sometimes inadvertently, and opponents make their campaign finance practices, legal or not, political issues in their campaigns.

The chapter proceeds in three main parts. I set the stage with some *factual context*. The second, much longer part analyzes the central campaign finance issues, most of them shaped by a handful of Supreme Court decisions. Sharpening the focus, I review the debate among political scientists about which forces determine electoral outcomes, drawing on their recent analyses. We shall see that almost all the debaters find the system pathological, citing the same unholy trinity of polarization, gridlock, and hyper-partisanship. Some add intraparty fragmentation[4] and unequal influence[5] to the list. Yet their diagnoses, remedies, and assessments of previous reforms differ markedly; no consensus on what should be done exists. In the third and final part, I present the major competing approaches to reform.

Some disclaimers are in order. I do not discuss some other elections-salient issues that are extremely important but that bear only tangentially on campaign finance. Examples include the Voting Rights Act, redistricting, negative campaigning, and state laws regulating registration, voting, and ballot access. Nor do I discuss other factors that some think contribute to political dysfunction such as reduced socializing among legislators, atomizing new media, overuse of filibusters, and diffusion of power within Congress.[6] I also ignore judicial elections, which do not occur at the federal level but have attracted the Court's attention,[7] and ballot referenda and initiatives, which are regulated entirely by state law and deal with policy issues, not individual candidates (except in the case of recalls).[8]

CONTEXT

Here, I discuss six important contextual conditions: the political salience of campaign finance; the First Amendment's role in campaign finance regulation; its legal-regulatory structure; the court decisions in the *Wisconsin Right to Life*,[9] *Citizens United*,[10] *McCutcheon*,[11] and *SpeechNOW.org* cases[12] (an important appellate court decision dovetailing with *Citizens United*); the trends in political contributions and spending; and political incivility. I discuss another important contextual element, the emergent online platforms for campaigning, in a later section.

The Political Salience of Campaign Finance

Never before in our history has the issue of federal campaign finance been so prominent in public debates over politics. This is not to say that the role of money in politics is a new one. To the contrary, it is as old as politics itself, going back at least to Plato's warnings in *The Republic* about politicians' susceptibility to corruption.[13] Our own nation's history is laced with corruption scandals.[14] What *is* new is that our current, democratically enacted, highly regulated system of campaign finance is routinely denounced in terms like "legalized bribery" (or worse),[15] and that the issue is perennially prominent in our public discourse, including that of politicians themselves. Some 84 percent of Americans say that there is too much money in politics.[16] As detailed below, recent election cycles prior to 2016 have indeed seen a huge increase in the amounts spent on federal campaigns. This growth, moreover, occurred in the face of—arguably *because* of—enactment of the landmark Bipartisan Campaign Reform Act of 2003 (BCRA, also known as "McCain-Feingold").

But surely the most provocative—indeed inflammatory—development was the Supreme Court's 2010 decision in the *Citizens United* case, "one of its most unpopular in history."[17] Briefly stated (I discuss it in detail below), it interpreted the First Amendment to bar any limits on independent expenditures by corporations and labor unions.* Five years after the decision, it remained among Google's most searched-for terms.[18] Although only 19 percent of respondents to a 2012 survey were familiar with it,[19] opinion polls find that they overwhelmingly oppose it. Indeed, a much higher percentage oppose *Citizens United* than oppose the Court's gay marriage and abortion rulings.[20]

Liberal politicians (and scholars) routinely denounce the Court's campaign finance rulings and advocate stricter regulation. Only days after *Citizens United* came down, President Obama used his State of the Union address to chastise the Court for "revers[ing] a century of

---

* "Independence" in the campaign finance context means not coordinated, controlled, or requested by candidates or their campaigns. "Expenditures" are funds spent by a candidate or a group to promote its views on a policy issue. I explicate these terms below.

law that I believe will open the floodgates for special interests—including foreign corporations—to spend without limit in our elections." Senator Chuck Schumer, who may become the Senate Minority Leader, called it the "worst decision since *Plessy v. Ferguson.*"[21] Hillary Clinton, the Democratic standard-bearer in 2016, constantly inveighs against *Citizens United* in equally strong terms. Conversely, the Republican leadership and many other conservative politicians support *Citizens United* and advocate further deregulation of campaign finance, invoking the First Amendment. But as election law expert Richard Hasen points out, most politicians' talk about campaign finance reform is little more than lip service and political theater, masking their satisfaction with the status quo—even (or especially) with *Citizens United.*[22]

The First Amendment and Campaign Finance Regulation

The First Amendment to the Constitution, which provides that Congress shall make no law "abridging the freedom of speech," casts an immense shadow over almost all campaign finance regulation.[23] The Supreme Court and nearly all constitutional scholars hold that *political* speech is at the very core of the First Amendment's protections, and that speech about candidates and public issues is core political speech. This "communicative interaction" between citizens and government, as First Amendment scholar Robert Post puts it,[24] is essential to self-government and must be protected even more than other kinds of speech are. (Although not a constitutional scholar, I strongly share this view.) Accordingly, virtually any restriction that Congress might enact in this area—whether it relates to campaign contributions, spending, disclosure, commentary (especially by traditional and social media, which the Amendment further protects as "freedom of the press"), or any other aspect of election activity—is under a constitutional cloud, so legal challenges to such restrictions are inevitable. Indeed, today's Supreme Court interprets the First Amendment's protection of political and other speech more broadly than any of its predecessors did.[25]

At the same time, however, the Court recognizes that Congress has a "compelling interest" in preserving the integrity of the electoral and political processes.[26] This interest, which is analyzed below, is one that *Citizens United*'s many critics think the Court has undervalued. In trying to reconcile these conflicting considerations and values, it has drawn distinctions that, although often opaque and debatable in application, lie at the very center of campaign finance regulation.

The most significant distinction, legally and politically, is that between "quid pro quo corruption" and what some—including critics of the Court's narrow approach to the subject—call "influence corruption." (Later in the chapter, I further discuss "undue access" corruption, which is often paired with its cognate, "appearance" of corruption.) But First Amendment constraints, the applicable statutes, and the ingenuity of campaign finance strategists have produced many other important distinctions: between "contributions" and "expenditures"; "independent" and "coordinated" expenditures; spending money and engaging in speech; "express advocacy" (for a candidate) and "issue advocacy" (for a policy idea); "political campaigns" and "party-building" activities; the related distinction between "hard money" and "soft money";* "substantial" and "insubstantial" (or "marginal") restrictions on free speech; "dark money" contributions (whose donors' identities need not be disclosed) and contributions whose donors must be disclosed;† human and corporate speech; and, especially salient today, "PACs" and "Super PACs."‡ Magnifying this

---

* The Court has defined "soft money" as "money as yet unregulated under FECA" (*McConnell v. FEC*, 540 U.S. 93, 128 [2003]). "Hard money" refers to regulated dollar contributions to a party or campaign. Parties use soft money for general party-building, get-out-the-vote, support of volunteers, consulting, and other purposes not expressly or implicitly linked to a particular candidacy.

† "Gray money" refers to contributions that must be disclosed but are hard to trace to their ultimate source. https://www.brennancenter.org/publication/secret-spending-states

‡ *PACs* are political action committees established by corporations and unions to channel their contributions to campaigns; they must register with the Federal Election Commission (FEC), are subject to specified contribution dollar limits, and must disclose their donors.

Super PACs are "independent expenditure-only" committees that can spend unlimited funds contributed to them by corporations, unions, associations, and individuals—so long as the Super PACs spend the money "independently" of the candidates and parties whom

complexity, primaries, general elections, and ballot initiatives are regulated differently.

I shall explicate these and other distinctions as they become relevant in the analyses that follow. For now, the important point is this: Almost every aspect of campaign finance (and of elections more generally) potentially implicates First Amendment constraints. Regulation in this area is so specialized and technically complex, and the distinctions drawn so legalistic and fine, that it may sometimes seem (or actually be!) at variance with common sense. And because the political stakes in campaign finance are so high, these issues are always bitterly contested.

The Legal-Regulatory Structure of Campaign Finance

The first federal campaign finance law, enacted in 1867, barred federal officials from seeking campaign contributions from Navy Yard workers.[27] Subsequently, laws have limited contributions, prohibited certain sources of funds for campaign purposes, controlled campaign spending, and required disclosure. In 1907, the Tillman Act barred corporations and national banks from contributing money to federal campaigns, and the Taft–Hartley Act of 1947 barred both unions and corporations from making expenditures and contributions in federal campaigns. The campaign finance provisions of these and other such laws were largely ignored, however, because none provided an insti-

---

they support. Super PACs can also accept and spend money from groups organized for tax-exempt social welfare purposes ("501(c)(4)" organizations, further defined in a footnote on page 203), and Super PACs must disclose their donors' identity if they engage in electioneering or independent expenditures on behalf of candidates. Otherwise, 501(c)(4) groups can contribute to Super PACs, which in turn can support candidates "independently" (i.e., without coordination). This practice facilitates "dark money," evading disclosure. See generally, Jane Mayer, *Dark Money: The Hidden History of the Billionaires behind the Rise of the Radical Right* (2016).

"527 organizations" are tax-exempt groups, organized under the same tax code provision as are parties, PACs, and Super PACs. 527 organizations seek to influence elections not by supporting individual candidates (which they are not permitted to do either directly or by coordinating with campaigns) but by engaging in issue advocacy and voter mobilization. There are no limits on who may contribute to them or what they may spend, but they must disclose their donors and report on where their money goes.

tutional framework to administer their provisions effectively. These laws had other flaws as well. For example, spending limits applied only to committees active in two or more states. Further, candidates could avoid the spending limit and disclosure requirements altogether by claiming to have no knowledge of spending on their behalf.

The evasion of disclosure provisions became evident in the second spasm of reform following the Watergate scandals when Congress passed the more stringent disclosure provisions of the 1971 Federal Election Campaign Act (FECA).* The FECA initiated fundamental changes: It not only required full reporting of campaign contributions and expenditures, but also limited spending. (This limit was later repealed.) The FECA also provided the basic legislative framework for separate segregated funds through PACs established by corporations and unions, along with disclosure of PACs' contributors. Although the Tillman and Taft-Hartley laws banned direct contributions by corporations and labor unions to influence federal elections, the FECA had an exception allowing corporations and unions to use Treasury funds to establish, operate, and solicit voluntary contributions for PACs; these contributions could then be used to contribute to federal races. Another 1971 law allowed citizens to check a box on their tax forms authorizing the government to use one of their tax dollars to finance presidential campaigns in the general election. By 1976, enough tax money had accumulated to fund the 1976 election, the first publicly funded federal election in U.S. history.

In 1974, comprehensive amendments to the FECA established the FEC, an independent agency, to write regulations and monitor compliance. These amendments also authorized partial federal funding, in the form of matching funds, for presidential primary candidates and in addition extended it to political parties' presidential nominating conventions. Congress also enacted strict limits on both contributions and expenditures applicable to all candidates for federal office and to political committees seeking to influence federal elections.

* In 1968, still under the old law, House and Senate candidates reported spending $8.5 million, while in 1972, after the passage of the FECA, spending reported by congressional candidates jumped to $88.9 million.

Another amendment relaxed a 1939 prohibition on contributions from federal government contractors. The amended FECA now permitted corporations and unions with federal contracts to establish and operate PACs.

After the constitutionality of key provisions of the 1974 amendments were challenged,[28] the Supreme Court handed down its 1976 ruling (almost 300 pages of it!) in *Buckley v. Valeo*.[29] Drawing a fateful distinction—one so pivotal that I discuss it at some length here—the Court upheld the law's contribution limits while at the same time rejecting its expenditure limits. "It is clear," the Court stated, "that a primary effect of these expenditure limitations is to restrict the quantity of campaign speech by individuals, groups and candidates. The restrictions . . . limit political expression at the core of our electoral process and of First Amendment freedoms." Acknowledging that both contribution and spending limits had First Amendment implications, the Court stated that the "expenditure ceiling imposes significantly more severe restrictions on protected freedom of political expression and association than do its limitations on financial contributions."[30]

Constitutional law, however, sometimes undermines policy coherence. Election law scholar Samuel Issacharoff is surely right to say that "no rational regulatory system would seek to limit the manner by which money is supplied to political campaigns, then leave unchecked the demand for that same money by leaving spending uncapped."[31] This "odd regulatory misalignment between the encumbered ability to raise money and the unfettered capacity to spend it" means that "candidates and campaigns would inevitably seek to spend—and therefore raise—more money."[32] The treatise goes on to quote from Frank Sorauf, a leading campaign finance scholar:

> We shall never know what kind of regulatory regime the FECA amendments of 1974 created because they were so drastically altered by the Supreme Court in *Buckley v. Valeo*. What was intended to be a closed system in which the major flows of money into and out of campaigns were fully controlled emerged as an open system of uncontrolled outlets when the Court struck down all limits on direct spending in the campaign by candidates, PACs,

and individuals. A tightly constrained regulatory system became a more relaxed, open-ended one. The modifications in *Buckley* meant that the original 1974 plan would never have to meet its two severest tests: the administration of spending limits in hundreds of races and the accommodation of excess money in a system with no effective outlets. Instead, the crippled FECA affected chiefly the recruitment of money, ending the freedom of the fat cats and encouraging the development of PACs.[33]

In response to *Buckley*, Congress amended the FECA in 1976 to repeal expenditure limits (except for candidates who accepted public funding), to reconstitute the FEC (the president now appoints six members subject to Senate confirmation), and to significantly restrict PAC solicitations (specifying who could be solicited and how solicitations must be conducted, and imposing a single contribution limit for all PACs established by the same union or corporation). The basic regulatory regime established by FECA continues today. It is one "that no legislature ever voted to create and, one may surmise, no legislature would ever have voted to create."[34] As we shall see, it is also *very* complex and has become much more so over time, as regulators have tried to keep up with new evasions by the parties, donors, and other regulated entities.

In the 1990s, fund-raising efforts began to rely increasingly on contributions to parties of soft money that was not then subject to FECA restrictions and was often used to support particular candidates in ways that *Buckley* failed to prevent. In 2002, Congress enacted the third major reform, the BCRA—a legislative effort jointly coordinated by Senators McCain and Feingold—which was intended to plug this loophole.* There is evidence that BCRA reflected more of a bipartisan elite effort than grassroots pressures;[35] future reforms may follow the same pattern.[36]† BCRA prohibited national parties,

---

* "Loophole" implies the existence of an integrated scheme with very narrow exceptions ("loopholes") that can be used to evade the scheme's general rules. It is hard to view campaign finance regulation as such since there are so many ways to stymie enforcement, most of them constitutionally protected. The better metaphor is to Swiss cheese with more holes than cheese.

† According to political analyst Mark Schmitt, the only other major bipartisan law in

candidates, and candidate- or party-affiliated nonprofits from solicit-
ing or spending soft money for any purpose (not just to promote particular candidates and their campaigns); barred state and local parties and committees from using soft money on federal elections;
prohibited expenditures by outsiders for "electioneering communication" within a certain period before an election; and required disclosure of any contribution in excess of $200 by donor's name. Today,
party and candidate committees and PACs must file periodic reports
disclosing what they raise and spend, and who their contributors
are.[37]* For example, candidates must identify all PACs and party committees that give them contributions, as well as all individuals who
give more than $200 in an election cycle. They must also disclose
expenditures exceeding $200 per election cycle to any individual or
vendor.[38] In *McConnell v. FEC*,[39] a 2003 ruling, the Court upheld
these provisions.

BCRA, like the FECA before it, quickly spawned evasive tactics,
once again proving an old adage even mentioned by members of the
Court: "Campaign money is very much like water flowing downhill on
the side of a mountaintop. It is going to find its way to the valley, and
you're not going to be able to build enough dams to keep the water
from getting [there]."[40]† To minimize BCRA's restrictions, campaign
donors increasingly directed funds to outside groups—PACs, 527
groups (defined above), 501c groups,‡ and later on, Super PACS (de-

---

the last fifteen years was the No Child Left behind Act of 2001. The parties, he believes, are
much more polarized than the voters. For a definition of "polarization" in this context, see
Nathaniel Persily, ed., *Solutions to Political Polarization in America* (2015), 4 and chaps. 2
and 3.

* PACs' ultimate contributors can be hard to identify. https://www.brennancenter.org
/publication/secret-spending-states. Other tax-exempt groups whose political activities are
strictly limited under the tax code must identify donors who give money to the group for
electioneering purposes.

† Experts of all political stripes acknowledge this "hydraulic" fact about money in politics. See, e.g., Samuel Issacharoff & Pamela S. Karlan, "The Hydraulics of Campaign Finance Reform," 77 *Texas Law Review* (1999). I join many reformers in thinking, metaphori-
cally, that dams cannot stop it but canals can channel it better. The question is: among the
limited alternatives, where should we want it to go? See Raymond La Raja & Brian F.
Schaffner, *Campaign Finance and Political Polarization: When Purists Prevail* (2015).

‡ These are nonprofit, tax-exempt groups organized under Section 501(c) of the In-

fined above)—that donors hoped were in practice unconstrained by BCRA's contribution limits and disclosure requirements. In the 2016 campaigns, these groups were where much of the financial action was, and they managed to evade full disclosure of their donors.[41]

The Decisions in Wisconsin Right to Life, Citizens United, McCutcheon, and SpeechNOW.org

Today's public debate over campaign finance is fundamentally shaped by the Court's 2010 decision in *Citizens United*, immediately followed by the DC Circuit's *SpeechNOW.org* decision, and the Court's 2014 decision in *McCutcheon*. The leading treatise in the field describes *Citizens United*'s effect:

> The case has defined the sharp divide in the Roberts Court on campaign finance cases. The divide spread across the scope of the First Amendment protections, the interests of corporations in speech, the definition and weightiness of the state's anti-corruption interest, and the deference owed to Congress on its findings on the ills of the political system—the deference that seemed to define the Court in *McConnell* began to ebb almost immediately. The controversy over *Citizens United* spread to Congress when President Obama criticized the decision during his State of the Union address, and appeared to provoke a response of denial from Justice Alito, seated just a few feet in front of him.[42]

Three elections have been conducted under the *Citizens United* regime; the 2016 election was the fourth.

---

ternal Revenue Code that can engage in varying amounts of political activity, depending on the type of group. For example, 501(c)(3) groups operate for religious, charitable, scientific, or educational purposes. These groups are not supposed to engage in any political activities, though some voter registration activities are permitted. 501(c)(4) groups are commonly called "social welfare" organizations that may engage in political activities, as long as these activities do not become their primary purpose. Similar restrictions apply to Section 501(c)(5) labor and agricultural groups, and to Section 501(c)(6) business leagues, chambers of commerce, real estate boards, and boards of trade. https://www.opensecrets .org/527s/types.php. For the rules on when 501(c)(4) groups must disclose their donors, see http://afjactioncampaign.org/wp-content/uploads/2012/08/501c4-Reporting.pdf

Here, I shall simply summarize these post-*McConnell* decisions' main holdings, deferring closer analysis of their specific rationales until later when they become relevant to particular issues.

Wisconsin Right to Life was a nonprofit, anti-abortion advocacy corporation that accepted contributions from for-profit companies. It sought to run ads—encouraging voters to contact their representatives and get them to oppose filibusters of judicial nominees—within the preelection blackout period during which BCRA prohibited electioneering communications. The FEC found that the ads violated BCRA's prohibition on ads referring to candidates within sixty days of the election, but the Supreme Court reversed in a 5–4 decision. It held that an ad during this blackout period not clearly advocating the election or defeat of a candidate could not be considered BCRA-barred electioneering. The majority issued a strongly-worded critique of the FEC's inquiry into the ad's motive and context; it insisted instead that the FEC must assess the ad on its face. In effect, BCRA could only limit ads expressly advocating a candidate's election or defeat.

Citizens United, a nonprofit organization with an annual budget of approximately $12 million raised from individual and corporate donations, produced a documentary critical of then-candidate Hillary Clinton ("Hillary: The Movie") which was aired to paying customers in theaters and on DVD during the 2008 primary campaigns. Citizens United wanted to release it through video-on-demand for wider viewership, but this would require that it broadcast the movie within thirty days of a primary election, which would violate the BCRA's restrictions (upheld earlier in *McConnell*) on the use of corporate and union treasury funds for an electioneering communication or express advocacy within a certain time period. Under the statute, corporations and unions may establish PACs for these purposes. The group challenged the BCRA's restriction on its electioneering as a violation of its First Amendment rights to engage in political speech independent of a campaign.

In a long-familiar 5–4 split, the Supreme Court held that the BCRA's restriction on using its own funds for electioneering communications that were not coordinated with a campaign violated the First

Amendment.* Justice Kennedy's majority opinion struck down various provisions of the BCRA. *Buckley*, he wrote, upheld FECA's contribution limits specifically to counter quid pro quo corruption, not to restrict mere access or influence that is not corruption at all and does not undermine public faith in our democracy. By definition, Kennedy continued, independent expenditures are not coordinated with a campaign and thus do not risk quid pro quo corruption. Because the film was an independent expenditure, therefore, Congress's restrictions on campaign contributions close to an election could not constitutionally limit it. A strong dissenting opinion by Justice John Paul Stevens, concurred in by the three more liberal justices, argued that Congress's compelling interest in avoiding even the appearance of corruption justified barring corporate spending in campaigns; such spending, he claimed, has "a distinctive corrupting potential."[43] Kennedy's opinion, however, also included *dictum*—that is, language going beyond what is needed to decide a case on its facts (its actual "holding")—to the effect that Congress's power to legislate against corruption in campaigns extends only to quid pro quo corruption, not undue influence corruption.[44] I discuss this dictum in the section on corruption.

In *McCutcheon*, the Court struck down the FECA and BCRA provisions that imposed *aggregate* limits on campaign contributions to federal candidates ($46,200) and political parties ($70,800) during a given campaign cycle, limits that *Buckley* had upheld on the ground that they were necessary to prevent donors from evading FECA's base contribution limits. Shaun McCutcheon, a Republican activist, had contributed to sixteen candidates and to the party during the electoral cycle and wanted to give to an additional twelve candidates, which would have exceeded FECA's aggregate contribution limits. The Court, again in a 5–4 decision with further splintering of opinions, found these limits to violate the First Amendment.

The fourth pivotal decision, *SpeechNOW.org v. FEC*, was decided in the wake of *Citizens United*—not by the Supreme Court but by the U.S. Court of Appeals for the DC Circuit, the nation's second most

---

* The Court did uphold the statute's disclosure and disclaimer requirements, and it did not disturb the century-old ban on corporate contributions directly to campaigns.

influential court. Extending *Citizens United*'s dictum, *SpeechNOW.*
org held that independent expenditures by Super PACs and other
groups formed to accept contributions are not subject to the statutory
limits on campaign contributions to candidates and party committees. They must register with the FEC as a political committee, but
because their expenditures are independent, they can accept unlimited contributions from anyone—even from entities like unions
and corporations whose direct contributions to parties and candidates are limited by statute—and can electioneer independently
without restriction.

Trends in Political Contributions and Spending

The 2016 elections occurred just a few days before this chapter went
to press. Solid information about contributions and spending in these
elections (especially for Congress) was not yet available—especially
given that disproportionate contributions and spending usually occur
just before Election Day. Readers should also bear in mind that the
2016 elections, like all others, were unique, reflecting the complex
interaction of issues, candidates, competition, closeness of the races,
voter interest and turnout, strategies for traditional and online media,
economic and political conditions in different regions, and many
other factors. Campaign finance is a central component of this mix,
of course, both shaping and reflecting the others. The data that we
already have on the 2016 *presidential* election suggests at least three
surprising facts:[45]

- *Campaign spending did not seem to matter much in either the pri-*
  maries or the general election. Donald Trump won the election
  handily despite having spent only a little more than half of what
  Hillary Clinton spent (and far less than what he had anticipated
  earlier in the campaign). He also won despite raising far less
  money than Clinton did. Clinton and her allies took in about $1
  billion; Trump and the groups working on his behalf raised only
  about $600 million.
- Trump relied mostly on a Twitter account, his own money, and

extensive news media coverage. Mrs. Clinton depended more on TV advertising, spending hundreds of millions of dollars on almost relentlessly negative attack ads.

- Although every presidential election tends to break the previous spending record, 2016 was a striking exception: *both candidates spent significantly less than their counterparts did in 2012.* Clinton's total expenses were $565 million, compared with $775 million for President Obama; Trump spent $322 million, about 70 percent of what Mitt Romney spent in 2012 ($460 million).

The following discussion of campaign finance trends is divided into three aspects: campaign spending, campaign contributions, and (very briefly) state and local campaigns. But several preliminary points are important in thinking about the information that follows.

- The numbers presented in this section represent the *aggregate* fund-raising figures of the parties and their candidates in order to discern the larger patterns in election spending. The parties spend a fraction of what candidates do in elections. In 2014, for example, candidates for Congress spent $1.5 billion, some five times more than the $291 million spent by the two parties' national committees.
- Spending and contributions do not fully measure a campaign's *resources.* Volunteers, for example, provide a crucial campaign input, not captured in contribution and spending data. Labor unions fielded an army of 128,000 volunteers in just the final four days of the 2012 Obama campaign![46] Although I could find no comprehensive study of the question, such volunteers evidently can have large effects on electoral outcomes.[47]
- A growing share of campaign spending is done by outside groups supposedly independent of the candidates and parties.
- Campaign spending and contributions are not the same as campaign effectiveness, a point developed later in the chapter.

Spending. Campaigns have grown much more costly in recent elections; spending now exceeds $6 billion in a presidential election and

$3 billion in an off-year election—and these numbers have surely escalated in the 2016 campaigns. On spending, *Citizens United*'s most notable aspect, especially in view of the jeremiads against it, is that the dire predictions about corporate spending have *not* been borne out in the four elections held since the decision. At this writing, data on the 2016 congressional election is not yet available.

In the 2012 *presidential* election, the first that it affected, spending did not increase very much, considering that presidential election years always attract and cost more money than off-year elections. Bradley Smith, a former FEC Chair who applauds *Citizens United*, makes several points: (1) very few business corporations donate to parties and most of those are closely-held family firms; (2) corporations' spending on elections is less than 5 percent of the total; (3) all outside spending (not just corporate) in 2014 was only 10 percent of the total (compared with 17 percent in 2000); (4) total political spending in 2014, adjusted for inflation, was only 1.5 percent higher than in 2006 (the last pre-*Citizens United* off-year election), whereas the spending increase over the previous eight-year period was 42 percent; and (5) it left donor disclosure rules unchanged.[48] Smith also argues, more dubiously, that the decision has increased competition and reduced the incumbent advantage.[49]

Citizens United has also had less effect on *congressional* election spending than was anticipated. In 2010, the first election after the decision, spending was $3.6 billion, a 27.3 percent increase from the 2006 midterms, but this was a smaller increase than the 30.75 percent between the 2006 and 2002 midterms, long before *Citizens United* came down.

For the 2012 presidential campaign, candidates, parties, and outside groups *reported* having spent $2.3 billion—$1.1 billion for Barack Obama, and $1.2 billion for Mitt Romney. The reported candidate spending was 47.6 percent of the total, national party spending was 29 percent, and outside spending was 23.4 percent.[50] In 2012, candidates allocated 58.4 percent of their spending to media, 13.7 percent to fund-raising, 8.3 percent to administration, 7.5 percent to salaries, 4 percent to unclassifiable, and 8.1 percent to "all other."[51]

In the 2014 congressional elections, total spending by candidates, parties, and outside groups was $3.7 billion. Candidates accounted for about 42 percent of this spending; parties, 30 percent; PACs and 527 organizations, 13 percent; and other sources, the remaining 15 percent.[52] As always, incumbents enjoyed large fund-raising advantages: Senate incumbents raised on average almost ten times more money than their challengers, and House incumbents averaged six times more![53] Traditional media costs were high.*

To be sure, *Citizens United* did unleash well-funded, high-spending Super PACs. (I discuss the implications of this fact for campaign finance below.) In 2010 when Super PACs first appeared (and were allowed by the *SpeechNOW.org* decision, discussed earlier, to make unlimited independent expenditures), 83 of them spent $62 million. In 2012, a presidential election year, 1,310 of them spent $609 million. In the 2014 midterms (with the White House not at stake), 1,360 of them spent $345 million.[54] Business Super PACs outspent labor union Super PACs 15 to 1.[55] In mid-2015, with the 2016 campaign just beginning, Super PACs had already raised $250 million, *more than sixteen times what they had raised at the same point in 2012 and twice what the campaign committees had raised.*[56]

The cost of elections *overall* (calculated only for presidential election years but including those years' congressional elections as well) has risen steadily—from 2000 ($3 billion) to 2008 ($5.2 billion) to 2012 ($6.2 billion).[57] (Two new candidates ran in 2008, so more spending was to be expected.) The average House winner spent $407,000 in 1990 and $1.5 million in 2012 (an almost 285 percent increase); the average Senate winner spent $3,870,621 in 1990 and $11,474,362 in 2012 (a 196 percent increase).[58] Donor demographics were relatively similar to those in 1990, with 0.11 percent of the population contributing more than $200 in 1990 and 0.4 percent doing so in 2012.[59]

---

* The total of $763 million for media broke down into the following subcategories: unspecified media buys ($594 million); web ads ($94 million); media consulting ($30 million); media production ($17 million); miscellaneous media ($15 million); broadcast ads ($8 million); and print ads ($2 million).

We can better understand this campaign spending by considering it in some comparative contexts. One comparison is to campaign spending in the United Kingdom. In the UK, party election expenditures are limited to 30,000 pounds ($45,000) per contested district and 19 million pounds ($29 million) per nationwide election.[60] With about 45 million registered voters in the UK, the expenditure limits work out to 2.36 pounds ($3.63) per voter for a nationwide election. The British system, of course, differs from ours in many ways: fewer voters, fewer and less costly media, perhaps more free TV time; smaller landmass, stronger parties, unified government, smaller area, shorter campaigns, and so forth.

A second contextual comparison is between our spending on campaigns and our spending on other items. Holiday shopping, for example, was forecast at almost $617 billion in 2014;[61] indeed, more than $31 billion would be spent on holiday gift cards alone.[62] The average shopper's holiday spending of $804[63] dwarfs the infinitesimal share of Americans (0.04 percent) who spend more than $200 in an election cycle. In 2015, the cosmetics industry's revenues were estimated to exceed $60 billion;[64] Americans also spent almost $6 billion on just the five most common cosmetic surgeries, and another $4 billion on the five top nonsurgical cosmetic procedures.[65] Consumers also spent more than $10 billion on movie tickets in 2014, almost triple what was spent on the congressional elections.[66]

Politics is inevitably expensive in a vast, diverse, media-driven country like ours. Town meetings, soapboxes, and water-cooler conversations are cheap and important, but most campaigning is done through televised debates, advertising, direct mail and other costly media, and increasingly the Internet. Money is necessary to communicate political ideas effectively; even negative advertising conveys useful information to voters.[67]

A strong case can be made, then, that we should spend more on elections than we do. Indeed, political scientists showed in 2003 that campaign spending as a share of GDP had not risen appreciably in more than a century![68] Even the $3.7 billion spent in the 2014 campaigns represented a mere 0.0002 percent of U.S. GDP that year.

Contributions. The parties, between them, raised $1.6 billion in hard money for the 2012 presidential election cycle. The two parties raised essentially equal amounts even though the Republicans were trying to unseat the incumbent, which generally requires much more spending. For the 2014 congressional elections, Democrats raised $736 million, and Republicans, $901 million. This Republican fund-raising advantage over the Democrats has diminished over time and may have disappeared in 2016.[69]

The donor population has grown significantly—3,138,564 individuals (10 percent of the population) made itemized contributions in 2012—but it remains small and very lop-sided. Less than 0.5 percent account for most of the money contributed by all individual donors.[70] Of the donations that are disclosed under the statute, only 0.23 percent of Americans contributed more than $200 in 2014, and a much smaller group (0.04 percent) contributed more than $2,400.[71] An elite corps of 769 bundlers, who collect contributions of at least $50,000, directed $186.5 million to the Obama reelection campaign.[72] Super PACs supporting specific presidential candidates spent $239 million.[73] The Open Secrets organization found 69 reported bundlers for Romney who raised $17 million and then 37 bundlers who were undisclosed by Romney but revealed in a variety of press reports.[74]

The 2014 *McCutcheon* decision applied to contributions (unlike *Citizens United*, which concerned expenditures). In *McCutcheon*, the Court struck down the statute's aggregate contribution limits, but the decision's actual effects on the concentration of donations among the very rich are less than one might think, once enforcement realities are considered. Adam Bonica and colleagues show that the FEC did not seriously enforce those limits: In 2012, with the limits ($117,000) still in effect, they identified more than 1,800 individuals and a smaller number of families who exceeded them. Studying the top 0.01 percent of the voting-age population (those listed in Forbes's list of the 400 wealthiest individuals), they found that the vast majority of these super-wealthy donors gave a lot and gave often,* steadily

---

* Bonica et al. treat these contributions as what economists call a normal consumption good: As their wealth has increased, they make larger donations, which constitute a smaller

increasing their share of the total contributions to 40 percent in 2012.[75] The same general pattern was already evident in the 2016 presidential campaign.[76]

Some of Bonica et al.'s empirical analysis of donations by the super-wealthy and smaller donors—their distribution by party and ideology, and their likely effects—are worth quoting at length for its wealth of information. (I omit citations, some examples, and methodological passages.)

> The Democrats have come to rely, increasingly, on contributions from individuals, particularly big money. Contributions from organized labor, never dominant, have fallen in importance. The relative proportions of funds raised by Democrats from the top 0.01 percent and from organized labor provide a telling comparison. The top 0.01 percent, whose donations had been roughly on par with those of labor during 1980s and early 1990s, outspent labor by more than a 4:1 margin during the 2012 election cycle. While Republicans had a slight advantage in fundraising from the top 0.01 percent during the 1980s, this trend had reversed by the mid-1990s, with Democrats raising more than Republicans from the top 0.01 percent in six out of eight election cycles between 1994 and 2008. Only in the last two election cycles did Republicans regain the advantage in fundraising from the top 0.01 percent. While it is difficult to gauge the effect of the Democrats' reliance on contributions from the wealthy, it does likely preclude a strong focus on redistributive policies.
>
> For individual campaign donors, we have explored who gives how much to whom in terms of the ideology of the donors and candidates. In 2012, 62 percent of contribution dollars raised from the top 0.01 percent went to Republicans, accounting for 40 percent of the party's total campaign dollars. . . . Although contributions from the Forbes 400/Fortune 500 skew somewhat to the right, a sizable percentage of their contribution dollars go to sup-

---

fraction of their income. On the electoral influence of the super-wealthy in some other countries, see Darrell M. West, *Billionaires: Reflections on the Upper Crust* (2014), chap. 5.

port candidates who are left of center. . . . As a rule, individual donors exhibit high levels of partisanship in their giving patterns, and the super-rich are no exception. The vast majority have given at least 90 percent of their contribution dollars to one or the other party. Of those who split their contributions between parties, most give predominantly to the moderate wings of both parties. As such, the bimodal density of contribution dollars reflects the ideological diversity in the contributors, rather than individuals purchasing access or otherwise acting strategically in ways that cause them to disperse their contributions widely. Only three of the 30—George Soros, Larry Page, and Sergey Brin—would be placed in the "progressive" wing of the Democrats. Similarly, only one of the 30, Charles Koch, is to the right of the mean Republican member of Congress. The big contributions [appear] as moderate only in the limited sense that they are less ideologically extreme than the small contributions.

The ideological diversity of corporate elites is not simply a function of firm-specific incentives that would cause a firm to stake out an ideological position. Bipartisan boardrooms are the norm. One way a firm maintains political access is to have both high-profile Democratic donors and high-profile Republican donors within the firm. A consequence of the ideological diversity of the corporate community is to help keep the political financing system competitive for both parties, while at the same time ensuring that firms remain well connected in both parties.

. . . [T]he 30 richest Americans are diverse but relatively moderate. The distribution of contributions from the top 0.01 percent of the voting age population is more extreme than the Forbes 400/ Fortune 500 but less extreme than the small donors. While Forbes 400/Fortune 500 individuals are more moderate than small donors, their contributions tilt toward Republicans. The top 0.01 percent of donors give pretty evenly to Democrats and Republicans. Why are big donors a bit less polarized than other donors? With regard to the left, the answer seems straightforward: those who are left and rich still have a limited tolerance for redistribution. For the right, the answer seems a bit more complicated. The wealthy are often more pro-business than pro-market . . . , and are often not anti-statist.

This section has emphasized political spending in the form of campaign contributions. We should also note that even more is spent on lobbying. While a good deal of lobbying reflects corporate competition . . . much of it gets directed in ways that increase inequality. . . .

We would also be amiss not to emphasize the role of the re-volving door between between politics and the private sector as another nontrivial form of political expenditure. [Examples omit-ted]. . . . Revolving door jobs, lobbying, and campaign contribu-tions by the rich, when coupled with free market ideological pro-clivities in the voting population, are likely to have abetted the increase in inequality.

We might wonder what these individuals receive for their con-tributions? A decade ago, Ansolabehere, de Figueiredo, and Sny-der asked in this journal, "Why Is There So Little Money in U.S. Politics?"* . . . The question we focus on is a little different: Why have total contributions and the share of total contributions from the top .01 percent risen so much in the last few decades? One possibility is that campaign contributions are just another fad for the rich in the twenty-first century. Standard economic arguments are that rational people won't make large contributions in the hope of different policy outcomes for the same reason that rational people will not expect their personal vote to influence the outcome of elections. However, when contributions become very large, then the notion that your contributions will be completely overshad-owed by others may not be as true. Large contributors may also be serving as "bundlers" (fundraisers who solicit checks from other individuals and then pass the checks along to candidates and com-mittees), similar to the collective funding of industry lobbies such as the American Bankers Association. Contributions may help

---

* This research is discussed later in the chapter.

carry the day on very specific issues that relate to income inequality—like the provisions that allow the "carried interest" income received by private equity investors to be taxed at a lower capital gains tax rate rather than the higher marginal income tax rate.

More broadly, there does seem to be evidence that members of Congress represent the views of their high-income constituents much more than those of low-income ones. . . . especially in policy domains where the opinions of rich and poor diverge. When the rich and poor (90th and 10th percentile incomes) disagree more than 10 percentage points on a policy question, the odds of a policy change are completely unresponsive to views of the poorer voters. But if 80 percent of high-income voters support the change, it has a 50 percent chance of passing compared to only a 32 percent chance of passing with 80 percent support from the poor. [77]

This and other evidence establishes some broad propositions.

- Any Republican Party fund-raising advantage over the Democratic Party (except when the latter controls Congress) has lessened and is no longer very significant. In the 2016 presidential election, it flipped.
- A tiny group of super-wealthy, mostly conservative individuals provide a vastly disproportionate share of total campaign contributions, but their overall giving, while tilting toward Republicans, is fairly bipartisan, as is much corporate giving.
- Individuals tend to be more ideologically extreme than PACs and other interest groups are.
- The candidates whom individual donors support are also more extreme (the opposite is true of those supported by corporate and union contributions to PACS).[78]
- Individuals' contributions comprise an ever-larger share of candidates' funds (almost 75 percent in 2012); indeed, an even higher share of those funds come from out-of-state donors (about 80 percent).[79]
- *McCutcheon* has had little practical significance because the FEC seldom enforced the aggregate limits when they existed.

- *Citizens United* probably made corporate spending more opaque by channeling some of it through 501(c)(4) entities that need not disclose their contributors, and such dark money accounts for a large proportion of outside group spending.[80] Still, the decision so far has affected campaign finance much less than its critics predicted. This is mainly because corporate contributions are subject to the low statutory limits on contributions, while corporate spending—as distinct from that of wealthy individuals—is very modest and not significantly partisan.*

- Although outside organizations—especially PACs that contribute to campaigns and Super PACS that spend in thinly veiled support of them—have proliferated since 2010, their actual electoral effects remain unclear. Super PAC funding comes mostly from wealthy individuals, not corporations or unions.[81] They cannot pay for a candidate's campaign costs like salaries, rent, travel, office expenses, opinion polling, legal fees, or ballot access efforts.[82] Insurgent and maverick candidates like socialist Bernie Sanders and retired neurosurgeon Ben Carson lack personal money but still were able to raise enough to be competitive without Super PACs. Scott Walker and Rick Perry got nowhere de-

---

* Shortly after *Citizens United* came down, Samuel Issacharoff noted:

> [T]he Court did not act at the behest of corporations eager to exploit the vagaries of campaign finance law. No corporation filed an amicus brief in the case, with only the Chamber of Commerce making the expansive case for the First Amendment. In states where corporate campaign contributions are legal (about half the states), the evidence of an urge to overwhelm elections with corporate spending is scant, at least thus far. For example, one study from California for 2001–2006 revealed that among the top ten contributors to state independent expenditure committees, there was not a single corporate interest. There were two wealthy individuals among the top ten, banking a friend who was running for governor, but the top ten were dominated by either Indian tribes or public employee unions. Even the trial lawyers—another widely disparaged group—barely eked onto the list at number ten. When all contributions among the top ten were added together for that period, the amount expended by public employee unions was about double that attributed to corporate sources. In some individual races, there were expenditures by associations of small businesses, such as real estate interests, but even they were secondary players overall.

Issacharoff, "On Political Corruption," 124 *Harvard Law Review* 118, 130–31 (2010).

spite large Super PACs, and Jeb Bush had little to show for his despite its having raised the most.[83] Indeed, total spending by candidates and their Super PACs was *inversely* proportional to the votes received in the 2016 New Hampshire and Iowa primaries.[84]

- Super PACs support liberal campaigns as well as conservative ones. In March 2016, a group led by George Soros committed to spending hundreds of millions of dollars to get out the Hispanic vote, which would presumably aid Democratic candidates.[85]
- Republican candidates traditionally dominated small donations, while Democrats led by Sanders in the 2016 race perfected the small donor online technology.[86] Indeed, relying on small donations, they sometimes vastly outraise the more establishment candidates who are aided by Super PACs.[87] Moreover, billionaire candidates like Donald Trump don't need these groups at all; indeed, they try to discredit opponents who receive Super PACs' support, demanding that they have the groups return any money received from donors.[88] (At least one Super PAC supported Trump anyway.)[89] In a variety of ways, then, candidates' financial support is a mixed blessing—indispensable but also a weapon that their opponents wield against them. Although independent expenditures can be important, parties and candidates—and small donors, in recent campaigns—still dominate campaign finance quantitatively.

State and Local Elections. This chapter focuses on federal elections. But because the Supreme Court's interpretation of the First Amendment constrains states and localities as well, the increases in dark money and independent spending in the wake of *Citizens United* are salient there as well. Indeed, *Citizens United* invalidated laws in the twenty-four states that had restricted or banned corporate election spending.[90] In these states, outside spending increased approximately 80 percent between 2006 and 2010. (States that had previously allowed such outside spending saw an increase in it of "only" 34 percent in that period.)[91]

Also, large donors have become increasingly prominent in state and local elections. In the 2011 San Francisco mayoral election, for example, tech mogul Ron Conway created a Super PAC that raised $600,000 for Mayor Ed Lee (who raised only $1.6 million himself). This development has increased coordination between candidates and the donors to these outside spending groups, especially since their fund-raising effect looms larger in local elections. Since 2010, election spending had increased four to twenty times in governors' elections, and disclosure laws do not make it easy to track the sources of this money. Some states have tried to minimize the effects of *Citizens United* by regulating such coordination in new ways, such as providing expanded lists of scenarios that might suggest collaboration. As we shall see in the later discussion of reform proposals, some states and localities have adopted public funding of elections.[92]

The Decline of Civility in Political Discourse

Democratic politics has always been rough-and-tumble and bitter, especially since the emergence of parties in the election of 1800 and its aftermath.[93] As humorist Finley Peter Dunne said a century later with typical understatement, "politics ain't beanbag." Today, incivility in politics may be worse than ever before. (Such things, of course, are hard to measure.) Political scientist Nathaniel Persily sees an "erosion of politics-constraining norms." He notes that extreme rhetoric, routine recall elections, mid-decade redistricting, legislators hiding to prevent a quorum, widespread efforts to disenfranchise voters, and much more—"actions previously considered 'nuclear' are now conventional."[94] This toxic, hyperpartisan atmosphere, replete with assertions that the other party started it and angrily invoked examples, makes campaign finance one of many hot-button issues whose resolution is that much more difficult. This is particularly true of campaign finance because, as discussed in the final part, there is little agreement on whether there is a problem that needs solving, much less what the problem is and which policy changes might remedy it.

ISSUES

In this section, I shall use two types of analysis—(1) the justices' debates in *Citizens United* and *McCutcheon*, and (2) the scholarly work (mostly in political science and law) scrutinizing the justices' approaches in these cases—to distill campaign finance issues and deepen our understanding of them. These issues turn on an interrelated set of conceptual, normative, legal, empirical, and policy considerations. Before discussing them, however, I present three propositions to which all members of the Court subscribed in *Buckley* (the seminal *per curiam* decision in 1976 that upheld modern campaign finance regulation's basic architecture), propositions that the Court has reaffirmed many times since—although its unanimity in *Buckley* disappeared long ago.

- Campaign spending is equivalent to speech for First Amendment purposes. They are not the same, of course, but the Court *treats* money as speech in the crucial sense that one cannot be heard in the national public sphere without spending money—usually a lot of it. As Robert Samuelson, a leading syndicated columnist, puts it: "Political speech is a public phenomenon. It aims to affect how people behave. It requires money to hire campaign staff, build a Web site, buy political spots and the like. Penniless politicians can't easily communicate."[95] Law professor Richard Briffault captures this point, saying that campaign spending is "speechy enough" to qualify for First Amendment protection.[96] The hard question, then—part constitutional law, part policy—is how much money-funded political speech is enough to serve the public interest in enabling voters to make informed decisions. This question, however, is one that the First Amendment allows politicians to decide for us *only if* they can satisfy the constitutional standard of review described next.
- Contributions and expenditures are, constitutionally speaking, entirely different. Contribution limits are permissible while expenditure limits are highly suspect. The Court's rationale for this dis-

tinction is that expenditure's size measures the quantity of speech and thus must be protected. In contrast, a contribution is only a general expression of support because it does not communicate the underlying basis for it, and the quantity of a donor's speech does not increase perceptibly as her contribution increases. It thus deserves less protection.

To implement this core distinction, the courts must apply a two-tier standard of review, assigning contribution limits to the lower, more relaxed tier where for the limits to be upheld (a) the governmental interest need only be "sufficiently important," and (b) the limit need only be "closely" tailored to serve that interest. For limits on expenditures (whether "independent" or not), assigned to the higher, more congressionally-restricting tier: (a) the government's interest must be "compelling" in order to justify those limits, and (b) the limits must be "narrowly" tailored to serve that interest. A coordinated (non-"independent") expenditure is treated as a contribution.

- Of the two interests traditionally invoked by the government to justify expenditure and contribution limits, only prevention of quid pro quo corruption satisfies the "compelling" test; preventing "influence corruption" does not. As the Court stated in *Buckley*, "the concept that government may restrict the speech of some elements of our society in order to enhance the relative voice of others is wholly foreign to the First Amendment."[97]

In the remainder of this section, I discuss eight fundamental, indeed defining, issues: (1) the nature of corruption in politics, and whether its avoidance is the only compelling interest that Congress may invoke to justify its regulation of campaign contributions and expenditures; (2) whether "independent" expenditures are indeed independent, and whether they counter the risk of corruption in ways that direct contributions to campaigns do not; (3) the role of incumbency; (4) whether some corporate speakers pose greater corruption risks than other corporate speakers do, such that Congress can regulate the former but not the latter; (5) whether money is decisive in elections; (6) how our campaign finance system affects the behavior of the major parties and other actors; (7) disclosure; and (8) regulation in the emerging world of online campaigning. In what I hope is a useful addendum to these issues, I then summarize the debate between the two leading camps on these issues before turning to the final section on reforms.

Corruption in Politics

All members of the Court and all commentators agree that Congress has a compelling interest in combating corruption and the appearance of corruption (a distinction discussed below).[98] But agreement ends there. Campaign finance policy debates and litigation often center on which kinds of conduct (or conditions*) constitute political corruption.

These competing definitions are manifest in the warring opinions in *McConnell, Citizens United,* and *McCutcheon.*† In *McConnell,* a sharply divided Court used the narrower, quid quo pro conception of corruption and the lower standard of review to uphold the BCRA's ban on soft money contributions. (As discussed later, the Court also upheld its regulation of "electioneering communications"). Finding that soft-money had fostered manipulation of the legislative calendar and other tactics that affected policy outcomes favoring industries' interests, the majority (Justices Breyer, Stevens, O'Connor, Souter, and Ginsburg) saw this as evidence of the kind of undue influence, unequal access, and appearance of corruption that the parties *sold* in exchange for soft money, practices that Congress could legitimately

---

* I add "conditions" to acknowledge Justice Thurgood Marshall's claim that political corruption in the political arena includes "the corrosive and distorting effects of immense aggregations of wealth that are accumulated with the help of the corporate form and that have little or no correlation to the public's support for the corporation's political ideas." *Austin v. Michigan Chamber of Commerce,* 494 U.S. 652, 666 (1990).

† Court opinions that review campaign finance statutes deal with somewhat discrete issues raised by the statutes, so I shall discuss only those parts of opinions that deal with the particular issue under analysis—here, corruption.

regulate. (It also held that the soft money ban was narrowly tailored enough to only marginally limit protected political speech.)

On the key definition of corruption, the *McConnell* minority strongly dissented. Justice Kennedy criticized the majority for having stretched the idea of quid pro quo corruption to include "any conduct that wins goodwill or influences a Member of Congress. . . . [In this view], access has the same legal ramifications as actual or apparent corruption of officeholders." More than thirty years after FECA, he observed, *McConnell's* trial record of more than 100,000 pages failed to cite a single direct example of votes being exchanged for independent expenditures, adding that there also was scant evidence of expenditure-related "ingratiation" that in any event—and like superior access—did not constitute corruption.[99] Kennedy further insisted that the majority, by defining corruption to include undue influence, "sweeps away all protections for speech that lie in its path." Indeed, he maintained, elected officials are *supposed* to be responsive to contributions by constituents urging them to promote certain outcomes. I discuss the notion of undue influence below.

Seven years later in *Citizens United*, Kennedy got his way. The majority was correct to hold on the specific facts of the case that (1) *Buckley's* dichotomy between expenditures and contributions applied to corporations and unions, and (2) Citizens United's film qualified as an independent expenditure. (It did not help the government's case that its logic would allow Congress to prevent the group even from using its own funds to publish a book criticizing Clinton, which seemed to sanction book-burning—a position that Justice Alito understandably found "pretty incredible.") But the majority went further— and further than necessary to decide the case. This dictum stating Congress could bar only quid pro quo corruption, not undue influence—and related language (naively or disingenuously, depending on how one views it) ignoring the reality of widespread campaign coordination of "independent" expenditures—account for much of the criticism of *Citizens United* by many legal scholars, including Laurence Tribe, perhaps the leading constitutional law expert in the country.[100]

This same question of what constitutes political corruption was again addressed in *McCutcheon*, which struck down the BCRA's limits on aggregate contributions by any single contributor. Writing for a plurality, Chief Justice Roberts insisted that Congress "may no more restrict how many candidates or causes a donor may support than it may tell a newspaper how many candidates it may endorse."[101] Only quid pro quo corruption, the plurality reaffirmed, is a legitimate target given First Amendment principles. Neither "[s]pending large sums of money [without] an effort to control the exercise of an officeholder's official duties," nor using contributions "to garner 'influence over or access to' elected officials or political parties," constitutes quid pro quo corruption. This line between corruption and general influence, Roberts wrote, may be vague but it is essential.[102]

The *McCutcheon* dissenters, through Justice Breyer, argued that corruption, properly defined, should include disproportionate access or influence, not just quid pro quo corruption; that aggregate limits do combat corruption; and that aggregate limits were also needed to prevent donors and parties from evading the contribution limits. Eliminating those limits, he wrote, created "a loophole that will allow a single individual to contribute millions of dollars to a political party or to a candidate's campaign. Taken together with *Citizens United*, today's decision eviscerates our Nation's campaign finance laws [and threatens democratic legitimacy]."[103]

The most recent Supreme Court analysis of corruption occurred in *McDonnell v. United States*,[104] a June 2016 decision involving a former governor of Virginia prosecuted for corruption for doing favors—arranging meetings, hosting events, and contacting other officials—for someone who gave him personal gifts, loans, and campaign contributions. The case was a federal criminal prosecution, not an enforcement action under the campaign finance laws. Still, the Court's narrow definition of corruption, endorsed by all eight justices including the *McCutcheon* dissenters, will surely affect the interpretation of campaign finance laws by making clear that providing favored access does not by itself constitute the requisite quid pro quo under the corruption statutes; the decision or action must be an official one that the official made, or agreed to make, on the donor's behalf.

What are we to make of this debate? The claims by both sides about the nature and risks of political corruption are remarkable for their uncompromising assertiveness, tendentiousness, and paucity of rigorous empirical support. Begin with the most fundamental questions: What is quid pro quo corruption, and how much of it actually occurs via campaign finance? Obviously, we cannot know how much actually occurs but goes undetected, like the dog that didn't bark. Nevertheless, there are reasons to think that such corruption is uncommon. Although it fits the legal definition of criminal bribery—indeed, "legalized bribery" is the leading epithet hurled by the system's many critics—relatively few members of Congress had been convicted of it before the campaign finance system was established in the 1970s. Since then, only two members of the House and no senators have been expelled.[105] This rarity is especially striking, as ambitious, media-hungry prosecutors have strong political and other incentives to indict politicians, especially from the other party. Bribery, to be sure, is hard to prove; it requires evidence that A tried to give something of value to official B in exchange for, or anticipation of, B's performing a specific official act that B would not have performed otherwise. Thus, it demands proof of some incriminating communication between them; as the Court in *Buckley* noted, bribery laws "deal with only the most blatant and specific attempts of those with money to influence government action."[106]

To those who assert "legalized bribery," of course, this equation with the traditional crime misses the whole point because the reality of campaign finance obviates any need for such a surreptitious transaction. Instead, it brings the bribery out into the open in the form of check-writing—and then blesses it. But someone looking for evidence of quid pro quos between donors and politicians should at least have to find them acknowledging the specific quids and quos. If all that happens is that (1) a contributor writes a check and asks the candidate to do something if elected, and (2) the candidate simply expresses gratitude for the contribution, it is not legalized bribery but a desirable process of democratic representation—unless the mere giving of money to a candidate is illegitimate, which no member of the Court (or Congress) believes.

To be culpable, then, a check-cum-thank-you must be something more. Yet political scientists, election law experts, and journalists, three groups of professionals deeply interested in unearthing corrupt exchanges, have found little of it.[107] And if a check, request for action, and gratitude constitute bribery, why can Congress permit a donor to bribe a candidate a certain amount[108]* and yet threaten an administrative (not criminal) penalty† if the donor exceeds it? Does this mean that such a small bribe (or risk of it) is okay? The system's answer, ratified by the Court, is an emphatic yes—although the justices would never put it this way. But what the justices *have* held is that a contribution limit can be unconstitutional if the limit is *too low*—on the theory that the law is unduly burdening the right to contribute a non-corrupting amount.[109] But the parameters of the Court's Goldilocks zone—not too high, not too low—remain uncertain.

Adding to the confusion concerning how quid pro quo corruption actually works in politics is the principle, uniformly accepted by the Court, that it is illegal not only if it *actually* exists but even if it merely *appears* to exist. Since appearance is in the eye of the beholder, who gets to decide whether a donation creates an appearance of corruption? Empirical studies present a confused picture of appearance of corruption.[110] No jury considers this question, so the FEC (in the first instance) and judges (if and when it gets to them) must decide it—and not after the fact based on the context of a specific donation, but instead through a generic ex ante rule—that *all* contributions above the statutory level *categorically* create the *appearance* of quid pro quo corruption. If this is so, then the contribution limits, albeit constitutionally valid, are arbitrary in the sense that there is no clear justifica-

---

* For the 2015–16 elections, the limit is $2,700 for individual donors and other amounts for various kinds of donor committees.

† The FEC's enforcement process is remarkably mild, replete with opportunities for delay and evasion. See "Enforcement Actions" at http://www.fec.gov/pages/brochures/fecfeca.shtml#anchor257909

tion for drawing the line at this amount rather than some other amount. Of course, most line-drawing—in law as in life—is arbitrary in this sense. (Some people are qualified to be president at age thirty-four, but the Constitution draws the line at thirty-five; the same is true of the legal drinking age, as different states prescribe different ages.) We usually rely on our elected representatives to draw lines as best they can. The First Amendment, however, makes it much harder to do so in the campaign finance context. It ordains that any contribution limits that Congress enacts must be "closely tailored" to prevent quid pro quo corruption or its appearance, and that any expenditure limits must be be "narrowly tailored" to that purpose.

Finally, there is the question of the other kind of corruption in politics, sometimes called undue influence.* This lies at the core of the public's concerns about campaign finance. But I am not at all sure what "undue" means here. Specifically, I do not see how we can distinguish it factually and morally from (a) the normal—and normatively accepted—practical politics of influence in a representative democracy, and (b) other sources of influence not necessarily connected to campaign contributions.

Normal politics in a healthy democracy necessarily entails tough, messy, horse-trading, favor-doing, and influence-peddling among politicians and interest groups with few holds barred. As one analyst puts it, "government is a blur of the high-minded and the petty, where it is often difficult to distinguish between rewards to constituents and matters of policy and principle."[111] Governmental activities are both preceded and followed by complex interactions among voters, interest groups, and politicians in which they all seek to influence each other. Short of bribery, blackmail, or some other criminal transaction, we deem these influences legitimate, salutary, and even essential. No

---

* Larry Lessig, a prominent legal scholar and briefly a candidate in the 2016 presidential election on a single-issue campaign finance reform platform, calls this "dependency corruption." He argues that politicians' dependence on "the funders" rather than "the People" corrupts democratic *institutions*. But while "dependency" surely occurs in many cases, it connotes an abject reliance that may or may not in fact result from a donor's dollars, whereas those dollars doubtless improve the donor's opportunities for physical or other access to the recipient or staff.

well-informed person doubts this, nor should anyone doubt that money is one legitimate instrument among others for conveying both the information and the influence. Were this not the case, it would make no sense at all to allow any contributions to politicians, yet we do so—up to a point. Reasonable people (and the justices) obviously disagree about the point beyond which a contribution becomes illegitimate because it tends (or appears to tend) to corrupt.

In thinking about this, consider a central, often-ignored fact: *Money is only one of many sources of influence over politicians.* While no one doubts that financial support is indispensable for candidates ("mother's milk," it is called), opponents often use their campaign spending against them, so it is a mixed blessing. Indeed, political scientists find that *other* resources are usually decisive—and help attract campaign contributions in the first place. They include: better organizational skills; friendship; past contacts or ties; the size, intensity, and thus influence of interest groups; tactical expertise; valuable information; media access and free (known as "earned") TV time;* personal charisma or eloquence; name recognition; dynastic power; persuasive arguments; propitious timing; a compelling life story; and still others—especially incumbency (discussed below).†

Campaign finance rules treat money altogether differently than any of these other levers of influence: Money alone is subject to legal limitation. Why is this? Money seems more measurable and controllable than these other advantages, and it enables campaigns to purchase many other things of political value that can then be converted into some (not all) of the non-monetary advantages I have just

---

* Donald Trump has vastly exceeded his rivals in this category, enabling him to run a relatively cheap campaign. In March 2016, the *New York Times* reported that he had already "earned close to $2 billion worth of media attention, about twice the all-in price of the most expensive presidential campaigns in history," and twice that of Hillary Clinton, the next best at earning media. Bernie Sanders had earned more media than any of the Republicans except Trump. Of course, not all of this attention is positive. http://www.nytimes.com /2016/03/16/upshot/measuring-donald-trumps-mammoth-advantage-in-free-media .html?emc=eta1

† Political scientist Norman Ornstein claims that money matters more in down-ballot elections where there is much less of it. http://www.aei.org/publication/in-politics-money -isnt-everything-but-it-still-matters/

listed—lobbyists, for example. The $3.24 billion spent on lobbying policy makers in 2014[112] dwarfs the $1.6 billion in campaign contributions spread over many candidates and only during election campaigns. Lobbying, however, cannot be limited constitutionally, while contributions can. A detailed study of the repeal of the estate tax in 2001 finds that campaign contributions played a much smaller role than money spent for core protected speech: research and publishing, political organizing, disseminating opinion, and lobbying. Washington insiders' "most frequently repeated view was that campaign contributions are overrated when it comes to getting legislation passed. [They] consider lobbying and interest groups far more important."[113] Political scientist Nolan McCarty thinks that any effort to further restrict campaign contributions or spending would simply divert the money to increased lobbying, where equalization and control are much more problematic.[114]

Another reason reformers focus on money, of course, is inequality: The rich have so much more of it than their fellow citizens do and can use it to gain greater access or influence, multiplying their existing advantages. To the *McCutcheon* dissenters, this "derails the essential speech-to-government-action tie [and frustrates] Congress' concern that a few large donations not drown out the voices of the many."[115] But as we saw earlier, *Buckley* (and more recently, *McCutcheon*) emphatically and *unanimously* rejected the notion that the First Amendment permits Congress to justify spending or contribution limits to achieve equal access or influence.

Nevertheless, many (perhaps most) critics of the current system find this egalitarian rationale to be more convincing than the corruption rationale; it is the outsized influence of moneyed interests that they most strongly decry and think is most corrosive of democratic legitimacy.[116] But emphasizing financial inequality is odd in two important respects. The amount spent on campaigns is less decisive than how efficiently it is spent;[117] after a certain point, the marginal returns to spending decline significantly. And many of the *non-monetary* assets listed above (especially earned media) are distributed *even more unequally* than wealth is.[118] We often ignore these crucial facts simply because money is so much easier to measure than these other assets are. I will discuss this misleading "monetization" of the reform discourse later.

Larry Lessig points out another fact bearing on this debate about undue-influence corruption: Many contributions come from donors who live outside the district and whom, strictly speaking, the candidate would not even represent.

> [T]he vast majority of contributions to a congressional campaign are not even from "the voters" in that district. At one point, Representative John Murtha (D-Pa; 1973–2010) had raised over $200,000, with only $1000 coming from his district. OpenSecrets.org reports that 67 percent of John Kerry's contributions in his 2008 reelection to the Senate came from out-of-state donors. His Republican opponent received 73 percent of his funding from outside Massachusetts.[119]

To summarize: Fundamental confusions pervade both the linkage between contributions and corruption, and the key concepts that define these terms and this linkage. Once we leave the rare outright bribery example, it is not at all clear what corruption is—and, as noted earlier, it is even less clear what the appearance of corruption (assuming no *actual* corruption) means.[120] As "small-d democrats," we want voters to try to influence the politicians who seek to represent them and we want them to press numerous levers of influence in order to do so. One particular form of influence—money—is approved for this purpose, yet the law deems it illegitimate only when it exceeds a certain dollar amount stated in the statute. Nor does the law tie contributions to the representative-constituent relationship; as Lessig explains, even those who are not eligible to vote for the candidates and are not directly represented by them can give them money. Supposedly, campaign finance regulation assures public confidence in the electoral and representative processes, but clearly it does just the opposite. Indeed, the more Congress has enacted new reforms to fix the loopholes left in the previous ones, the more cynical the public has become about the system.[121] An intriguing question, then, is why reformers think that new reforms, discussed in the chapter's final section, can somehow erase the growing cynicism that earlier reforms failed to dispel and may even deepen.

Independent Expenditures

The Supreme Court held in *Buckley* that Congress cannot restrict "independent" expenditures, and has reaffirmed that principle on many occasions. The Court's rationale, as noted earlier, was that expenditure limits restrict the freedom of speech and association far less than contribution limits do. They do so, according to the Court, because the quantity of the expenditure directly correlates with the quantity of speech and because its communication value is greater than that of merely writing a check for a contribution.

Both of these reasons are debatable. Although the amount spent may *tend* to correlate with the quantity of speech, this is not certain. And it is hard to see how giving money to a PAC that uses it to urge voters to "elect Smith" communicates any more than does giving money directly to Smith, who goes out and says the same thing. Of course, the PAC might instead use the money to communicate a more substantive, nuanced justification for supporting Smith, which would likely convey more (and more valuable) political information. This possibility may help explain why the Court demands greater leeway for expenditures than for contributions.

But there are several other serious problems with this distinction. One is that spending on behalf of candidates or the positions they espouse can easily become functional equivalents of direct contributions to them and thus undermine the anticorruption-based contribution limits (unless expenditures were also subjected to such limits and those limits were enforceable). For this reason, the Court only accords a higher (more constitutionally protected from regulation) status to expenditures if they are "independent" of the campaign—defined, as we saw earlier, as not being coordinated with it, directly or indirectly. This basic distinction, we also saw, lies at the very heart of the regulatory system, for two reasons: The Court deems it essential to the integrity and effectiveness of the contribution limits, and the First Amendment prohibits other limits on political speech or on spending that constitutes political speech.

Another problem with the distinction is this: Even spending that is in fact independent of the campaign "exacerbate[s] the already disturbing trend toward politics being divorced from the mediating influence of candidates and political parties. . . . Without mediating institutional buffers, money becomes the exclusive coin of the realm as politics pushes toward issue advocacy by groups not engaged in the give and take of party and coalitional politics."[122] Also, it is not clear why a distinction based on fear of corruption should apply at all to spending by parties whose very purpose, which is so essential to our political system, is to influence and promote their own candidates. Here, the notions of independence and corruption seem quite out of place, yet the Court (sharply divided, of course) has applied the distinction to party spending as well.[123] This is a classic case of a regulation begetting more regulation designed to prevent evasion of the first one: If Congress is to limit *parties'* spending for candidates, then it must also limit contributions by individual citizens to either parties or candidates.*

The fact that so much, legally, turns on the independence of these expenditures raises an obvious question: In reality, how independent are "independent" expenditures? Much depends on how assiduously the FEC can and does police this boundary. Here, the agency is (by congressional design) notoriously toothless, usually deadlocked by a 3–3 partisan division on important issues. In practice, campaigns and Super PACs use a variety of well-known ploys and loopholes to circumvent the FEC's restrictions on coordination of spending and message, while the agency temporizes[124] or looks the other way.[125] Consider just two recent examples. Hillary Clinton was still testifying before the House committee investigating the Benghazi incident when her Super PAC responded in detail to committee members'

---

* Chief Justice Roberts referred to this dynamic as "prophylaxis-upon-prophylaxis." *Wisconsin Right to Life v. F.E.C.*, 551 U.S. 449, 479 (2007).

criticisms of her conduct.[126] And Super PACs are now going far beyond sponsoring advertisements, actually conducting many basic
ground operations—field work, data collection, voter registration—
for candidates[127] and increasing their control over candidates.[128] The
coordination ban is meaningless in a political world where parties,
interest groups, candidates, media, and many other sources constantly interact in and manipulate an extremely complex field of sub-
tle influences, intimate relationships among the players, anticipated
reactions, and winks and nods.

Issue ads are an important example of this enforcement dilemma.
These ads, after all, are core political discourse. They are not linked
explicitly to a candidate, yet they effectively aid those candidates who
share the substantive position that the ads advocate at the expense of
their opponents who oppose it. And the ads' sponsors, of course, intend precisely this competitive effect. Yet even if they contain little
actual substantive discussion of issues, they are constitutionally protected from regulation unless they use certain "magic words" that ex-
hort their audience, explicitly or implicitly, to support particular candidates. These words are seldom necessary; it is ordinarily quite
obvious which candidate the sponsor supports.

Indeed, candidates' parties and other supporters exploited this
loophole so easily that the BCRA was enacted partly to close it. Among
other things, the statute limited electioneering communications—
broadcast ads that refer to a "clearly identified candidate" within
thirty days of a primary or caucus or within sixty days of a general
election, and that is also "targeted to the relevant electorate." Invoking
the distinction between impermissible "express advocacy" on behalf
of a candidate, and permissible "issue advocacy" on behalf of an idea,
the Court in *McConnell* upheld this BCRA limit on electioneering
communications.

Also straining any commonsense notion of independence are certain practices of Super PACs, whose expenditures must be independent lest they be deemed contributions subject to the statutory limits.
The *Harvard Law Review* has described these practices:

This basic notion of Super PACs as independent of candidates is becoming increasingly attenuated with the growth and development of Super PACs, especially a new form of Super PAC focused on electing a single candidate. Single-candidate Super PACs are often set up and funded by former aides, family, or close friends of the favored candidate for the express purpose of electing that candidate. For example, the "Restore Our Future" Super PAC dedicated to electing Governor Mitt Romney as President in 2012, and "Priorities USA," a similar Super PAC focused on reelecting President Barack Obama, were run by former aides of the candidates the Super PACs were dedicated to supporting. Beginning with the 2012 election, major candidates were put at a serious competitive disadvantage if they were not supported by at least one Super PAC. In the 2012 elections, all of the serious presidential candidates had single-candidate Super PACs supporting them.* ... Super PACs are often able to outspend the candidates they support, without contribution limits as an imposition. The major role Super PACs have come to play in U.S. elections over a short span of time has only served to diminish candidates' incentives to remain completely independent from these new groups and to fuel the fire behind collaborative fundraising efforts.... After the major impact these new Super PACs had in the 2010 elections, candidates rushed to take advantage of any opportunity to assist these groups in their fundraising efforts, and the FEC obliged. Candidate assistance with Super PAC fund-raising has taken several forms.

Candidates may attend Super PAC–hosted fundraisers, and may solicit contributions up to the federal limits on behalf of those groups. Candidates may use common vendors with Super PACs, such as fundraising consultants, which often raises questions about whether these vendors are improperly sharing nonpublic information between the candidates and Super PACs. Super PACs

---

* Bernie Sanders is the proverbial exception that proves the rule. His presidential campaign, eschewing any Super PACs, raised a huge sum in small donations.

also may solicit contributions from the wealthy family and friends of a candidate above the amounts the candidate would be able to solicit directly, sometimes even using lists of potential donors supplied by the candidate.[129]

Responding to these sorts of ploys, California's Fair Political Practices Commission adopted rules in October 2015 to prohibit these evasions of the coordination ban in state and local elections.[130] But whether they too will be evaded by winks and nods among candidates, parties, and their supporters remains to be seen.

Another kind of faux "independence" designed to avoid the contribution limits takes the form of 501(c) (4) groups, organized under that section of the tax code to promote "social welfare." The tax code allows them to spend some portion of their funds on public education about politics, and they are not required to identify their donors/ members. While barred from spending to back particular candidates, they may under certain conditions donate to groups that do. According to the *New York Times*, at least one 501(c)(4) was obviously advocating for Senator Marco Rubio during his 2016 presidential campaign, running little risk of enforcement action by either the tax authorities or the FEC.[131] Surely, other such dark money groups will do (or are already doing) the same for other candidates.

Incumbency

The relationship between incumbency and the campaign finance debate is pivotal. Most campaign contributions go to incumbents in Congress* or the White House (during a first term): donors want to return incumbents to powerful positions where they can (continue to) benefit the donors and their causes. And this incumbency advantage compounds others: seniority in Congress, name recognition, franking

---

* In 2012, the average incumbent House member raised nearly six times the amount raised by the average challenger. For the Senate, the average incumbent raised 8.5 times as much as the average challenger (based on data from https://www.opensecrets.org/big picture/incumbs.php?cycle=2012). Corresponding data for the incumbency effect in the 2014 elections were presented earlier.

privileges, knowledge of the district, experienced staff, favorable districting maps, voter partisanship, and others. Partly for this reason, representatives win reelection at very high rates (as do presidents).* (Another reason is that constituents tend to like their own representatives even while scorning the institution as a whole.) From 1976 to 2010, reelection rates in the House have averaged more than 90 percent, while Senate rates have fluctuated between 79 and 96 percent.[132] In 2014, the reelection rate was 95 percent in the House and 82 percent in the Senate.[133] Ironically, as noted above by Bradley Smith, the much-reviled *Citizens United* decision seems to have *reduced* the incumbency advantage somewhat.

Respectable arguments can be made that high incumbent reelection rates serve us well. As Persily puts it, "high turnover and a constant fear of replacement may lead to fewer representatives with the expertise and the long-term relationships necessary to build trust. Paradoxically, the more effective the electoral check on incumbent behavior, the less willing the average legislator may be to compromise."[134] To this, I would add that incumbents are likely to be better than newcomers at understanding the politics and policy of government programs, and thus better at controlling the bureaucrats who administer them. Trade-offs are unavoidable here as everywhere else in political design.

For present purposes, however, the most salient facts about incumbents are these: They write the campaign finance rules, influence how the FEC will enforce them, and have strong incentives and opportunities to use that power to shape campaign finance regulation to enhance their own electoral prospects and weaken those of potential challengers. In *Buckley*, those challenging the contribution limits cited these incumbency advantages as reasons to invalidate the limits, but the Court rejected this argument on the ground that the limits were the same for all candidates,[135] which of course raises the question of whether this formal equality in the face of immense incum-

---

* To be sure, incumbents are not the only ones who benefit from the high reelection rate. The greater legislative experience, policy continuity, and influence on legislation and with the agencies that goes along with incumbency all can benefit the electorate as well.

bency advantage misses the real point. These realities help to explain why past reforms have been so easily evaded, why the public has little confidence in what past reforms have wrought, and why future reforms should be approached with extreme skepticism.

Although the Court's reason for treating incumbency advantages as constitutionally irrelevant is unpersuasive, another justification for doing so has more heft. Incumbency is just one of many variables that may favor or disfavor candidates electorally, albeit a very important one, as we have seen. (Incumbency can sometimes be riskier, especially in a severe economic downturn or a Watergate-type scandal.) But although it is usually very advantageous, I see no principled reason to insist that Congress design the various contribution and other limits to compensate for this factor while leaving the others unregulated. Nor can the Court determine reliably just how much of an advantage incumbency is, either in general or in any particular campaign.

Distinctions among Types of Speakers

The Court's campaign finance decisions have included some statements that are at least superficially inconsistent. On the one hand, as noted earlier, it has emphasized that the First Amendment prohibits "restrictions distinguishing among different speakers; Congress can't allow speech by some but not others."[136] On the other hand, the campaign finance statutes have long drawn such distinctions—for example, prohibiting both contributions and independent expenditures by foreigners and agents of foreign governments, and banning both corporations and unions from using their general treasury funds to make campaign contributions.* In another example of differentiation, Con-

---

* The reasons for banning the use of treasury funds are both the large potential infusions coming from those funds and the view that politically diverse union members and corporate shareholders should not have their common funds used for political purposes.

The Court's position may remind some readers of Anatole France's quip about the law's "majestic equality [that] forbids the rich as well as the poor to sleep under bridges, to beg in the streets, and to steal bread."

gress imposes different contribution limits on donors depending on whether they are parties, PACs, or other groups.

This issue came to a head in *Citizens United* where the Court divided on, among other things, whether corporations enjoyed full First Amendment rights. (The Court had earlier recognized the importance of voters receiving information from corporations about issues affecting business,[137] but not corporations' *own* speech rights per se.)[138] Many critics of *Citizens United* insist that corporations are merely artificial persons, not real, flesh-and-blood ones, and that their resources are so vast that they can in effect buy elections. In the decision, the Court allowed corporations to make unlimited independent expenditures on campaigns, holding that "[t]he Government may regulate corporate political speech through disclaimer and disclosure requirements, but it may not suppress that speech altogether."[139] In doing so, it overruled a 1990 decision, *Austin v. Michigan Chamber of Commerce*,[140] that had allowed a state to ban political speech based on the speaker's corporate identity. The Court in *Citizens United* held that *Austin* contradicted the line of cases barring restrictions on political speech based on the speaker's corporate identity or its wealth. *Austin's* logic, it reasoned, would allow Congress to bar wealthy media companies from paying for their own political speech* even though a corporation must publicly disclose its campaign spending but need not disclose most of its other efforts to influence government. Tracking *Buckley's* finding that contributions and expenditures have different relationships to quid pro quo corruption, the *Citizens United* majority held that corporations' independent expenditures did not cause it, and that the fact that some shareholders might disagree with the corporation's political speech through independent expenditures could not justify banning it. For all these reasons, it also overruled the part of *McConnell* that had limited such expenditures.

The dissenting justices, in a forceful opinion written by Justice Stevens (his last on the Court), noted that prior laws and the Court's

---

* Congress has not yet done this; a BCRA provision exempts such companies from the corporate expenditure ban.

own decisions had restricted corporations' political activities more than the activities of others in order to reduce the special risks of corruption posed by the use of corporate treasury funds. In any event, Stevens argued, the Citizens United group remained free to speak by contributing to its own PAC or by electioneering before BCRA's time limits kicked in. But Stevens challenged an even more fundamental tenet of the Court's canon: its "crabbed view of corruption" under which quid pro quo corruption was the only compelling concern that could justify regulation, thereby preventing Congress from targeting the "undue influence" on politics exerted by corporate money. In reality, he insisted, such influence was immense, with "distinctive corrupting potential" and the risks of drowning out noncorporate voices and "undermining self-government."

Again, powerful arguments exist on both sides of this issue of whether Congress can regulate some speakers but not (or more than) others. In favor of regulation, we do not want our electoral and political systems unduly influenced by wealthy individuals and corporations. As we have seen, such individuals donate a very high fraction of campaign contributions, and there can be no doubt that their contributions give them greater access to politicians; these donors both demand and command their attention and presumably assume that they are getting value for their money.[141] Some presumably view this as a political investment.[142] In this sense—and also in the sense, discussed earlier, that speech today requires money in order to reach and persuade an audience—money does talk. When one adds to these individual donations the large amounts spent by PACs, Super PACs, and other putatively independent entities—linked to already powerful corporate, labor union, and other well-organized interests—the danger of drowning out the voices of the vast majority of ordinary Americans becomes profound and perilous to our democracy. Indeed, even very large individual campaign contributors say that they no longer plan to contribute to campaigns because even their contributions are submerged in campaigns now dominated by Super PAC spending.[143]

But there are also strong arguments against giving Congress the power to distinguish among types of speakers.

- Some speakers, especially media, already have their own mega-phones—usually highly tendentious ones—that cannot constitutionally be constrained. It is hard to see why some speakers should be limited when the *New York Times*, *Wall Street Journal*, Fox TV, MSNBC, social media, and countless other publications are free to spend as much money as they like to speak and exercise political influence.

- Apart from the serious First Amendment issues that legislative efforts to control money in elections raise, such efforts inevitably create distortion and favoritism. For example, they make it harder for challengers to mount effective challenges to incumbents, magnify the effects of non-monetary factors in elections, and constrain candidates' communications with voters.

- As discussed in the next section, the factual premise of the concern about plutocracy appears to be false, or at least greatly exaggerated.

Money and Electoral Outcomes

The discussion of the amounts, sources, and types of campaign contributions and spending raise perhaps the most important question: How does this money actually affect electoral outcomes? Campaign reform advocates routinely insist that money buys elections and votes in Congress, and that it goes disproportionately to conservative candidates. Yet political scientists who study these questions consistently find that the effect of campaign spending at the margin is either small or shows no regular, discernible pattern. Raymond La Raja and Brian Schaffner, for example, studied states that allowed unlimited spending by corporations and/or unions and found that this spending had little or no effect on partisan outcomes and incumbency reelection rates.[144] In fact, for contributions that the parties report to the FEC (not including their informal networks), the Democrats have been raising more money than the Republicans: In the 2008 presidential election, the Democrats' margin was $41.8 million and this widened to $47.3 million in 2012 and promises to be even larger in 2016. In the 2014 congressional elections, the gap was $189.3 million; in 2010 it was even larger, $230.4 million.[145] What best explains outcomes—even more than the many *non-monetary* resources listed earlier in the section on incumbency—are the politician's (and his or her party's) ideology, voting record, campaign "ground game," and constituents' preferences.

The canonical study was conducted by Stephen Ansolabehere and colleagues and published in 2003.[146] The study's conclusion (omitting methodological discussion) is straightforward—and contradicts the common claims:

> An extensive literature exists that attempts to measure the political efficacy of interest group donations. Almost all research on donors' influence in legislative politics examines the effects of contributions on roll call votes cast by members of Congress. Dozens of studies have considered the effects of contributions on legislative votes, across hundreds of pieces of legislation. We surveyed nearly 40 articles in economics and political science that examine the relationship between PAC contributions and congressional voting behavior. . . . Overall, PAC contributions show relatively few effects on voting behavior. In three out of four instances, campaign contributions had no statistically significant effects on legislation or had the "wrong" sign—suggesting that more contributions lead to less support. . . . Overall, our findings parallel that of the broader literature. As regressions like these make clear, the evidence that campaign contributions lead to a substantial influence on votes is rather thin. Legislators' votes depend almost entirely on their own beliefs and the preferences of their voters and their party. Contributions explain a miniscule fraction of the variation in voting behavior in the U.S. Congress. Members of Congress care foremost about winning re-election. They must attend to the constituency that elects them, voters in a district or state and the constituency that nominates them, the party. . . . This finding helps to explain why there is so little money in politics relative to the enormous payoffs to organized interests in influencing government policy

[known as "Tullock's puzzle"].* Money has little leverage because it is only a small part of the political calculation that a re-election oriented legislator makes. And interest group contributors—the "investors" in the political arena—have little leverage because politicians can raise sufficient funds from individual contributors. It is true that when economic interest groups give, they usually appear to act as rational investors. . . . However, this "investor" money from organized groups accounts for only a small fraction of overall campaign funds. Since interest groups can get only a little from their contributions, they give only a little. As a result, interest group contributions account for at most a small amount of the variation in voting behavior. *In fact, after controlling for legislator ideology, these contributions have no detectable effects on the behavior of legislators.* (emphasis added)[147]

A 2012 literature review by Ansolabehere on the same issue reached the same conclusions.[148] Other political scientists—most notably in a

---

* The study's authors deepen this puzzle by noting the billions of dollars contributed in each campaign cycle, the proliferation of corporate PACs (and now Super PACs), and the many millions of individuals who make campaign contributions (almost all of which are small, as we have seen). They then go on to explain this conduct using a number of different datasets to test whether campaign contributions are more affected by income growth and thus are a form of consumption, or instead by government spending growth and thus are political investments:

> In our view, campaign contributing should not be viewed as an investment, but rather as a form of consumption—or, in the language of politics, participation. Recall that almost all money in the existing campaign finance system comes ultimately from individuals and in relatively small sums. We therefore expect that the factors that determine why individuals give are the factors that drive total campaign spending. The tiny size of the average contribution made by private citizens suggests that little private benefit could be bought with such donations. Instead, individuals give because they are ideologically motivated, because they are excited by the politics of particular elections, because they are asked by their friends or colleagues and because they have the resources necessary to engage in this particular form of participation. In short, people give to politics because of the consumption value associated with politics, rather than because they receive direct private benefits. Those who give to politics are also disproportionately likely to participate in other ways, including attending meetings, writing letters, talking to others and voting. . . . They account for most of the campaign money in politics. Political giving should be regarded as a form of consumption not unlike giving to charities, such as the United Way or public radio.

2014 article by Martin Gilens and Benjamin Page—find that economic elites and business-oriented groups have much more impact on policy decisions than average citizens and mass-based interest groups do.[149] This article, however, does not challenge (or even cite) the Ansolabehere et al. analysis. Indeed, their article is not about campaign finance at all, so it does not discuss the effect, if any, of contributions and spending on policy outcomes. The substantial elite influence on policy outcomes that Gilens and Page find has many possible sources; after all, wealthier people engage in *every* form of political activity more than poorer ones do: writing letters, attending meetings, voting in primaries and general elections, contributing, lobbying, and much else.[150] And as noted earlier, the amount of money spent on lobbying, which is not regulated, vastly exceeds that spent on campaign contributions.

Finally, there is the vital question of what causes what. Because correlation does not prove causation, campaign contributions *might* occur because potential contributors are attracted to winning candidates (not just incumbents) and their positions, rather than because contributions cause their electoral victories. Of course, both of these propositions could be, and likely are, true to some extent and at the same time.

Effects of Campaign Finance Regulation on Parties and Other Actors

The laws that regulate campaign contributions and spending affect the political system and its actors in various ways. Perhaps the most important effect is to diminish the role and effectiveness of parties. Today, the parties cannot control the flow of money into campaigns, which gives them that much less leverage over the candidates, their messages, and their tactics in elections.

In preparation for the primaries before the 2016 conventions, for example, the candidates had to move quickly to attract media attention and tie up large donors early, declining exploratory committees and opting for Super PAC fund-raising instead.* *New York Times* ana-

---

* But contributions to campaigns and to Super PACs are to some extent a zero-sum game. Wealthy traditional donors say that they are withholding donations from the former

lyst Nate Cohen finds that "[a]long with Internet fund-raising, Super PACs are helping to form an alternative campaign finance model that is eroding party control over the primary process."[151] Other party-weakening factors such as the growing bloc of independent voters and the rise of non-party media platforms (discussed below) also induce candidates to rely less on the party apparatus to approve or shape their campaigns. Candidates rely increasingly on non-party staff and resources: media handlers, campaign consultants, voting data analysts, election and campaign finance law experts, special accountants, contribution bundlers, etc. Independent candidacies, always hard to mount, are even more so now due to these and other (e.g., ballot access rules) high barriers to entry.

This marginalization of parties by non-party staff and resources is not new, and its causes go well beyond campaign finance patterns. Hostility to parties goes back to the earliest days of the Republic, captured most famously in James Madison's critique of factions in Federalist No. 10,[152] and later institutionalized in Progressive Era reforms designed to weaken parties, reforms that remain with us particularly at the state and local levels (where parties are strongest). These anti-party measures—always promoted as "more democracy"—included referenda and recall procedures; non-partisan elections; judicial elections; direct election of U.S. senators; requirements that delegates to national conventions be selected through primaries and caucuses over which party leaders have little influence; "sunshine" laws that ban closed-door meetings; bans on legislative earmarks; and the kinds of campaign finance rules analyzed in this chapter.[153]

Today's parties are in particularly bad odor due to gridlock[154] in Congress (although, as discussed below, this gridlock probably reflects their weakness more than their strength); growing disaffection with Washington; voters' higher levels of education and sophistication; more self-styled independents; and the new online platforms

---

because the latter dwarfs their efforts. http://www.wsj.com/articles/big-obama-donors-stay-on-sidelines-in-2016-race-1447375429

that sow disdain for parties and have replaced some of their traditional functions.

Even so, the case for strong parties remains even more compelling today than it was in 1950 when the American Political Science Association issued its important "Toward a More Responsible Two-Party System"[155]—more compelling because we now know what happens when party control is attenuated. A politics dominated by entrepreneurial candidates—unmediated, unvetted, untested, and unconstrained by parties—conduces to disorganization, irresponsibility, opportunism, and inability to deliver on promises. For all their flaws, parties perform their crucial, traditional functions, albeit in a different environment. They have the strongest possible incentives to recruit solid, marketable candidates, provide coherent ideological choices, develop realistic policy options, organize legislative activity, and simplify voter choice. Given limited voter information and interest, party identification makes voter choice more rational than otherwise (e.g., just voting for the first name on the ballot). In a country in which politics is merely a sideshow for most voters most of the time (as political scientist Jack Citrin has noted), parties maintain a steady commitment to it. In contrast to today's many narcissistic, flash-in-the-pan candidates (including Donald Trump), the parties are oriented to the long term, determined to maintain their brands. They provide stabilizing ballast against transient follies and enthusiasms.

In the summary below I distill the debate about parties and suggest how they can be strengthened.

Disclosure

Today's campaign finance disclosure rules were enacted long before *Citizens United* and the proliferation of unregulated independent expenditures by non-party groups that need not disclose their memberships. They were also enacted before the Internet made cheap, rapid, easily accessible information dissemination possible. Such changes make disclosure policy an even greater area of contention than before.

Opponents maintain that mandatory disclosure violates donors' privacy rights and, on highly controversial issues, may even cause adverse publicity and intimidation, thus burdening their acts of citizenship and reducing their giving. Disclosure advocates, in contrast, tend to downplay the importance of donors' privacy interests. They emphasize that *public* office is at stake, after all, and that transparency will increase the legitimacy of, and public confidence in, a campaign finance system in which private donors provide most of the campaign funds used by parties and candidates.* This view also taps into a common concern, discussed earlier, about excessive influence by moneyed interests in politics. Finally, disclosure enables citizens who must decide how to vote to take into account which candidates accept money from which donors, according that factor whatever weight they wish. But even when disclosure requirements are favored, their particular design—what must be disclosed and in how much detail, reports' format, frequency, and user-friendliness, the penalties for non- or tardy compliance, their enforceability, and so forth—remain important regulatory issues.

Many states and localities impose their own disclosure requirements, which vary considerably among jurisdictions. In reviewing these laws under the First Amendment, the Supreme Court—including in *Citizens United*—has largely sided with the disclosure advocates, upholding mandated disclosures against constitutional challenge. In *Doe v. Reed*,[156] a 2010 ruling, it upheld a state law requiring disclosure of petition signers for a referendum on a measure to protect domestic partnerships. Subjecting disclosure requirements to a less demanding standard of review than the Court applies to restrictions on speech, the justices (with Justice Thomas dissenting) upheld the requirement despite claims that it would invite anti-gay harass-

---

* The statute authorizes public funds to help pay for conventions and, if candidates accept them, presidential campaigns.

ment of disclosed signers. The Court found no specific evidence to support this fear, but it noted that a future challenger might show that compelled disclosure would subject signers to "threats, harassment, or reprisals from either Government officials or private parties," perhaps tipping the constitutional balance against disclosure. The empirical evidence on how disclosure laws actually affect behavior is thin, but a new study that exploits state-state and before-and-after differences in these laws and practices finds that they affect contribution patterns only negligibly, regardless of donation size and ideology.[157] Another study, however, indicates that setting a disclosure threshold too low, as many states now do, can discourage small donations (a $50 threshold caused past donors to decrease giving by 50 percent), and urges focusing instead on larger ones.[158]

To what extent is disclosure of campaign contributions and spending a substitute for direct controls on those activities? If sunlight is the best disinfectant (as Justice Brandeis claimed), perhaps fuller disclosure in real time would enable watchdog groups and the public to monitor these transactions, expose questionable financial relationships between donors and candidates, and cast votes better informed about these relationships. If direct controls on contributions and spending are unavailing—because, say, they are unconstitutional, unenforceable, too restrictive or costly, or otherwise undesirable—then disclosure mandates may be the best available policy option. Still, it seems perverse to require disclosure of $200 contributions while allowing unlimited anonymous spending by outside groups.

Even where direct controls are constitutional, of course, people will still have different answers to key policy questions about optimal trade-offs among conflicting values—for example, between transparency and conflict-of-interest rules, on the one hand, and the secrecy needed for political bargaining, on the other. Some values may not conflict much or at all (e.g., limiting large contributions and requiring disclosure), but policy trade-offs in campaign finance policy abound.

Indeed, one might think that transparency through greater disclosure would be a no-brainer—but one would be wrong. Indeed, Congress's omnibus 2016 budget law barred regulators from even considering tougher disclosure rules for corporate donors and Super PACs.[159] And as noted earlier, existing disclosure rules for these groups are easily evaded or rendered opaque when their donors are entities rather than individuals.[160]

Regulation of Online Campaign Activity

Much core campaign work—communication with potential voters and donors about candidates, issues, fund-raising, and mobilization—has moved online since the 2008 campaign, and this movement has snowballed since then. We are only beginning to grapple with the implications of this change, and of related developments such as the massive collection by Facebook and other social media of personal data about voters. With an estimated 78 percent of Americans now having a social network profile of some kind and receiving much of their news through those portals, the risk that this data will be used to influence elections cannot be ruled out. Indeed, anti-Trump employees at Facebook reportedly explored using this data to weaken his candidacy, only to be rebuffed by their superiors.[161]

In an aptly titled essay, "The Campaign Revolution Will Not Be Televised,"[162] Persily argues that our thinking about campaign finance—and about its regulation—is rooted in what is becoming a technological relic: the thirty-second TV ad. Lost in the furor over *Citizens United*, he says, is that the film at issue there (an "ideologically motivated hatchet job") was online and accessible only to those who sought it out, unlike the traditional partisan- and PAC-sponsored TV spot. Online voter-targeting platforms such as Google, Facebook, Amazon, and their ilk, Persily shows, are the main future vehicles for campaign money. As election law expert Richard Hasen explains, regulating them will raise even more constitutional and practical problems than regulating traditional media.[163]

This is a revolutionary change with vast implications for campaign finance. Reformers, Persily notes, have seen TV advertising as a special target for two main reasons that made it a focus of BCRA: its putative power to persuade (and mislead), and the fact that it can be regulated. Internet advertising is altogether different:

> In general, the FEC (and Congress) have left the internet alone when it comes to campaign regulation. [Apart from limited disclosure requirements] online communications are uniquely unregulated. . . . The concern about regulating online communication is well placed. Certain critical concepts in campaign finance law become especially contested in the cyberspace setting. Moreover, any domestic election authority, from whichever country, will find it difficult to enforce regulation on the web—which is worldwide, after all.

Congress and the FEC cannot control online campaign ads as either a practical or legal matter. No federal agency can control a foreign website, nor can it easily distinguish domestic websites from traditional media whose election coverage and endorsements (and the money spent on this) are constitutionally impervious to regulation. Indeed, as Persily points out, any rule that depends on establishing the identity of the speaker would be hard to implement in the online context; "the internet is potentially even more fertile ground for anonymous, unaccountable spending . . . [A] website video could come from any source anywhere in the world. . . . The internet . . . provides the perfect breeding ground for the most polarizing, least accountable, and most finely targeted forms of political communication."

Persily concludes from all this *not* that regulation of online campaign activity is impossible but rather that effective regulation will have to come from the online portals themselves as they refine their existing rules for commercial and other users—about nondiscriminatory access, tone, disclosure, misrepresentation, and fairness—in light of the many new challenges posed by online campaigning and the limited constitutional power of the government to prescribe these rules directly. In this new world, he speculates, "private regulation . . . may be better positioned to preserve democratic values than the government ever could."

SUMMARY

Where does our exploration of these eight issues leave us? In the last section of the chapter, I shall review the leading proposals and approaches for reforming the campaign finance system. But before doing that, it is worth considering how political scientists, election law experts, and other well-informed specialists on American electoral politics come down on these issues and their policy implications. In this debate, one side claims to be "realists" about both the nature of the campaign finance problem and how to reform it, while dismissing the other side as "romantics."* (The so-called romantics in turn claim that they are the *true* realists.)

The modern version of the debate began back in the 1950s when leading political scientists began to conduct detailed theoretical and empirical studies of political parties as distinctive organizational types. Any organization, they argued, is constrained and defined by three types of incentives—material, ideological, and solidary—each with its characteristic advantages and disadvantages. Parties deploy different versions and mixes of these incentives to attract and motivate their workers and supporters enough to win elections, to govern once in office, and to perpetuate the party's effectiveness.† Traditionally, parties in many states and cities (Albany and Chicago, for example) were political machines that relied mainly on patronage (jobs, contracts, favors) and other material benefits to secure and retain power, often in unprincipled, corrupt ways. Their leaders were political professionals skilled at bargaining behind closed doors. Opposing them were predominantly middle-class, "clean government" reformers who, like Progressive-Era reformers, wanted to use antiparty measures to dismantle the machines and replace them with more public-spirited, honest, policy-oriented, transparent, participatory, efficient government.

---

* Other analysts label them "pragmatists" and "purists." Raymond J. La Raja & Brian F. Schaffner, *Campaign Finance and Political Polarization: When Purists Prevail* (2015).

† Especially in the old days, party leaders also used these resources to enrich themselves and their allies.

When scholars like Edward Banfield, James Q. Wilson, and Martin Meyerson at the University of Chicago studied both kinds of organizations (and their variants), they found that the machine organizations tended to govern more effectively than the more idealistic reformers did. The pathologies of the former (e.g., graft) were well understood, but those of the latter were less familiar. In a remarkably prescient 1962 book, Wilson carefully analyzed how these antiparty reform groups ("amateur Democrats," he called them) actually worked in three large cities. He found certain endemic, politically dysfunctional patterns. Given their members' more idealistic, antiparty beliefs, they found it harder than machines did to overcome free-rider and other obstacles to collective action, to impose internal discipline and hierarchical decision making and thus avoid divisive primary and leadership battles, and to compromise enough to get their platforms enacted and implemented. To mobilize voters and resources, they had to rely heavily on hard-to-control media and inflexible ideological appeals rather than the kinds of material and other incentives that are not tied closely to abstract principles (Wilson called them "issue-free resources"). This bias produced frequent schisms. It made it harder for the Democrats in amateur-dominated cities to attract the mass of less educated voters who cared more about their material needs, because the reformers, constrained by their distinctive mode of politics, often could not deliver the goods.

This perspective deeply informs the current debate among social scientists and policy makers about the trends, actual effects, and reform of campaign finance. The most recent chapter occurred in 2015 when Jonathan Rauch, a Brookings Institution analyst, published "Political Realism: How Hacks, Machines, Big Money, and Backroom Deals Can Strengthen American Democracy."[164] In this essay, Rauch presented an updated version of the old Chicago defense of strong party organizations controlling their candidates with top-down discipline, policy direction, staff support, and money. Calling this a "realist" defense of "transactional politics," he sharply contrasted it with "idealistic political reforms." Government needs a modern version of machines, Rauch argued, because only professional deal-makers (often dismissed by reformers as "party hacks") can "negotiate compromises and make them stick." Echoing Wilson, he recalled the long war waged by progressive, populist, and libertarian reformers against machines "by weakening political insiders' control of money, nominations, negotiations, and other essential tools of political leadership. . . . *Reforms' fixations on corruption and participation, although perhaps appropriate a long time ago, have become destabilizing and counterproductive*, contributing to the rise of privatized pseudo-machines that make governing more difficult and politics less accountable" (emphasis mine).

Rauch quoted Wilson's prescient prediction about how such reforms would cause gridlock: "The need to employ issues as incentives and to distinguish one's party from the opposition along policy lines will mean that political conflict will be intensified, social cleavages will be exaggerated, party leaders will tend to be men skilled in the rhetorical arts, and the party's ability to produce agreement by trading issue-free resources will be reduced." Rauch has a strong critique of how FECA, BCRA (he and many other realists opposed it), and other recent reforms have perversely rendered money's role in politics more corrosive, not less. I quote him at some length just below for three reasons. His provocative view of how campaign finance reforms have magnified the role of unaccountable money—well before *Citizens United*—is shared by many if not most of the nonpartisan experts in the field. It accords with my own views of how our politics does and should work (views honed as Wilson's student and erstwhile coeditor). And it helps one assess many of the reform proposals discussed in the final section.

> The first wave of progressivism, a century ago, took aim at dishonest graft, like bribery and extortion, and also at some forms of "honest graft," such as featherbedding and patronage, but it left ordinary political donations mostly alone. Disappointed by the results, a second wave, beginning in the 1970s, spread the net much more widely, establishing a web of legalistic rules and regulations which have made it much harder for candidates and par-

ties to raise money, on the general theory that fundraising and dependence on big-dollar donors are inherently corrupting. The result was not to reduce the amount of money in politics or to reduce the influence of special interests but to drive money to unrestricted channels, such as party committees. When progressive legislation restricted those channels too, the result was to push money into so-called "independent" spending by super PACS, nonprofit organizations, billionaires, and other actors who are less accountable, less pragmatic, and less transparent than Tammany ever was. To be sure, many social and political changes, not just progressive laws and regulations, have contributed to the growth of the gray market for political money. Some of what is happening would have happened anyway. But to acknowledge as much does not get the progressive paradigm off the hook: its raison d'être for four decades or more has been to sequester political professionals from political money, opening the way for amateurs to take over the job. Raymond La Raja, a political scientist, . . . points out that money raised by party committees almost tripled in real dollars from 1988 to 2004. After [BCRA] banned unrestricted donations to parties, party fundraising went into a mild decline—and spending by outside groups rushed in to fill the gap, going from trivial in the 1990s to $1 billion or so by 2012. "The campaign finance system has strengthened the hand of partisan activists by limiting the flow of financial resources to the formal party organization and its technocratic staff," he writes. "The campaign finance rules constrain coherent, party-based organizing to such an extent that partisans have sidestepped the rules to create organizations such as super PACs." To organize coalitions and deals, political machines need to talk to and organize their networks and supporters. But that imperative runs afoul of the weirdest and most perverse of modern progressive obsessions: the attempt to restrict "coordination" of campaign efforts between political parties and either their own candidates or their outside supporters. In the progressive worldview, limiting the money which private interests can give directly to candidates and parties does little good if the interests can pretend to spend independently while quietly letting candidates and parties direct the spending. For progressives, in other words, coordination is a way of circumventing the quarantine on political contributions. For a machine, of course, coordination with a party is something else: the whole point of politics. If a machine can't organize, assist, and direct its politicians and supporters, it might as well not exist. "The restrictions on party coordination force parties to spend 'independently' of candidates," writes La Raja. "This arrangement is not only a parody of what parties are about in most democracies, but encourages inefficient use of resources (hence ever more money is needed), legal gamesmanship, and diminished political accountability."

Predictably, trying to disconnect politicians and parties from each other and their supporters has created a gray market in coordination; driven resources, professional talent, and influence to unaccountable outside groups; hindered candidates' and parties' ability to control and transmit their message; and underwritten the growth of a burgeoning independent political infrastructure which is difficult (at best) for leaders to organize and influence. Even in principle, efforts to define and ban unacceptable "consultation" and "cooperation" criminalize politics arbitrarily. For example, conservative groups in Wisconsin have been investigated and raided by state prosecutors for spending money on issue ads in consultation with Governor Scott Walker, a form of political collaboration which a federal judge ruled is perfectly legal. Overturning that ruling, a federal appeals court threw up its hands: "The Supreme Court has yet to determine what 'coordination' means." The kinds of questions which the appeals court said await resolution are hopelessly metaphysical: for example, "What if the [coordinated] speech implies, rather than expresses, a preference for a particular candidate's election?" It's hard to assemble power in government if consulting or cooperating with the people you are assembling is a criminal act—or if you can't tell whether it's a criminal act.[165]

This, then, is the essence of the "realist" case for rejecting the basic thrust of FECA and BCRA, modulating transparency in order to facilitate political negotiations, and returning to a system in which parties are strengthened by channeling more of the money and competitive resources through party institutions controlled by party professionals who define its policy positions and political behavior. This case has been embraced by many prominent scholars of American politics such as James Q. Wilson, Nelson Polsby, Bruce Cain, Francis Fukuyama, Jack Citrin, Nathaniel Persily, Richard Pildes, Raymond La Raja, Nolan McCarty, and Stephen Ansolabehere. I shall say a bit more about this party-strengthening approach in the final section.

The "realist" view has not gone unchallenged. Perhaps the sharpest response comes from political scientists E. J. Dionne (who is also a leading columnist) and Thomas Mann, both affiliated with the Brookings Institution and prominent advocates of the BCRA reforms.[166] They criticize the self-styled realists as "romantics" who ignore the public's reasons for rejecting machine politics and who are "fundamentally mistaken in much of their diagnosis of what ails our democracy and in many of the treatments they suggest." Acknowledging that parties and transactional politics have their place in our system and that citizens vary in their attentiveness to politics, they accuse the realists of naivete about the parties that Mann and Dionne see as "more receptacles of money than the pragmatic, center-seeking, coalition-building mechanisms the realists describe."

The real problem with FECA and BCRA, say Mann and Dionne, is not the reforms but how the Supreme Court perverted them in *Citizens United* with its false description of the current system. Many other commentators agree.[167] Political scientists Jacob Hacker and Paul Pierson, along with Mann, Dionne and others, add that Congress's polarization is now *asymmetric*: The Republican Party has become far more conservative and extreme than the Democrats have become more liberal.[168] It eschews compromise more than the Democrats do and uses the filibuster in the Senate irresponsibly. Hacker and Pierson predict that the ideological nature of today's parties and the fierce partisanship this produces will remain for the foreseeable future. The realists, they say, cannot reverse this but should instead deal with it. To Mann and Dionne, the great evil is corruption, and they impugn the realists' argument by identifying it with "Gilded Age politics, a period when political party leaders managing the large sums of money that came their way from well-endowed political interests had far more control over political outcomes."

> On this matter, our views could not be more distant from theirs. The threat to our system comes precisely from the growing power of concentrated political contributions. Redirecting these to the parties will not improve either the responsiveness or the efficiency of the political system. And the truth is that the parties themselves are already deeply complicit in the new money system. Giving more money to formal party structures would make little difference to the operation of government or the conduct of campaigns, but it would further tilt the system toward large donors. . . . If the goal of the realists is to strengthen parties, they should join rather than resist reformers in rolling back the Wild West world of political money that Citizens United and lax-to-non-existent regulation by the FEC have created. . . . Many of our governing problems are rooted precisely in machine-like political behavior: partisan gerrymanders, proliferating legal barriers to voting, a gutted Voting Rights Act, a primary system that fosters low-turnouts, and the oversized role of moneyed interests in shaping legislation. . . . The breakdown in governing that the realists are trying to cure was not caused by the reforms they so fervently criticize. Our system hit a crisis point later, most dramatically during President Obama's time in office, when asymmetric polarization took hold and the intense competition between the parties for control of Congress and the White House drove the oppositional politics of today.

Mann and Dionne especially dispute realist claims that the campaign finance reforms have weakened the parties. Today's Congress, they say, exhibits "the highest rate of party voting in the electorate and in

Congress in at least a century,"* and today's parties are "bigger players in the financing of federal elections than any time since the beginning of the Progressive Era more than a century ago." Mann and Dionne also dispute the claim that the reforms have simply moved the money outside of party control:

> It is a mistake to assume that all or most non-party independent spending committees are separate from the parties. Here, too, the parties have adapted. Both parties have informally affiliated super PACs run by former party officials and operatives who act as surrogates for the party leaders. Another group of party-aligned super PACs established by traditional allies has, with few exceptions, followed the spending lead of party central. Even the non-aligned groups play almost exclusively in one party or the other, including those like Club for Growth and the Koch's Americans for Prosperity that got their starts well before BCRA and were spurred by differences with the "mainstream" party leadership. The major exception is single-candidate super PACs, which operate mostly in the battles for presidential nominations and account for much of the outside spending.

Other reformers join Mann and Dionne in criticizing the view of many realists that transparency and conflict-of-interest rules are often ineffective and have been oversold.[169]

The divide between these two camps, then, is wide indeed and applies to a whole range of empirical and normative issues. It is not surprising, then, that they, along with other analysts, differ as well about how best to approach campaign finance reform as a policy matter. This is the subject to which I now devote the final section of the chapter.

---

* Some political scientists who acknowledge this fact about party-line voting see it instead as institutional weakness. Under conditions of divided government, "such strong parties pose particular obstacles (all else equal) because the president then has fewer members of the ruling party in Congress that he or she can peel off to help enact preferred legislation." Nathaniel Persily, ed., *Solutions to Political Polarization in America* (2015), 5.

REFORM PROPOSALS

The notion that our campaign finance system is "broken" and desperately needs fixing is so commonplace as to be conventional wisdom. It is routinely denounced as grotesque, plutocratic, cancerous, and barely disguised corruption—an excrescence on American democracy. At a time when popular agreement about important policy directions is notoriously elusive, this pervasive contempt for the campaign finance system and demand for reform approaches a consensus.

David Strauss, a law professor whose analysis is discussed below, notes a "curious feature" of these reform proposals: "the cure often precedes the diagnosis; and the diagnosis, when provided, is often a little vague."[170] He is right; neither the consensus nor the jeremiads against the system tell us much about just *why* or *how* it should be reformed. The critiques come from different directions and invoke diverse normative premises and inconsistent factual claims—as the debate between the realists and their opponents shows. Those disputants differ on whether (among other things) there is too much money in politics, more of it should flow through the parties, transparency is always a good thing, contributions corrupt politics, and politicians can alter the status quo. Many politicians, to be sure, join the reform chorus. They claim to find "dialing for dollars" demeaning, time-consuming, and a perverse diversion from their more important legislative work. But an entirely separate question is whether enough incumbents would actually vote to change a system that they have mastered, that helped put them in office, and that keeps their future challengers at a serious disadvantage.

I now discuss eight possible reforms: (1) overrule *Citizens United*; (2) redefine "independent expenditures"; (3) provide public funds; (4) require donor anonymity; (5) strengthen the parties; (6) require greater disclosure; (7) encourage small donations; and (8) allow free TV time. (Another reform—adapting regulation to the new world of online campaigning—was discussed earlier.) In considering them, we must bear in mind, as leading political scientists have put it, "how little we genuinely know about the operation of complex political processes and institutions, and, consequently, how likely it is that proposed reforms will prove ineffectual or, worse, counterproductive."[171] The history of campaign finance reforms, we saw, confirms this prudent caution.

Overrule Citizens United

As noted earlier, the decision is extraordinarily unpopular with the general public, so many politicians and others want to see it overruled. But I also argued that its actual holding was correct: The First Amendment does protect a group's right to spend its own funds criticizing a candidate for public office if it acts independently of the candidate's campaign rather than making a thinly veiled campaign contribution. Instead, its objectionable feature is its dictum that independent expenditures can never create an appearance of undue influence and that even if it did create such an appearance, this would not be a legitimate target of Congress.

Still, my earlier analysis shows how hard it would be to frame and enforce such a law defining and punishing undue influence. Political influence, we saw, has numerous sources, of which money is only one—and not necessarily the most decisive. The incumbents who would enact such a law have powerful self-protection biases. Even if the Court allowed Congress to act prophylactically against undue influence corruption, the strict scrutiny standard would cast a long shadow over the difficult line-drawing needed to design such a law. Finally, as Laurence Tribe has argued, the real culprit here is not the holding in *Citizens United* or even its dictum. Rather, it is *SpeechNow.org* and the DC Circuit's "utterly implausible" reading of that dictum to foreclose any restrictions on Super PACs' independent expenditures. Overruling *SpeechNow.org*, he suggests, would be easier for the Court. It would also be more important, to the extent that Super PAC spending is independent of campaigns,[172] an issue that I discuss immediately below. Denying Super PACs tax-exempt status is also possible.

Redefining "Independent Expenditures"

My earlier discussion of independent expenditures revealed four important facts. They are constitutionally protected by four decades of Supreme Court decisions. The key criterion of independence is defined as coordination with a campaign. The operational distance between campaigns and their Super PAC and other group supporters is often illusory, consisting of obfuscatory tactics that any crafty campaign finance lawyer can design. Finally, the FEC, assiduously neutered by Congress, does not patrol this line.

Two quite different changes to the treatment of independent expenditures are worth considering. One is to tighten the definition of coordination to render such evasions illegal, while also banning not only those but also any other practices that have that evasive effect, regardless of intent. Even without altering its precedents, the Supreme Court might well uphold such a law, perhaps modeled on the California Fair Political Practices Commission rules noted earlier. Such a law would "simply" enforce the existing system's congressionally and judicially-approved rules, so it is hard to see any serious, principled objections to it other than by those who also object to the *existing* contribution and expenditure limits. In reality, however, it would surely be difficult (especially under the current FEC regime) to enforce such a scheme and risk crossing the uncertain lines that the Court has drawn to protect independent expenditures.[173]

A better, far more realistic reform would turn the independence-enforcement approach on its head, doing the very opposite. Instead of trying to police the boundary between the parties and the outside groups that purport to spend "independently" of the party candidates they support, this reform would make a virtue of necessity. It would *ratify and legitimate* the coordination between outside groups and the parties, give the latter ultimate control over the spending, and end the hypocrisy, obfuscation, and Alice-in-Wonderland distortion of the pretended separation. It is not clear whether Congress could *require* outside groups to coordinate given the Court's interpretation of the First Amendment, but surely it could incentivize them to do so, perhaps through matching funds for coordinated donations. But it seems likely that many of these groups would welcome the chance to coordinate openly with the parties so as to increase the effectiveness of their funds. Increasing this coordination would be one of a number of important ways to strengthen the parties, a strategy discussed below.

Public Funding

A common reform idea proposes mandatory or, more often, optional public funding of campaigns. In practice, this has meant public funding of candidates, not of parties—although public funding could be used to buttress parties rather than candidates, as is the case in Germany, France, Australia, and Israel.[174] I discuss this below under "Strengthening the Parties."

For federal elections, FECA makes public funding available only to presidential campaigns. The Supreme Court upheld this scheme in *Buckley*, however, only because it was voluntary and thus consistent with candidates' constitutional right to spend money on campaigns. FECA allows presidential candidates to receive federal funds for the primaries according to how much they raise in contributions in at least twenty states. Major party candidates can receive a flat grant for the general election, while other parties can receive grants only if they won at least 5 percent of the vote in the previous general election. This federal money, however, is conditional on a candidate's agreement to comply with spending limits in both the primaries and general elections. A similar grant system exists for party nominating conventions, subject to a convention spending limit. The public funding system is financed by taxpayers who check a box on their tax returns allowing for a $3 contribution to the fund.[175]

This system has atrophied in recent elections, as candidates—most notably, Barack Obama in 2008—rejected this quid pro quo in favor of the default regime, unlimited spending. This enabled him to raise and spend many times more money than his opponent, John McCain. The 2016 candidates did likewise, and it seems almost certain that future presidential candidates will do the same, rendering this particular public financing scheme irrelevant.

Many states and a few localities have adopted their own public funding systems for their elections. Again, these schemes must be voluntary to comply with the Court's interpretation of the First Amendment; indeed, it has struck down some that penalize additional spending by candidates who decide not to participate in it and thus forego public funding.[176] Two main approaches to public funding exist: full public financing, and matching funds. These systems have been described as follows:

> The full public funding approach, with a trigger formula . . . provides qualifying candidates with an initial grant of public funds and offers additional matching funds that may be triggered by a high-spending privately-funded opponent or independent group. A candidate who qualifies and opts into the system agrees to spend only public funds from that point forward. . . . The centerpiece to these systems is the trigger, which increases the amount of public money a candidate receives based on how much his privately financed opponent spends and, in some jurisdictions, based on how much third-party actors independently spend on behalf of the privately financed candidate. . . . The other popular public financing approach eschews the initial grant in favor of matching funds, in some cases offering a multiple match of small contributions. [Some of these schemes, like New York City's, contain triggers.][177]

Some jurisdictions provide tax credits, deductions, or even refunds to small donors, and some offer public funds to qualifying political parties. And foreign countries have a variety of campaign finance schemes, though many of them would raise clear constitutional objections under our Supreme Court's precedents.[178]

A different use of public financing has been proposed by my Yale colleagues Bruce Ackerman and Ian Ayres.[179] The ingenious Ackerman-Ayres proposal has two parts: public funding (discussed here) and donor anonymity (discussed next). Reviews by prominent law professors Pamela Karlan and David Strauss raise serious questions about some of its underlying assumptions and likely effects.[180] As it happens, Strauss's questions are relevant to most other reform proposals, so I present some of them—and his answers—here.

The public funding part of their scheme draws on the idea of vouchers, so popular in other settings like education and housing, by having the government issue all registered voters a certain number of "Patriot dollars" on a digital card that they could dispense to candidates, parties, or PACs of their choice at ATM machines. Private contributions of other dollars would still be allowed and contribution limits would be raised. In order to keep private contributions from swamping the Patriot dollars, however, a "stabilization algorithm" would kick in when the private contributions amounted to half the Patriot dollars being contributed; the algorithm would increase the number of Patriot dollars in the next election cycle. As already noted, voters could give Patriot dollars to PACs as well as candidates or parties, but the PACs would in turn have to give those dollars to candidates or parties; they could not use those dollars for independent expenditures or other PAC activities. A 2015 ballot initiative in Seattle authorized the city to distribute $100 in vouchers to all registered voters, which candidates could use if they abided by certain contribution and spending limits.[181]

Strauss thinks that providing public funding through Patriot dollar vouchers would improve on FECA by basing funding for third parties on current voter preferences rather than on FECA's existing prior-election-performance formula. Still, he wonders whether the Patriot dollars would, like other public funding schemes, risk further entrenching incumbents. Indeed, incumbent entrenchment is a serious constraint on the efficacy of most reforms, including public funding. After all, as discussed earlier, incumbents inevitably control the shape and terms of a reform because they write the rules.* With pub-

---

* Justice Scalia, dissenting in *McConnell v. FEC* (which upheld the BCRA), made this point powerfully:

> *any* restriction upon a type of campaign speech that is equally available to challengers and incumbents tends to favor incumbents. Beyond that, however, the

lic funding specifically, one would naturally expect the incumbents to keep the funding for challengers low enough, and its availability regulated enough, to maintain their own fund-raising and other advantages. Indeed, one may well doubt whether today's taxpayers, so disgusted with politics, will ever again agree to spend public funds for political campaigns, whether recipients be incumbents or challengers. Another question is whether people would allocate Patriot dollars as carefully as they would if the dollars were instead coming out of their own pockets.

Donor Anonymity

Strauss's analysis of the proposal for donor anonymity is also illuminating, as is Karlan's. Although anonymity could be intended to prevent special-interest deals, secrecy doesn't prevent such deals. If instead the point is to prevent contributions being used by the wealthy as bribes in return for special-interest deals, Strauss counters that contributors do not enrich politicians personally, as bribes do. Instead, donors contribute in order to get them elected—and in that case even anonymous donors achieve their objective. Since groups often promise their votes in exchange for desired policies, Strauss asks, why is it wrong for a group to provide "not votes but campaign contributions—bearing in mind that campaign contributions are . . .

---

present legislation *targets* for prohibition certain categories of campaign speech that are particularly harmful to incumbents. Is it accidental, do you think, that incumbents raise about three times as much "hard money," the sort of funding generally *not* restricted by this legislation, as do their challengers? Or that lobbyists (who seek the favor of incumbents) give 92 percent of their money in "hard" contributions? Is it an oversight, do you suppose, that the so-called "millionaire provisions" raise the contribution limit for a candidate running against an individual who devotes to the campaign (as challengers often do) great personal wealth, but do not raise the limit for a candidate running against an individual who devotes to the campaign (as incumbents often do) a massive election "war chest"? And is it mere happenstance, do you estimate, that national-party funding, which is severely limited by the Act, is more likely to assist cash-strapped challengers than flush-with-hard-money incumbents? Was it unintended, by any chance, that incumbents are free personally to receive some soft money and even to solicit it for other organizations, while national parties are not? 540 U.S. at 249 (citations omitted) not a means of enriching a candidate but only a means of enabling the candidate to try to get more votes? . . . And if it is all right for officials to respond to contributions, then what's wrong with the quid pro quo exchanges that [the] anonymity requirement is designed to prevent?"[182] Strauss concludes that anonymity aims to prevent not special-interest deals but unequal influence. Yet if candidates want to pursue contributions from the rich by supporting policies that favor them, anonymity won't stop them. "It will be easy for officials to determine how to benefit wealthy people—either directly, by tax cuts for example, or indirectly, by policies that favor groups in which well-off people are disproportionately represented. Wealthy individuals will know who is acting in their interest and will contribute accordingly. Anonymity does not seem to be a very promising solution to the problem of inequality."[183] Strauss does concede that anonymity would prevent outright extortion.

Still, if Congress enacted a system that infused public funds into presidential or congressional campaigns based on some government match of small contributions, the Court would almost surely uphold it. If it included a trigger for public funds based on the opposition's spending, however, the Court (barring a change in membership) would likely strike it down as an effort to "level the playing field," which the Court has explicitly refused to recognize as a compelling governmental interest (the constitutional test in such cases). Indeed, it would likely strike such a measure down even though it arguably increases the amount of protected political speech, arguably reduces the risk or perception of corruption, and arguably reduces the burdens of fundraising on candidates.[184]

I say that these effects "arguably" occur because such effects are hard to measure even though many public funding schemes are already operating. Also hard to predict or prove—the studies are mostly inconclusive[185]—is whether and to what extent such reforms would increase electoral competition and diversity of candidates, reduce large (but within-limits) contributions, affect independent expenditures, increase public confidence in the system, or alter other features of the campaign finance status quo.

Strengthening the Parties

Many "realists" propose to encourage coordination, not prohibit it. They would redesign campaign finance regulation so as to give parties at both the state and national levels more control, not less, over their donors and their candidates' messages, campaigns, and behavior once in office.[186] As Persily explains, this strategy has trade-offs:

> [T]he pro-party approach gives up on electing moderates and focuses more on reining in extremists. . . . Party organizations need to be richer and more powerful to counteract the polarizing tendencies of outside groups, and party leaders need to have a greater array of tools to whip recalcitrant members into shape. . . . Such an approach takes as a given the huge demand for campaign funds and the inevitable influence of large independent expenditures in the post-*Citizens United* world. However, instead of trying to clamp down on the influence of all participants in the campaign finance system, the pro-party approach seeks to rectify the imbalance between insiders and outsiders by amplifying the voice of the parties so they can compete with outside groups.[187]

Law professor Rick Pildes sees, and welcomes, another "tragic trade-off" in this party-strengthening approach—between the populist's claim to "certain modes of popular participation and the parties' capacity for effective governance."[188] Another tricky balance in a stronger-party system would be to retain some space for intraparty challenges by mavericks and insurgents with broad support, although the parties would have strong incentives to get that balance right.

The pro-party group readily acknowledges how hard it would be to achieve this change; after all, the trends have moved in the opposite direction for more than a century. Ever since the Progressive Era's antiparty reforms, powerful forces have conspired to keep them weak. Candidate selection, necessarily at the heart of parties' power, has devolved to party primary electorates. Primaries' outcomes are shaped by a relatively small, unrepresentative subset of each party's voters. They tend to be the most narrowly focused, ideologically extreme among the parties' adherents, those who most strongly resist bargaining and compromise *even within the party itself.* In recent years, this intraparty warfare has most toxically infected the Republican Party, but at other times (e.g., in the 1968–72 period) the Democrats were prone to it[189] (and might be again, having lost the party-unifying White House in 2016). The nominating convention delegates reflect this powerful tilt: 28 percent of Democratic convention delegates in 2008 were teacher's union members[190] and more than 38 percent of Republican delegates in 2016 were from majority-evangelical districts.[191] Almost half the states now have some form of election law in which independents and even members of the opposing party can, and often do, vote in a party's primary, further diluting its autonomy, coherence, and solidarity.[192] Those who advocate these more open primaries, including California's recent "Top Two" system, usually argue that it will make the parties more moderate, but the evidence does not yet confirm this prediction.[193]

If the state and national parties are to be strengthened vis-à-vis their own candidates and the outside groups, then certain restrictions on the parties must be eased or eliminated, and more campaign money—either from contributions (with full disclosure) or public funding— must go directly to them. La Raja and Rauch recently advanced workable proposals for both approaches.[194] This accords with "realist" claims that the BCRA ban on soft money contributions to parties simply starves the parties of needed funds while enabling wealthy donors to exert more influence through unaccountable nonparty groups.[195]

McCarty, a prominent realist, summarizes the pro-party view as follows: "Strong parties have autonomy from and bargaining advantages over special interest groups. Weak parties are those whose elected officials are free agents who can build electoral coalitions around narrow and extreme interests."[196] There is ample evidence to support this broad generalization. The key policy questions are these: Does extreme polarization in Congress (and the states) actually exist? The strong consensus among political scientists is yes.[197] Is this party polarization bad for our democracy? Again, almost all agree that it is.

What has caused it? Here there is strong disagreement, with the "realists" blaming it partly on party-weakening reforms (especially campaign finance) and their critics blaming it instead mostly on growing Republican extremism and *Citizens United*. What can be done about this situation (the subject of this subsection)? And is it too late? Some argue that the popular culture, which lionizes personalities, has simply changed too much to nourish trust in parties.[198]

Expanded Disclosure

Reformers often propose greater disclosure of campaign contributions and expenditures. Their focus on disclosure has at least three rationales. The virtues of transparency are relatively non-controversial because the benefits seem obvious and the costs seem trivial. Enforcement seems fairly straightforward, with each party monitoring the other's (non-) compliance. And the Supreme Court, starting with *Buckley* and even in *Citizens United*, has deferred to Congress on disclosure mandates on the theory that disclosure increases the public's information without suppressing speech (except where serious reprisals might ensue, unlike the situation it faced in its *Doe v. Reed* ruling described earlier).

Ever since *Citizens United* allowed unlimited independent expenditures by outside groups (absent coordination), bipartisan coalitions in Congress have tried but failed to enact legislation, known as the DISCLOSE Act, to mandate disclosure of this dark money and other information. The act would require covered organizations that spend money in federal elections to promptly disclose donors of $10,000 or more during an election cycle.* A "covered organization" would include any corporation, labor organization, Section 501(c), 527 organization, or Super PAC (but not a party or candidate committee). It would exempt Section 501(c) (3) charitable groups whose tax status bars them from spending money to influence elections.† Other provi-

---

* Under existing rules, PACs only need to file reports periodically. This allows them to wait until after an election to disclose contributions that pour in just before it.

† The California Attorney General's order requiring such groups to disclose their do-

sions aim to prevent political operatives from using complex arrangements or transfers to hide donor identities or otherwise game the system. Any covered organization that spends $10,000 or more on election ads would have to file a disclosure report with the FEC within twenty-four hours, and to file a new report for each additional $10,000 or more that it spends. The disclosure report must include the sources of all donations of $10,000 or more that the organization received during that election cycle. The act would also expand existing bans on foreign contributions.

New disclosure issues sometimes arise, fueling new demands for reform. "Bundling," mentioned earlier, is an example. Under a 2007 law, federal candidates and party committees must disclose the identity of registered lobbyists who have bundled $17,600 or more, but this doesn't apply to non-lobbyist bundlers, so campaigns need not disclose their names. In October 2015, Jeb Bush's presidential campaign decided to list the names of non-lobbyists who bundle that amount or more, a lower disclosure threshold than that used then by Hillary Clinton ($100,000) and other candidates. Even so, Bush was criticized because his list will not disclose what each bundler raised, making it harder to identify the major bundlers.[199] Reformers want to increase disclosure of bundlers' identities and amounts. And strengthening FEC enforcement of disclosure requirements is essential to their effectiveness.

Increasing Small Donations

Increasing the number and influence of small donors is a perennial goal of reformers who believe that the unequal influence blessed and arguably magnified by the existing system poses a serious threat to our democracy. This common concern is manifested in a 2010 joint report by scholars associated with both Brookings and the American Enterprise Institute (left-of-center and right-of-center, respectively)

---

nors in order to solicit donors in the state was upheld by the Ninth Circuit. *Center for Competitive Politics v. Harris*, 784 F. 3d 1307 (9th Cir. 2015). The Supreme Court declined an appeal.

to "foster citizen participation through small donors and volunteers" (in the words of the report's title).[200]

This report begins with the premise that campaign finance has become a "stale two-sided battleground" between those who seek to use limits to curb corruption—seen as the influence of wealthy interests—and those who seek to protect free speech. Hoping to "leap over the 'undue influence' v. free speech gulf,'" the report would empower small donors rather than restrict large ones. If enough people enter the system at the low end, it argues, there may be less reason to worry about the top. Moreover, increased participation is "healthy for its own sake." The report seeks to accomplish this by using new technologies like expanded broadband and access to digital media to increase open access to communications, lower information costs of participation, and improve transparency. It also urges the government to ensure that carriers provide access for political speech, and to create and maintain a website with voter registration information, candidate information with links to the candidates' websites, and real-time, downloadable electronic disclosure. Any radio or television statement would be required to publish real-time advertising logs for political spots with the FCC and on the voter website where all disclosures would be posted. Greater transparency would also enhance enforcement.

Most important, the report proposes a partial public financing system centered on matching funds on a multiple basis but only for small contributions. By imposing lower contribution limits but no expenditure caps, this system would increase prospective small donors' incentive to contribute. The public funding would be available to candidates as soon as they met a qualifying monetary threshold, and the matching funds would have a ceiling. Contributions by low-income donors would be supported by tax credits or rebates.

There are reasons to be skeptical about reformers' enthusiasm for encouraging small donations. As noted earlier, small donors tend to cluster at the ideological extremes, as their support for candidates Bernie Sanders, Ben Carson, and Donald Trump indicate. Small donors, moreover, *already* participate disproportionately in politics;

they tend to be the same people who contact politicians, organize at the grassroots, and turn out for caucuses, primaries, and general elections.[201] As for transparency, small donors need not disclose their contributions to federal candidates until the amounts exceed $200. Even if, as the reformers hope, small donors' significance increases, requiring such disclosure by small donors may not be cost-effective and would have little effect on the perceived problem of undue influence.

Free TV Time

Purchasing TV time has grown ever more expensive, and TV exposure can be an important political advantage (or disadvantage, depending on the candidate's performance). Reformers often propose that Congress or the FCC require networks to provide free or reduced-fee time to candidates for public office (not their parties, as is done in many peer democracies). These proposals have never attracted much support. Broadcasters oppose them for obvious reasons. Incumbent politicians, who enjoy media access by reason of their prominence and official positions, have no incentive to provide it free to their challengers. The traditional argument for free TV time—that the broadcast spectrum is a public resource granted by the FCC and that its use by networks is not a private property right but a privilege to be allocated for public purposes—has become more tenuous with the spread of other media. In addition, a free time system would necessitate difficult judgments distinguishing between bona fide candidates and mere publicity hounds.

Federal law does impose an "equal time" rule requiring broadcasters to provide equal opportunities to all political candidates, but First Amendment concerns have qualified the rule with several important exceptions for documentaries, bona fide news interviews, scheduled newscasts, or on-the-spot news events, which in practice mitigate the rule's significance. Broadcasters are required to offer time to candidates at the rate charged to the "most favored advertiser," but that rate is still likely to be very high.

CONCLUSION

Our campaign finance system is stalemated by the collision among four groups. The first consists of incumbents and powerful groups with deep interest in maintaining the campaign finance status quo. They think that it serves them well enough, especially those donors who are able to spread their political contributions around to reach both parties, hire lower-visibility lobbyists, and support friendly interest groups—as in the earlier campaign to repeal the estate tax, mentioned above. They resist opening the campaign finance system to wholesale changes outside their control.

A second group includes many journalists, some political scientists, and other reformers disgusted by a system they consider execrable, corrupt, and subversive of democracy and equality. To this group, the notions that money is speech and that corporations have important speech rights are nonsensical smokescreens concocted by the Supreme Court and its plutocratic allies to deform the First Amendment and preserve the status quo.

The third group includes reform skeptics and political scientists who emphasize the complexity of the political ecosystem in which campaign finance is embedded. They despair about the prospects for significant change (except perhaps in the disclosure area) and fear that new reforms, like earlier ones in FECA and BCRA, would produce unintended, sometimes perverse consequences. Campaign finance reformers, they warn, should be very careful what they wish for. After all, political actors' stratospheric stakes means that they will invest a great deal in manipulating the system to serve their interests. The hydraulic force of money in politics strongly propels it toward its intended destination. Non-monetary factors also shape political behavior and outcomes, casting doubt on the notion—an idée fixe for most in the first group—that campaign contributions and spending largely determine electoral outcomes. Constitutional principles constrain many proposed reforms. Incumbents, concerned more with their own short-term reelection prospects, control both the rules and their implementation. Political entrepreneurs increasingly operate on their own, largely beyond the parties' control. The FEC was designed by politicians to be a toothless cipher, making strong enforcement unlikely.

The last group—call them meliorists—consists of those who largely agree with this grim description of the status quo but are cautiously optimistic that reforms can improve on it. Recent reforms, they believe, have tried to use Canute-like fiats to abolish political realities and to prevent politicians from doing what they must in order to do their work effectively in an increasingly complex system— with predictably bad results. Instead, these meliorists want to use the inescapable political hydraulics of our system to restore and renovate the long-traditional system of parties and negotiation that recent reforms, in an effort to discredit this system, have only made more dysfunctional. Rauch, a leading meliorist, predicts that respecting those hydraulics rather than suppressing them will make unintended consequences less likely.[202]

These four groups subscribe to quite different normative, empirical, and policy claims about campaign finance but largely agree that the political system as a whole is dysfunctional. As they debate how politics should be organized and funded, the Court will, for better or worse, constrain future reforms. Its campaign finance jurisprudence is laced with constitutional interpretations that have become deeply embedded and resistant to change—although many of its key decisions were decided by only one vote! Two central pillars of this jurisprudence—a narrow conception of the kind of corruption that might justify restrictions, and a broad conception of independent expenditures that must be protected from limits—mean in effect that reformers can hope to work only at the margins of campaign finance activity, such as disclosure rules. Congress, an assembly of incumbents, is not about to rock the boat. And as campaign activity moves inexorably to the Internet, the most important rules will increasingly be prescribed there—and not by Congress or the Court.

CHAPTER 5

AFFIRMATIVE ACTION

AMERICANS ARE DEEPLY COMMITTED to equal opportunity. This is evidenced not just by public rhetoric but by our law, the policies of leading private institutions, and the values endorsed by the general public. This public philosophy, with its strong support for ethnic diversity in almost all areas of American life, has helped to propel unprecedented progress by minorities, including blacks. Yet no informed person could possibly maintain that this progress has produced anything approaching genuine equal opportunity: The vast gulf between the life prospects of blacks and whites, taken as groups, mocks such a claim.[1] This gulf raises legitimate questions about this national commitment—whether it is sufficient, whether it has taken the right forms, and the reasons why we have not yet fully vindicated it.

Affirmative action (or preferences; I use the terms interchangeably) is not mandated by federal law (except for federal contractors); most states do not require it; and some even prohibit it. Indeed, the fact that different states, and perhaps different institutions within those states, take their own approaches to affirmative action is a great strength, reflecting the nation's diverse attitudes about it. Many leading public and private institutions—selective universities and colleges, most notably and controversially—use affirmative action. Yet today, preferences are even more divisive and unsettled than they were fifty years ago when first instituted under the Nixon administration. Here is the skein of disagreement that this chapter seeks to unravel.

The serious criticisms of ethno-racial affirmative action that I shall present here go not to its constitutionality, which I have long accepted,* but instead to its policy wisdom and efficacy as a remedy for racial disadvantage. Why, then, do I still consider it a hard policy issue? Major institutions in American life have invested in it, continue to defend it ardently, and will probably retain if not expand it no matter what.[2] Despite strong empirical evidence casting doubt on its effectiveness, this evidence (which, of course, is contested) has not changed the minds of affirmative action's strongest advocates.[3] The historical injustices suffered by blacks and their continuing disadvantages cry out for a remedy, and many Americans see affirmative action as a relatively easy, essentially costless one.

I present the analysis of affirmative action in two main sections: first, its policy context, and second, the policy issues that affirmative action raises. A brief conclusion follows.

CONTEXT

Context is crucial to a sophisticated understanding of affirmative action, as with any hard issue. The following discussion analyzes nine aspects of this context: definitions and distinctions; history; moral principles; ideology; domains; public attitudes; politics; the dearth of blacks in elite institutional settings; and the constitutional status of preferences after the Supreme Court's 2016 ruling in the *Fisher* case.

---

* Long before the Supreme Court in *Fisher II* upheld it (albeit narrowly: "The University's program is *sui generis*"), I argued that it was indeed constitutional, but for a different reason; I discuss this below. *Diversity in America: Keeping Government at a Safe Distance* (2003), 135.

Definitions and Distinctions

In affirmative action programs, institutions that control access to important social resources offer particular groups preferential access to those resources because those groups (minorities, except when the group is women) are thought to need or deserve more favorable treatment. Typically, affirmative action programs use decision rules or weightings that can be outcome-determinative. (I discuss the issue of weightings below.) This chapter focuses on ethno-racial preferences, and particularly those that favor blacks (especially black men; black female applicants have much more competitive credentials on average)[4]—rather than, say, preferences based on income, age, gender, or disability. No one doubts that blacks present by far the strongest case for affirmative action—historically, morally, and politically. If that case fails, as I believe my analysis will demonstrate, then the case for favoring other groups must fail as well. The chapter will also focus on higher education, the arena in which affirmative action is most controversial and actively contested and in which empirical evidence on its effects is most available.

I distinguish affirmative action from nondiscrimination, a more passive practice in which the normative principle is simply to refrain from treating people differently on the basis of their ethno-racial characteristics. The distinction between affirmative action and nondiscrimination is clear and important both in politics and in principle, though not always in practice.[5] Nondiscrimination, in sharp contrast to affirmative action, is no longer controversial in American society except among bigots and some libertarians. Public discourse severely condemns any hint of anti-black or anti-minority attitudes,[6] and rightly associates nondiscrimination with the universally praised norm of equal opportunity while generally disparaging preferences as a demand for equal outcomes or special treatment. Some strong egalitarians favor affirmative action precisely because they think that it will equalize results, but most affirmative action proponents make a more limited argument—that it is essential for genuine equal opportunity.

Both proponents and opponents of affirmative action define non-discrimination in ways they hope will exploit its greater legitimacy. Proponents claim that affirmative action, by leveling the playing field, is simply another form of nondiscrimination. Opponents define non-discrimination to include greater outreach to minority communities in hopes of going beyond the "old boy" network and expanding the pool of minority applicants who will then have an equal opportunity to compete on the basis of merit (a term I discuss below). This distinction between nondiscrimination and affirmative action is clear enough analytically and normatively, but two factors can propel us down the slippery slope from nondiscrimination to preferences. First, as I have explained elsewhere,[7] increasing outreach is neither cost-free nor neutral; it too is affirmative action of a sort, though we do not usually equate it with preferences.[8]

Second and much more important, evidentiary problems can move decision makers toward rules that look and operate less like nondiscrimination and more like outright preferences. Antidiscrimination enforcers need baselines or other indicia of bias to help them gauge its extent, the need for remedial measures, and those measures' effects. They naturally prefer numerical benchmarks—in employment, for example, a group's share of the working-age population in the relevant labor pool—as a basis for inferring whether the employer actually discriminated against the group. These benchmarks may take the form and rhetoric of mere "goals" toward which firms and institutions should strive but which do not necessarily trigger sanctions if they are not met. This "not necessarily" qualifier is what can push an antidiscrimination program toward using preferences. For legal and psychological reasons, soft, tentative goals tend to become harder, more rigid standards that raise a presumption of bias if not reached. The strength of the presumption, the kind of evidence that can rebut it, the effect of the rebuttal on the burden of proof, and other technical issues are the province of a very complex body of antidiscrimination law. Goals that at their inception were merely aspirational become more binding and consequential. These goals may mark "safe harbors" where organizations that meet them can expect protection from liability. Or the goals may condemn organizations that do not meet them, or may at least shift the burden of proof to those organizations.

In this enforcement context, three related distinctions—between nondiscrimination and affirmative action, between equality of opportunity and equality of result, and between goals and preferences—can blur at the edges as the opposing ideas bleed into one another. Some affirmative action advocates use this blurring to deny that the distinctions even exist; others recognize the distinctions but then define nondiscrimination, equal opportunity, and goals in ways that imply greater normative and programmatic scope for affirmative action. In contrast, I see these distinctions as foundational—though again, blurry at their edges—and Americans overwhelmingly agree. Indeed, they have organized their public philosophy on this issue around these three distinctions. This consensus, of course, could still be wrong. Our history is replete with collective delusions (e.g., norms favoring racism, homophobia, and subordination of women). My claim here is a limited one: These distinctions matter a lot to almost all of us.

The idea of *merit* also needs clarification, as it is central not only to these three distinctions but, more importantly, to most people's attitude toward affirmative action.[9] Most advocates of preferences challenge opponents' basic assumption about what merit means, about how it should be measured, and about whether merit selection (as conventionally understood and actually implemented) is a compelling principle of distributive justice with respect to the particular social goods at issue.

Affirmative action advocates' position on merit takes at least three forms; some use all of them. First, they contend that accepted understandings of merit are arbitrary, unduly narrow, and unjustly disadvantage certain minorities. "Merit," Nicholas Lemann writes, "is various, not unidimensional. Intelligence tests, and also education itself, can't be counted on to find every form of merit. They don't find wisdom, or originality, or humor, or toughness, or empathy, or common sense, or independence, or determination—let alone moral worth."

Stanley Fish adds that when disputes arise over merit, "the dispute is between different versions of merit and not between merit and something base and indefensible." Like Lemann and Fish, advocates of preferences particularly reject notions of merit that rely heavily or exclusively on certain kinds of mental and physical tests or that demand certain academic, experiential, and other traditional credentials.[10] This argument for (re)defining merit may invoke efficiency as well as fairness values. The claim is that those who administer conventional merit standards ignore or reject many individuals who, if merit were properly defined, would turn out to possess it and would perform the task perfectly well. By excluding them, some advocates say, the ostensibly race-neutral merit standard actually operates as a "white-people's affirmative action" program.

A second critique is that conventional definitions of merit are actually composites of different ingredients, some of which have little or nothing to do with the kinds of virtues that society should reward with material or status advantage. Ronald Dworkin, for example, condemns the notion that what he calls "wealth-talents" (which would include scholastic aptitude or achievement) should be rewarded because they are praiseworthy attributes. "What counts as a wealth-talent," he writes, "is contingent in a hundred dimensions. . . . Luck is, anyway, by far the most important wealth-talent in this catalogue—being in the right place is often more important than being anything else at all." Even apart from luck, he argues, it is wrong to confer such social advantages on those whom such contingencies happen to favor. In short, merit is not an appropriate principle of distributive justice for the social rewards that wealth-talent receives.

Third, advocates of preferences maintain that conventional merit standards are routinely violated by other preference practices that bear little or no relation to any defensible conception of merit and that exhibit few if any of affirmative action's virtues. Examples in higher education include lower admissions standards for athletes, legacies, and geographic diversity. Other exceptions to the merit principle abound in areas like employment, where governments and pri-

vate firms often recruit, hire, and promote through veterans' preferences, "old boy" networks, nepotism, and favoritism. (I discuss these
exceptions below in the discussions of stereotypes and of the size of
preferences.)

Some defenders of preferences do not so much challenge traditional notions of merit as they argue pragmatically that the likely alternatives to preferences would be even worse. In legal commentator
Jeffrey Rosen's view, for example, state universities' programmatic
responses to the end of preferences coupled with continuing political
pressures to keep minorities on flagship campuses threaten "to turn
the leading state universities into remedial academies. . . . [A]ffirma-
tive action represents a lesser compromise of meritocratic standards
than the alternatives that are almost certain to follow its elimination."
(I discuss these alternatives below.)

The willingness to disregard, dilute, or redefine the merit principle
knows no ideological and partisan boundaries. Does this bespeak a
context-sensitive flexibility in the notion of merit, as Fish maintains,
or is it just plain hypocrisy? The answer is—it depends. Universities,
employers, and other decision makers are in the best position to define and measure merit in whatever terms they deem most relevant to
their own institutions because they must bear most if not all of any
efficiency losses and other costs arising from any errors in definition
or measurement. Thus, what outsiders may view as arbitrary and
hypocritical exceptions to the merit principle presumably advance the
institutions' broader interests. In this sense, these "exceptions" can be
seen as part of a defensible, institution-specific conception of merit.
For example, preference for legacies and athletes—which one study
indicated were significant (for athletes, comparable to that for Hispanics but lower than for blacks)[11]—may maximize the alumni contributions and loyalty that in turn support the institution's academic
mission. By the same token, an ethno-racial preference may reflect an
institution's belief that the beneficiaries' presence will somehow enrich campus life—a belief that I analyze at length below under the
rubric of "diversity." If so, the merit principle remains inviolate, al-

though its precise definition depends on the particular social context in which it is invoked and the mix of values that the institution seeks to promote.*

Defenders of traditional merit make several dignity-based and consequentialist arguments against preferences. One of them contends that Dworkin's contingency argument gives too little weight to the role that individual efforts play in academic and other success. Such efforts, they maintain, should be rewarded on both efficiency and fairness grounds; those rewards send socially desirable signals to others in the community that self-help in cultivating meritorious habits will lead to success.[12] If society deems the rewards excessive, it can best reduce them by taxing the excess, not by disparaging a principle that helps motivate socially valuable activity. Once this merit principle is abandoned or discredited, it cannot readily be restored or replaced. No alternative principle, in this view, is as socially functional or morally attractive as merit.

---

* This contextualized conception of merit is not just window-dressing. A university president may well believe that admitting athletes, legacies, and minorities who do not meet the school's normal academic standards would nonetheless advance its overriding academic and social missions. Indeed, many university presidents do take this view. For myself, I could not support this without strong evidence that admitting them was both necessary and sufficient to advance those missions without eroding those standards. Given the academic and fiscal success of elite schools that abandoned single-sex admissions over initial alumni opposition, and given the scandalously low academic standards for athletes on many campuses, I suspect that such evidence does not exist and that most special treatment for athletes and legacies bears no relation to a defensible conception of merit. Evidence on the contribution of minorities to campus life and other institutions does exist, however, and I discuss it below. In defining the academic mission at the elite institutions where preferences are most controversial, I personally place a very high weight on intellectual achievement or promise. I say "very high," not exclusive; I might also give points to applicants who play in the school orchestra, come from rural backgrounds or foreign countries, or exhibit unusual leadership abilities. Doubtless others, mindful of their own institutions' distinctive goals and traditions, would strike these balances somewhat differently, and variations of this kind are to be encouraged. An institution's choice should be considered hypocritical (as opposed to misguided) only when it manifestly violates the institution's proclaimed values or when the institution does not demand hard evidence to justify departure from those values. The important point is not merely that, as Lemann and Fish rightly argue, different institutions (and the people within them) can plausibly define merit in different ways, but also that the integrity of those definitions depends partly on the underlying facts.

Another merit-based argument against preferences holds that departures from merit, as traditionally understood, tend to demean and stigmatize the program's beneficiaries—including those who would have qualified under the traditional merit standard. Since preferences' categorical (and usually concealed) nature prevents others from telling which members of the favored group were hired or admitted on the basis of merit and which on the basis of the preference, observers will tend to assume the worst. (This assumption, of course, might itself be considered discriminatory but it may instead reflect a non-discriminatory aversion to risk.) In a reverse twist on the economic theory that explains why "lemons" are hard to detect in the market,[13] a preference tends to reduce the returns to true merit and the effort required to achieve it. A similar argument of this kind notes that many who take advantage of preferences will perform poorly or fail, further stigmatizing the group and demoralizing its individual members. As we shall see, much evidence bears out this prediction.* And as we shall also see, affirmative action programs do not fare well under *any* plausible, non-circular conception of merit.

The last idea that needs clarification before developing the analysis of affirmative action is *program*. Any affirmative action program combines a number of distinct features (some more explicit than others). First, it specifies one or more *favored groups*. Typically, it tracks what David Hollinger calls the "ethno-racial pentagon": blacks, Hispanics, Native Americans, Asian and Pacific Islanders, and women,[14] but other groups have demanded, and sometimes obtained, inclusion.[15] (In October 2016, the White House announced its controversial proposal to add a new racial category to the Census for people from the

---

* Even so, this cannot in itself be a decisive argument against affirmative action. As Stanley Fish has argued: "Some beneficiaries of affirmative action will question their achievements; others will be quite secure in them; and many more will manage to have low self-esteem no matter what their history. Affirmative action is a weak predictor of low self-esteem, and even if there were a strong correlation, you might prefer the low self-esteem that comes along with wondering if your success is really earned to the low self-esteem that comes from never having been in a position to succeed in the first place. At any rate, low self-esteem is at least in part the product of speculation about it."

Middle East and North Africa (MENA), who up to now have been considered white.[16] This proposal risks further reifying the system of racial classifications. Policy experts like former Census Bureau Director Kenneth Prewitt advocate dropping current race questions altogether in favor of questions on nationality, parental place of birth, and the like that more accurately capture our demographic diversity.[17]) Which groups should be covered and how they should be defined are of course deeply controversial issues. Blacks and Native Americans are always included, but the consensus ends there.

A program specifies the *kinds of actions* that may or must be taken. The possible actions range from the relatively uncontroversial (collecting and reporting data) to the most contentious (outright quotas). A program also specifies whether such actions are *mandatory*, *voluntary*, or *prohibited* (as quotas often are); which kinds of *benefits* the preferences will confer (e.g., jobs, broadcasting licenses, college admissions, loans); and possibly how weighty, the preferences will be (e.g., whether it will merely function as a tie-breaker when competing claimants are otherwise equally qualified).

Programs differ in how they *measure membership* in the favored groups, *rank claimants* according to various eligibility or performance criteria, and so forth. Programs may exempt small businesses, permit religious institutions to employ only coreligionists, or include other special provisions. Most are open-ended but some can be time-limited, becoming inapplicable once certain conditions are met. And some, such as race-based districting under the Voting Rights Act (discussed below), are essentially affirmative action programs but are seldom denominated as such.

History

The most salient aspect of affirmative action's context, of course, is America's execrable history of slavery and racial disadvantage for blacks, deeply embedded in law, social practice, and culture. Legions of historians, sociologists, economists, and legal scholars have exhaustively analyzed the depredations of slavery, Jim Crow, pervasive institutionalized racism, and the enduring legacies of these regimes of subordination even today, more than 150 years after Emancipation.

This shameful and turbulent history is the starting point for the policy debate over what to do about it. Today, most Americans who lament the legacy of slavery and discrimination do not feel personally responsible for it, believing that it was perpetrated not by them but by others long ago. Nor do many whites and other non-blacks feel that they personally benefit from black disadvantage. Yet, the vast majority do believe that *something* should be done to rectify this injustice. The disagreement is about the nature of the remedy.

Moral Principles

The fact that morality demands rectification of this egregious historic injustice tells us little because different moral principles compete for our allegiance and often point in different policy directions. Some, like Kant's categorical imperative, are premised on abstract moral claims. Others, like Rawls's difference principle, speak to distributive justice. Still others, like Bentham's utilitarianism, look to the consequences of a particular action or policy. Even the term *rectification*, etymologically derived from the notion of right, raises some hard moral questions. For example, some insist that the descendants of blacks victimized by the historical crimes deserve reparations, even though reparations cannot undo what has been done—after all, the crimes were already committed and most of their direct victims are long dead. Advocates say that reparations would nevertheless be the next best remedy.[18] Others (including me) think that reparations would actually violate several important moral values.[19]

Another aspect of moral thinking about affirmative action, noted earlier, is the distinction between equality of opportunity and equality of outcome and their tendency to bleed into one another. Putting aside the difficult questions of how to define and measure equality, almost all Americans agree with two propositions concerning it: (1) equal opportunity is a basic, indeed constitutive, value in American society and one that government must pursue in some fashion;

and (2) even equal opportunity would yield unequal outcomes because of our diverse abilities, preferences, and behaviors. The point, again, is that moral argument about affirmative action is inevitably affected by how one perceives the relationship between these two propositions.[20]

Ideology

Affirmative action debates—and the history of the programs themselves[21]—are also shaped by ideology, which in turn reflects cultural differences. Political scientist John Skrentny distinguishes three approaches to it in the context of workplace affirmative action but his analysis also applies in its other venues (discussed below). The first, "classical liberalism," calls for a color-blind approach to employment in which race should play no role whatsoever in how individuals are treated. "Affirmative action liberalism" holds that race is significant, but only for the purpose of ensuring equal opportunity—the idea is to use race "to get beyond race." The third approach, "racial realism," is instrumental; it holds that race is an important aspect of a person's identity that an organization can use to achieve its goals by recognizing race-specific abilities and by signaling its commitment to diversity.[22]

Domains

Federal affirmative action programs were not adopted until the 1960s, and their main target has been workplaces.[23] In 1961, President Kennedy issued an executive order requiring affirmative action in hiring by federal contractors, an order extended by President Johnson in 1965. The Nixon administration expanded this scheme following the assassination of Martin Luther King, Jr., major urban riots, campus violence, and social upheaval that caused widespread fear that the nation was becoming ungovernable. The administration desperately sought quick remedies such as affirmative action, and also hoped that it would drive a wedge between white and black

Democratic voters divided over racial issues. Congress expanded Equal Employment Opportunity Commission (EEOC) enforcement authority in 1968, after which the agency used it to challenge private-sector employers whose facially neutral rules and practices caused low levels of black and minority employment. In 1971, the Supreme Court interpreted the equal employment opportunity statute to authorize EEOC challenges to these practices,[24] followed by numerous lawsuits (which continue today, sometimes as class actions) against employers on behalf of minorities and women.[25] When employers responded with new rules and practices, white workers sometimes sued, alleging "reverse discrimination" unfairly favoring black and minority workers.[26]

Today, affirmative action extends to much of the nation's workforce in both public and private employment, and it protects not only the ethno-racial pentagon but religious, national origins, disability, and other conditions and affiliations. It also extends beyond recruitment and hiring decisions to include promotions, terminations, in-service training, and other workplace practices. The U.S. military is the work setting in which affirmative action has been most pervasive and arguably most successful. In public and private contracting, federal, state, and local laws often impose set-asides, quotas, and other preferences for minority contractors and subcontractors.

Many of these programs, however, now operate under a legal cloud. *Federal* set-asides were upheld by the Supreme Court in 1980,[27] but subsequent developments—the Court's insistence on more demanding "strict scrutiny" standards of judicial review (discussed below) and other changes in judicial doctrine, as well as more conservative justices—cast doubt on their legality, culminating in the 1995 *Adarand* decision invalidating a federal set-aside.[28] And an earlier decision, *City of Richmond v. Croson*,[29] invalidated such preferences granted by state and local governments.

Affirmative action also operates in all parts of the educational system; no other domain, save the military, practices and supports it so enthusiastically. Public education systems often mandate it to assign pupils to different schools and school districts and to structure their programs in order to achieve and then maintain some ideal of racial or ethnic balance in the face of enrollment changes that might "tip" this carefully engineered balance and precipitate white flight. These assignment policies have generated bitter political and legal conflicts in many cities, prompting the Supreme Court in 2007 to bar almost all race-specific pupil assignment schemes.[30]

Colleges and universities with selective admissions criteria—a minority of institutions, but exercising disproportionate social influence—often use affirmative action to select students, balance residential units, award financial aid, employ administrators, recruit and promote faculty, run athletic programs, staff student organizations, award contracts, and conduct other aspects of their institutional lives. In a backlash against affirmative action in public university admissions, however, eight states, beginning with California in 1996, have banned it by statute, initiative, or constitutional amendment; the Supreme Court upheld the latter in 2014.[31] Even so, selective public and private institutions, including their alumni, are among its most committed advocates. Affirmative action may even extend to how scientists must design their research in university and other settings. A 1993 law requires the National Institutes of Health to ensure that women and minorities are involved in clinical studies as researchers, not just as research subjects (where such designs can have a scientific rationale).

Financial institutions are required to use affirmative action in their programs, including mortgages, construction and auto loans, and the like. Under the Community Reinvestment Act, these institutions must, on pain of losing their public charters, assure that their facilities and investments are located in minority and low-income communities. Small Business Administration (SBA) loans and grants are also subject to affirmative action requirements, as are public housing projects. Private developers receiving public credit, funds, or other public assistance must assure that members of favored groups enjoy equal access to their projects, sometimes including set-asides and quotas.

Legislative districting is another affirmative action domain. Federal courts have interpreted the Voting Rights Act of 1965 and its

1982 and 2006 amendments to require the states, under certain conditions, to draw federal, state, and local electoral lines for legislative districts and other decision-making bodies so as to maximize the number of "majority-minority" districts, those with a sufficient concentration of the favored minority group that one of its members is very likely to win. Since 1993, however, Supreme Court decisions have cast doubt on the extent to which districting may take race into account. This situation is complicated by the fact that the Court allows the line-drawers to use partisanship, which is easy to predict for blacks, who overwhelmingly vote for Democratic candidates. Again, the Court's mixed signals have sowed enormous uncertainty and confusion in this area.

The Federal Communications Commission (FCC) administers affirmative action programs governing the agency's awarding of television and radio broadcasting licenses. The agency extends its diversity requirements to programming content, the employment and investment practices of potential and existing licensees, and the financing of auction bids by potential licensees. The size of FCC preferences for favored groups is huge. By awarding licenses for the spectrum it controls, it confers enormously valuable economic rights on a very small number of individuals and firms, including subsidizing minority bidders at license auctions. In 1990, the Court narrowly upheld FCC preferences of this kind,[32] but the *Adarand* decision mentioned above makes their continuing legality doubtful.

Private groups often promote or engage in affirmative action even when the law does not require it. To cite but one example: The American Bar Association presses the courts to increase minority representation among judicial law clerks—surely among the most privileged young people in America.

Public Attitudes

Americans have thought about affirmative action for a long time; it has been a prominent policy issue for almost a half-century. And Americans decisively oppose it. In the higher education context, a

Gallup poll published in July 2013 found that 67 percent of all adults, 59 percent of Hispanics, and 44 percent of blacks agreed that "applicants should be admitted solely on the basis of merit, even if this results in few minority students being admitted." Only 28 percent of all adults, 31 percent of Hispanics, and 48 percent of blacks agreed that "an applicant's racial and ethnic background should be considered to help promote diversity on college campuses, even if that means admitting some minority students who otherwise would not be admitted."[33] Most recently, a Gallup poll was conducted shortly after the Court's 2016 decision in *Fisher II* (discussed below), which upheld the Texas system's program.[34] The public, it found, was even more opposed to the use of ethno-racial preferences in college admissions than in 2013: 63 percent of blacks disagreed with the Court's decision, only slight below whites' 66 percent disapproval rate. More generally, the use of ethno-racial preferences was opposed by 70 percent of respondents; only 26 percent favored it. Half of blacks opposed taking race and ethnicity into account, while 44 percent of blacks favored it.[35]

One leading study of public attitudes found that, consistent with other studies, "the most fundamental factor behind opposition to affirmative action is one of principle."[36] That is, the opponents view preferences, rightly or wrongly, as contrary to the ideals of equal opportunity and merit that almost all Americans strongly endorse. Those who research attitudes about affirmative action agree, of course, that how questions are phrased and other contextual factors can affect survey results, and that multiple interpretations of the data are often possible.[37] A majority of people favor affirmative action when it seeks to encourage minorities through more outreach to them, but all researchers find that the public remains decidedly and intensely opposed to "preferences" or "quotas."[38] This has changed little since 1978 when the *Bakke* case was decided. Public support for "racial preferences" has declined, particularly among blacks.[39]* Nor

---

* Black intellectuals are divided on the issue. Some, like Glenn Loury and Randall Kennedy, support affirmative action, while others, like John McWhorter, Thomas Sowell,

does this opposition seem to depend on how the "preferences" question is framed, the state of the economy, or the age, sex, financial conditions, or general political inclinations of those polled. Here are the conclusions of a 1997 analysis by political scientists Paul Sniderman and Edward Carmines, who employed a variety of survey-based experiments in order to tease out public attitudes in a more nuanced way:

(1) The role of racial prejudice in promoting opposition to affirmative action is minor. (2) Rather than opposition to affirmative action signaling a refusal to acknowledge the discrimination and exploitation that black Americans have suffered, a substantial majority of white Americans believe that an extra effort should be made to see that blacks are treated fairly. (3) Opposition to affirmative action is not peculiar to Americans. (4) Opposition to affirmative action does not hinge on the race of the group who benefits but rather on whether the procedures involved are judged to be fair. (5) In addition to dislike of blacks leading to dislike of affirmative action, dislike of affirmative action fosters dislike of blacks. (6) Opposition to and resentment over affirmative action has burst conventional political channels. It is now as prevalent on the left, among liberals and Democrats, as on the right, among conservatives and Republicans.[40]

Politics

The interesting question about affirmative action, then, is why it has managed to survive for so long in the face of such widespread opposition. More than thirty-five years after Nathan Glazer first posed this question, there still is no simple answer.

---

and Walter Williams, oppose it. Sowell has examined the effects of affirmative action programs in other countries, which he finds to be consistently negative. Thomas Sowell, *Affirmative Action around the World: An Empirical Study* (2004). In India, violent protests in 2016 marked efforts by a relatively prosperous ethnic group, Jats, to be classified as a "backward class" and thus eligible for preferences. http://www.nytimes.com/2016/02/23/world/asia/new-delhi-jat-water-protest.html?_r=0

Interest-group politics, analyzed in the light of public choice theory, surely provides some of the explanation. Affirmative action may be a classic case of what James Q. Wilson called clientist politics, in which a policy's benefits are concentrated on a relatively small but intense group while its costs are spread among a much larger but more diffuse, hard-to-organize group for which the issue is less salient. The number of white workers, white nonfavored college applicants, and other whites potentially disadvantaged by affirmative action is large, but relatively few report actual disadvantage, perhaps because the statistical probability of such disadvantage *to an individual white* is quite small.* The probability is higher for Asians, which augurs greater opposition by them in the future, as evidenced by a complaint filed with the federal government against Harvard University, alleging a quota system under which they must score vastly higher on the SAT for their chances of admission to equal those of whites and preferred minorities.[41] SAT disparities are discussed below.

In contrast to the general public, powerful political interests support affirmative action. Nicholas Lemann notes that the "new meritocratic elite . . . didn't resist affirmative action at all—in fact it voluntarily established affirmative action in every institution under its control." In time, liberal advocates for minority groups placed it high on their policy agendas. The status quo has been sustained by strong support by ethnic organizations, national media, leading educational institutions, large corporations, government bureaucracies, mainstream foundations, and other opinion leaders. It has been further fortified by the acquiescence (and in the electoral districting area, connivance) of national Republican politicians, as well as by the inertial advantages of any long-established policy.

Large corporations' strong support for affirmative action might seem counterintuitive. After all, employers must bear most of the di-

---

* On the other hand, as political scientist Shep Melnick suggests, "it is possible that the opposite is true—for each black or Hispanic student who benefits from preferences there are many more white students who believe that otherwise they would have gotten that slot."

rect compliance costs, and affirmative action often places them be-tween contending employees in an awkward damned-if-you-do, damned-if-you-don't quandary. Nevertheless, some large companies support affirmative action even in nonbusiness settings. Their leaders emphasize the benefits of ethno-racial diversity in a global market, and the programs are promoted by powerful internal and external constituencies, including some customers. The programs also tend to advantage large companies by imposing onerous reporting, staffing, and other compliance costs on smaller competitors who cannot bear them as easily. Firms also see affirmative action as a safe harbor shel-tering them from Title VII claims, helping them to "keep the peace" and avoid adverse publicity. Absent allowable preferences, these claims would come not only from black workers but also from the vastly larger number of white workers who might allege reverse dis-crimination. In a notoriously uncertain system, firms favor almost anything, even some regulations, that can clarify their legal duties.

All of these corporate interests, as well as strong support by mili-tary leaders, surely help to explain the failure of President Reagan and both Presidents Bush to move vigorously against affirmative action—except in their judicial appointments—despite numerous opportuni-ties to do so. (Presidents Johnson, Nixon, Carter, Clinton, and Obama supported it in varying degrees.) Today, most politicians, with their eyes on Hispanic and Asian voters (and money) are unwilling to rock the affirmative action boat and risk being pilloried by ethnic group advocates as racist or insensitive to minority interests on an issue that is highly salient to the advocates but not to most minority voters. This helps to explain why the battles against affirmative action (and bilin-gual education) in California and elsewhere have been led primarily by private political entrepreneurs in ballot referenda, not by elected politicians.

Finally, affirmative action's political survival reflects more than the interests of particular groups and politicians. Many who are skeptical of preferences simply do not see any viable alternative. As noted earlier, advocates of preferences have drawn upon a deep res-ervoir of white guilt about past discrimination and its continuing effects on black representation in elite educational and economic institutions. Many see affirmative action as the only way to prevent a "re-segregation nightmare."[42]

Dearth of Blacks in Elite Institutions

Despite dramatic social, economic, and political gains in many areas of American life producing a sizeable black middle class, blacks (especially males) are conspicuously absent from important areas relative to their share (about 15 percent in 2015) of the overall population. This is most notable in the ranks of the leading professions, top corporate management, and high-ranked educational institutions. In particular, the percentage of black physicians, dentists, architects, and those in other elite professions has stagnated over the past ten years.[43] These numbers have not grown much since 1990. Only about 1 percent of Fortune 500 companies have a black chief executive. The share of black lawyers dropped in 2010 for the first time. Even black graduates of elite colleges reportedly have more difficulty than similarly educated whites (and are on par with whites educated in non-elite institutions).[44]

The pressure for affirmative action programs is particularly intense on highly ranked campuses due to a combination of egalitarian ideology and low numbers of blacks among faculty and students. Blacks constitute only 4 percent of the student body in the top decile of four-year institutions, while accounting for 26 percent of students in the lowest decile institutions.[45] These low numbers partly reflect black enrollees' dropout rates, which are much higher than for whites at all kinds of institutions, differences that are not entirely attributable to family income.[46] The numbers are also low on the other side of the rostrum. In 2011, degree-granting institutions that knew their full-time faculty's ethnicity reported that blacks were only 4 percent of those at the rank of full professor, 6–7 percent at the lower professorial ranks, and 8 percent among instructors.[47] And even these numbers are inflated by counting as black faculty the many who are clinicians at university teaching hospitals.[48]

Whether one should view this disturbing pattern (and its analogues in other fields) as "under-representation" depends, of course, on the reasons why it persists despite efforts to overcome it. Advocates of affirmative action tend to blame it on inadequate recruitment, past and current racism, educational disadvantage, culturally biased criteria, negative stereotypes, and off-putting elite cultures. In contrast, opponents point to black applicants' failure, for whatever reasons, to meet legitimate meritocratic standards. In this view, blacks' under-representation on selective campuses is no more remarkable or unjust—though infinitely more disturbing—than the under-representation of short people in the NBA. This debate over how to define merit and the reasons for group differences was discussed earlier.

Constitutionality

The path to the current constitutional status of affirmative action is a long and tangled one. This reflects the shifting membership of the Supreme Court since the *Bakke* decision, the persistently sharp divisions among the justices on this issue, and the narrow, fact-based, and often opaque opinions that they have written on this subject, leaving key concepts ill-defined. Even so, the constitutional context can be briefly summarized.

Affirmative action programs at public institutions or those receiving government funds implicate the Fourteenth Amendment's Equal Protection Clause, which prohibits a state from denying "any person within its jurisdiction the equal protection of the laws."* Under the Court's equal protection doctrine, the government may distribute benefits or burdens on the basis of race—the prototypical "suspect classification"—only if it can satisfy the "strict scrutiny" test that the Court applies to such classifications. This test requires the government defending the program to show two things: that the suspect

* The same principle, essentially, limits the federal government—but under the Due Process Clause of the Fifth Amendment. And private institutions that receive federal or state funds face most of the same restrictions.

classification is necessary to serve a "compelling governmental interest," and that the classification is as "narrowly tailored" as it can be while still serving that interest.

Ironically, the Court has held that the very rationale for preferences that many Americans find most morally powerful—the need to remedy the continuing effects of past discrimination—is legally unavailable. Such remediation is *not* considered a compelling governmental interest unless that university, employer, or other institution intentionally discriminated against the group in the past in ways that continue to disadvantage the group. Thus, the institution cannot use preferences in order to remedy the effects of more general social practices or conditions.[49]

In the educational context, the Court has upheld only one general rationale for affirmative action—institutional diversity—which Justice Powell had endorsed in his decisive opinion way back in *Bakke* and which every justice has embraced except for Clarence Thomas and the late Antonin Scalia. In *Bakke*, the Court allowed a university to consider race in medical school admissions if it was only one of several factors, was used to advance student-body diversity, and avoided specific racial quotas for admission. The Court reaffirmed these three principles in the 2003 cases of *Grutter v. Bollinger* and *Gratz v. Bollinger*. In *Grutter*, involving the admissions policy of the University of Michigan's law school, the majority ruled that an admissions process giving some advantage to "underrepresented minority students," but also taking into consideration a variety of other factors applied (so the Court found) strictly on an individual basis for each applicant, did not amount to a quota system and so satisfied constitutional requirements. But in *Gratz*, which examined the university's undergraduate admissions policy, the Court found that, because the program gave a set number of admission points to any racial-minority applicant rather than considering each applicant individually as the law school did, it amounted to an impermissible quota system.

The Court reaffirmed this standard in its 2013 decision (*Fisher I*) involving the University of Texas's admissions program, remanding the case to the lower court because it had incorrectly applied the strict

scrutiny standard, applying (in the Court's later words) "an overly deferential 'good faith' standard in assessing" the program's constitutionality. On remand, the lower court essentially reiterated its earlier
analysis, contending that it had now satisfied the Supreme Court's
criteria.* The case returned to the Supreme Court in *Fisher II*. In a
June 2016 opinion authored by Anthony Kennedy (the swing justice
on affirmative action and many other cases), a truncated Court relied
on the diversity rationale to uphold the same Texas program. Because
he viewed it as one in which " 'race is but a factor of a factor of a factor
in the holistic-review calculus," Kennedy opined that the Texas program satisfied strict scrutiny. Although affirmative action proponents
applauded this decision, it is fair to say that Justice Alito's long, rigorous dissenting opinion was analytically much stronger. Relentlessly,
Alito showed how Kennedy's analysis in *Fisher II* was consistently
inconsistent with many aspects of his earlier opinions on this issue—
and, indeed, with his *Fisher I* analysis—concerning what strict scrutiny requires when applied to the Texas program and the state's own
defense of it. Perhaps Alito was right to suggest that Kennedy, having
grown "tired" of the case, did not want to remand it once again.

As will be evident in the policy discussion immediately below, I
find the diversity rationale for affirmative action to be conceptually
incoherent, refuted by the facts of the programs and of campus life,
and thus an unconvincing foundation on which to rest its constitutionality. This is why I once referred to the diversity rationale as a
"rhetorical Hail Mary pass, an argument made in desperation now
that all other [constitutional] arguments for preferences have
failed."[50]

Many legal scholars probably agree with my critique of the diversity rationale but still defend the programs' constitutionality. Usually,
they emphasize the need to rectify the injustices wreaked on blacks
by slavery, Jim Crow, and pervasive discrimination—but this is a
moral and policy argument, not a constitutional one. I addressed this

---

* In the intervening period, the Court held in another case that Michigan did not violate equal protection when it adopted a constitutional amendment banning affirmative
action. *Schuette v. Coalition to Defend Affirmative Action*, 134 S. Ct. 1623 (2014).

earlier—agreeing that these injustices occurred and trigger moral obligations even today, but showing that other legitimate moral arguments cut against ethno-racial preferences that rest on, and magnify, corrosive racial stereotypes—indeed, the very ones that strict scrutiny is supposed to root out—and create new injustices without really remedying the old ones. In any event, the Court has repeatedly rejected a general social-remedial justification for preferences.

A second argument for their constitutionality is that the courts should view preferences adopted by legislative majorities who do not benefit from them as "benign," judging them more permissively. While there is much to be said for this argument, benignity is in the eye of the beholder. A very large number of people are disadvantaged by preferences: those who tell the Census Bureau and others that they are white (that is, whites, 48 percent of Hispanics, similar proportions of Asians, and 80 percent of Native Americans); anyone else (dark-skinned Middle Easterners, for example) who is not included in the ethno-racial pentagon; and the more than seven million people (many with black ancestry) who consider themselves multiracial and wish to be identified as such (if they must be racially identified at all). These people are unlikely to think of this disadvantage as benign. Prima facie, at least, members of these groups are at least as deserving of special treatment as the non-black members of the favored pentagon.

The third argument for the constitutionality of preferences—the strongest, in my view—is based not on morality or majoritarian process but on historical precedent. At the very same time that Congress adopted the Fourteenth Amendment, it was also enacting programs favoring the former slaves.[51] This historical argument has been criticized,[52] but the Supreme Court has not really addressed it. Perhaps it has finessed this because it is simply impossible to imagine that the Congress that enacted the Freedmen's laws would have supported a system of preferences in which most of the potential beneficiaries are recent immigrants and their descendants.* Indeed, civil rights scholar

---

* In fact, immigrants are disproportionately represented (27 percent) among black students at selective institutions. Douglas S. Massey et al., "Black Immigrants and Black Natives Attending Selective Colleges and Universities in the United States," 113 *American Journal of Education* 243 (2007).

Hugh Davis Graham, finding this extension to post-1965 immigrants a "strange" result of bureaucratic politics, estimated that more than 75 percent of them—tens of millions—became eligible for preferences the moment they received their green cards, competing with the descendants of black slaves whose families have been (and suffered) in America for centuries.[53] This grotesque lack of fit between the Freedmen's laws and today's programs should give the Court considerable pause, particularly under the strict scrutiny standard that it now applies to them.

POLICY ISSUES

Assuming that the Court will now uphold the constitutionality of at least some affirmative action on the authority of *Fisher II*, a more important question remains: Even if it is constitutional, is it wise as a matter of policy? We can best pursue this question by taking the diversity rationale as seriously as the Court has taken it. This means analyzing the rationale's logic on both conceptual and empirical grounds. If it turns out to be unconvincing, as I maintain, then those who promote affirmative action bear the burden of defending it on some other policy ground. (The burden rests on them, I maintain, not only because the Court has placed it there as a matter of constitutional law by applying "strict scrutiny" to ethno-racial classifications of this kind, but also because they have failed to win widespread public support for these preferences in their five decades of existence.) Accordingly, I then consider three other rationales, somewhat related to diversity, which its defenders often invoke: black *role models* in positions of influence, *representation* of blacks in elite institutions, and *legitimation* of our social institutions. (Economists have also noted a possible efficiency argument in favor of preferences, if the social returns to raising human capital are particularly high for those minorities.)[54]

The diversity rationale raises at least six sets of crucial questions:

- What does diversity mean, and how does it confer value in the educational setting?

- How coherent is the "critical mass" argument made by proponents and accepted by a majority of the Court, and how does it relate to the diversity rationale?
- Do ethno-racial preferences in the name of diversity undermine the stereotypes that proponents (and the Court) claim to abhor, or do they instead reinforce those stereotypes?
- How can race be made a "plus factor" without the kind of racial balancing that the Court prohibits?
- Do race-neutral alternatives exist?
- How long will preferences continue? (*All* rationales for preferences—not just diversity—raise this question.)

*The Meaning and Value of Diversity.** Affirmative action programs, despite professions to the contrary, aim largely or only at ethno-racial diversity. From a diversity-value perspective, the programs' designation of beneficiary groups is arbitrary and incoherent, even silly. The status of blacks today, as well as their historical experience, differs greatly depending on whether they are native-born or immigrated from Africa or the Caribbean. Hispanics are a language group, not a race; they come from all over the world, mostly self-identify as whites, intermarry with other groups at a high rate, are residentially more dispersed, and have endured nothing like the systematic oppression and subordination experienced by blacks. Asians are an extraordinarily heterogeneous group whose only commonality is that they or their ancestors once lived on an immense continent. They have entirely distinct historic, linguistic, religious, immigration, and political identities. (Indeed, many Asians have compiled such strong academic credentials that Harvard and other elite schools may—the matter is in litigation—be subjecting them to a quota system to *limit* their presence on elite campuses, much as Jews were once limited.)[55] A significant, growing number of Americans—almost 7 percent, according to a Pew Center report (more than triple the Census Bureau estimates)—

---

* Sources for most of the following analysis of the diversity rationale for preferences can be found in Schuck, *Diversity in America* (2003), at 160–69.

are ethnic hybrids, falling into two or more of these categories, with the largest such group (half the total) being a mix of whites and Native Americans. An estimated 26 percent of Hispanics and 28 percent of Asian Americans marry a spouse of a different race or ethnicity.[56] The Pew report also confirms what many studies have found—that these identities are far too fluid to conform to affirmative action's rigid pigeonholes.[57] The programs make little or no effort to take *intragroup* diversity into account.[58]

Also making little sense from a diversity perspective is affirmative action programs' disregard of the many anomalies, evasions, and confusions that attend most ethno-racial discourse in America. The attributes that define the programs are relatively poor predictors of the experiences, outlooks, and ideas that an individual is likely to bring to campus. Indeed, partisan and religious affiliation account for the largest viewpoint cleavages, certainly more than race does, yet the programs select for the latter, not the former. A priori (which is how programs select the groups to be preferred), doesn't the perspective of a white Muslim or fundamentalist Christian have at least as much diversity value as that of a middle-class black or Hispanic?

The claim that members of the preferred minority groups actually create diversity value on campus rests on certain essentialist premises that not only are false as a general matter but also tend to ratify the very stereotypes that the programs are intended to combat—a tendency I discuss below. Leading defenses of preferences, such as the Bowen-Bok study,[59] assume that black students, for example, bring to campus special histories and viewpoints that are common to almost all of them—even though these are not racially or genetically hardwired into them. Because these students have the common experience of growing up black in America and gaining the special perspectives that go with that experience, this view suggests they help non-blacks to comprehend all of this, thus strengthening the foundations of good citizenship in a pluralist democracy. Affirmative action, in this view, cultivates interracial socialization skills valued by both white and black students, skills they can enhance by attending racially diverse institutions.

This set of assumptions can be challenged from many directions. In fact, most students and faculty place little weight on ethnic diversity as a cause of positive educational outcomes; indeed, peer-group racial composition has no positive effect on any of the eighty-two outcome variables used by the American Council on Education. A comparison of interracial friendships on campus and among adults finds that such friendships are more common in other social arenas. The evidence of growing interracial friendships among pre-college youngsters today would likely strengthen the finding that college makes the difference.

Another challenge focuses on what actually goes on in the classroom. Even assuming that minorities' values and experiences are different, these differences turn out to be irrelevant to most of what students study as undergraduates, even in the humanities and social sciences. Many teachers observe that white and Asian students tend to express the same ideas that black students do, which is not surprising given that admissions officers don't ask how salient race is to applicants' ideas or perspectives, nor would we want them to. And when the U.S. Air Force Academy conducted a controlled experiment in which it assigned new cadets to peer group squadrons designed to maximize the lowest-ability students' academic performance, it found that "students avoided the peers with whom we intended them to interact and instead formed more homogeneous subgroups," with the "social mismatch" effects swamping the intended academic benefits of the diversification.[60] I shall return to the mismatch issue below.

The Air Force Academy study is not alone in finding persistent racial self-isolation on campuses that give preferences, which also casts doubt on the interracial socialization idea. Orlando Patterson, a supporter of a complex structure of affirmative action,[61] laments that "no group of people now seems more committed to segregation than Afro-American students and young professionals." Political scientist Jack Citrin found that the 250-point white-black gap in SAT scores created an academic "caste system" at Berkeley in which the preferred students major in different—and frankly, easier—subjects. (Significantly, this ethnic academic gap among students narrowed once California banned preferences in 1996.)

Critical Mass. Institutions argue that a "critical mass" of favored minorities assembled through preferences is crucial to achieving educational diversity, and the Court has accepted this notion. But what does it mean? It must be a function of either the number or proportion of students needed to produce it, yet the Court, as explained below, has flatly barred any numerical or proportional quotas; even *Fisher II* demands individualized assessments. Moreover, the critical-mass criterion is only intelligible if one specifies the level of university activity at which racial assignments are permissible in order to achieve the critical mass. Is the level campus-wide? academic program–wide? each major, or only some? seminars? lectures? dormitories? sports teams? Neither the schools nor the Court says which it is. Finally, what constitutes a critical mass depends on the individual school, yet the Court in *Fisher I* emphatically refused to defer to schools' judgment in this matter.

Stereotypes. In *Grutter*, the Court majority saw a very close link between critical mass and stereotype destruction: "[W]hen a critical mass of underrepresented minority students is present, racial stereotypes lose their force because nonminority students learn that there is no 'minority viewpoint' but rather a variety of viewpoints among minority students."[62] But just the reverse is much more likely. A school cannot prefer students on the basis of skin color or surnames without at the same time endorsing the notions of ethno-racial essentialism and viewpoint determinism. By admitting minority students with academic records that are much weaker (whatever the school's metric) than those of their competitors, the school can only reinforce the stereotype of academic inferiority. The faculty and non-preferred students notice what is going on and draw the logical and stigmatizing inference that the preferred group's academic abilities are inferior.* This inference often takes the form of insidious innu-

---

* To recognize the importance that elite schools give to academic factors is emphatically *not* to say that test scores and GPA are, or should be, decisive in determining admission. A sensible institution will consider a variety of factors in selecting its student body, although elite schools hoping to maintain their positions will weigh academic potential or performance most heavily. Schools do give preference to athletes and legacies, which can

endo about the deserts of almost all but the most unquestionably superior performers in the preferred group—and, as the "lemon" phenomenom suggests, perhaps even of them. This innuendo tends to perpetuate the very stereotypes that affirmative action is supposed to dispel.

A group *qua* group (which is how preferences treat it) can confer diversity value only if it possesses certain desired qualities—and it can only do that if those qualities inhere in all of its members. (If it doesn't, then the program should redefine the group to exclude those who lack those qualities, but affirmative action programs do not do this.) But to affirm that a quality inheres in a racial group is to "essentialize" race, utterly contradicting liberal, egalitarian, scientific, and religious values. These values hold that all individuals are unique and formally equal regardless of genetic heritage, and that their race per se causally determines little or nothing about their character, intelligence, experience, or anything else that is relevant to their diversity value. Indeed, if an employer used racial stereotypes in this way, it would clearly violate the law—whether or not the stereotypes were generally true. This use of stereotypes would also justify racial profiling by police if the stereotypes were used to fight crime and were accurate enough.

Another defense of affirmative action asserts that applicants with manifestly inferior academic performance are superior to others with respect to non-academic virtues such as leadership, character, community commitments, and overcoming obstacles. But this too is a patronizing and pernicious stereotype. Their superiority in these "soft" variables may be true in particular cases, of course, but there is simply no a priori reason to believe that applicants from a favored group are more likely to exhibit these qualities than are applicants from other groups. Indeed, it would be very surprising if this were true.

---

engender stereotypes of academic inferiority ("dumb jocks"). But the constitutional and historical valences of these groups and their experiences are different. These differences do not justify their preferences (at least to me), but they do help to explain why these stereotypes are not as corrosive and stigmatizing as those attaching to preferred ethno-racial minorities.

The Size of the "Plus Factor." The Court majority in *Grutter* held that "each applicant must be evaluated as an individual and not in a way that makes an applicant's race or ethnicity the defining feature of his or her application." This, the Court reasoned, will place members of all groups on the same admissions track, where they will compete "on the same footing." Race and ethnicity can be a "modest plus factor" in a system of "individualized assessments," but this must not constitute either a "rigid quota" or "racial balancing."[63] *Fisher II* reaffirmed this.

But are the ethno-racial plus factors merely "modest"? In fact, they are huge. In the program at issue in *Grutter*, as the dissenters showed statistically, the plus factor was weighted so heavily that it effectively created a two-track system, tantamount to racial balancing, in order to reach its racially defined "critical mass." And what was true in *Grutter* is essentially true of most if not all other affirmative action programs. In 2003, I reviewed the empirical studies on the size of preferences, which showed that the programs gave enormous weight to ethno-racial status[64]—much larger, for example, than the preferences given to legacies and athletes.

This situation is unchanged, judging by more recent analyses of admissions patterns.[65] For example, a study of all students admitted to the nation's medical schools in 2014–15 found that blacks and Hispanics were vastly more likely to be admitted than whites and Asians with comparable MCAT scores and GPAs. And this was true in every credential range: average, below average, or above average.[66] Writing in 2009, researchers Thomas Espenshade and Alexandra Radford reported that the admission "bonus" for being black was equivalent to 310 SAT points relative to whites and even more relative to Asians.[67] The GPA differences are even greater than for SAT scores. An earlier analysis by another researcher, Thomas Kane, found that black applicants to selective schools "enjoy an advantage equivalent to an increase of two-thirds of a point in [GPA]—on a four point scale—or [the equivalent of] 400 points on the SAT."[68] That enormous preferences-conferred advantage seems to have grown even larger since then. In a review article commissioned by the prestigious *Journal of Economic Literature* and published in March 2016, Peter Arcidiacono and Michael Lovenheim found virtually no overlap between white and black admits' credentials, especially but not only at law schools:

> The median black admit had an academic index at the second percentile of the white distribution, and the seventy-fifth percentile of the black admit distribution was at the eighth percentile of the white distribution. The difference between the black and white admit distributions is not all due to affirmative action: if the African American academic index distribution is below the white distribution, this would produce a difference in the incoming qualifications of black versus white students even in the absence of affirmative action. However, the fact that these distributions are almost non-overlapping is suggestive of a large amount of race-based preferences in admissions being given to African American students. . . . The data also reveal that affirmative action works differently for blacks and Hispanics. While affirmative action is very much present for Hispanics (the median Hispanic admit at Michigan is at the 9th percentile of the white admit distribution), the median Hispanic admit is at the 78th percentile of the black admit distribution. Hispanic admission rates were also lower than those for blacks, despite having on average better test scores and undergraduate grades.[69]

Moreover, the SAT test, which has long been criticized as being culturally biased against blacks, is actually an overly optimistic predictor of how they will perform in college. Once on campus, they do worse than the SAT would predict.[70] Finally, 2015 data on SAT scores, broken down by ethnicity, show that the scores of whites and minorities have declined significantly since 2006, while Asians' scores have risen in all three skills categories, not just math.[71] (The National Assessment of Education Progress [NAEP] scores, while less discouraging, are nothing to celebrate either.)[72] This suggests, ominously, that those who administer preferences will have to increase their size even more in the future in order to admit low-scoring minorities.

These findings raise a crucial question: Are the students who receive these enormous preferences in order to be admitted to elite schools likely on average to be in over their heads academically? This phenomenon, known as "mismatch," is discussed below.

Race-Neutral Alternatives. The Court majority has repeatedly insisted that ethno-racial preferences may not be used if workable race-neutral alternatives exist. In an earlier opinion by Justice Kennedy, the Court also refused to endorse race-based assignments to public schools where race-neutral assignment methods are available to accomplish the same end.[73] In *Fisher II*, Justice Kennedy reaffirmed this principle, while concluding that no such alternative existed there.

Race-neutral criteria are no panacea, of course, especially when the question is not the one that the Court asks (i.e., whether the Constitution requires it) but instead is about which criteria make the most policy sense if the goal is increasing opportunity for the disadvantaged—which Americans overwhelmingly support. Given this goal, the most straightforward criterion is to determine disadvantage directly rather than use ethnicity or race as an extremely crude proxy for disadvantage. This approach is more difficult than it sounds for conceptual, administrative, and target efficiency reasons—and it might not yield the ethnic mix that those favoring race-based affirmative action want; indeed, one analysis finds that it would increase the share of whites and Asians on campus and reduce blacks by almost 50 percent![74] Conceptually, we generally equate disadvantage with economic deprivation, usually measured by income or assets—but disadvantage can be social, not just economic; they are not always congruent and social disadvantage is harder to define and measure. Administratively, determining economic need directly for a very large number of applicants would be at least as challenging as it has been in the operation of need-based social welfare programs. And the difficulty of targeting the neediest is captured by questions posed by Michael Kinsley (a supporter of affirmative action): "Is it worse to be a cleaning lady's son or a coal miner's daughter? Two points if your father didn't go to college, minus one if he finished high school, plus three if you have no father? (or will that reward illegitimacy which we're all trying hard these days not to do? . . . Officially sanctioned affirmative action by 'disadvantage' would turn today's festival of competitive victimization into an orgy."[75]

Determining who is truly needy is difficult, surely, but not impossible. Richard Sander, a law professor at the University of California at Los Angeles, reports that he actually devised and implemented a sophisticated system of preferences for UCLA law school based on economic need, and that the system worked "exceedingly well. Audits against financial aid statements showed little abuse; the preferences substantially changed the social makeup of the class and never to our knowledge, prompted complaints of unfairness."[76] Such approaches need to be tried and assessed more broadly, of course, but they may offer one kind of race-neutral alternative to ethno-racial preferences.

A second kind of race-neutral alternative is a program that automatically admits students in the upper echelons (say, the top 5 or 10 percent) of their high school classes. Texas, Florida, and California have adopted such percentage programs (although Texas, unsatisfied with the number of minorities its percentage plan yielded, added to it the race-based program challenged in the *Fisher* litigation). Percentage programs do seem to increase racial diversity on college campuses, but two realities about such programs should be kept in mind. As Justice Kennedy noted in *Fisher II* (quoting Justice Ginsburg's point in *Fisher I*), these programs, far from being race-neutral, are designed and adopted with race very much in mind.[77] And, given differences among the high schools in different communities, such programs inevitably bring to these campuses many students whose academic preparation is relatively poor.

A third alternative, which has attracted much interest, would not only increase the number of minority students attending selective institutions but also ameliorate a different, more tractable, and even more socially wasteful kind of problem—the substantial pool of high school students who are perfectly capable of performing well at selective colleges but do not even apply to them—or indeed to any college at all! Caroline Hoxby and her colleagues have shown that applications by these students, many of whom are minorities, can be increased through better information about how to apply, about available financial aid opportunities, and about other assistance available on campus. Moreover, increasing applications from this group can be accomplished at trivial cost—as little as $6 per student.[78]

Finally, as Justice Alito tartly observed in his dissent in *Fisher II*, "the most obvious race-neutral alternative" is "race-blind, holistic review that considers the applicant's unique characteristics and personal circumstances."[79]

The Duration of Preferences. Writing for the *Grutter* majority, Justice O'Connor expressed hope that "25 years from now, the use of racial preferences will no longer be necessary."[80] Much has been made of her expectation. In his dissent, Justice Thomas recited the grim statistics on comparative academic performance, evidence that makes Justice O'Connor's hope seem very unrealistic. And the studies of ethno-racial preferences in other societies provide no support for it either, as the economist Thomas Sowell has shown in his cross-national studies.[81] To the contrary, the studies show that such preferences, once established, tend to endure and perhaps even expand to new groups and new programmatic benefits. The Court's blessing of affirmative action in *Fisher II* seems more likely to perpetuate it than to herald their eventual demise.

It is true that six politically diverse states (Arizona, California, Michigan, Nebraska, Oklahoma, and Washington) have banned these preferences by voter referenda, while New Hampshire has done so through statute and Florida through executive order. But California's experience after its voters banned the preferences suggests that such bans do not end them but simply drive the preferences underground. The California system engaged in a series of stratagems in the early 2000s expressly designed to circumvent the state's ban. Some of the more egregious ones involved channeling minority students to new "critical race studies" programs with lower admissions standards; awarding special admissions credit for foreign-language fluency to minority students who were already native speakers of the language; adopting "percentage" plans; and using unspecified (and unspecifiable) "holistic" criteria as well as winks and nods by admissions officials.[82] The evidence suggests that affirmative action advocates will never abandon it but will always find new ways to preserve it. And their arguments will always have a surface plausibility so long as full equality eludes us, which in the real world it surely will—however we define it.

The Role Model Rationale. Affirmative action advocates commonly argue that it is effective in producing a cadre of black professionals who can form a nucleus of group leaders and serve as role models for other group members, especially the young who need to have high aspirations and confidence that others have succeeded despite their common legacy of group disadvantage. This rationale, which has its skeptics even among ardent liberals,[83] applies most strongly in the domain of higher education, which of course is an important training ground for future leaders of society. Studies on how well such programs perform this function have been chewed over by proponents and opponents of affirmative action alike.

There is something to the role model argument. Group members who have succeeded are surely a source of encouragement to young people thinking about their futures. If this is true, however, it is true not just for the groups preferred by affirmative action but for *all* low-status groups, not just the preferred ones. This argument, moreover, cannot be separated from questions about the other social signals that youngsters receive from role-modeling. A role model might signal: "If you study hard and work hard and keep your nose clean as I did, you too can succeed." But in a society in which preferences have become both pervasive and normative, another signal might be: "You get points for having a certain skin color or surname, so you should emphasize that identity and learn to play the ethno-racial card." How do youngsters in such a society in fact read role-model signals, and how do they integrate conflicting ones? These are important questions to which we have not really sought, and as a methodological matter may not be able to obtain, reliable answers.

The Representation in Elite Institutions Rationale. Like the other rationales, this one has some force. Most Americans want to see disadvantaged minorities better represented in major firms, select universities, high public office, nonprofit organizations, and so forth—if these minorities earn this recognition by meeting the institutions' legitimate standards, whatever they might be. Affirmative action proponents believe that admitting minorities to these prestigious and advantageous precincts will level the playing field, reducing inequality by providing the advantages that these institutions can confer, including greater satisfaction and future advancement.

To what extent are these hopes actually borne out? The answer has a lot to do with the size of the preferences. In elite institutions, as we have seen, they are very large indeed—so large that they may do more harm than good to many of the putative beneficiaries. An important body of empirical research suggests that this unhappy outcome is occurring, at least in higher education, as a result of a mismatch between the institution's demands and the preferred students' academic performance. It indicates that although some affirmative action beneficiaries will surely succeed at the select institutions to which preferences gain them admission, *on average* they will perform relatively poorly, yet they would probably have succeeded at less select institutions.

In their book-length analysis of this mismatch problem,[84] Richard Sander and Stuart Taylor, Jr., conclude that it largely explains "why, even though blacks are more likely to enter college than are whites with similar backgrounds, they will usually get much lower grades, rank toward the bottom of the class, and far more often drop out; why there are so few blacks and Hispanics with science and engineering degrees or with doctorates in any field; and why black law graduates fail bar exams at four times the white rate."[85]

Two important facts about these bad outcomes and human costs are especially notable—and disturbing. First, according to an authoritative review of mismatch research (discussed below), no programs give under-represented groups needed information about their prospects of success at different tiers of institutions.[86] Second, the resulting failures are wholly unnecessary. Sander and Taylor observe: "[N]early all of these students *do* have what it takes to succeed" in the absence of affirmative action preferences; they would just gain this success at the less demanding schools to which they could gain admission without preferences. They continue:

> [T]he main victims of large racial preferences . . . are not the many whites and Asians who get passed over but rather the many blacks and Hispanics who receive preferences and do badly. . . . Their intellectual confidence has been undermined, their career aspirations have in many cases been derailed, and they must deal with the stigma of being "affirmative-action admits." In the words of liberal scholar Christopher Jencks, "A policy that encourages the nation's future leaders to believe that blacks are slow learners will . . . do incalculable harm over the long run, because blacks cannot shed their skin after graduation."[87]

In fact, any declines in minority enrollments in the flagship campuses in state systems where affirmative action admissions are banned tend to be offset by their attendance at less selective schools in the system (or elsewhere)—what Sander and Taylor call a "cascade effect." This outcome is not at all surprising. Several econometric studies of minority enrollments in state systems after bans on affirmative action in those states confirm this empirically: Only the students' *distribution* among system campuses is affected, not their total enrollments or graduation rates.[88] In fact, Sander and Taylor's data indicate that the academic performance of minority students in the University of California system substantially improved after Proposition 209 banned explicit affirmative action policies in the state. Their four-year graduation rate rose 55 percent; the number who earned degrees in STEM fields rose 51 percent; the number who had GPAs of 3.5 or higher rose by 63 percent; and the number who earned doctorates and STEM graduate degrees rose by 25 percent.

Under any reasonable accounting, these immense gains to minority students under race-neutral admissions systems vastly outweigh whatever loss of diversity value has occurred at the most selective campuses, Berkeley and UCLA. And logically, no diversity value should be lost; this cascade effect merely redistributes it, as any losses of diversity benefits to students at more selective colleges absent preferences are offset by diversity gains at the less selective ones that minorities will now attend. Indeed, Sander finds that the overall level of integration of both blacks and Hispanics across the eight UC undergraduate campuses increased significantly after Proposition 209. Before Proposition 209, Berkeley and UCLA used racial preferences to attract blacks and Hispanics, and as a result half the blacks in the UC system had been concentrated on those two campuses. After the ban, when those schools could no longer officially employ such policies, this skewing largely disappeared; the distribution of both groups more closely approximated the distribution of whites across all of the other campuses in the system.

On the other hand, a number of prominent scholars strongly challenge the mismatch theory and data, particularly as applied to legal education (the focus of Sander's original study), on various methodological grounds. Indeed, they filed an amicus brief in *Fisher II*, and the day it came down, one of them (Richard Lempert, a law professor and leading proponent of preferences) published a *New York Times* op-ed urging that mismatch theory be "dumped" now that preferences had been upheld.[89] Sander has replied in detail to these critics, and he and Taylor devoted a chapter of their book to reviewing and refuting their objections. The 2016 peer-reviewed Arcidiacono-Lovenheim analysis of the mismatch studies, mentioned above, largely confirms Sander's findings that the long-run outcomes of preferred students in the most selective schools are relatively poor—not only on average but through most of the distribution.[90] Their analysis also observes that "[i]f, indeed, affirmative action harms long-run outcomes of minority students, it suggests that returns to diversity within an institution would need to be quite large in order to justify these programs."[91] In fact, my own critique of the diversity rationale suggests that the actual returns to diversity ("diversity value," as defined above) on these campuses are insubstantial.

As we have seen, the preferences are so large that it would be rather astonishing if substantial academic mismatch did not in fact occur. Still, colleges could reduce the amount of potential mismatch in several ways. Remedial programs on campus, if effective, could help. Colleges could also reduce the size of their preferences. For example, Sander and Taylor propose that if preferences are to be used, their magnitude should be no larger than the ones that the same school uses for socioeconomically disadvantaged students of all races. Finally, schools that use preferences could substitute transparency about their affirmative action programs for what has been their calculated secrecy and opacity on the subject (which Sander and Taylor have documented in detail in their book and other work). This would place students and their parents in a better position to assess the benefits and costs of preferences at particular schools when deciding which schools to attend. The Court, most recently in *Fisher II*, has insisted that the schools conduct this sort of analysis in order to justify preferences under strict scrutiny if challenged in the courts, yet schools have evidently done little serious analysis of this kind.[92] A recent survey of several dozen flagship state universities shows that fewer than one in five even collects systematic data on the socioeconomic background of their applicants, while virtually all not only collect data on applicants' race, but give heavy weight to it.[93]

The Social Legitimacy Rationale. Affirmative action proponents also contend that the presence of minority group members in visible roles of leadership and influence is conducive, if not essential, to the legitimacy of America's social and political institutions. For minorities to accept their outcomes as minimally just or at least acceptable, the argument goes, they (and others) must view those institutions as inclusive and procedurally fair. Being governed by minority legislators, taught by minority teachers, and tried by minority judges, for example, may advance that goal. A slightly different argument, which is particularly applicable to public universities, is that minorities pay taxes for these mobility-enhancing public services, entitling them to fair representation in those programs.

There are at least three problems with this argument. The first concerns the casual way in which many commentators deploy the concept of legitimacy. For many, it is not merely a handy rhetorical trope. It also serves as an indispensable prop, a kind of all-purpose, gap-filling, *deus ex machina* that we* often use to rescue arguments that lack much empirical support or that merely reflect our deeply held convictions. We can all readily agree that any sound democratic regime must be perceived as legitimate in the sense that those subject to it accept and feel bound by its law, quite apart from whether they agree with the law's merits.

Affirmative action advocates assert that democratic legitimacy requires preferences, not just non-discrimination, and that preferences even increase this legitimacy. But there is no evidence either that Americans, including those favored by preferences, did not view the United States as a legitimate regime until affirmative action became widespread in the mid-1970s, or that the citizens of those states (nine as of 2016) that have abolished it in public programs regard their governments as any less legitimate than do the citizens of those states that have retained it. As noted earlier, the vast majority of Americans, including more than a third of blacks and 70 percent of Hispanics, oppose ethno-racial preferences in the workplace and on college campuses, and this level of opposition has risen somewhat over time.[94] So the legitimacy argument in favor of preferences turns out to be one more Hail Mary pass.

At the same time, the public does support the general idea that government should try to improve the status of racial minorities. When Gallup in 2015 polled opinions about affirmative action programs for racial minorities without mentioning preferences, 58 percent expressed support.[95] But this has no bearing on whether they regard a polity that lacks affirmative action as illegitimate. So far as I know, supporters of affirmative action have not protested its abolition in certain states by engaging in the kind of civil disobedience or mo-

---

* I say "we" because sometimes I too invoke the notion of legitimacy, although usually to express skepticism about our ability to know its absence when we see it, except perhaps in revolutions or other extreme cases.

bilized actions that, during the civil rights era, signaled the widespread perception that regimes practicing Jim Crow or denying the vote to blacks were indeed illegitimate. Substantial disagreement with a policy, even on moral grounds, does not thereby make the policy illegitimate. If it did, no diverse democratic policy would be legitimate. Accordingly, when affirmative action advocates insist that the policy is essential to democratic legitimacy, what they really mean is that they feel very strongly about it. Their opponents, of course, feel just as strongly, yet this fact does not render the policy illegitimate.

A second argument against the social legitimacy rationale is that the vast majority of black students admitted to these institutions are already from middle- and upper-class families (although on average they are still poorer and more needful of financial aid than their white peers). One study found that 86 percent of African Americans at selective colleges were either middle- or upper class.[96] In another study of Ivy League universities, sociologists found that 41 percent of black freshmen were immigrants, who are typically more socioeconomically advantaged than non-immigrant blacks.[97] This relatively privileged background correlates with both participation and leadership.

Third, a study of many public colleges and universities suggests that absent affirmative action, these minority students would have attended *other* institutions that graduate many more blacks who succeed both professionally and civically.[98] Today's 105 historically black colleges and universities (HCBUs) account for only 3 percent of America's colleges, yet enroll 11 percent of its black students.[99] Indeed, a striking fact is that, while HBCUs account for only a small percentage of total black college enrollment, they produce a substantial share of black members of Congress, military officers, religious and social action leaders, and MacArthur "genius" grantees.[100] Although these successful graduates were educated some time ago, their alma maters are now more intensively recruiting and often enrolling the most outstanding black students (and now even other minorities, particularly Latinos),[101] many of whom could gain admission to predominantly white elite institutions through affirmative action programs—or in some cases, without preferences.[102] The non-flagship campuses of public university systems, where most of the direct affirmative action beneficiaries would end up absent affirmative action, also produce large numbers of successful graduates.[103] In short, the vast majority of those admitted to select institutions may well have succeeded and been leaders *anyway* even without the preferences. (This is not to deny that the level of success of some of them might have been lower, perhaps because of reduced financial aid opportunities at less selective institutions).

CONCLUSION

This chapter began by explaining why affirmative action is a hard issue despite the fact that the chapter's analysis—on public opposition, constitutional vulnerability, weak rationales, moral ambiguity, and evidence of harm to many of its intended beneficiaries—argues strongly against it. Affirmative action inflames social conflict in the already sensitive area of race relations. (It surely accounts for some of Donald Trump's support). Yet any marginal gains for black group advancement from preferences are slight or non-existent. Admittedly, conflict and ineffectiveness afflict many of our public policies (as I have shown elsewhere).[104] But such results are especially problematic here because plausible policy alternatives exist that promise to improve outcomes for blacks and other disadvantaged minorities, and with fewer negative effects. Moreover, the conflict over affirmative action tends to draw attention away from the real problem—the dire effects of poverty and family pathology (the subject of chapter 2) on the next generation of black Americans. Affirmative action on campus is wholly irrelevant to this, as we saw in examining who benefits from it. If preferences were better-targeted and effective, we could do both—retain preferences while *also* seeking to ameliorate poverty's corrosive effects. But because political and moral resources are scarce, issues compete with one another for attention, energy, resources, and effort. Affirmative action, then, is not merely problematic for the many reasons discussed in this chapter; it also constitutes a costly distraction from what should be our top domestic priority.

CHAPTER 6

RELIGIOUS EXEMPTIONS FROM SECULAR PUBLIC POLICIES

THE AMERICAN POLITY IS a mighty engine of public policies generated by all levels of government, policies that affect us all in myriad ways. Each of these policies is usually framed in general terms so the policy will apply equally to everyone subject to its terms. This goal of equal treatment under the law, however, is vastly complicated by a singular fact about America: It is the most diverse Western society on earth—regardless of how one defines diversity, or what kinds of diversity are under discussion.[1]

Among the many aspects of American diversity, perhaps the most distinctive (compared with other modern democracies) is our rich array of religious beliefs and practices.[2] These beliefs and practices are deeply valued not only by their adherents but also by the many more secular Americans who believe that religious values are good for our society.* Unlike most other types of diversity, religious belief

* By secular, I mean an attitude or orientation that is not grounded primarily in religious convictions.

and practice are both constitutionally protected. This protection is conferred by two parts of the First Amendment—the Free Exercise Clause and the Establishment Clause—that are in significant conflict or tension with each other, especially with regard to accommodation decisions.* (The Fourteenth Amendment's Equal Protection Clause also applies, but to a lesser extent.) This tension sometimes occurs when the government's very efforts to accommodate a religious practice (e.g., when it funds chaplains or exempts religious groups from taxes, land use controls, equal employment, and other generally applicable laws) might be deemed excessive government entanglement in the religious sphere under the applicable legal tests for prohibited establishments.

The Supreme Court has elaborated certain doctrines designed to bring the constitutional values enshrined in the two clauses into a proper balance with other constitutional values and social interests, almost all of which are essentially secular, sometimes explicitly so (e.g., the Constitution's ban on any religious test for office[3]). These balancing doctrines seek to preserve the conflicting values and interests while also protecting precious rule-of-law norms: coherence, consistency, predictability, and even-handedness. This delicate balancing act presents a "hard issue," in this book's parlance. Few experts in the field think that the Court has gotten it right. Many believe that it should defer more to the balance that legislatures have already struck in the statute or rule under challenge. One thing seems abundantly clear: The combination of a more expansive regulatory state, and more diverse views about which behaviors are appropriate or offensive, is engendering more—and more complex—social and legal conflicts.

---

* Some constitutional law scholars argue that there is really but one religion clause and that this fact affects how it is interpreted. See, e.g., Akhil Reed Amar, "The Supreme Court, 1999 Term Foreword: The Document and the Doctrine," 114 *Harvard Law Review* 26, 120 (2000). Others argue that the Free Exercise Clause is essentially redundant because of the large zone of protection afforded to religious exercise by other constitutional provisions, especially the Fourteenth Amendment. See Mark Tushnet, "The Redundant Free Exercise Clause?" 33 *Loyola University of Chicago Law Review* 71 (2001); Kenji Yoshino, "Covering," 111 *Yale Law Journal* 769, 927–30 (2002).

The chapter consists of five parts. The first presents the larger context in which the issue arises—specifically, our religious diversity and rights culture. The second part explores three key concepts—separation, accommodation, and neutrality—that the Court and other discussants use when analyzing accommodation claims. Next, I discuss judicial methodology, focusing on two legal doctrines—the "standard of review" and the test for "establishment"—that the Court uses to resolve such disputes. (I do so as briefly and non-technically as possible.)

The next part, "Emerging Accommodation Issues," has three sections. The first analyzes the Court's controversial 2014 decision in the *Hobby Lobby* case holding that certain closely-held, for-profit employers could claim religious exceptions (or exemptions; I use the terms interchangeably) from generally applicable laws—there, the Affordable Care Act mandate that employer-provided insurance cover contraceptives.[4] The second section discusses the proliferating demands for exceptions in the wake of the Court's 2015 *Obergefell* decision upholding same-sex marriage.[5] Here, sexual and gender minorities' claims to equal treatment clash with claims by those who refuse to provide services to these minorities, citing religious objections and *Hobby Lobby*. And most recently, civil rights disputes have arisen over which bathrooms and locker rooms transgender people may use, disputes that presage many others. Finally, I discuss how we might best accommodate the conflicting interests going forward.

CONTEXT

Two fundamental features of American life intensify the conflicts between religion and secular public policies (and between one religion and others). The first is its *religious diversity* (as well as its growing secularism). The second is our distinctive *rights culture*—mostly legal but also informal—which complicates such conflicts by pressing them into adversarial and uncompromising forms.

Religious Diversity*

America is an anomaly among modern postindustrial societies: It is more religious, its religiosity is more diverse, and its separation of state and religion is more rigorous. This religiosity, diversity, and separation—which contrast sharply with the European experience on all three points—did not come immediately or naturally. The zealous Puritans who founded American society were soon reduced to a minority even in the Plymouth colony, and their descendants engaged in a constant and mostly unsuccessful struggle with secularism, indifference, and declining church attendance. The only doctrine they valued was their own—or, as the nineteenth-century minister Henry Ward Beecher put it, "Orthodoxy is *my* doxy and heterodoxy is *your* doxy, if *your* doxy is not like *my* doxy." Many colonists, themselves anti-establishment dissenters, nonetheless did not shrink from persecuting, expelling, even killing those whose worship differed from theirs—an intolerance widely practiced in Massachusetts, Maryland, Virginia, New Amsterdam, and other colonies.

What brought religious diversity to America was not so much toleration as immigration, which the colonies desired primarily for its economic value to thinly settled frontier communities and their entrepreneurial merchants and real estate speculators. Toleration for the strange beliefs and practices of other Christians, not to speak of non-Christians and nonbelievers, came only slowly and even then, incompletely. Americans, literally repelled by the religious wars (which actually were about much more than religion[6]) that had butchered and benighted so many of their ancestors in Europe, gradually found their way to the live-and-let-live acceptance of heterodox beliefs and disparate practices that mark our constitutional tradition—and, today, our dominant social ethos. The dramatic declines in

---

* Much of this section on religious diversity is taken more or less verbatim from my book *Diversity in America: Keeping Government at a Safe Distance* (2003), 264–71, with some updates. Sources can be found in the endnotes to that discussion. Readers not interested in exploring this topic can skip to the next section without losing the thread of the larger analysis.

anti-Catholicism and anti-Semitism during the last half of the twentieth century were important signs of this attitudinal change. If any more proof of the new ethos were desired, one need only look to President Bush's speech to the nation only two days after the September 11 terrorist attacks, praising Arab Americans and Islam while declaring war on their violent co-religionists. President Obama also celebrated Islam in his Cairo speech, not long after his inauguration. Yet intolerance (occasionally, even violence) toward atheists, agnostics, Muslims, and other non-Christians still intrudes into the public square at times—perhaps never more so than in Donald Trump's presidential campaign. At the same time, however, public opinion polls find that attitudes toward Muslims are more positive than ever, even after incidents like the June 2016 mass shooting by an Islamic terrorist in Orlando.[7]

America's religious diversity also reflects the fierce, fractious ethos of its Protestantism, an ethos refined through almost four centuries of sectarian struggle as well as by American society's distinctive racial, class, ethnic, and regional cleavages. This history has precipitated a vast number of sects and denominations (a term loosely used here to mean large, confessionally-related groups). This heterodox pattern was apparent as early as the seventeenth century with the migration of Huguenots, Quakers, Mennonites, and other dissenting groups to the American colonies. Nor is this fragmentation diminishing. During the twentieth century, the Pentecostal movement produced more than three hundred distinct denominations, and a significant dissident faction has recently arisen within the Southern Baptist Convention, by far the largest Protestant group. Indeed, further fragmentation seems likely as the forces of secularism, pluralism, and bureaucratization transform the nature, function, and relationships of religious groups. Almost fifty years ago, Peter Berger described them as "marketing agencies" working in a "system of free competition very similar to that of *laissez-faire* capitalism," one in which "[r]eligious contents become subjects of 'fashion.'" On the supply side, denominations seek more distinctive niches or "brand identities" with which to hold and attract members. On the demand side, people in what Wade Clark Roof calls the "questing culture" pursue a bewildering variety of customized mixes of meditation, therapy, counseling, self-help, behavior modification, fellowship, and a search for "spirituality without religion." The power of this competitive, individuating impulse helps to explain why so little has come of formal ecumenical efforts among American churches, most of which have involved restoring relations broken by the Civil War more than a century earlier.

These centrifugal forces extend far beyond Protestantism. American Judaism, for example, long ago split into four major streams— and a fifth, "humanistic Judaism," is now seeking recognition. Some of these, like Reconstructionism, have no real counterparts in other countries, while others such as Orthodoxy are divided into so-called black hat, Lubavitcher, modern, and many other sects led by particular rabbis, with the greatest growth occurring in the more conservative sects. As this example suggests, the fragmentation is by no means confined to liberal, congregational-oriented, and decentralized groups; it also extends to the more hierarchical Catholic and Orthodox Christian churches and especially to the evangelical and Pentecostal sects, which are the fastest growing of all in the United States and are rapidly expanding overseas. Indeed, the largest gains in the evangelical sector have occurred in nondenominational groups, which have tripled as a percentage of the total since 1965. The degree of fragmentation is further underscored by the fact that once we set aside a few large denominations—Catholics, Baptists, and Methodists—no single religious group exceeds 5 percent of the population.

Even within the most hierarchical of American religions, diverse views abound. Today's Catholic Church has been described, perhaps hyperbolically, as "a federation of internally divided quasi denominations.... [P]eople who identify as Catholic are more liberal on sexual morals than Protestants as a whole. Birth rates and opinions on abortions are virtually the same. Like Protestantism, the American Catholic Church today seems to be many denominations, loosely united."[8] Thus, Catholics split fairly evenly between "traditional" and "progressive" views on basic issues of faith, and much the same is true among other putatively conservative groups:

For example . . . one-third of committed evangelicals and 41% of committed Catholics believe that legal abortions should be available to women in at least some circumstances other than rape, incest, or to save the life of the mother, and well over half of the members of these two groups support the distribution of birth control information in public schools. Thirty-three percent of committed evangelicals—and nearly as high a percentage of Mormons—believe that government regulation is necessary for the public good, and 28 percent of both groups think that the federal government does a better job than it is often given credit for. Similarly, about one-fourth of committed black Protestants believe that the government cannot afford to do more for the needy, and almost one-third feel that African Americans are largely responsible for their own economic circumstances.[9]

American Protestantism's *intra*-denominational divisions over public policies, then, are greater than their *inter*-denominational ones over religious practices and doctrines.

The religious practices and views within most religious groups in America are far more heterogeneous—liturgically, doctrinally, organizationally, demographically, and in their geographic distributions—than are the same groups elsewhere in the world, and this diversification is accelerating. For each church that amalgamates with others today, many more are born afresh or separate from their parent congregations. An estimated 1,600 religions and denominations exist in the United States, a far cry from the "three-religion country" proclaimed by Will Herberg in the 1950s. About half of them were founded since 1965. Indeed, as Richard Ostling points out, each of two dozen denominations has as many local congregations today as made up the whole of American religion in 1776. Here, as elsewhere in American life, technological and market forces have played their part in spawning diverse forms of worship—tele-churches, mega-churches, and pastoral teachings on the Internet.

Reflecting international trends, the mainline Protestant denominations—predominantly white, relatively affluent, ecumenical, affiliated with the National Council of Churches, and leaders in college and seminary education—have experienced marked decline since the 1960s. The American Episcopal Church, for example, has lost more than a quarter of its members in the last thirty years. Some religions and denominations, of course, have lost more than others. Catholicism is maintaining its numbers, aided by immigration; about 3 percent of its seminarians are Vietnamese. In contrast, Judaism's share declined during the 1990s and that of the Baptists and Methodists did not change. At the same time, the shares of fundamentalist, evangelical, Pentecostal, and charismatic sects (especially Mormons, the Assemblies of God, and the Church of God in Christ) have grown dramatically; ecstatic Christianity is resurgent. About 10 percent of adults raised in another tradition now identify as evangelical Protestants.

Christianity, if increasingly fragmented and prone to denominational shifting, still utterly dominates Americans' religious affiliations. More Christians live here than in any other country in the world; Christianity predominates in virtually every U.S. county. Roughly seven in ten Americans identified with some Christian denomination in 2014. Protestants made up 46.5 percent of those identifying as Christian, while Catholics made up 23.9 percent. This large share of Christian identifiers, however, had declined by 8 percent since 2007. This is partly because religions other than Christianity have grown rapidly. Approximately one million Hindus live in the United States, compared with only 70,000 in 1977; most of the world's diverse Hindu traditions are practiced here, as are the Sikh, Jain, and other offshoots of Hinduism. The Muslim population is now roughly 3 million. Like Protestants, they are divided by ethnicity, race, and language; one-third are from South and East Asia, 30 percent are African American, and 25 percent are Arabs, with significant political tensions existing within and among these groups. There soon will be more Muslims in the United States than in the small Arab countries— although Islamic State attacks in Europe in 2015 will make it harder to resettle Muslim refugees here.[10] As with Hinduism, all branches of Islamic worship exist in the United States. More than 4 million practicing Buddhists live here, representing the full range of Asian Buddhist traditions, along with many indigenous American ones. Only twenty-one Buddhist study centers existed here from 1900 to 1964, but more than a thousand exist today; in 2001, American-born Buddhists consecrated an immense stupa in a Rocky Mountain valley. There are many Zoroastrian temples here, and more Baha'i live in the United States than in Iran. Even pagan religions seem to be flourishing; in 2000, the Pagan Educational Network estimated 600,000 practitioners here.

But even this does not quite capture the religious diversity in America because it fails to capture the steady devolution of worshipful energy, liturgical innovation, and even governing authority from national religious organizations to their regional and local units. (Secular organizations have also experienced such devolution.) Even the Jesuits, a relatively disciplined and hierarchical Catholic group, have come under the spell of these fragmenting, individualizing conditions of modern American religious life. This devolution of even highly centralized religious authority rests on practical, structural, and ideological considerations. The Episcopal Diocese of New York, for example, conducts its Sunday worship in fourteen languages, and Catholics, who are increasingly Spanish- and Asian-language speakers, come from twenty-three different countries of origin. Another devolutionary factor is Americans' traditional personalization of their religious practices, whether as members of organized denominations or not—a remarkable phenomenon famously analyzed by philosopher William James more than a century ago in *The Varieties of Religious Experience*.

The United States is unique in its vast proliferation of sects, which usually break away from more mainstream denominations, and "new religions" or cults, usually centered around charismatic leaders. In Alan Wolfe's study of middle-class suburbanites, he found that "this strong strain of individualism ... helps explain why, as religious as Americans are, they also distrust organized religion: in 1990, as few as 23 percent of the American population expressed a great deal of confidence in religious institutions. ... Americans would be more comfortable living next to blacks than to religious sectarians." Even traditional sectarianism cannot wholly satisfy this radical religious individualism, which Wolfe sees as distinctively privatistic, voluntaristic, nondogmatic, and separate from organized religion.

Indeed, sociologists have argued that all religions in America, including those with strong hierarchical organizations, become de facto congregationalist in form and practice. Even the Catholic Church, which for centuries resisted devolving power over diocesan decisions, may have to cede more authority to parish and lay groups in the United States in the wake of the pedophilia scandals covered up by bishops and other central authorities. In Protestant congregations, a liberal-conservative divide often forms, and "special-purpose groups," which reflect members' diverse interests but also create more divisions, abound. Even more fragmented are the apparently growing number of "home churches" where a single family, sometimes joined by a few others, constitutes its own unique congregation and liturgy. This chronic dissatisfaction with religious institutions bears a striking resemblance to the populist, anti-hierarchical, maverick, questing, and competitive impulses of Americans in other spheres. Their mistrust of mainline religions probably springs from many of the same social, psychological, and ideological sources as their suspicion of large corporations, political parties, professional expertise, and government.

Americans do profess strong religious convictions. Fully 96 percent of them say that they believe in God—about the same as fifty years ago—with 90 percent believing in heaven, 65 percent in the Devil, and 75 percent in angels that affect human affairs. More than 40 percent of Americans have been telling pollsters for six decades that they attend religious services each week. Some observers doubt the accuracy of this figure, but its consistency over time is striking. In any event, church attendance is higher, often much higher, than in any industrialized country other than Ireland and Poland, as are other indicia of religiosity. The United States is the only advanced Western industrial society with a strong fundamentalist movement. In 1996, religion accounted for 16 percent of all TV programming in the United

States and appeared on 257 stations, up from 1 percent and nine stations in 1974. Sales of "Christ-honoring products" had quadrupled to $4 billion since 1980. Even back in 2001—before the vast growth in Internet use, 25 percent of adult users, about 28 million people, had gone online to find religious and spiritual material—more than the number who had visited gambling sites, participated in online auctions or traded stocks online, and a sharp increase from the number in 2000.

All this religious fervor among Americans makes their theological ignorance all the more remarkable. They appear to know little about basic religious ideas and facts. Although 93 percent of their homes contain at least one Bible and a third claim to read it at least once a week, 54 percent cannot name the authors of the Gospels, 63 percent do not know what a Gospel is, 58 percent cannot name five of the Ten Commandments, and 10 percent think Joan of Arc was Noah's wife! Indeed, a recent survey found an astonishing number of born-again Christians whose views seem to flatly contradict the Bible.

The number of atheists, agnostics, and "no preference" (or "nones") in the United States seems to be rising.* According to Pew, those who self-identify as such have almost doubled since 1965, and a large, growing minority of younger Americans call themselves "spiritual" rather than religious. Pew finds that even among the religious, a large drop has occurred in traditional religious beliefs, practices, and commitment. For example, only 46 percent of U.S. Catholics said in 1993 that they regularly attended mass, down from 74 percent in 1958. This marked decline is occurring even among white evangelical Christians.[11]

These changes are strikingly generational. As Millennials enter adulthood, they become less religiously affiliated than older generations. Nearly a quarter of Generation Xers now claim to have no par-

---

* Rodney Stark, a leading religion scholar, disputes this. Citing low response rates, he doubts the accuracy of the widely cited Pew surveys from which most of this paragraph's statistics are taken. And he contends that many of the "nones" were already atheists when earlier surveys were done but only now are acknowledging it. Stark, *The Triumph of Faith: Why the World Is More Religious Than Ever* (2015).

ticular religion or describe themselves as atheists or agnostics, up four points in seven years. Baby boomers also are now more likely to identify as "nones." Religious intermarriage is on the rise: Among those who married since 2010, nearly four in ten are in mixed marriages; for pre-1960 marriages, the share was 19 percent.[12] Indeed, Americans seem more tolerant of other religions than of atheism.* Pew found that 49 percent would be "unhappy if a family member were to marry someone who doesn't believe in God," whereas only about 15 percent would be unhappy having someone from the other party join their family.[13]

Americans increasingly support bringing religious voices into the political sphere. About half (49 percent) of those polled in 2014 supported having houses of worship express views on political and social questions (up from 40 percent in 2012), and 32 percent felt that religious leaders should endorse political candidates (up from 24 percent in 2010). Perhaps they support more religion in politics because so many fear that religion's influence is diminishing; 72 percent believe this—and they may be right. Indeed, America's great cultural divide is not among different religions. It is between believers and nonbelievers.

Whether all of these social facts amount to paradox, a deeper consistency, poor survey techniques, or arrant hypocrisy is uncertain. But Americans clearly profess respect for the religious diversity around them,† as Wolfe finds:

When we consider how many people have died in the name of religion over the years, the acceptance of so many different kinds of belief in America is remarkable. One is tempted to call it real diversity, not because the idea of diversity in inappropriate to race,

---

* The state constitutions of seven states ban atheists from holding public office, and Maryland's provides that belief in God is a requirement for jurors and witnesses. These provisions are almost certainly unconstitutional. *Torcaso v. Watkins*, 367 U.S. 488 (1961).

† Religious diversity as an *ideal* (as distinguished from it as a fact) is very recent, as is the *ideal* of immigrant diversity, with its religious implications. Only in 1965 did Congress end the national origin immigration quotas and Vatican II issue *Dignitatis Humanae*, urging religious freedom for all.

gender, or sexual orientation, but because religion claims to speak to what really and truly matters in life. I confess that at some level I did not fully understand the non-judgmentalism of middle-class Americans. . . . [but] what comes along with it [is] a strong commitment to the principle that a wide variety of religious views ought to be allowed to flourish.

Protecting religious diversity in American life might seem straight-forward. Historically, Steven Smith notes, "the ferment that caused religious diversity to flourish—and that is largely responsible for the condition of religious freedom we enjoy today—was a product of pluralism; it owed little or nothing to judicial review, or to the legal elaboration and enforcement of any constitutional 'principle of religious freedom.'"[14] Religious minorities, many of them recent immigrants with traditions (such as Santeria[15]) that seem exotic to Americans, now have vast breathing space where they can cultivate their distinctive beliefs and practices. We saw that Catholicism, our largest single denomination, accounts for a declining share of the population. And other conditions also favor religious pluralism: the religion clauses, dominant social norms, and officials' responsiveness to even small groups of deep religious faith.

Rights Culture

For centuries, American and foreign commentators have noted that American culture (not just law) is more steeped in the notion of individual rights than perhaps any other. In the United States, individuals assert these rights strongly not only against government but also against each other. Law professor Mary Ann Glendon traced the rigidities, hyper-individualism, and other consequences of this "rights talk."[16] Several points about this rights culture are important for present purposes.

- The proliferation and assertion of religion-based rights by A necessarily reduces the rights-free space in which B, C, D . . . can exercise their freedom to act without affecting A's rights. Unless rights-holders are willing to redefine their rights claims to avoid a clash (as through accommodation, discussed below), conflict is inevitable.

- Where the conflict concerns religion-based rights—those thought necessary to worship God and protect a religious community against outside influences—rights-holders are likely to be most determined to exercise them in the most uncompromising fashion.

- The assertion of these claims occurs within a system of what lawyer-sociologist Robert Kagan calls "adversarial legalism."[17] This system has many rule-of-law virtues, as Kagan explains, but its costs are also many. It encourages a rigid, aggressive, legalistic approach to resolving social disputes. This means, among other things, conflict resolution that is costly, protracted, contentious, party-dominated (in practice, lawyer-dominated), technical and procedural, winner-take-all and thus crushing to the loser. It is also a poor way to make complex public policy, as I have explained elsewhere.[18] (Some disputes over religious rights are narrow and localized, but others—for example, the *Hobby Lobby* and *Obergefell* cases discussed below—have far broader implications affecting many people beyond the litigants and the nature of important public programs.)

- In the cultural, legal, and political wars, a common argument is that those who seek an exemption from a general requirement for one or another religious practice are claiming special rights, placing them "above the law" by denying the rights of others who oppose the exemption. What is and is not lawful, of course, depends on the legal principles that govern a specific conflict. Here, the point is that such an argument resonates strongly with popular demands for legal equality. I analyze this question later in the chapter.

- Our constitutional structure—particularly separation of powers and federalism—makes cooperation and conciliation essential to government's effective functioning.[19] The rights culture, however, tends to cut against this, impeding both political and social capital formation. Although conflict, like the diversity that inevitably causes it, advances social learning, too much of it can generate dangerous levels of gridlock, mistrust, despair, and even violence.[20]

THREE KEY CONCEPTS: SEPARATION, ACCOMMODATION, AND NEUTRALITY*

We can best map this contested terrain by exploring what divides the disputants. The polar positions are "separation" and "accommodation." Each of these positions, however, ultimately depends on how each defines and applies the idea of "neutrality" (discussed in the next section), which the Court requires the government to observe when it regulates religion. For example, Supreme Court justices William Brennan and Thurgood Marshall were strong separationists in Establishment Clause cases but vigorously favored accommodation in Free Exercise cases.

Separationists tend to think that religion is a potentially divisive force when brought into public life; they wish to consign it to the private realm where, like other forms of expression and activity, law should protect it on the same neutral terms that liberalism applies to these other forms. Invoking Jefferson's famous metaphor, which the Court adopted only as recently as 1947, separationists believe that both religion and politics gain when the law erects between them "a wall . . . which must be kept high and impregnable." They also draw on Jefferson's equally famous distinction between belief, which the government cannot regulate, and conduct, which in this view it can sometimes regulate. In 1990, the Court affirmed this distinction in *Employment Division, Department of Human Resources of Oregon v. Smith* after having criticized it in the *Wisconsin v. Yoder* and *Sherbert v. Verner* cases. These three decisions are discussed below.

---

* Much of this section is taken more or less verbatim from my book, *Diversity in America: Keeping Government at a Safe Distance* (2003), 274–76. Sources can be found in the endnotes to that discussion. Readers not interested in exploring this topic can skip to the next section without losing the thread of the larger analysis.

Acommodationists believe that religion generates enormous public and private benefits (a claim many separationists concede—up to a point) but insist that it can only retain its meaning-creating, value-conferring force and integrity if religious persons have leeway in which to pursue distinctive beliefs and practices. Nevertheless, accommodation in the religious realm is more elusive than in other areas of public policy, especially where religious claims conflict with equally strong claims grounded in largely secular moralities for which universalizing rights-talk seems appropriate—for example, abortion (the "right to choose" versus the "right to life"), and equal treatment (the right to avoid condoning conduct that a religion considers sinful versus the right to equal treatment). In such cases, both sides may view compromise as an accommodation with evil. (Think of William Lloyd Garrison's denunciation of the 1850 Compromise as a "pact with the Devil.") Even short of that extreme position, accommodation will often seem to sacrifice important values—which sometimes may indeed be true.

The law, accommodationists say, should create a strong presumption favoring even those practices that seem illiberal or in some cases are illegal—although just how strong that presumption should be is a question that, as we shall see, divides Congress and has set it against the Court. Separationists reply that such accommodations do not just tolerate religion but "establish" it in violation of the Constitution—that accommodation is not neutral as between religion and non-religion or perhaps even as among religions. So what does neutrality mean?

Neutrality. Americans value two kinds of *neutrality*: neutrality (1) among religions, and (2) between the religious values of a largely pious people and the secular values of a liberal civic culture. But this is still too simple. Stanley Fish observes that any effort to define neutrality without appealing to some non-neutral value is "mission impossible" because one can only decide hard cases by appealing to a non-neutral principle. (Of course, the Court will gussy up the decisive principle so that it appears neutral.)[21] In speaking of neutrality, then, I take Fish's point: Some understandings of neutrality are more plausible and persuasive than others in specific cases, but they are not neutral in a more universal or rigorous sense. Neutrality's meaning also depends on how one frames the particular comparisons in the neutrality analysis—an instance of a more general difficulty encountered when we reason by analogy. Judgment, not logic, determines which features of the supposedly analogous cases should be regarded as salient to the comparison.

Neutrality, then, is a norm whose meaning and application to actual conflicts can be highly contestable.* Just to get the discussion rolling, I define neutrality (following Professor Douglas Laycock) in substantive terms: The government should not use burdens or benefits to influence people's religious choices.[22] Legally, this has come to mean that a law must accommodate any religious practice or claim that does not threaten "compelling governmental interests." (The Religious Freedom Restoration Act [RFRA][23] and its state-level counterparts essentially adopt this standard, as we shall see.) This legal definition underscores the public value of preserving a broad private sphere of religious autonomy even when a religious practice may offend general public policies and civic sensibilities. In this view of neutrality, government may not coerce a religious practice. Neither may it sponsor or endorse the practice, favor one religion over another, or favor religion over non-religion (or vice versa).† But in choosing among competing standards of judicial review (analyzed in the next section), the Court must put its thumb on one side of the scale or the other. By holding that a government interest can carry the day even if it is less than "compelling," the Court could make it

* Other liberal democracies with strong secularizing trends but no Establishment Clause face similar dilemmas. See, e.g., Stephen Castle, "Refusal to Run a Church Ad Has Britain in an Uproar," *New York Times*, November 24, 2015, A4.

† As the "In God We Trust" motto on U.S. currency suggests, the neutrality norm recognizes exceptions. They are usually rationalized in terms of the Framers' usage, hoary tradition, or de minimis offense. For a non-exhaustive list of this kind of "ceremonial deism," see John T. Noonan, Jr., *The Lustre of Our Country* (1998), 236–37.

harder for a challenger to demand that the government grant a religious accommodation.

Separationists and accommodationists have conceptual, empirical, normative, and political differences about neutrality. To begin with, separationists and accommodationists disagree about what neutrality means, whether it is really possible in religiously diverse America, and if so whether it is a defensible public value or legal standard in this context. Because these three issues are not always distinguished, separationists like political theorist Stephen Macedo, a liberal defender of civic values against the inroads of religion, and accommodationists like law professor Stephen Carter, a religious conservative who wants to broaden religion's role in public life, can end up agreeing on a number of points even though they present their positions as strongly antagonistic. In what follows, I use their work to sharpen and illuminate the debate.

Their first commonality is that, as Carter approvingly puts it, "religion has no sphere. It possesses no natural bounds. It is not amenable to being pent up. It sneaks through cracks, creeps through half-open doors . . . and it flows over walls. . . . Rushing past boundaries is what religion does." Macedo acknowledges this leakage but decries it, warning that it poses a mortal danger to the ideal of civic liberalism. They also agree that state neutrality—basing government policy solely on secular ideas without regard to its effects on religion—is illusory. Religion is inevitably political in that it helps shape our public and private values. To Carter, "[n]eutrality is a theory about freedom of religion in a world that does not and cannot actually exist" because the state cannot act without taking account of religion. A pretense of neutrality, Carter argues, is used to override deep convictions for little state gain, as when the Supreme Court invoked neutrality to uphold military discipline against an Orthodox Jew for wearing a yarmulke while in uniform. Macedo too doubts the possibility of strict neutrality but wants to contain this leakage lest it contaminate both sides, especially the liberal polity, which needs inoculation against certain sect-values. The state, he argues, must promote civic virtues, not comprehensive ideals of the good life, but even this civic promotion affects religious beliefs and practices in non-neutral ways.

Carter also claims that the neutrality norm favors big, influential religions over small, defenseless ones. Interestingly, separationists say the same about accommodations, although some Free Exercise decisions granting accommodations to small sects seem to refute this theory.* Carter's larger hostility claim, however, is very weak. Traditionally, many federal and state laws gave special consideration to religions in general and small sects in particular. *Smith* denied an accommodation, but the RFRA statute was enacted to overrule such denials. It is true that courts tend to be less accommodating than legislatures, almost always upholding the government even under the "compelling interest" test that *Smith* rejected but the REFRA restored. This is discussed later in the chapter.

Most separationists like Macedo agree with accommodationists like Carter on religion's virtues. Indeed, Macedo maintains that the separatist project "depends upon the support of religious reasons and religious communities—a support that can be encouraged by a liberal public philosophy but not altogether justified by it." Liberalism, he says, depends on the reasons, norms, and moral convictions generated by religious communities, and also on the political and moral education that such communities provide. Even Catholicism, whose earlier illiberalism he strongly condemns, has strengthened the American polity, in his view. Its natural law doctrine checks the moral excesses of democratic majoritarianism; its "subsidiarity" principle supports devolution of power; and it rightly insists that human values transcend the political, justifying why one should not invest politics with all one's moral energies.

---

* For example, in *Wisconsin v. Yoder*, 406 U.S. 205 (1972), the Court granted an exception to the Old Order Amish, hardly a political powerhouse even in Pennsylvania. It gave one to an even smaller, more obscure sect in *Gonzales v. O Centro Espirita*, 546 U.S. 418 (2005). *Smith* did go the other way, denying an exception for even a minor, peyote-eating Native American sect, but as I explain, Congress in the RFRA emphatically rejected *Smith*.

Beyond these convergences, however, separationists and accommodationists disagree sharply. To someone like Carter, the state that Macedo wants to protect poses a far greater threat to religion than religion does to the state, and the state's putatively civic projects, which Macedo wants to promote, are in fact pervaded by assumptions of value and fact that can be hostile to religion. To Carter, these assumptions cohere to constitute a comprehensive, secular worldview that not only competes with religion in defining the meaning of life but remorselessly deploys its monopoly of coercive power, together with a conviction of the state's superior rectitude, to establish and maintain its dominance. To Macedo, in contrast, this competition is disciplined by the ground rules of separation, and the hegemony of an activist state is required to sustain his vision of "liberalism with spine," which goes beyond promoting tolerance, freedom, order, and prosperity. It must also secure "the preconditions of active citizenship," including the state's "educative" interests in citizens' character, in order to pursue society's collective ends. Some religions, notably fundamentalist groups that insist on subordinating the state's educational and moral authority to that of the group and family, are anathema to this vision and must be overridden in the name of civic liberalism. Which values civic liberalism includes, of course, is itself a hotly disputed issue.

I am tempted to suggest that despite these sharp rhetorical conflicts, and except at the extremes, most separationists and accommodationists differ only in degree. Militants of both stripes doubtless will reject this pacific suggestion. Unlike Macedo, for example, many separationists categorically oppose use of vouchers in religious schools; unlike Carter, many accommodationists demand school prayer. Nor do I deny that such differences can produce quite disparate views about particular cases or policy disputes, as with school choice proposals. I suggest, rather, that in the end the precise location of the lines that the law must draw depends on principles that come down to matters of degree, of more or less.

Carter, for example, concedes that there are limits "beyond which no claim of religious freedom will be recognized," citing the case of religiously-mandated murder. One could cite more difficult cases like church-sanctioned child and spousal abuse, racial segregation, and female genital mutilation, but the point would be the same: Lines must be drawn and someone with temporal authority must draw them. But having acknowledged this, Carter then complains that it is the courts that eventually will do this, and that they inevitably "center their concern on the needs of the state, not the needs of the religionist." But Congress and the states, as we have seen, often do precisely the opposite. Courts, moreover, must review these legislative choices. The real issue for the courts, then, is the legal standard for reviewing them.

And here is where the *casus belli* between separationists and accommodationists dissolves into a difference of degree, albeit a consequential one, involving the standard of judicial review in religion cases discussed in some detail in the next section. Both Macedo and Carter support tests under which courts draw lines by identifying, weighing, and balancing competing interests much as legislatures do. They differ only over whether the state's interest must be "compelling" or merely "important" and whether the burden must be "the least restrictive means" or merely "reasonable." Outcomes in particular cases may turn on these differences.[24]

Diverse religious beliefs "are as infinite as the imagination," and once the genies of opt-outs and exceptions to general rules (or standard school curricula) are out of the bottle, they cannot easily be confined. Among some academics, this was a leading argument against the RFRA in which Congress resurrected the more religion-accommodating "compelling interest" standard that *Smith* had jettisoned. (Congress had no such qualms; the RFRA passed almost unanimously!) The Court's concern about the RFRA reflects a similar and legitimate anxiety about line-drawing in an area fraught with constitutional constraints imposed by the religion clauses and federalism's vertical division of power. These constraints are the subject to which I now turn.

JUDICIAL METHODOLOGY: STANDARD OF JUDICIAL REVIEW, AND THE TESTS FOR "ESTABLISHMENT"*

The constitutional setting for religious accommodation issues consists of the Establishment and Free Exercise clauses of the First Amendment: "Congress shall make no law respecting an establishment of religion, or prohibiting the free exercise thereof." Two judicial doctrines, developed over the last ninety years or so, constitute what we might think of as "meta-doctrines" that frame the way the Court then goes on to decide specific religious accommodation disputes. These meta-doctrines are: (1) the standard of judicial review used to decide Free Exercise Clause cases, and (2) the tests used to decide Establishment Clause cases.† My brief explanation of them sets the stage for the next section of this chapter, where I shall examine how the Court has resolved specific disputes under these clauses in various areas of social conflict.

Standard of Judicial Review. In deciding cases under the Religion Clauses (and many other constitutional provisions), courts must decide how much deference they will accord to the legislative (and administrative) judgments embodied in the governmental rule or practice that is being challenged as unconstitutional. Depending on the kind of constitutional claim that is being asserted against the government, the Court has applied one of three standards of review. The default standard is called "rationality" review. The most lenient or relaxed (pro-government) standard, it requires only that the governmental action be reasonably related to a legitimate government objective. Age-based claims, for example, are reviewed under this standard. The second standard is "intermediate scrutiny," under which the law

---

* Readers not interested in exploring the legal architecture of "establishment" can skip to the next section without losing the thread of the larger analysis.

† Two other meta-doctrines are standing and incorporation. Standing prescribes who may sue an Establishment Clause violation. Incorporation holds that the Religion Clauses limit the states as well as the federal government.

being challenged must further an "important" governmental interest by means "substantially related" to that interest. Examples include most gender classifications and undocumented immigrant children's right to attend public schools.[25] The most stringent (pro-claimant) standard of review is "strict scrutiny"; here, the government's action must further a "compelling" governmental interest and do so in a way that is least restrictive of the right that the claimant asserts. (This is called "narrow tailoring.") Strict scrutiny review applies to government actions that impinge on a "fundamental right" (religion, for example) or that treat people differently based on certain "suspect classifications," of which the main ones are race, national origin, and—central to this discussion—religion.

In religion cases, the Court has developed its standard of review through a series of cases involving "exotic" or minority religious practices that believers, invoking the Free Exercise Clause, defended against criminal prosecutions. In *Reynolds v. United States*, decided in 1878, Mormons challenged a federal statute making polygamy a crime. In this, its first application of the Clause, the Court did not spend much time worrying about the standard of review in upholding the statute. It sufficed that polygamy had always been treated as "an offence against society. . . . [I]t is impossible to believe that the constitutional guaranty of religious freedom was intended to prohibit legislation in respect to this most important feature of social life."[26]

The modern evolution of the standard of review in religion cases begins with the 1963 decision in *Sherbert v. Verner*,[27] involving a state's denial of unemployment benefits—there, to a Seventh Day Adventist who refused to work on Saturday. In *Sherbert*, the Court required the accommodation; denying it would "substantially burden" her religious freedom and the state had no strong reason not to grant it. This "*Sherbert* test" is essentially a strict scrutiny standard of review.*

---

* Even so, the Court once upheld a federal action that the dissenting justices thought "promise[d] to destroy an entire religion." *Lyng v. Northwest Indian Cemetery Protective Assn.*, 485 U.S. 439, 476 (1988).

The next evolutionary step came in 1990 with a decision discussed earlier: *Employment Division, Department of Human Resources of Oregon v. Smith*. There, the Court upheld a state law denying unemployment benefits to a man fired for using peyote as part of a religious ceremony, which constituted "misconduct" under the state's illegal drug law. Because the law was neutral, generally applicable, and not targeted at any particular religion, the Court upheld it, seeing no threat to free exercise in the denial of an exemption for peyote use, and thus no need for heightened review. For such a law, *Smith* held, the state need not grant a religious exception.

Religious groups strongly denounced this "*Smith* test" for allowing the state too much leeway to punish believers. They persuaded Congress not only to pass laws granting religious exceptions but also to enact a more general reform, the RFRA, in 1993. This statute mostly rejected the *Smith* test and revived the *Sherbert* test—even as applied to neutral, generally applicable rules. The RFRA formulated this test as follows: "Government shall not substantially burden a person's exercise of religion even if the burden results from a rule of general applicability, except as provided in subsection (b) of this section." Subsection (b) provided that "Government may substantially burden a person's exercise of religion only if it demonstrates that application of the burden to the person (1) is in furtherance of a compelling governmental interest; and (2) is the least restrictive means of furthering that compelling governmental interest." This is sometimes called an "enhanced *Sherbert* test"; subsection (b) (2) replaced the "narrowly tailored" element of the test with an arguably more demanding, pro-exception test of the "least restrictive means."

But even the RFRA—crafted by a Congress that strongly (indeed, almost unanimously) rejected *Smith*—was not to be the final word. Four years later, in 1997, the Court in *City of Boerne v. Flores*[28] struck down the RFRA as applied to state laws. This delighted those, like law professor Marci Hamilton, who had condemned the RFRA for giving religion special privileges while countenancing genuine harms to others.[29] Hamilton argued this before the Supreme Court, which held that by legally basing the RFRA on its Fourteenth

Amendment remedial powers against the states, Congress had in effect redefined a substantive constitutional right—something that only a court or a constitutional amendment could do. Accordingly, the RFRA applies only to *federal* laws; the states are bound by the Religion Clauses as interpreted by the Court, not by the RFRA. As to *state* laws, *Smith* would continue to uphold general, neutral criminal laws that did not grant a religious exception even if those laws burdened religion.*

This evolution of the standard of review in Free Exercise cases was still not over, for two reasons:

- Many states (twenty-one as of late 2016) passed their own RFRAs; other states are considering them; and some, including California, have rejected them. While intended to echo the federal RFRA, state RFRAs differ from one another.[30] Some of them, for example, dilute the substantial burden requirement, require more onerous scrutiny of the governmental interest, and expand the notion of "religious exercise."[31] (North Carolina and Michigan were also considering RFRA legislation in 2016.) Many of these state RFRAs are embroiled in controversy about whether they protect religious objections to same-sex marriage and gay rights statutes. I discuss these disputes in the next section.

- In 2000, three years after *City of Boerne*, Congress—invoking its power under the Spending and Commerce Clauses—enacted the Religious Land Use and Institutionalized Persons Act (RLUIPA). Like the RFRA, the RLUIPA was strongly promoted by religious groups seeking to restore the special protections threatened by *City of Boerne*. The RLUIPA governs state and local government decisions that affect land use and institutionalized persons in ways that burden religion. It not only requires strict scrutiny of such decisions, but also allows successful challengers to recover their

---

* Notably, some states have refused to use a *Smith* framework to interpret the Free Exercise provisions of their own constitutions, instead providing more expansive, *Sherbert*-type protection. Paul Benjamin Linton, "Religious Freedom Claims and Defenses under State Constitutions," 7 *University of St. Thomas Journal of Law and Public Policy* 103 (2013).

attorney fees, which Professor Hamilton believes encourages governments to concede.[32]

Thus, the *Sherbert* test lives on in both the RFRA and RLUIPA, limiting government actions that affect religious exercise.

EMERGING ACCOMMODATION ISSUES

In 2014, the Court decided a highly controversial RFRA case, *Burwell v. Hobby Lobby Stores, Inc.*,[33] whose bearing on difficult religious accommodation issues will be bitterly contested and litigated for years to come. The next year, the Court upheld same-sex marriage in *Obergefell v. Hodges*, decided on due process and equal protection, not RFRA, grounds. Both have already generated many accommodation demands, most invoking various civil rights laws. In this section, I briefly discuss these two decisions and some of the hard issues (some would call them "culture wars") arising in their wake. Before doing so, however, it is important to keep the larger context in mind. As scholars who closely examine the disputes arising in this area note, the vast majority of RFRA-type claims have nothing to do with such hot-button issues; instead, they involve the religious practices of vulnerable minorities (e.g., Amish, Muslims, prisoners)—exemption claims that, as Professor Christopher Lund puts it, "liberals should welcome."[34] Thus advocates *for* religious accommodation should think twice before upending federal and state RFRA laws based on atypical high-profile cases like *Hobby Lobby*.[35]

Hobby Lobby. At issue were regulations issued by the U.S. Department of Health and Human Services (HHS) under the Patient Protection and Affordable Care Act of 2010 (ACA). These regulations required non-exempt employers to provide coverage for the twenty contraceptive methods approved by HHS, including four that "may have the effect of preventing an already fertilized egg from developing any further by inhibiting its attachment to the uterus." HHS granted exemptions to religious employers (churches and other religious nonprofits) with religious objections to the contraceptive coverage mandate. Under such exemptions, insurers must "exclude contraceptive coverage from the employer's plan and provide plan participants with separate payments for contraceptive services without imposing any cost-sharing requirements on the employer, its insurance plan, or its employee beneficiaries."

The owners of two closely-held business corporations who have sincere Christian beliefs that life begins at conception sued HHS under RFRA and the Free Exercise Clause, challenging this mandate insofar as it required them to provide the four contraceptives to which they had religious objections.* The Court did not decide the case on constitutional grounds; instead, it interpreted the terms of the federal RFRA statute, applying its "substantial burden" and "least restrictive alternative" tests to *Hobby Lobby*'s facts. For the Court majority, Justice Alito first held that RFRA's protections for "persons" extended to for-profit firms, noting that for-profit firms were not required "to pursue profit at the expense of everything else, and many do not do so." Hobby Lobby was owned and controlled by members of a single family, so their beliefs were the same as the company's, obviating concerns about determining the company's sincere beliefs.

Applying RFRA's tests, the Court held that the ACA "substantially burdened" Hobby Lobby by requiring it to "engage in conduct that seriously violates [the family's] religious beliefs." It reasoned that noncompliance with the ACA or dropping the insurance altogether would risk severe economic harm resulting from penalties, taxes, and competitive disadvantage if the firm dropped the insurance altogether. Rejecting HHS's claim that the link between providing contraceptive coverage and destroying an embryo was too attenuated to constitute a substantial burden under RFRA, the Court held that its Free Exercise precedents precluded inquiry into the reasonableness of any sincerely-held belief, and Hobby Lobby's was clearly sincere. But even assuming that the ACA mandate served a compelling gov-

---

* Pharmacies are another venue in which religious objections to contraceptives are being litigated. In June 2016, the Court declined to hear such a case, over a strong dissent by three justices. *Stormans, Inc. v. Wiesman*, 136 S. Ct. 2433.

ernment interest, the Court held, it failed RFRA's "least restrictive means" test: HHS could have chosen more accommodating alternatives, provided the offensive contraceptives to women at no cost to religiously objecting employers, or extended to Hobby Lobby–type firms the ACA's exception for houses of worship and accommodation for other religious nonprofits allowing them to self-certify their religious objection and requiring their insurers to exclude contraceptive coverage from the policy. HHS, the Court found, had failed to provide a good reason for not extending such exceptions to a firm like Hobby Lobby.

Justice Ginsburg's powerful dissenting opinion, joined in most respects by the three other liberal justices, rejected the majority's assurance (reinforced by Justice Kennedy's concurring opinion) that its decision could be limited to *Hobby Lobby*'s facts. Congress, she argued, only intended RFRA to overrule *Smith*—not to effect the radical change that the majority opinion would produce; religious exceptions were proper only for individuals and nonprofit firms, which is why Title VII had never granted them to for-profit corporations. She argued that the ACA mandate satisfied both RFRA tests. Its insurance scheme served compelling governmental interests, and the tenuous link between firms' religious convictions and the contraceptive coverage mandate did not substantially burden firms' free exercise rights. Nor would the less restrictive alternatives cited by the majority actually serve Congress's objectives.* Most troubling, she predicted, the majority's logic would eviscerate numerous civil rights laws by inviting anyone who could cite a sincerely held religious objection to claim—and receive—an exception to those laws. And future courts, she observed, could only decide such claims by making judgments about the merits of particular religious claims, judgments that courts

---

* The Obama administration, eager to avoid a confrontation over contraceptive coverage, developed a rule that it hoped would be an end run around *Hobby Lobby*. Under the rule, employers like Hobby Lobby can state their objections to HHS, which will transmit it to the insurer, which must then provide the coverage at no additional cost to the firm. I discuss this rule, which remains under challenge (*Zubik v. Burwell*, 136 S.Ct. 1557 [2016]) in the final section of this chapter.

could not constitutionally make. Many other commentators have joined Justice Ginsburg in warning about *Hobby Lobby*'s invitation to demands for religious exceptions in many areas other than contraception coverage, with some seeing the decision as a threat "to the entire regulatory state."[36] And while *Hobby Lobby* formally applies only to federal RFRA claims, it may well affect how the states interpret their own RFRA statutes.[37] Finally, as law professor Ira (Chip) Lupu explains, the decision "appears to provide *constitutional* legitimation as well," insofar as RFRA purported to restore constitutional norms (i.e., the *Sherbert* strict scrutiny test) that the Supreme Court had abandoned (in *Smith*).[38]

Obergefell and Its Aftermath. One year after its *Hobby Lobby* decision, the Court in *Obergefell v. Hodges* upheld the constitutionality of same-sex marriage, which it found to be a fundamental right protected by the Due Process Clause. Unquestionably among the most important Court rulings in modern history, *Obergefell* directly affects the lives, identities, and family arrangements of millions of people historically subject to harsh discrimination and blighted existence in many areas of American life. The decision's basis in the federal Constitution precludes state-level erosion of that right.

By dismantling the legal barrier to marriage equality for gays, *Obergefell* may have paved the way to broader protections for all LGBT people in civil rights statutes more generally. Few federal civil rights laws cover sexual and gender orientation minorities,* nor do most state civil rights laws cover them (although more states are already doing so).[39] Notably, as Lupu observes, racial minorities won legal equality in employment, education, and other public services well before they gained it in marriage, the most intimate realm, in *Loving v. Virginia*.[40] In contrast, LGBT people have won this harder-to-achieve equality *first*, which may mean that gaining their legal

---

* The exceptions are the Violence Against Women Act, and President Obama's broadening of an executive order to protect LGBTs from discrimination by government contractors.

equality in areas less intimate and more conventional than marriage will come more easily and swiftly.[41]

But *Obergefell* is a two-edged sword. On the one hand, it supports expanding LGBT rights into the workplace and areas other than marriage—often with the strong support of business groups and other prominent institutions that sometimes threaten to boycott recalcitrant jurisdictions. The NBA,[42] the NCAA,[43] PayPal,[44] Salesforce,[45] and the Atlantic Coast Conference,[46] for example, have all exerted pressure on North Carolina in the wake of its anti-LGBT legislation. But on the other hand, *Obergefell* is galvanizing strong, religiously-based objections to these protections and fueling demands for constitutional, statutory, or regulatory exceptions in some states. And because most civil rights laws now include religion as a protected attribute, employers and other objectors can invoke their own free-exercise rights to buttress their demand for exception by citing the state or federal RFRAs as well as *Hobby Lobby*'s extension of religious exceptions into the commercial and corporate spheres. Further, the RFRAs' key tests are ambiguous enough to make such demands legally plausible. As Lupu notes, "RFRAs are a Rorschach test, on which everyone can project their hopes and fears, and cannot be proven wrong until the courts resolve particular questions. Even when courts do so, the resolutions are highly fact-specific, so RFRA-based judicial precedents are rarely generalizable."[47]

Indeed, this process is already well under way. At the federal level, a proposed "First Amendment Defense Act" would bar the government from taking any "discriminatory action" against people who believe that same-sex marriage is wrong on moral or religious grounds,[48] while an Equality Act bill would extend civil rights protections to LGBTs in various contexts. The states and localities naturally present a much more diverse and arguably important field for these battles because state law governs many more of the contexts in which LGBTs seek equal treatment. Just how important the federal-state difference is will partly depend on how states and localities resolve the following issues. For example:

- *Hobby Lobby* interpreted only the federal RFRA and so is not binding on states, although many states will likely follow it in reading "persons" in their own RFRAs to protect some for-profit entities.

- A state or locality may not have an RFRA statute (or if it does, the statute may differ from the federal one). In either case, the state or locality may still choose to look for guidance to the federal RFRA, to *Hobby Lobby*'s interpretation of it, or both as it formulates new laws or interprets existing ones. (Many state RFRAs were enacted long before marriage equality was on the horizon.)

Lupu's description of this complex pattern remained accurate as of July 2016:

> [T]wenty-two states (and D.C.) have jurisdiction-wide laws that forbid discrimination based on LGBT status in employment, housing, and/or public accommodations. Twenty-one states now have RFRAs modeled on the federal Act. The overlap between these two sets is four—Connecticut, Illinois, New Mexico, and Rhode Island are currently the only states that have RFRAs and state-wide anti-discrimination laws that include LGBT status. In addition, another eight states have the combination of broad anti-discrimination laws and state constitutional provisions that have been construed in ways akin to the pre-*Smith*, pre-RFRA regime of free exercise adjudication. Accordingly, under current law, only twelve states—four with RFRAs plus eight with constitutional norms—present the possibility of strong conflict between state-wide LGBT anti-discrimination laws and statewide religious freedom laws.
>
> Local law offers another dimension to the possible clashes. In a considerable number of states that have RFRAs, are considering RFRAs, or have strong constitutional protections for religious exercise, local jurisdictions have enacted LGBT anti-discrimination laws. These include (among many others) Phoenix, Arizona, where proposed amendments to the state's religious freedom law produced a political uproar, nearly costing the state the 2015 Super

Bowl; and Atlanta, Georgia, where a proposed state level RFRA generated considerable controversy, and eventually died as a result of concern that it would promote discrimination against members of same sex couples and others.[49]

As of then, Lupu reported, the much-publicized disputes between LGBTs and various wedding florists and bakers had been resolved in favor of the LGBTs; the specific legal rationales reflected (1) a state's own religious freedom law, which may or may not include an RFRA (and one inflected by *Hobby Lobby*), and (2) its anti-discrimination law, which may or may not extend to LGBTs or to the specific contexts or markets (e.g., housing, goods and services, child welfare) in which disputes arise. Actual resolution of such disputes will turn on these two legal variables. *Obergefell* is marriage-specific, so it remains unclear how it will affect emerging disputes in other realms in which religious claimants demand accommodation. One such realm is access by transgender people to bathrooms, locker rooms, and other public facilities based on their chosen sexual identity rather than their gender at birth. In July 2016, Massachusetts became the nineteenth state to protect transgender people in this way.[50] Another important arena, which has received less attention so far, is child welfare services.[51]

In May 2016, the Obama administration directed that Title IX of the federal Civil Rights Act, which prohibits discrimination on the basis of sex in federally funded programs or activities, requires schools and other recipients to allow transgender students to use bathrooms aligned with their current gender identity rather than their gender at birth. Almost half the states as well as some private groups promptly sued to challenge this directive, and in August 2016 a federal district judge in Texas enjoined it.[52] Although some of the private challenges are free exercise claims based on religious requirements of modesty in undressing before members of the opposite sex, most challenges are based on other theories—that "sex" discrimination under Title IX does not cover gender identity; that the directive failed to comply with the Administrative Procedure Act; and that it overrides constitutional protections of state sovereignty.[53] Quite apart from the legal issue, the administration rolled out the directive in a way that has already sowed public misunderstanding, opposition, and partisan wrangling.[54]

Another potential dispute could involve challenges to the tax-exempt status of religious groups that refuse to accept same-sex marriage. The stakes in this challenge would be high; the groups value tax-exempt status, while others see it as a government imprimatur that a group's activities are consistent with public policy and values. Such a challenge would rely on *Bob Jones University v. United States*,[55] a 1983 ruling in which the Supreme Court allowed the government to revoke the tax-exempt status of a religious university that barred interracial dating by students. (The Court did not address "churches or other purely religious institutions.") Since then, the government has not revoked any religious entity's tax exemption on such grounds, and the Obama administration said that it would not do so in the wake of *Obergefell*. In my view, tax exemption should not be denied to an otherwise-eligible religious group simply because it limits access to its activities and facilities based on fundamental, good-faith religious tenets inconsistent with a still-controversial government policy. Tax exemption aside, other disputes will surely arise over whether governments can deny otherwise-eligible religious groups access to public funds or other benefits if they discriminate against LGBTs. In the final section, I suggest some general principles to guide our approach to disputes of this kind.

GOING FORWARD

Conflicts between the religiously devout and other people whose beliefs and behaviors offend them go back to the earliest human communities. Today, the almost limitless ways of living differently from the majority in our society—as well as the vast increase in the number and scope of government policies that regulate people's behaviors—multiply these conflicts. Liberal norms of tolerance and conciliation can help to reduce these conflicts' intensity to manageable levels. In an earlier book, I advocated two informal "punctilios"—more candor, and thicker skins—that can ease (not solve) these diversity-generated disputes.[56] But I also noted that such norms will often be inadequate to avert conflicts between fervent religious convictions and equally fervent demands (some partly theological) for equal treatment, dignity, and respect. Indeed, they may even exacerbate them.

When these norms and punctilios fail to manage the conflict, we are left with law, the essential democratic tool of last resort albeit one with intrinsic limitations.[57] Those who contest hard issues, of course, always negotiate solutions in the law's shadow. When law represents and then enforces workable solutions between conflicting interests, it can legitimate those solutions and help implement them. Still, the fraught politics of many accommodation issues and the new contexts in which evolving legal principles must be applied produce much uncertainty and conflict. Moreover, some techniques to encourage compromise on these issues—for example, finding more money, splitting the difference, making side payments to offset losses, redefining the conflict, and pushing it to a different governmental level—are often unavailable here.

How, then, can a liberal, diverse, constitutionally constrained democratic society hope to resolve these proliferating disputes? Many thoughtful students of religious accommodation issues have considered this question, and LGBT claims give it a renewed urgency. I begin with Professor Steven Heyman's point that these conflicts proceed from the fundamentally different "identities and ways of life" of religious traditionalists and LGBT people (many of whom, of course, are religious).[58] Finding his view useful but somewhat question-begging, I then present a number of other approaches.

Heyman first rejects two decision rules in which either the most powerful group or the political majority gets its way. Mere dominance, he argues, "does not mean that it should be allowed to promote its own identity and way of life at the expense of another group." He then rejects RFRA's pro-religion tilt because it treats LGBT status not as an inherently valuable way of life but merely as a placeholder for a "governmental interest." This, he suggests, may be appropriate in a case like *Smith* where the government's interest is to enforce a general public welfare law (there, narcotics control), but not in a clash that pits two ways of life against one another. Trying to balance values that are really incommensurable, he claims, does not sufficiently protect rights, and a tolerant "live-and-let-live" approach provides no guidance as to which should prevail when the disputants interact in public spaces or when the state is regulating public services or benefits. Heyman's preferred approach is "mutual recognition" by both sides of the full and equal citizenship of the other and the right of each to hold and live according to their own beliefs.

But suppose the identity and way of life of one group are inconsistent with that of the other? Heyman posits some "easy" cases—the law cannot compel religious objectors to perform same-sex marriages,* nor must churches change their teachings or use their property for acts that offend them. He then poses a "hard" one, mentioned earlier, in which a vendor refuses to perform a wedding-related service (e.g., photography, cake, flowers) for LGBT couples, one that it willingly provides (and that the law does not permit it to withhold) from mixed-sex couples on the basis of certain characteristics. Heyman would resolve this conflict in favor of LGBTs because the vendor is defining its identity in a way that "denies the legitimacy of" the couple's identity.

This conclusion, however, is conclusory, side-stepping the central question of what legitimacy means (an issue also discussed in the previous chapter on affirmative action). Perhaps the vendors in such cases are not denying the couple's marital "legitimacy" but are instead saying in effect: "You have the right to marry but because I oppose and am offended by it, I simply don't want to deal with you, so go in peace and find another provider who isn't offended." Law professor Douglas Laycock made a similar point in a brief filed in *Obergefell*: "Burdens on religious exercise arise only when the state demands that religious organizations or believers *recognize or facilitate* a marriage

---

* A court has so held in the high-visibility case of Kentucky count clerk Kim Davis. *Miller v. Davis*, 2015 U.S. Dist. LEXIS 105822 (E.D. KY, Aug. 12, 2015). North Carolina and some other states have adopted "Kim Davis" rules that protect same-sex marriage licenses but allow religiously objecting officials to recuse themselves from participating.

in ways that violate their religious commitments. . . . [G]ay couples ought to be free to be married, and religious dissenters ought to be free to refuse to recognize these marriages."[59]

Consider further that civil rights law allows A to discriminate against B so long as A's decision is not based on specific prohibited grounds like race, sex, disability, and in most states, religion. A may refuse to deal with B if A is motivated by dislike of B's appearance, perceived immorality, rude conduct, or any other factor not prohibited by the statute. Distinguishing those reasons from a religious one, of course, can be difficult, as they commonly overlap and intent is an elusive state of mind. The law, by treating these reasons differently, seeks to strike a delicate balance between A's interest in autonomy and B's interest in equal treatment. But in many other areas of the law, an actor's intent likewise determines outcomes. Here, A's possible religious motivation simply adds a constitutionally-inflected wrinkle to the balancing.

In short, Heyman's mutual recognition approach does not tell us how to apply the RFRA balancing factors, much less how to resolve hard cases. In what follows, I propose other principles or considerations that may provide more guidance in such cases.

Dignity. Any analysis of a proposed accommodation (under RFRA's various prongs, say) should assess how it would affect the dignity of those affected. Although considering dignitary effects should not be controversial in principle—indeed, dignity is as fundamental a norm in many well-functioning foreign legal systems as "due process" and "equal protection" are in ours—it (like legitimacy) is easier to assert than to define.

Champions of LGBT rights stress the dignitary harms that may result when, for example, a wedding baker cancels a tasting upon finding out that the couple is gay[60]—a harm magnified by the ancient obloquy LGBTs have had to endure and by the fragility of their recent gains. Yet religious persons may also have strong claims of dignitary harm if their accommodation demands are denied. As Sherif Girgis writes:

[I]n many disputes, both sides could claim with equal force that a decision against them would morally stigmatize them. Grant that exemptions from baking same-sex wedding cakes tell gay couples that intimacies central to their identity are immoral. What about denying the bakers' claims? Won't that tell them—and traditional Muslims, Orthodox Jews, and Christians—that beliefs central to their identity are bigoted? If exemptions from performing abortions tar women who've had them, coercing prolife doctors must brand them enemies of women's equality. On most serious issues, any side might feel deeply stigmatized by rival actions or policies.[61]

The fact that dignitary claims may exist on both sides does not necessarily diminish their significance. In the end, decision makers must assess each such claim and weigh it against competing ones. For example, I imagine that merely selling a product to be used in a gay wedding to which one objects is not "participation" in any obvious sense and thus is at most a minor indignity, if that. But other factors could alter that assessment. (One might also note that a group's power to obtain the legal accommodation in the first place implies that its members' dignity is already well respected by the state.)

While decision makers should weigh dignitary harms on both sides of conflicts over religious freedom, they might be wary of overemphasizing such harms. As Girgis explains, a claim of stigma can actually be self-fulfilling: "The more that we—or officials, in weighing complicity claims—say that a policy or belief expresses disdain for a group, the more it will take on that social meaning. Lawmakers or judges trying to fight the harm might thus extend it."

Choice. Policy makers and courts can ease some conflicts over religious freedom by taking individual choice into account when fashioning the legal rules applied to such disputes. Americans place a very high value on choice—in families, markets, religion, and most other social settings—for well-understood reasons. Choice protects individual autonomy and freedom from state coercion that would compromise their will or conscience. In many disputes, A's choice can only be upheld by rejecting B's; there, coercion is unavoidable. But in a society whose social and legal architecture is usually flexible enough to accommodate competing values, we can sometimes minimize coercion by invoking the more general principle of choice.

If choice is to be a weighty factor in analyzing a proposed accommodation, we must determine how much choice actually exists. Consider the now-familiar example of a same-sex couple denied a wedding cake or other service by a vendor with a genuine, strong religious objection to such marriages. The jurisdiction's antidiscrimination statute, of course, may have resolved the conflict between the choice of the couple and the choice of the vendor in favor of one or the other. But even if the statute does prohibit this kind of discrimination, the vendor may claim a constitutionally-required or RFRA-based exception (citing *Hobby Lobby*). In this case, the decision maker's task is more difficult. It might take choice into account by determining whether the couple can obtain the same or comparable service from another vendor. (In most but not all cases, comparability of price, quality, and convenience should be easy to determine.) If so, the couple's desire for the service can be met without having to compel the objecting vendor to provide it. Choice, of course, is no panacea: Either decision will disappoint one side or the other. Even so, maximizing choice might reduce that harm or make it more palatable.

School curriculum and prayer provide other familiar contexts where valuing choice can reduce coercion and conflict yet still accommodate the competing values (e.g., neutrality among religions and between religion and secularism; and state responsibility for the welfare of children whose parents are incompetent, neglectful, or abusive). Although the specific facts will matter a lot—simple or categorical answers are seldom possible—some cases are easier than others. Small children's conduct and religious views are largely controlled by the parents, presumably (not always) dictated by what they think is in their child's best interests. In *Yoder*, the parents' choice grew out of a deep, responsible Amish tradition in which that community replaced the state in many areas of life.[62] Reasonable people can assess these situations differently, of course, just as the justices did in *Yoder*. But the inevitable interest-balancing should accord great, perhaps decisive, weight to parental choices about their children's welfare.

School cases often involve young adults. Here, the value of their own choices should be important, perhaps dispositive, in resolving disputes; young adults are far better equipped than younger children to exercise informed choice. The Court's recent prayer decisions have blurred the relevance of maturity. *Lee v. Weisman* [63] barred a school-sponsored clerically-led prayer at a middle school graduation ceremony, and *Santa Fe Independent School District v. Doe*[64] barred a student-delivered prayer over the school's public address system before high school football games. Reasonable people may disagree about whether the state was sufficiently neutral on the facts of these cases and whether each group of students was mature enough to choose, but I am troubled by how the Court defined choice and coercion in these cases. The students were free to remain seated or silent if they did not wish to participate, yet the Court still held that they were deprived of choice and harmed *psychologically*.

This reasoning, I think, trivializes the ideas of coercion and harm, presumes that young adults are more psychologically fragile than the vast majority probably are, and seeks to protect them from possible peer disapproval if they hold to their convictions and choose not to participate. If the school maintains the requisite neutrality and merely recognizes and fairly accommodates many students' observance on certain occasions, that should suffice. The mere possibility that non-observant students might feel some social discomfort is not coercion—it is inevitable in a religiously diverse society—and there should be no constitutional right to avoid it. By limiting their exposure to any risk of such discomfort, the Court may actually increase their vulnerability to it when they are exposed, as they surely will be, to other unfamiliar practices later in life. (The bizarre controversy over "trigger warnings" in the college context comes to mind.)[65] As the dissenting justices in *Lee* urged, the idea of unconstitutional coercion should be limited to the threat of official sanctions, intimidation, or clear psychological harm.

In cases involving young children or in which parental choice arguably threatens a child's life or public safety, courts must strike a somewhat different balance and deny a religious accommodation. *Prince v. Massachusetts*,[66] a 1944 decision, is the classic example. There, the Court upheld the state's power to vaccinate a child against communicable disease despite religious and other objections, invoking a traditional distinction between a belief and conduct. Belief is almost always protected,[67] but conduct is increasingly subject to regulation based on a majoritarian view of the child's interests rather than that of parents with exotic or deviant beliefs. Still, the vast majority of parents have a sustained and informed moral, physical, and financial commitment to their child that no state can match and that warrants great deference. Such deference is a price we rightly pay for the advantages of family autonomy, which typically (not always, alas) serves the child's interests well enough—especially compared with many foster care alternatives. The state, of course, must always prohibit parental abuse and neglect, but it should only overrule parents' religious choices when they create serious, well-established, and unacceptable risks to their children—for example, female genital mutilation.[68]

Conduct versus Status. Some demands for accommodation proceed from an aversion to having to act in a religiously repellent way, while others base their claim on a religious objection to the target's very status. Professor Lupu analyzes how this conduct-status distinction might affect accommodation claims under RFRA. He imagines an employer with a genuine religious objection to the worker's same-sex marriage claiming an exemption from the Family Marriage and Leave Act (FMLA), which requires firms to grant unpaid leave to workers with seriously ill family members. In *Hobby Lobby*, the Court granted the accommodation under the RFRA balancing test but here, Lupu argues, no exemption should be granted. Whereas the ACA would have forced Hobby Lobby to *act* in ways that promote the objectionable contraception, the FMLA would require the employer to *recognize* a worker's objectionable marriage *status*. To Lupu, it is more harmful to victims of discrimination if it pertains to many aspects of their family life, not just to contraception:

> [T]he objection is broader and far more troubling [than in *Hobby Lobby*] because its target is a relationship, an ongoing status protected in many ways by law. If the employer, acting on religious grounds, can treat a marriage as invalid, the employer can presumptively exclude the spouse from all benefits that federal law requires private employers to provide to employees' spouses. . . . It is difficult to see how this kind of claim of a religious burden could be limited to same sex marriages. Why would it not also extend to other marriages to which the employer had religious objection (e.g., inter-racial, inter-faith, purely secular), or to parent-child relationships to which the employer had religious objections (e.g., a child born out of wedlock, or through some form of assisted reproduction)? An employer might assert that any of these relationships are unnatural, disordered, contrary to God's plan, or evil. These kinds of objections, to status rather than acts, extend far beyond any singular act of "sinful" behavior, and are sweepingly hostile to the life plans of those whose family connections are being denied.[69]

Even so, Lupu notes, the Court's abject deference in *Hobby Lobby* to the firm's own subjective characterization of its religious conscience may render the conduct-status distinction useless in an RFRA analysis—a difficulty that Justice Ginsburg emphasized in an early decision allowing a public university to deny official recognition to a student group that excluded LGBT students.[70]

Least Restrictive Alternative. Another path to accommodation is already built into the law: RFRA's requirement that a secular government rule that conflicts with a specific religious practice can only be upheld if the rule is the "least restrictive" way to achieve a secular government purpose that is "compelling." This implies that a religious exception can only qualify to the extent that it is specific and clearly limited. As we saw, RFRA took this prong from the *Sherbert* test (which the *Smith* decision had briefly supplanted). It was dispositive in the Court's 2015 ruling in *Holt v. Hobbs,* which cited *Hobby Lobby* in striking down a prison's overly broad restriction on inmates' beards.[71] As noted in my summary of the *Hobby Lobby* ruling, the Court there found that the ACA failed this test: The law already had a less restrictive alternative for religious nonprofits—i.e., an exception that HHS could easily have extended to Hobby Lobby without further impairing the government's interest in covering contraceptives. This least restrictive alternative test has the important virtue of minimizing the clash between secular and religious interests.

But the other way to limit these conflicts is for the law to narrow the scope of the religious exemption. As Lupu explains, the Court has often held that a religious exception can be no broader than is necessary to protect those roles and activities that have a "distinctively religious" character. Much of what goes on in for-profit businesses, and even in religious organizations, will lack this religious connection. In addition, striking the correct balance between allowing government to pursue compelling public values and allowing a specific religious exception should take into account the full range of potential third-party effects, positive or negative.* Several other factors can affect the least-restrictive-alternative analysis. Expanding the choices available to either or both sides is one. Another is the scope of the exception: The narrower it is, the more likely it is to be the least restrictive of secular interests. An exception's scope can vary along several dimensions: the number of people it covers, the magnitude of its various effects on them, the breadth of its subject matter, its duration, and so forth. Whether it is indeed the least restrictive alternative or not depends on how it scores in each of these dimensions compared with possible alternative exceptions. Narrower exceptions tend to have a clearer purpose and meaning, and a more predictable effect. (For this reason among others, some statutes require public notice of exceptions.)

---

* Even before RFRA, the Court emphasized the third-party burdens aspect in a 1985 ruling finding that a statute favoring Sabbath-observing workers regardless of any adverse effects on other workers and the employer violated the Establishment Clause. *Estate of Thornton v. Caldor, Inc.,* 472 U.S. 703 (1985).

Lupu provides an example: the exemption from Title VII for co-religionist hiring by religious entities. Such specific exceptions "are typically not subject to interest-balancing. More significantly, they clearly identify their beneficiaries and specify the norms against which the exemptions may be invoked. So, for example, if non-profit religious entities were to be fully exempted from a federal law prohibiting LGBT discrimination in employment, the exemption would be clear and absolute. . . . [It] protects only entities with primary religious purposes, and hence presumptively excludes for-profit firms. Moreover, that exemption does not extend to exclusions based on race, sex, national origin, or any forbidden ground of discrimination other than religion."[72]

Decentralizing Accommodation. As we have seen, states and localities sometimes enact religious accommodations in their own constitutions, RFRAs, civil rights statutes, and other laws. Roderick Hills makes a strong argument that this decentralization is socially desirable and should be protected.[73] His premise is that many accommodation issues constitute "reasonable and deep disagreements" about liberty that cannot be reconciled in principle or empirically. Both are worthy of respect because, as in a *Hobby Lobby*–type situation, "social and legal consensus provides no commonly acknowledged baseline against which the disputing parties can measure their rights, [thus] one side of the dispute can plausibly claim that any resolution of the [dispute] constitutes an invasion of their fundamental rights. There is no neutral ground between coercing the organization into violating its religious scruples or allowing that organization to coerce its constituents (employees, customers, contractors, etc.) into obeying the organization's religious commitments. . . . Each side has plausible arguments to back their position, giving them all the more reason to dig in their heels."

Hills urges that subnational jurisdictions not be preempted by national rules on accommodation but be permitted to modify or waive them. The Court already did some of this work in *City of Boerne*, spawning a multiplicity of state RFRAs. "The federal system as a whole," he contends, "extends equal concern and respect to rival and reasonable conceptions of religious liberty by giving each conception a larger area in which it can be acknowledged as authoritative. Such federalism broadens what philosopher Jeremy Waldron calls the "right of rights"—that is, the right of citizens to say what their rights mean, where disagreement about the rights' content is reasonably disputed.[74]

The de minimis *Principle.* The English and American common law developed the principle of *de minimis non curat lex,* usually translated as "the law does not concern itself with trifles." This is a norm of judicial economy but more important, it also recognizes a more widely-relevant precept: In an increasingly crowded, diverse, sharp-elbowed society like twenty-first-century America, each individual should be expected to absorb some *limited* degree of intrusion, imposition, even offense if we are to live together without endless conflict and litigation. How limited? This is where the *de minimis* idea comes in. Like many vital principles, it is neither self-defining nor self-applying but requires case-by-case judgment. It does not deny the genuine, deeply-held feelings and values that the *de minimis* principle may decline to remedy. It simply means that one cannot look to the law to prevent or assuage the offense.

The *de minimis* principle often arises in the law of nuisance where A's and B's activities interfere with one another's use and enjoyment of their neighboring properties. For example, A may be offended by the appearance of B's house, the junk that B leaves in the yard, the smells that emanate from B's kitchen, and so forth, and we may conclude that we would react the same way. But up to some level of offense (often uncertain in advance), A cannot look to the law to protect his sensibility. If A has chosen to live in a crowded urban community, A is expected to absorb the kinds of intrusions that "go with the territory." The fact that an offense A experiences arises out of a religious commitment rather than a secular one (e.g., privacy, esthetic taste) should not make the *de minimis* principle inapplicable to A's offense, though it might affect how one assesses the *de minimis* level in particular cases. What constitutes a *de minimis* burden is often in the eye of the beholder. It ultimately turns on the decision maker's judgment, informed by analogous decisions in the past.

In the religious accommodation context, the *de minimis* principle would ordinarily come into play in applying an RFRA statute or a *Sherbert*-type strict scrutiny test to a government requirement affecting religion. The Supreme Court recently considered such a case, *Zubik v. Burwell*.[75] It involved a regulation issued under the ACA requiring employers to provide health insurance to their employees, including contraceptive coverage. The Obama administration proposed a number of different processes and criteria under which religious employers might obtain an exemption to the contraceptive element of the coverage, some more onerous than others. Ultimately, it imposed a requirement that those claiming a religious exemption submit a form to their insurer or to the government (which will then transmit it to the insurer) stating their religious objections. Religious employers argued that having to submit the form to the government violated RFRA because it would substantially burden their religious exercise. To them, it was not *de minimis*. Rather than decide this issue, the Court punted, remanding the case in hopes that a compromise would be reached under which the groups would not have to submit the form. In my view, having to submit a simple form in order to obtain the exemption should be treated as *de minimis*—as a reasonable way to satisfy the contending interests in a notoriously complex and controversial program, while fully respecting the groups' religious views.

Free Speech to Reduce Conflict. Law professor Andrew Koppelman has proposed allowing religious objectors to gay marriage and other secular policies to forthrightly express their objections without incurring liability under antidiscrimination laws that prohibit conduct that creates a "hostile environment" for protected minorities.[76] Under his approach, business owners could articulate their views but could not threaten to discriminate or treat any individual customer worse than others. "[E]ven if they have no statutory right to refuse to facilitate ceremonies they regard as immoral, they are unlikely to be asked to participate in those ceremonies. On the contrary, same-sex couples will almost all want nothing to do with them." In this way, the conflict between the groups can be avoided to the extent that they are kept far apart from one another and the disputed service is not demanded.

Koppelman notes that his approach would vindicate important First Amendment values in disputes in which A experiences and expresses A's moral distress at the conduct or beliefs of B, a member of a minority protected by equal-treatment and hostile-environment rules. One such value is the protection of religious disagreement, which, he reminds us, was a core concern of the Framers. Another is to promote mutual transparency among persons by encouraging their speech. A third value is the social learning that ethical confrontations can engender, which is particularly important when traditionally despised practices are at issue. Koppelman emphasizes that his approach can reduce and manage such conflicts better but is unlikely to eliminate them.

Compromise. A combination of these approaches can facilitate compromise. In March 2015, a Republican legislature and governor passed a law that received national attention, now known as the "Utah compromise." Its gist is to extend the state's civil rights law to bar housing and employment discrimination against LGBTs based on their gender identity, sexual orientation, and gay marriage. At the same time, it prohibits employer reprisals against religious objectors who express their opposition to these practices so long as their speech does not interfere with the company's business. It allows public employees, like marriage license clerks, who object on religious grounds to recuse themselves so long as the service is not denied to the couple. As for religious nonprofit organizations, they already enjoy broad exemption from the state's employment discrimination law, including from its prohibition of race and sex discrimination. The compromise thus allows religious nonprofits to refuse to hire LGBTs, just as it can refuse to hire other minorities.

Like most compromises, this one does not satisfy all participants and will be hard to replicate. It permits vendors to refuse service to LGBTs. Indeed, although the Mormon Church supported the compromise, it also affirmed "the rights of a religious community to set its standards and live according to them" by adopting new rules barring young children of gay couples from Church membership and disciplining members in same-sex marriages.[77] That said, the negotiations and compromise in Utah were widely praised by both sides and by commentators throughout the nation. Whether its protections of objectors will mollify them in other states, and whether LGBTs will accept other practices that they feel treat them as second-class citizens, remains to be seen.

A compromise that leaves both sides frustrated can engender bitterness among committed, intransigent opponents; this can make the compromise harder to sustain, legitimate, and institutionalize. In some cases, this determined opposition may succeed in partially reversing it, as with abortion rights, or forestall its full realization, as with gun control. Even so, some reformers believe that religious accommodation can be a powerful tool to mollify opposition by showing it respect and by relieving it from what it sees as offensive impositions. Professor Robin Wilson, for example, maintains that providing *Hobby Lobby*-type religious exemptions has facilitated the enactment of same-sex marriage laws by many states and has even furthered women's access to health services. (It is telling that same-sex marriage proposals are never enacted unless they include exceptions for religious objectors and cover clergy and houses of worship.[78] On the other hand, the enacted laws have not given exceptions to wedding vendors or public employees.)

Unsurprisingly, commentators differ over political strategy, predictions about how an accommodation is likely to affect third parties, and judgments about how American society does—and should—work through its cultural and legal conflicts. Some fear that religious groups' success in winning such accommodations will just inflame the culture wars and further embolden the groups' efforts to reverse the change.[79] Lupu predicts that both things may happen simultaneously: *Obergefell* will energize the movement to expand civil rights protection of LGBTs *and* this effort will stoke religious resistance to that movement.[80] Needless to say, outcomes will depend on the breadth, specificity, and exact wording of a proposed exception.

CONCLUSION

This chapter's analysis of the law and policy concerning accommodation of religion in the face of secular policies leads to important conclusions. In hard cases, the deep tensions—between protecting religious liberty through the Free Exercise Clause, preventing excessive government entanglement with religion through the Establishment Clause, and nourishing First Amendment values—yields few obvious answers. If government continues to expand its regulation of social conditions, it inevitably coerces more people, intensifying the conflicts between religious and secular values and extending those conflicts to more areas. The issue of accommodation, therefore, is bound to become more prominent and complex—especially as America's social diversity continues to grow.

Ensuring that accommodation respects the integrity and humanity of all participants while protecting their fundamental rights poses an immense social and legal challenge. With rights at the core of our public discourse, accommodations are bound to compromise them as they are redefined and tailored in light of particular conflicts. To some this trimming and compromise dilute rights' essence—a view that I believe misconceives how a liberal, diverse, competitive polity like ours must govern itself. In the realm of hard issues, the notion of a clear, absolute right is a fantasy—and a dangerous one at that. We wisely put a thumb on the scale to protect one value or another. But when we do so, we actually weigh and compromise them in order to preserve what the Court long ago called our system of ordered liberty.[81]

CHAPTER 7

CONCLUSION

EVERY HARD POLICY ISSUE is its own battleground, a field of fierce contestation over the future of one corner of our collective lives. Although its dramatis personae and contours may change, the hard issue has over time acquired a recognizable shape, an entrenched politics, an encrusted legal framework, and public frustration with the lack of "progress," which of course is defined in different ways. Each hard issue even has its own tropes and lingua franca, as we talk about it in ways that are often constrained by their familiarity. Its long history casts a large, often dark shadow over those who now struggle to resolve it.

In chapter 1, I identified ten attributes that are common to hard issues, distinguish them from easier ones, make them such enduring sources of conflict, and limit the range of possible solutions. I defined those attributes abstractly, as befits an introduction. But having now analyzed five of these hard issues in great detail, we can more easily see how in each case those common attributes express themselves differently, even uniquely. To put it another way, those five detailed analyses now enable us to look across them in order to see why each of them is hard in its own distinctive way (as Tolstoy famously said of unhappy families). In this conclusion, then, I return to those common features of "hardness"—now as a way to highlight their differences rather than their similarities, thus adding a comparative dimension to our understanding of them.

Public and Federal. Each of our five issues is public and federal, of course, but in quite different ways. Immigration policy is almost entirely a creature of federal law; indeed, the Supremacy Clause of the U.S. Constitution generally invalidates even indirect or peripheral efforts by states to regulate it. Poverty is a hybrid case, shaped today by both federal and state policies. Until the New Deal, it was hardly federal at all and became a focus of federal policy only in the 1960s. Campaign finance is regulated at both the federal and state levels, and often quite differently. Affirmative action is a hybrid of a different sort. The federal government has adopted it for some federal programs, federal contractors, and recipients of federal funds, but the most controversial programs—and the main subjects of legal challenge (largely in the federal courts)—are state-designed programs at state universities. Religious accommodation is perhaps the most unusual case of federalism, partly due to the novelty of recent legal changes at the federal, state, and local levels. These changes are very much in flux but have already transformed what were previously private decisions by employers, vendors, institutions, and individuals into matters of public policy.

Salience. All five issues greatly concern a large number of people, but in different ways. Campaign finance is salient primarily during election seasons, which are now endless, but a major obstacle to reform is that most people have little sustained interest in it (as with gun control). Much the same is true of poverty, which directly affects only a small minority of Americans. Religious accommodation issues directly affect relatively small minorities (the best estimates of the transgender share of the population are well under 1 percent[1]), but are exquisitely salient to them. Although immigration was a hot-button issue for millions of voters in the 2016 presidential campaign, its salience has usually been lower in most parts of the country.

Affirmative action has a symbolic significance for Americans, both pro and con, that seems far greater than the number of people directly affected by it.

Interrelatedness with Other Hard Issues. Affirmative action, campaign finance, and religious accommodation are all relatively autonomous from other hard issues; they can be resolved on their own merits without directly affecting other policy systems and issues. (Campaign finance, of course, indirectly affects many other things linked to political decisions.) This contrasts sharply with immigration and poverty. Immigration directly affects domestic politics, foreign policy, race relations, labor markets, religious patterns, social programs, and a host of other policy issues. Antipoverty programs affect budgetary issues, politics, work incentives, family structures, inequality, private philanthropy, housing patterns, and much more.

History. History affects all of our hard issues, but some much more than others. Affirmative action and poverty are both dogged by the tangled skeins and embedded legacies of slavery, subordination, and inequality. Americans acknowledge these legacies to some degree but differ sharply about how relevant this history is today after many decades of government programs, private efforts, and social changes. As we have seen, great progress has been made in alleviating deep poverty and expanding educational opportunity. In some policy settings (e.g., food stamps), the poor have influential allies. With affirmative action, the most enthusiastic advocates are powerful institutions—universities, the military, large corporations—that wield the popular mantra of diversity and enjoy broad discretion to adopt programs.

Immigration's history has bequeathed both advantages and disadvantages. Most Americans are proud of their own families' immigrant legacy and the many ways in which immigration has enriched our society. Our national identity is bound up with immigration history (some of it misunderstood or sanitized, like most histories). Immigration also has potent constituencies—employers, religious groups, ethnic advocates, influential media, and Democratic politicians—while restrictionists are more diffuse. Given this broad support, the public divides mainly over the kinds of difficult but relatively discrete, well-defined issues discussed in chapter 3: how many immigrants to admit, what their credentials should be, and how to conduct border, interior, and overseas enforcement more effectively. And because the large undocumented population creates serious, conspicuous social and legal conflicts, policy reforms are urgent, although their timing and shape remain uncertain.

The history of the poverty issue in America reveals that reformers lack these political advantages. Indeed, in a deeply individualistic society that values equal opportunity over equal results, people disagree about how much opportunity the poor actually have, how responsible they are for their low estate, which conditions and behaviors cause our inequalities, and how tractable those conditions and behaviors are to policy remedies. Although these controversies have not prevented antipoverty programs from expanding, their political footing is less secure. The poverty issue reveals another burden of history: The passage of time itself may magnify the problem, making it that much harder to resolve.* As we saw, much poverty in families and in communities is transmitted from one generation to another, making solutions that much more elusive.

The historical footprints of the campaign finance and religious accommodation issues are blurrier. Whether the FECA, BCRA, and the Supreme Court interpretations of them have improved or worsened the federal campaign finance system is hotly disputed, as we saw: The "realists" argue that history teaches that the reforms have weakened the parties and the system, while their opponents draw a different lesson from history, usually blaming economic inequality and the Court's decisions. In contrast, the history of religious accommodation disputes, which go back at least to the late-nineteenth-century disputes over Catholic schools and polygamy, casts little light on current controversies. Each side invokes historical precedents to

---

* This is not always the case. For some problems, the passage of time may produce newer, cheaper solutions, often technological. One hopes that climate change will prove to be an example.

support its position, with disputes being resolved (or exacerbated) through discrete debates, litigation, and politics.

Empirical Disputes. Poverty, as chapter 2 explained, is an unusually vexing issue, not least because of intense disagreement about so many of its empirical and methodological dimensions: its causes; how best to measure it; how to define a decent subsistence; how public and private provision of goods affects it; how various programs shape work incentives; and many others. Likewise, immigration engenders constant controversy over the number of undocumented immigrants in the country; immigration's effects on culture, demography, economic growth, wages, schools, other social services, and communities; the effectiveness of various enforcement strategies; its impact on elections; the need for detention; and many other empirical questions. With campaign finance, the empirical debate revolves around the actual effects of contributions and expenditures on electoral outcomes and on politicians' decisions, and on the likely effects of various reforms—with no consensus in sight. The affirmative action debate centers on many important factual questions: the size of preferences; their actual diversity value; the existence and size of a mismatch effect; how socially disadvantaged the program's beneficiaries are; and whether they are stigmatized on campus, among others. Religious accommodation disputes raise hard empirical questions about how much discrimination exists; its effects on minorities; the offense to religious values if accommodation is denied; and so forth.

Normative Disputes. Our five issues exhibit a wide range of divisions rooted in conflicting values. The analysis of poverty found almost universal agreement among Americans, regardless of class, on the importance of individual responsibility, family stability, and hard work—but much more division over the actual causes of poverty, especially in certain categories (e.g., unmarried mothers, absent fathers, criminals, high school dropouts). On immigration, putting xenophobes and racists aside, the normative conflicts are far outweighed by the empirical ones. Much the same is true of campaign finance, where empirical disagreements dwarf the normative ones (after all, everyone opposes corruption and unfair advantage in principle). On affirmative action, almost everyone agrees that merit should govern admission and hiring decisions and that diversity is usually desirable, but much disagreement remains over how to define merit and what kind of diversity is most valuable.

Of the issues analyzed in the earlier chapters, religious accommodation—the appropriate relationship between government and religion—presents the most clear-cut normative disagreements, as they involve conflicting worldviews. Sometimes, the courts have resolved disputes of this kind by invoking another abstract value—separation of church and state, concretized in the "wall" metaphor—that the disputants may be willing to accept. This principle, however, only raises further questions—mostly normative but partly empirical—about how high or firm the wall must be to protect both government and religion from each other, whether an exception will undermine its integrity, and so forth. Although the RFRA statutes are designed to raise and answer these questions, the proliferating disputes over providing services to LGBT people reveal the depths of these differences.

Fine Distinctions. In chapter 1, I explained how issues become harder as new, unanticipated fact situations engender finer, and thus more complex distinctions. Of our five hard issues, campaign finance is probably the clearest example of this. In chapter 4 I elaborated a number of the distinctions (some statutory, some judicially developed) that have become central to the administration of campaign finance policy. To critics, some of them—for example, the distinction between quid pro quo corruption and undue access and influence—make little sense and indeed are perverse in their effects. To other commentators, however, these same distinctions not only are essential to a sound campaign finance system but in some cases are (and should be) constitutionally required. The immigration statute contains hundreds of fine distinctions—often in the form of categories, criteria, and exceptions—that are pivotal to immigration administration and enforcement. These distinctions have steadily proliferated and make immigration one of the most complex areas of federal law. In poverty policy, the significant line-drawing is less in the statutes themselves than in the key distinctions that are applied in the countless low-visibility decisions of program administrators (e.g., between those who can be expected to work and those who cannot). Likewise with religious accommodation issues, the key distinctions are elaborated in the course of applying the RFRA criteria to determine which accommodation may—or must—be made under those statutes. Finally, the role of distinctions in affirmative action programs is something of a mystery because of the programs' continuing lack of transparency, one that *Fisher II* seems likely to worsen.

Institutional Density. Poverty and immigration are the most institutionally dense of our issues. Efforts to combat poverty involve a host of federal, state, and local agencies, countless private nonprofit groups, and of course millions of families and individuals. Immigration policy is shaped at every step by Congress, several federal departments and agencies, the federal courts, state and local police departments (in interior enforcement), public and private social service agencies (with immigrant families and children), other countries, and employers' innumerable hiring decisions. This helps to explain the many failed attempts to reform immigration policy by presidents of both parties in recent decades. In sharp contrast, affirmative action exhibits little institutional density, being designed and administered by a fairly small number of relatively autonomous public or private institutions. The institutional density of campaign finance policy is somewhere in the middle, involving national party committees, fifty autonomous state party organizations, numerous traditional and online media, and countless individuals, groups, and candidates seeking to influence elections.

Severe Constraints on Solutions. Perhaps the most obvious hallmark of a hard issue is officials' limited ability to adopt or implement promising solutions. As I noted in chapter 1, the reasons for this are typically fiscal and political but are sometimes legal, or even constitutional. This last constraint is most important in the areas of campaign finance, religious accommodation, and affirmative action. We saw in chapter 4 that the Court's readings of the First Amendment preclude some campaign finance reforms that might reduce money's influence in politics. (We also saw deep divisions over whether on balance this would be a good thing for our democracy.) The Court's rulings also preclude certain approaches to reconciling religious freedom and civil rights in disputes over health insurance, contraceptives, gay marriage, and transgender equality. And on affirmative action, as chapter 5 explained, the Court's view of the Fourteenth Amendment's equal protection principle constrains the types of minority preference programs that can pass legal muster.

The Constitution, of course, is only one of the nonfiscal barriers that make some issues especially hard to resolve. For example, Americans' overriding commitment to family autonomy from government intrusion precludes certain policy interventions that arguably might reduce poverty. The length and porosity of our southern border is what makes effective immigration control there nearly impossible. And, to cite one more example not discussed in this book: Even if there were no Second Amendment, any proposal to reduce gun violence would run into certain realities: Americans already own some 300 million guns—and many millions more being obtained in anticipation of renewed gun control efforts, and through 3-D printing of guns. These guns would be impossible to confiscate even if that were politically feasible, which it manifestly is not.[2]

A PARTING THOUGHT

If our journey through these five hard issues teaches us anything, it is that reasonable people who care deeply about the public interest (as they understand it) can and do disagree about how to define, approach, and resolve each of them. This simple but far-reaching fact may not be obvious to the warriors on the political battlefield, but at least it should now be evident to you, my readers.

If you accept this fact of deep disagreement—one underscored in the 2016 election—then three important implications follow. First, the elements of clear thinking can be applied to *any* hard public issue, not just the ones analyzed here. Second, if advocates of one or another position can acknowledge the empirical and normative complexities that make issues like these so hard, then they may come to see their opponents' arguments as at least plausible and thus worthy of grudging respect. If so, then this respect may cool and elevate the debate enough to encourage the disputants to seek solutions acceptable to all. But if advocates instead perceive their opponents' positions not just as wrong but as irrational, arbitrary, and even malevolent, then the search for common ground where broadly acceptable and workable policies are likely to be found becomes much harder to justify and motivate.

Finally, even in the common situation when reasoned, empirically informed, normatively open-minded analysis of the kind presented in this book cannot effectively resolve hard issues, it can, it is hoped, narrow the range of disagreement, which in turn can facilitate compromise. The only alternative to compromise, after all, is some form of coercion that threatens the perceived legitimacy of the victors and leaves the defeated bitter, vengeful, and determined to undermine the victorious party and policy. Sound familiar?

NOTES

CHAPTER 1. INTRODUCTION

1. The classic analysis is John W. Kingdon, *Agendas, Alternatives, and Public Policies* 2d ed. (2010).
2. For a discussion of this problem, see Peter H. Schuck, *Diversity in America: Keeping Government at a Safe Distance* (2003) (hereafter *Diversity in America*), pp. 332–37.
3. See, e.g., John H. Aldrich, *Why Parties? The Origin and Transformation of Party Politics in America* (1995); Andrew W. Robertson, "'Look on This Picture . . . And on This!' Nationalism, Localism, and Partisan Images of Otherness in the United States, 1787," 106 *American History Review* 1263 (2001).
4. See David Herbert Donald, *Lincoln* (2001); http://www.theatlantic.com/magazine /archive/2013/06/abraham-lincoln-is-an-idiot/309304/
5. See, e.g., Yuval Levin, *Our Fractured Society* (2016).
6. See generally, Nathaniel Persily, ed., *Solutions to Political Polarization in America* (2015).
7. Levin, *Our Fractured Society*.
8. See generally, Peter H. Schuck, *Why Government Fails So Often, and How It Can Do Better* (2014) (hereafter *Why Government Fails So Often*), chap. 9.
9. Daniel Yankelovich, *Coming to Public Judgment: Making Democracy Work in a Complex World* (1991), chap. 3.
10. On policy implementation, see ibid., chap. 8.
11. http://www.nytimes.com/2016/04/08/opinion/sanders-over-the-edge.html
12. On the meaning of legitimacy, see Schuck, *Why Government Fails So Often*, at 13–15.
13. See generally Schuck, *Why Government Fails So Often*, chaps. 5–10.
14. See, e.g., Rosa Mule, *Political Parties, Games and Redistribution* (2001), chap. 1.
15. http://press-pubs.uchicago.edu/founders/documents/v1ch13s7.html
16. http://www.manhattan-institute.org/html/teach-civics-and-citizenship-9271.html

17. For greater detail, see Schuck, *Why Government Fails So Often*, at 156–57 and sources cited there.

18. http://www.aei.org/files/2013/11/06/-public-opinion-on-conspiracy-theories_18164 9218739.pdf

19. For a more detailed explanation of these sources of citizens' irrationality, and the supporting references, see Schuck, *Why Government Fails So Often*, at 156–60.

20. Dan Kahan, "Climate-Science Communication and the Measurement Problem," 36 *Political Psychology* 1 (2015); Dan Kahan, Hank Jenkins-Smith, & Donald Braman, "Cultural Cognition of Scientific Consensus," 14 *Journal of Risk Research* 147 (2010).

21. Ibid., at 161–72 and sources cited there.

22. See, e.g., Schuck, *Why Government Fails So Often*, at 105–10, 113, 215–16, and sources cited there.

23. Ibid., at 163–64, and sources cited there.

24. See, e.g., Peter H. Schuck & James Q. Wilson, eds., *Understanding America: The Anatomy of an Exceptional Nation* (2008), chap. 7 (by S. Robert Lichter).

25. See, e.g., Robert A. Dahl, *Controlling Nuclear Weapons: Democracy versus Guardianship* (1985); Charles E. Lindblom & David K. Cohen, *Usable Knowledge: Social Science and Social Problem-Solving* (1979); Bryan Caplan, *The Myth of the Rational Voter: Why Democracies Choose Bad Policies* (2007).

26. Bruce Ackerman and James Fishkin have both theorized and orchestrated such events in various democracies. Ackerman & Fishkin, *Deliberation Day* (2004).

27. Schuck, *Why Government Fails So Often*, at 8–17.

28. See, e.g., Peter H. Schuck, *Diversity in America*, chap. 4.

29. See Schuck, *Why Government Fails So Often*, at 159–60 and chap. 12.

30. Ibid. at 34–35. See also Peter H. Schuck, *Meditations of a Militant Moderate: Cool Views on Hot Topics* (2006).

CHAPTER 2. POVERTY

1. Deuteronomy 15:11.

2. Mark 14:7.

3. Michael B. Katz, *Improving Poor People: The Welfare State, the "Underclass," and Urban Schools as History* (1997).

4. Edward D. Kleinbard, *We Are Better Than This: How Government Should Spend Our Money* (2015), p. 98.

5. On the (im)morality of poverty, see, e.g., Alexis de Tocqueville, "Memoir on Pauperism," 70 *National Affairs* 102 (1983); Michael Harrington, *The Other America: Poverty in the United States* (1962); Pope Francis, "Misericordiae Vultus," Bull of Indication of the Extraordinary Jubilee of Mercy (April 2015). https://w2.vatican.va /content/francesco/en/apost_letters/documents/papa-francesco_bolla_20150411 _misericordiae-vultus.html.

6. Thomas Piketty, book review of Anthony B. Atkinson, *Inequality: What Can Be Done*, "A Practical Vision of a More Equal Society," *New York Review of Books*, June 25, 2015.

7. Thomas Piketty, *Capital in the Twenty-First Century* (2014).

8. http://eml.berkeley.edu/~saez/saez-UStopincomes-2014.pdf, table 1.

9. Ibid.

10. http://www.brookings.edu/about/projects/bpea/papers/2016/bricker-et-al-income -wealth-top

11. https://www.brookings.edu/opinions/income-growth-has-been-negligible-but -surprise-inequality-has-narrowed-since-2007/

12. http://www.nytimes.com/2016/09/14/business/economy/us-census-household -income-poverty-wealth-2015.html?_r=0

13. "Buttonwood," *The Economist*, June 20, 2015, p. 68.

14. https://scholar.princeton.edu/sites/default/files/mgilens/files/gilens_and_page _2014_-testing_theories_of_american_politics.doc.pdf. See also https://www .washingtonpost.com/news/monkey-cage/wp/2014/04/08/rich-people-rule/

15. http://www.wsj.com/articles/behind-rising-inequality-more-unequal-companies -1446665769?alg=y

16. Atkinson, *Inequality: What Can Be Done?*.

17. James Ryerson, "Ivory Tower," *New York Times Book Review*, December 20, 2015, p. 27.

18. http://www.nytimes.com/2015/12/27/upshot/marriages-of-power-couples-reinforce -income-inequality.html (citing Jeremy Greenwood et al. study).

19. https://www.whitehouse.gov/sites/default/files/docs/2015_erp_chapter_1.pdf

20. E.g., *Inequality for All* (72 Productions 2015).

21. Noam Scheiber & Dalia Sussman, "Inequality Troubles Americans across Party Lines, Times/CBS Poll Finds," *New York Times*, June 3, 2015.

22. Matthew Hutson, "Measuring Up," *The Atlantic*, October 2015, p. 23 (describing studies).

23. Richard Reeves & Nathan Joo, "How Much Social Mobility Do People Really Want?" *Brookings*, January 12, 2016.

24. Leslie McCall, *The Undeserving Rich: American Beliefs about Inequality, Opportunity, and Redistribution* (2013).

25. William Galston, "Republicans and Democrats Divided on Important Issues for a Presidential Nominee," *Brookings*, June 3, 2015.

26. Alberto Alesina & Edward Glaeser, *Fighting Poverty in the U.S. and Europe: A World of Difference* (2004).

27. Remarks by the president on Economic Mobility (2013). https://www.whitehouse .gov/the-press-office/2013/12/04/remarks-president-economic-mobility

28. See, e.g., http://www.warren.senate.gov/?p=op_ed&id=1071; https://berniesanders .com/issues/income-and-wealth-inequality/

29. Ben Bernanke, "Monetary Policy and Inequality," *Brookings*, June 1, 2015.

30. See, e.g., Nicholas Kristof, "It's Not Just about Bad Choices," *New York Times*, June 13, 2015.

31. Jennifer L. Hochschild, *What's Fair: American Beliefs about Distributive Justice* (1981).

32. Arthur Okun, *Equality and Efficiency: The Big Tradeoff* (1975).

33. On how policy is confounded during the implementation process, see Peter H. Schuck, *Why Government Fails So Often*, chap. 8.

34. Noam Scheiber, "Why a Meaningful Boost for Those at the Bottom Requires Help from the Top," *New York Times*, July 6, 2015.

35. William G. Gale, Melissa S. Kearney, & Peter R. Orszag, "A Significant Increase in the

Top Income Tax Rate Wouldn't Substantially Alter Income Inequality," *Brookings*, September 28, 2015.

36. http://www.capx.co/external/why-are-wages-lagging-productivity-in-the-us/

37. http://www.pewresearch.org/fact-tank/2013/12/18/the-many-ways-to-measure -economic-inequality/

38. Gary Burtless, "Are Middle Class Incomes Shrinking? Census Statistics Tell a Different Story Than National Income Statistics," *Brookings*, September 22, 2015; Scott Winship, "Being a Member of the 'Hollowed Out' Middle Class Never Felt So Good," *Manhattan Institute: National Review Online*, December 14, 2015.

39. http://www.wsj.com/article_email/how-progressives-drive-income-inequality -1457132837-lMyQjAxMTI2NDA1NTIwMzU4Wj

40. http://www.oecd.org/social/income-distribution-database.htm, table 1.A1.1 (update May 19, 2015).

41. http://www.oecd.org/social/inequality.htm

42. http://www.wsj.com/articles/oecd-sees-continued-rise-in-growth-harming -inequality-1432198801

43. Harry G. Frankfurt, *On Inequality* (2015).

44. Ibid. at 71–72.

45. Ibid. at 78.

46. Readers interested in how it was developed should consult http://aspe.hhs.gov /poverty/papers/hptgssiv.htm

47. E.g., Sheldon H. Danziger, "The Mismeasure of Poverty," *New York Times*, September 17, 2013 (liberal); Nicholas Eberstadt, *The Poverty of the Poverty Rate: Measure and Mismeasure of Material Deprivation in Modern America* (2008) (conservative).

48. http://pubs.aeaweb.org/doi/pdfplus/10.1257/jep.26.3.111

49. http://www.nytimes.com/2015/09/17/us/politics/census-bureau-poverty-rate -uninsured.html?_r=0

50. Christopher Jencks, "The War on Poverty: Was It Lost?," *New York Review of Books*, April 2, 2015 (reviewing Martha J. Bailey & Sheldon Danziger, *Legacies of the War on Poverty* [2013]).

51. http://www.forbes.com/sites/scottwinship/2015/08/26/whether-and-how-to-adjust -income-trends-for-declining-household-size-part-2/

52. Email to author from Christopher Jencks, December 1, 2015.

53. Thomas Gabe, "Welfare, Work, and Poverty Status of Female-Headed Families with Children, 1987–2013" https://www.fas.org/sgp/crs/misc/R41917.pdf, p. 54.

54. http://www.cbo.gov/publication/49440

55. http://www.project-syndicate.org/commentary/are-us-middle-class-incomes -stagnating-by-martin-feldstein-2015-07

56. https://www.aei.org/wp-content/uploads/2015/10/MeyerMittag-Combined.pdf

57. http://www.nber.org/programs/ag/rrc/08–12%20Meyer,%20Mok,%20Sullivan% 20FINAL.pdf

58. E.g., Kathryn Edin & Laura Lein, *Making Ends Meet: How Single Mothers Survive Welfare and Low Wage Work* (1997); Sudhir A. Venkatesh, *Off the Books: The Underground Economy of the Urban Poor* (2006).

59. Bruce D. Meyer & James X. Sullivan, "Winning the War: Poverty from the Great Society to the Great Recession," in *Brookings Papers on Economic Activity* (2012).

60. Eberstadt, *The Poverty of the Poverty Rate.*
61. Franklin E. Zimring, *The Great American Crime Decline* (2006); Franklin E. Zimring, *The City That Became Safe: New York's Lessons for Urban Crime and Its Control* (2012); Michael Friedson & Patrick Sharkey, "Violence and Neighborhood Disadvantage after the Crime Decline," 660 *Annals of the American Academy of Political and Social Science* 341 (2015).
62. https://www.washingtonpost.com/graphics/national/2015-homicides/?hpid=hp_no-name_graphic-story-a%3Ahomepage%2Fstory
63 https://www.aei.org/wp-content/uploads/2015/06/Street-homelessness.pdf, fig. 1. On Utah's much-reported progress, see http://www.aei.org/publication/think-utah-solved-homelessness-think-again/?utm_source=paramount&utm_medium=email&utm_content=AEITODAY&utm_campaign=030816
64. http://www.heritage.org/research/reports/2011/07/what-is-poverty; John Iceland, *Poverty in America: A Handbook* 3d ed. (2013), p. 72.
65. Gary Burtless, "Generational War over the Budget? Hard to See It in the Numbers," *Brookings,* December 2, 2015.
66. http://www.cbpp.org/research/poverty-and-inequality/safety-net-for-poorest-weakened-after-welfare-law-but-regained
67. Robert I. Lerman, "US Wage Inequality Trends and Recent Immigration," *American Economic Review: Papers and Proceedings* (May 1999), 23–28.
68. Personal communication with the author, November 30, 2015.
69. Jencks, "The War on Poverty: Was It Lost?," fig. 1.
70. Christopher Jencks, "Why the Very Poor Have Become Poorer," *New York Review of Books,* June 9, 2016 (reviewing Kathryn J. Edin & H. Luke Shaefer, *$2.00 a Day: Living on Almost Nothing in America* [2015]).
71. Scott Winship, "Poverty after Welfare Reform," Manhattan Institute, August 2016.
72. http://www.aei.org/publication/hunger-finally-fell-in-2015-is-poverty-rate-next/
73. Gabe, "Welfare, Work, and Poverty Status of Female-Headed Families with Children."
74. Dionne Searcey & Robert Gebeloff, "America's Seniors Find Middle-Class 'Sweet Spot,' " *New York Times,* June 14, 2015. On retirees' continuing financial risks, see Eduardo Porter, "Doing More, Not Less, to Save Retirees from Financial Ruin," *New York Times,* June 16, 2015.
75. Bruce D. Meyer, "Unemployment Insurance and Unemployment Spells," 58 *Econometrica* 757 (1990); Lawrence Katz & Bruce D. Meyer, "The Impact of the Potential Duration of Unemployment Benefits on the Duration of Unemployment," 41 *Journal of Public Economics* 45 (1990); http://economix.blogs.nytimes.com/2010/03/17/do-jobless-benefits-discourage-people-from-finding-jobs/
76. Robert Pear, "Social Security Disability Benefits Face Cuts in 2016, Trustees Say," *New York Times,* July 22, 2015.
77. "Reflections on the Effects of Immigrants on African Americans—and Vice-Versa," in *Help or Hindrance? The Economic Implications of Immigration for African-Americans,* ed. D. S. Hamermesh & F. D. Bean (Russell Sage Foundation, 1998), pp. 361–75.
78. http://www.pewsocialtrends.org/2015/04/09/chapter-1-statistical-portrait-of-the-u-s-black-immigrant-population/; http://www.pewsocialtrends.org/2015/04/09/a-rising-share-of-the-u-s-black-population-is-foreign-born/
79. http://www.economist.com/news/united-states/21657392-americas-fastest-growing

-migrant-group-may-challenge-countrys-fraught-race?zid=304&ah=e5690753dc78c
e91909083042ad12e30

80. http://www.nytimes.com/2015/09/23/business/economy/education-gap-between
-rich-and-poor-is-growing-wider.html?emc=eta1

81. See, e.g., "When Marriage Disappears: The New Middle America" (National Marriage Project, eds.) (2010); Emma Garcia and Elaine Weiss, "Early Education Gaps by Social Class and Race Start U.S. Children Out on Unequal Footing," *Economic Policy Institute*, June 17, 2015; Gina Kolata, "Death Rates Rising for Middle-Aged White Americans, Study Finds," *New York Times*, November 2, 2015.

82. Kay S. Hymowitz, "Class Is Now a Stronger Predictor of Well-Being Than Race," *New York Times*, January 28, 2016.

83. *An American Dilemma: The Negro Problem and Modern Democracy* (1944).

84. https://www.census.gov/prod/2013pubs/acsbr11-17.pdf

85. Greg J. Duncan et al., *Years of Poverty, Years of Plenty: The Changing Fortunes of American Workers and Families* (1984), pp. 41, 75; Rebecca M. Blank, *It Takes a Nation: A New Agenda for Fighting Poverty* (1997), pp. 22–25.

86. http://www.washingtonpost.com/blogs/wonkblog/wp/2015/06/15/how-section-8
-became-a-racial-slur/

87. Dan M. Kahan & Donald Braman, "Cultural Cognition and Public Policy," 24 *Yale Law and Policy Review* 149 (2006); Mary Douglas & Aaron Wildavsky, *Risk and Culture: An Essay on the Selection of Technological and Environmental Dangers* (1982).

88. See, e.g., Nicholas Wade, *A Troublesome Inheritance: Genes, Race and Human History* (2014); Richard J. Herrnstein & Charles Murray, *The Bell Curve: Intelligence and Class Structure in American Life* (1994); Arthur R. Jensen, "How Much Can We Boost IQ and Scholastic Achievement?," 39 *Harvard Educational Review* 1 (1969).

89. The debate is fairly summarized in Christopher Jencks & Meredith Phillips, eds., *The Black-White Test Score Gap* (1998), chap. 1, summarized at http://www.nytimes.com /books/first/j/jencks-gap.html

90. http://www.brookings.edu/research/papers/2003/09/childrenfamilies-haskins

91. Paul Prettitore, "Adding a Legal Dimension to Multidimensional Poverty," *Brookings*, May 19, 2016.

92. See, e.g., Henry Aaron, *Politics and the Professors: The Great Society in Perspective* (1978).

93. Frank J. Sulloway, *Born to Rebel: Birth Order, Family Dynamics, and Creative Lives* (1996).

94. Richard R. Peterson, "A Reevaluation of the Economic Consequences of Divorce," 61 *American Sociological Review* 528 (1996).

95. "The Negro Family: The Case for National Action" (1965), at https://www.dol.gov /oasam/programs/history/webid-meynihan.htm

96. Sara McLanahan & Christopher Jencks, "Was Moynihan Right?" 15 *Education Next* (Spring 2015).

97. Gabe, "Welfare, Work, and Poverty Status of Female-Headed Families with Children," at 1.

98. http://www.equality-of-opportunity.org/

99. *The Economist*, May 9, 2015, p. 23, chart 1.

100. http://datacenter.kidscount.org/data/tables/107-children-in-single-parent-families
-by#detailed/1/any/false/869,36,868,867,133/10,11,9,12,1,185,13/432,431; http://
washingtonmonthly.com/magazine/janfeb-2013/the-new-white-negro/

101. Naomi Cahn & June Carbone, *Red Families v. Blue Families: Legal Polarization
and the Creation of Culture* (2010). http://family-studies.org/red-families-vs-blue
-families-which-are-happier/ (controlling for demographics).

102. http://family-studies.org/red-families-vs-blue-families-which-are-happier/ (controlling for demographics); http://www.aei.org/publication/a-red-family
-advantage-marriage-and-family-stability-in-red-and-blue-america/?utm_source
=paramount&utm_medium=email&utm_content=AEITODAY&utm_campaign
=070215

103. https://en.wikipedia.org/wiki/Divorce_demography

104. http://www.theatlantic.com/politics/archive/2016/02/soul-mates-black-church
-marriage/470760/

105. http://www.nytimes.com/interactive/2015/04/20/upshot/missing-black-men.html
?abt=0002&abg=1

106. Patterson, *Rituals of Blood: Consequences of Slavery in Two American Centuries*
(1998), p. 12.

107. "Exceptionally Deadly," *The Economist*, July 18, 2015, p. 28.

108. http://www.pewtrusts.org/en/research-and-analysis/reports/0001/01/01/family
-structure-and-the-economic-mobility-of-children

109. Patterson, *Rituals of Blood*, at 60–61.

110. http://www.nytimes.com/2015/06/15/opinion/charles-blow-jeb-bush-and-single
-mothers.html

111. Patterson, *Rituals of Blood*, at 61.

112. Ibid. at 148.

113. *The Economist*, May 9, 2015, p. 24.

114. Isabel V. Sawhill, "Is There a Shortage of Marriageable Men?," *Brookings*, September 22, 2015.

115. Orlando Patterson, *The Ordeal of Integration: Progress and Resentment in America's "Racial" Crisis* (1998).

116. http://www.economist.com/news/united-states/21657392-americas-fastest
-growing-migrant-group-may-challenge-countrys-fraught-race?zid=304&ah=e569
0753dc78ce91909083042ad12e30

117. http://www.fragilefamilies.princeton.edu/documents/FragileFamiliesandChildWell
beingStudyFactSheet.pdf; *The Economist*, May 9, 2015, p. 24.

118. http://educationnext.org/actingwhite/

119. Gabe, "Welfare, Work, and Poverty Status of Female-Headed Families with Children," at 17.

120. http://www.pewresearch.org/fact-tank/2015/07/14/black-child-poverty-rate-holds
-steady-even-as-other-groups-see-declines/

121. http://www.heritage.org/research/reports/2012/09/marriage-americas-greatest
-weapon-against-child-poverty

122. Email to author from Christopher Jencks, December 1, 2015

123. https://www.aei.org/publication/what-malcolm-gladwell-gets-wrong-about
-poverty/

124. https://www.census.gov/hhes/www/cpstables/032015/pov/pov22_100.htm

125. http://www.nytimes.com/2015/07/03/upshot/the-new-jobs-numbers-are-weaker
     -than-they-look.html?ref=business&_r=0&abt=0002&abg=0
126. http://www.bls.gov/news.release/empsit.t12.htm, table A12.
127. William Julius Wilson, *When Work Disappears: The World of the New Urban Poor*
     (1996); William Julius Wilson, *The Truly Disadvantaged: The Inner City, the Un-
     derclass, and Public Policy* (1987).
128. David J. Deming, "The Growing Importance of Social Skills in the Labor Market,"
     NBER Working Paper No. 21473.
129. Natalie Holmes & Alan Berube, "Close to Home: Social Mobility and the Growing
     Distance between People and Jobs," *Brookings*, June 9, 2015.
130. Daria Roithmayr, *Reproducing Racism: How Everyday Choices Lock In White Ad-
     vantage* (2014).
131. Joseph R. Fishkin, *Bottlenecks: A New Theory of Equal Opportunity* (2014).
132. Roger Waldinger, *Still the Promised City? African-Americans and New Immigrants
     in Post-Industrial New York* (1996).
133. Mary C. Waters, *Black Identities: West Indian Immigrant Dreams and American
     Realities* (1999); Ta-Nehisi Coates, "Why Do Black Immigrants Do Better Than
     Native Blacks?" *The Atlantic* (March 23, 2009). http://www.theatlantic.com
     /entertainment/archive/2009/03/why-do-black-immigrants-do-better-than-native
     -blacks/6891/.
134. Patterson, *The Ordeal of Integration*, at 163.
135. Gabe, "Welfare, Work, and Poverty Status of Female-Headed Families with
     Children."
136. Emily Badger & Christopher Ingraham, "The Striking Power of Poverty to Turn
     Young Boys into Jobless Men," *Washington Post*, January 29, 2016.
137. Lawrence M. Mead, *The New Politics of Poverty: The Nonworking Poor in America*
     (1992), chaps. 4 and 5.
138. http://www.census.gov/content/dam/Census/library/publications/2015/demo/p60
     -252.pdf
139. http://www.ed.gov/news/press-releases/us-high-school-graduation-rate-hits-new
     -record-high
140. http://www.nytimes.com/2014/09/11/business/economy/a-simple-equation-more
     -education-more-income.html
141. http://www.manpowergroup.us/campaigns/talent-shortage-2015/index.html
142. http://gpseducation.oecd.org/CountryProfile?primaryCountry=USA&treshold=10
     &topic=AS
143. http://www.wsj.com/articles/small-business-owners-work-to-fill-job-openings
     -1404940118; http://money.cnn.com/2015/09/09/news/economy/us-economy-job
     -openings/
144. http://www.nytimes.com/2015/11/04/business/economy/school-vs-society-in
     -americas-failing-students.html
145. http://www.aei.org/publication/to-narrow-the-digital-divide-the-fcc-should-not
     -simply-extend-lifeline-to-broadband/?utm_source=paramount&utm_medium
     =email&utm_content=AEITODAY&utm_campaign=033116
146. http://www.nytimes.com/2015/05/05/upshot/why-the-new-research-on-mobility
     -matters-an-economists-view.html?abt=0002&abg=0
147. Ibid.

148. Fishkin, *Bottlenecks: A New Theory of Equal Opportunity*, at 213, n 44 (citing studies).

149. http://www.nytimes.com/2016/03/27/upshot/growing-up-in-a-bad-neighborhood -does-more-harm-than-we-thought.html?smid=nytcore-iphone-share&smprod =nytcore-iphone

150. "With a Little Help from My Friends," *The Economist*, June 6, 2015, p. 66.

151. Venkatesh, *Off the Books: The Underground Economy of the Urban Poor*.

152. Mark S. Granovetter, "The Strength of Weak Ties," 78 *American Journal of Sociology* 1360 (1973).

153. Ibid.; Mark S. Granovetter, *Getting a Job: A Study of Contacts and Careers* (1995).

154. These blacks are middle-class in income, not wealth: The median black family had a net worth of only $11,000 in 2013, compared with $142,000 for the median white one. *The Economist*, May 9, 2015, p. 26, chart 5.

155. Patterson, *The Ordeal of Integration*, at 152–54.

156. Ibid. at 157.

157. For a more detailed discussion of stereotypes, see Peter H. Schuck, *Meditations of a Militant Moderate* (2006), essay 23.

158. *Texas Dept. of Housing vs. The Inclusive Communities Project*, 135 S. Ct. 2507 (2015).

159. http://papers.ssrn.com/sol3/papers.cfm?abstract_id=2684114

160. *Boddie v. Connecticut*, 401 U.S. 31 (1971).

161. U.S. Constitution, Amendment 24 (1964).

162. This analysis is explored in detail in Peter H. Schuck, *Diversity in America: Keeping Government at a Safe Distance* (2003), pp. 213–14.

163. Elizabeth Kneebone & Natalie Holmes, "U.S. Concentrated Poverty in the Wake of the Great Recession," *Brookings*, March 31, 2016.

164. http://ann.sagepub.com/content/660/1/78.full.pdf+html

165. Thomas Sowell, *Migrations and Cultures: A World View* (1996), pp. 118, 124, 226. For additional source and page references, see my lengthy review of Sowell's book in Peter H. Schuck, *Citizens, Strangers, and In-Betweens: Essays on Immigration and Citizenship* (1998), chap. 12.

166. Schuck, *Citizens, Strangers, and In-Betweens*.

167. http://www.aei.org/publication/watts-ferguson-and-the-state-of-race-relations-in -america/

168. http://www.gallup.com/poll/162362/americans-down-congress-own-representative .aspx

169. For a close-up, anecdotal account of bad choices, see J. D. Vance, *Hillbilly Elegy: A Memoir of a Family and Culture in Crisis* (2016).

170. Sendhil Multinathan & Eldar Shafir, *Scarcity: Why Having Too Little Means So Much* (2013).

171. http://www.economist.com/news/briefing/21654578-americas-bloated-prison -system-has-stopped-growing-now-it-must-shrink-right-choices

172. The statistics are summarized at http://www.wsj.com/articles/obamas-tragic-let -em-out-fantasy-1445639113?alg=y

173. Mark A. R. Kleiman, Jonathan P. Caulkins, & Angela Hawken, *Drugs and Drug Policy: What Everyone Needs to Know* (2011), p. 58; email to author from Jonathan P. Caulkins, July 29, 2015.

174. http://www.nytimes.com/2015/08/12/upshot/how-to-cut-the-prison-population
      -see-for-yourself.html?abt=0002&abg=0
175. Peter Baker, "Obama Takes Steps to Help Former Inmates Find Jobs and Homes,"
      New York Times, November 2, 2015.
176. http://www.wsj.com/articles/the-flawed-missing-men-theory-1439159236
177. Schuck, *Citizens, Strangers, and In-Betweens*, at 268–71; *Culture Matters: How Val-
      ues Shape Human Progress*, L. Harrison & S. Huntington, eds. (2002).
178. Ibid., at xxviii.
179. http://www.aei.org/wp-content/uploads/2016/08/2016-Poverty-Survey_AEI_Los
      -Angeles-Times_Topline.pdf
180. http://www.prrac.org/pdf/WJWMayJune2009PRRAC.pdf
181. http://www.nytimes.com/2010/10/18/us/18poverty.html. See also Theodore Dal-
      rymple, *Life at the Bottom: The Worldview That Makes the Underclass* (2001).
182. https://www.fas.org/sgp/crs/misc/R44574.pdf
183. Christopher Howard, *The Hidden Welfare State: Tax Expenditures and Social Pol-
      icy in the United States* (1997).
184. Jacob Funk Kirkigaard, "The True Levels of Government and Social Expenditures
      in Advanced Economies," March 2015, pp. 1–2; https://piie.com/publications/pb
      /pb15-4.pdf
185. Jencks, "The War on Poverty: Was It Lost?."
186. Schuck, *Why Government Fails So Often*, pp. 20–25.
187. Eric M. Patashnik, *Putting Trust in the U.S. Budget: Federal Trust Funds and the
      Politics of Commitment* (2000).
188. http://www.manhattan-institute.org/html/redistribution-fallacy-7935.html
189. Schuck, *Why Government Fails So Often*, chap. 8.
190. http://www.nytimes.com/2016/08/12/us/politics/trump-clinton-poverty
      .html?_r=0
191. See generally, David B. Muhlhausen, *Do Federal Social Programs Work?* (2013),
      chap. 3.
192. Ibid., chap. 2.
193. Schuck, *Why Government Fails So Often*, chap. 5.
194. See generally, Peter H. Schuck & Richard J. Zeckhauser, *Targeting in Social Pro-
      grams: Avoiding Bad Bets, Removing Bad Apples* (2006).
195. http://www.washingtonpost.com/blogs/federal-eye/wp/2015/08/17/a-family-in
      -public-housing-makes-nearly-498000-a-year-and-hud-wants-tenants-like-this-to
      -stay/
196. http://www.nytimes.com/2015/07/17/us/obama-el-reno-oklahoma-prison.html
197. Ibid. at 261.
198. Beth Akers & Liz Sablich, "The Economics of Hillary Clinton's Higher Education
      Plan," *Brookings*, August 11, 2015.
199. http://www.wsj.com/articles/buffalo-wild-wings-ceo-sally-smith-on-minimum
      -wages-1445824931?alg=y
200. http://www.nytimes.com/2015/08/24/business/economy/as-minimum-wage-rises
      -restaurants-say-no-to-tips-yes-to-higher-prices.html?_r=0
201. Kay Lehman Schlozman, Sidney Verba, & Henry E. Brady, *The Unheavenly Chorus:
      Unequal Political Voice and the Broken Promise of American Democracy* (2012).

202. Judith M. Gueron & Howard Rolston, *Fighting for Reliable Evidence* (2013), pp. 6–7.

203. Email to author from Henry Aaron, Senior Fellow, Brookings Institution, July 21, 2015.

204. http://www.nybooks.com/articles/archives/2015/apr/23/did-we-lose-war-poverty-ii/

205. Martha Bailey & Sheldon Danziger, eds., *Legacies of the War on Poverty* (2013).

206. Gabe, "Welfare, Work, and Poverty Status of Female-Headed Families with Children."

207. Robert Doar et al., "Comments on the House Ways and Means TANF Reauthorization Discussion Draft," July 24, 2015, p. 2.

208. Isabel Sawhill, *Generations Unbound: Drifting into Sex and Parenthood without Marriage* (2014), p. 91.

209. Richard V. Reeves, "Non-resident Fathers: An Untapped Childcare Aarmy?," *Brookings*, December 9, 2015.

210. Gabe, "Welfare, Work, and Poverty Status of Female-Headed Families with Children," at 17.

211. Kathryn J. Edin & H. Luke Shaefer, *$2.00 a Day: Living on Almost Nothing in America* (2015), p. 169.

212. Ron Haskins, "TANF at Age 20: Work Still Works," *Journal of Policy Analysis and Management* (2015).

213. Ibid. at 228.

214. Ibid. at 9, n 20.

215. Jencks, "The War on Poverty: Was It Lost?."

216. http://www.gao.gov/assets/670/669026.pdf

217. http://www.fns.usda.gov/sites/default/files/SNAP-ET-Pilot-Evaluation-RFP.pdf, Sec. C.2.2.

218. Muhlhausen, *Do Federal Social Programs Work?* at 152–55.

219. "Free Exchange," *The Economist*, July 4, 2015, p. 64. Studies at http://www.economist.com/taxcredits15

220. Natalie Holmes & Alan Berube, "States Adopt and Adapt the EITC to Address Local Need," *Brookings*, July 29, 2015.

221. Lawrence M. Mead, "Overselling the Earned Income Tax Credit," *National Affairs* (Fall 2014), pp. 20–33.

222. Hilary W. Hoynes & Ankur J. Patel, "Effective Policy for Reducing Inequality? The Earned Income Tax Credit and the Distribution of Income," NBER Working Paper No. 21340, July 2015.

223. http://www.gao.gov/assets/670/669026.pdf

224. http://www.aei.org/publication/are-the-costs-of-the-eitc-worth-it/?utm_source=paramount&utm_medium=email&utm_content=AEITODAY&utm_campaign=062915

225. Email to author from Christopher Jencks, December 3, 2015.

226. http://www.aei.org/publication/are-the-costs-of-the-eitc-worth-it/?utm_source=paramount&utm_medium=email&utm_content=AEITODAY&utm_campaign=062915

227. This passage closely follows Schuck, *Why Government Fails So Often*, at 170–71 and

the sources cited there. For a much more detailed analysis of the data on Head
Start, see Muhlhausen, *Do Federal Social Programs Work?* at 104–25. For AEI
scholars' take on the data, see http://www.aei.org/publication/does-pre-k-work-the
-research-on-ten-early-childhood-programs-and-what-it-tells-us/?utm_source
=paramount&utm_medium=email&utm_content=AEITODAY&utm_campaign
=041216

228. http://peabody.vanderbilt.edu/research/pri/VPKthrough3rd_final_withcover.pdf
229. http://www.nber.org/digest/jun06/w11832.html
230. http://equitablegrowth.org/report/the-benefits-and-costs-of-investing-in-early
-childhood-education/
231. Muhlhausen, *Do Federal Social Programs Work?* at 125.
232. Jencks, "The War on Poverty: Was It Lost?."
233. Email to author dated November 29, 2015, attaching James Heckman et al., "Understanding the Mechanisms through Which an Influential Early Childhood Program Boosted Adult Outcomes," http://pubs.aeaweb.org/doi/pdfplus/10.1257/aer
.103.6.2052; Elizabeth Cascio & Diane Schanzenbach, "The Impacts of Expanding
Access to High-Quality Pre-School Education," Institute for Policy Research, North-
western University, WP-14–01.
234. http://www.brookings.edu/research/reports/2015/11/20-title-i-spending
-disadvantaged-students-dynarski-kainz#.VlMqwADGSu0.email
235. Muhlhausen, *Do Federal Social Programs Work?* at 144–52.
236. Ibid. at 211.
237. Ibid. at 155–211.
238. Ibid.
239. Schuck, *Why Government Fails So Often*, and the sources cited there.
240. Jencks, "The War on Poverty: Was It Lost?."
241. http://www.nytimes.com/2015/09/17/upshot/californias-university-system-an
-upward-mobility-machine.html?hpw&rref=education&action=click&pgtype
=Homepage&module=well-region&region=bottom-well&WT.nav=bottom-well
242. http://www.gao.gov/assets/320/314551.pdf, p. 11.
243. http://www.nber.org/papers/w21659
244. Email to author from Robert J. La Londe, professor of economics, University of
Chicago Harris School of Public Policy, September 12, 2013.
245. Muhlhausen, *Do Federal Social Programs Work?* at 266–77.
246. Barry P. Bosworth, Gary Burtless, & Kan Zhang, "What Growing Life Expectancy
Gaps Mean for the Promise of Social Security," *Brookings*, Febuary 12, 2016.
247. Jeffrey B. Liebman, "Understanding the Increase in Disability Insurance Benefit
Receipt in the United States," 29 *Journal of Economic Perspectives* 123 (2015).
248. http://www.nationalaffairs.com/publications/detail/how-to-fix-disability
-insurance
249. http://www.cbpp.org/research/policy-basics-introduction-to-supplemental-security
-income
250. http://www.gao.gov/assets/670/669026.pdf
251. http://www.nber.org/papers/w21071.pdf
252. http://www.city-journal.org/2015/25_4_snd-public-housing.html
253. http://www.theatlantic.com/politics/archive/2015/09/the-surprising-optimism-of
-african-americans-and-latinos/401054/

254. http://www.aei.org/wp-content/uploads/2016/01/Hunger_Commission_Final _Report.pdf, p. 10.

255. Martha Ross & Nicole Prchal Svajlenka, "Employment and Disconnection among Teens and Young Adults: The Role of Place, Race, and Education," *Brookings*, May 24, 2016.

256. Arthur C. Brooks, "Philanthropy and the Non-Profit Sector," in Peter H. Schuck & James Q. Wilson, eds., *Understanding America: The Anatomy of an Exceptional Nation* (2008), p. 542.

257. See, e.g., Marvin Olasky, *The Tragedy of American Compassion* (1992).

258. http://www.giving-usa.org/giving-usa-2106

259. Arthur C. Brooks, *Who Really Cares: America's Charity Divide* (2006), p. 80.

260. http://graphics.thomsonreuters.com/12/12/Inequality-Indiana.pdf

261. http://www.nytimes.com/2015/11/18/business/economy/electing-to-ignore-the -poorest-of-the-poor.html

262. http://www.nytimes.com/2015/07/29/business/economy/wall-st-money-meets -social-policy-at-rikers-island.html?_r=0. But see http://www.nytimes.com/2015 /11/04/business/dealbook/did-goldman-make-the-grade.html (success measure- ment problem).

263. Annie Duflo & Dean Karlan, "What Data Can Do to Fight Poverty," *New York Times*, January 29, 2016.

264. http://www.cbo.gov/sites/default/files/114th-congress-2015–2016/reports/50250 -LongTermBudgetOutlook-3.pdf

265. http://www.aei.org/publication/sequester-doesnt-hurt-the-poor/?utm_source =paramount&utm_medium=email&utm_content=AEITODAY&utm_campaign =092115

266. Kleinbard, *We Are Better Than This: How Government Should Spend Our Money*, at 251–54.

267. Christopher G. Faricy, *Welfare for the Wealthy: Parties, Social Spending, and In- equality in the United States* (2015), cited in Ryerson, "Ivory Tower."

268. http://www.wsj.com/articles/hillary-bernie-tax-fantasists-1459206869

269. http://taxfoundation.org/blog/top-1-percent-pays-more-taxes-bottom-90-percent

270. Alison Burke, "New Research Shows Raising the Top Income Tax Rate Won't Re- duce Inequality," *Brookings*, October 1, 2015.

271. Schuck, *Why Government Fails So Often*, at 192–97; http://www.nytimes.com/2015 /07/30/us/as-medicare-and-medicaid-turn-50-use-of-private-health-plans-surges .html?_r=0.

272. http://www.aei.org/publication/tanf-has-been-a-success-lets-make-it-better/

273. http://www.brookings.edu/~/media/research/files/papers/2014/07/aging%20 america%20increasing%20dominance%20older%20firms%20litan/other_aging _america_dominance_older_firms_hathaway_litan.pdf

274. http://reports.weforum.org/global-competitiveness-report-2015–2016 /competitiveness-rankings/

275. See, e.g., Robert E. Litan & Ian Hathaway, "The Other Aging of America: The In- creasing Dominance of Older Firms," *Brookings*, July 31, 2014.

276. http://www.nytimes.com/2015/07/23/opinion/socialism-american-style.html

277. http://www.businessinsider.com/43-of-americans-dont-pay-federal-income-tax -2013-9

278. Milton Friedman, *Capitalism and Freedom* (1962).

279. Friedrich von Hayek, *Law, Legislation, and Liberty* (1973), pp. 55–56.

280. Bruce Ackerman & Anne Alstott, *The Stakeholder Society* (1999).

281. Charles Murray, *In Our Hands: A Plan to Replace the Welfare State* (2006); Charles Murray, "A Guaranteed Income for Every American," *Wall Street Journal*, June 3, 2016, http://www.wsj.com/articles/a-guaranteed-income-for-every-american -1464969586.

282. http://www.heritage.org/research/testimony/2012/05/examining-the-means-tested -welfare-state

283. http://www.nytimes.com/2015/04/22/opinion/obamacare-hands-off-my-medicare .html?emc=eta1&_r=0

284. Email to author from Henry Aaron, Senior Fellow, Brookings Institution, July 23, 2015.

285. *The Economist*, June 4, 2016, pp. 12, 21–24.

286. https://tcf.org/content/report/doing-more-for-our-children/

287. http://www.mdrc.org/sites/default/files/CEOSIF_Family_Rewards%20Report -Web-Final_FR.pdf

288. https://www.fas.org/sgp/crs/misc/R44327.pdf (December 30, 2015).

289. Richard Reeves & Edward Rodrigue, "Cutting Poverty by Increasing Program Participation," *Brookings*, June 11, 2015.

290. http://www.aei.org/publication/should-we-expect-full-participation-in-benefit -programs/

291. http://www.aei.org/publication/to-narrow-the-digital-divide-the-fcc-should-not -simply-extend-lifeline-to-broadband/?utm_source=paramount&utm_medium =email&utm_content=AEITODAY&utm_campaign=033116

292. Edin & Schaefer, *$2.00 a Day: Living on Almost Nothing in America*, at 168.

293. Haskins, "TANF at Age 20: Work Still Works," at 228.

294. http://www.aei.org/publication/reinvigorating-child-support-enforcement-as-an -anti-poverty-program/

295. http://cdn.theatlantic.com/newsroom/img/posts/Sabia_Burkhauser_SEJ_Jan10 .pdf

296. David Neumark, "The Evidence Is Piling Up That Higher Minimum Wages Kill Jobs," *Wall Street Journal*, December 16, 2015, A17.

297. Martha Ross & Nicole Prchal Svajlenka, "Worrying Declines in Teen and Young Adult Employment," *Brookings*, December 16, 2015.

298. David Card & Alan B. Krueger, "Minimum Wages and Employment: A Case Study of the Fast-Food Industry in New Jersey and Pennsylvania," 84 *American Economic Review* 772 (1994).

299. http://www.nber.org/papers/w5224

300. https://www.cbo.gov/sites/default/files/44995-MinimumWage.pdf

301. http://www.nber.org/papers/w21830

302. "When What Comes Down Doesn't Go Up," *The Economist*, May 2, 2015, p. 18.

303. "Destination Unknown," *The Economist*, July 25, 2015, p. 61.

304. "A Middle-Class Mirage," *The Economist*, July 4, 2015, p. 63.

305. David Autor, Alan Manning, & Christopher L. Smith, "The Contribution of the Minimum Wage to U.S. Wage Inequality over Three Decades: A Reassessment," February 25, 2015.

306. E.g., Elizabeth Kneebone & Natalie Holmes, "Strategies to Strengthen the Earned Income Tax Credit," *Brookings*, December 9, 2015.

307. Lawrence M. Mead, *Expanding Work Programs for Poor Men* (2011).

308. http://www.nytimes.com/2016/03/13/upshot/how-wage-insurance-could-ease -economic-inequality.html?emc=eta1

309. Eric Hanushek, Paul Peterson, & Ludger Woessman, *Endangering Prosperity: A Global View of the American School* (2013). In what follows, I have omitted their citations.

310. Brookings Series: Evidence Speaks—Harnessing the Value of "Failure," December 3, 2015.

311. Ibid. at 102.

312. Ibid. at 96–98.

313. Ibid. at 90–91.

314. Ibid. at 91–92. See also Raj Chetty et al., "Measuring the Impacts of Teachers II: Teacher Value-Added and Student Outcomes in Adulthood," NBER Working Paper No. 19424; http://educationnext.org/rewarding-and-employing-teachers-based-on -their-value-added/.

315. https://urbancharters.stanford.edu/download/Urban%20Charter%20School% 20Study%20Report%20on%2041%20Regions.pdf

316. Ibid.

317. http://www.rand.org/pubs/research_briefs/RB9433.html

318. http://www.brookings.edu/research/reports/2016/05/26-on-negative-effects-of -school-vouchers-dynarski?rssid=Evidence+Speaks

319. Hanushek et al., *Endangering Prosperity*, at 99–100.

320. http://www.brookings.edu/~/media/projects/bpea/spring-2013/2013a_hoxby.pdf

321. http://www.wsj.com/articles/big-gap-in-college-graduation-rates-for-rich-and -poor-study-finds-1422997677

322. http://www.bloomberg.com/news/articles/2015-02-24/the-college-dropout -problem-may-not-be-as-bad-as-the-government-says

323. http://www.theatlantic.com/business/archive/2012/03/why-do-so-many -americans-drop-out-of-college/255226/

324. Richard Arum & Josipa Roksa, *Academically Adrift: Limited Learning on College Campuses* (2010).

325. Timothy Ready, "Free College Is Not Enough: The Unavoidable Limits of the Kalamazoo Promise," *Brookings*, June 24, 2015.

326. https://www.whitehouse.gov/blog/2015/01/08/president-proposes-make -community-college-free-responsible-students-2-years

327. Joshua Goodman et al., "College Access, Initial College Choice and Degree Completion," NBER Working Paper No. 20996, February 2015.

328. http://www.nytimes.com/2015/06/09/education/us-to-forgive-federal-loans-of -corinthian-college-students.html?_r=0

329. http://www.nytimes.com/2015/11/18/us/government-to-expand-program-to -forgive-student-loan-debt.html?_r=0

330. http://www.brookings.edu/about/projects/bpea/papers/2015/looney-yannelis -student-loan-defaults

331. David Wessel, "How to Find Out What Graduates of That Cosmetology Program Actually Make," *Brookings*, June 25, 2015.

332. "Business High School," *The Economist*, July 18, 2015, p. 26. See also http://www .nytimes.com/2015/07/14/business/economy/a-new-look-at-apprenticeships-as-a -path-to-the-middle-class.html?emc=eta1

333. http://www.brookings.edu/~/media/research/files/reports/2015/07/20-young -adults-jobs/bmpp_srvy_unemploymentyouth_july20.pdf

334. http://www.gothamgazette.com/index.php/opinion/5786-certificate-programs -offer-opportunity-for-at-risk-youth-cuny-cherry

335. See, e.g., Robert I. Lerman, "Can Expanded Apprenticeship Prevent the Erosion of Middle-Class Jobs?," paper for the Association of Public Policy and Management, November 2014.

336. Sara B. Heller et al., "Thinking, Fast and Slow? Some Field Experiments to Reduce Crime and Dropout in Chicago," NBER Working Paper No. 21178.

337. Raj Chetty et al., "Where Is the Land of Opportunity? The Geography of Intergen-erational Mobility in the United States," NBER Working Paper No. 19843 at 4 (2014).

338. http://www.brookings.edu/research/papers/2003/09/childrenfamilies-haskins

339. Email to author from Ron Haskins, July 6, 2015.

340. Richard V. Reeves, Edward Rodrigue, & Alex Gold, "Following the Success Se-quence? Success Is More Likely If You're White," *Brookings*, August 6, 2015.

341. http://www.brookings.edu/~/media/research/files/papers/2015/11/campaign-2016 -ccf/sawhill_final.pdf

342. Haskins & Sawhill, "Work and Marriage: The Way to End Poverty and Welfare," at 1–2.

343. Ron Haskins & Isabel Sawhill, *Creating an Opportunity Society* (2009).

344. http://www.brookings.edu/blogs/social-mobility-memos/posts/2015/06/26 -teenage-pregnancy-republican-evidence-haskins#.VZLnrjRiq0w.email

345. Muhlhausen, *Do Federal Social Programs Work?*, at 138–44.

346. http://www.acog.org/Resources-And-Publications/Committee-Opinions /Committee-on-Gynecologic-Practice/Increasing-Access-to-Contraceptive -Implants-and-Intrauterine-Devices-to-Reduce-Unintended-Pregnancy

347. http://www.nytimes.com/2016/03/08/science/unplanned-pregnancies-hit-lowest -level-in-30-years.html?_r=0

348. http://www.economist.com/news/united-states/21660176-dislike-abortion-and -support-planned-parenthood-should-go-together-tissue-trade

349. http://www.nytimes.com/2015/07/06/science/colorados-push-against-teenage -pregnancies-is-a-startling-success.html?emc=eta1

350. http://well.blogs.nytimes.com/2015/10/26/iuds-and-hormonal-implants-remain -underused-contraceptives/?_r=0

351. Email to author from Christopher Jencks, December 5, 2015.

352. Sawhill, *Generations Unbound: Drifting into Sex and Parenthood without Mar-riage*, at 91–91.

353. Ibid. at 92–93.

354. https://hbr.org/1989/07/what-business-can-learn-from-nonprofits/ar/1

355. http://www.nursefamilypartnership.org/proven-results

356. Gillian Tett, "Land of Free Markets, Tied Down by Red Tape," *Financial Times*, July 30, 2015.

357. https://www.aei.org/publication/ask-candidates-about-these-5-charts/?utm

_source=paramount&utm_medium=email&utm_content=AEITODAY&utm
_campaign=022416

358. https://www.ij.org/cases/economicliberty;http://thefederalist.com/2015/08/06
/interior-design-doesnt-kill-but-regulating-it-does/

359. https://www.whitehouse.gov/sites/default/files/docs/licensing_report_final
_nonembargo.pdf

360. Fishkin, *Bottlenecks: A New Theory of Equal Opportunity*, Part IV.

361. http://www.nytimes.com/2015/07/08/business/economy/housing-program
-expansion-would-encourage-more-low-income-families-to-move-up.html?_r=0

362. See examples in Schuck, *Diversity in America*, chap. 6.

363. Some of the problems with affordable housing requirements are analyzed in Robert C. Ellickson, "The Mediocrity of Government Subsidies to Mixed-Income Housing Projects," in Ingrid & Hong, eds., *Property Rights and Land Policies* (2009), chap. 16.

364. http://www.nytimes.com/aponline/2015/07/08/us/politics/ap-us-fair-housing
.html?emc=eta1&_r=0

365. Discussed in Malcolm Gladwell, "Starting Over," *New Yorker*, August 24, 2015, p. 32.

366. http://www.nyc.gov/html/ceo/downloads/pdf/nns_15.pdf

367. http://nationalinterest.org/feature/new-homestead-act%E2%80%94-jumpstart
-the-us-economy-14618

368. http://www.nytimes.com/2016/02/13/health/disparity-in-life-spans-of-the-rich
-and-the-poor-is-growing.html?emc=eta1&_r=0

369. http://jama.jamanetwork.com/article.aspx?articleid=2513561

370. https://www.cms.gov/Research-Statistics-Data-and-Systems/Statistics-Trends-and
-Reports/Reports/downloads/bonito_part2.pdf

CHAPTER 3. IMMIGRATION

1. Mary C. Waters & Marisa Gerstein Pineau, eds., *The Integration of Immigrants into American Society* (2015).

2. Aristide R. Zolberg, *A Nation by Design: Immigration Policy in the Fashioning of America* 1 (2006).

3. Kerry Abrams, "The Hidden Dimension of Nineteenth-Century Immigration Law," 62 *Vanderbilt Law Review* 1353 (2009).

4. Ibid. at 4 (emphasis original).

5. For an analysis focusing on anti-Mexican bias, see Neil Foley, *Mexicans in the Making of America* (2014).

6. Gabriel J. Chin & Douglas M. Spencer, "Did Multicultural America Result from a Mistake? The 1965 Act and Evidence from Roll Call Votes," 3 *University of Illinois Law Review* 1239 (2015).

7. Peter H. Schuck, *Diversity in America: Keeping Government at a Safe Distance* (2003), 87–94.

8. E.g., Tom Gjelten, *A Nation of Nations: A Great American Immigration Story* (2015).

9. http://www.wsj.com/articles/u-s-says-deportations-rose-2-in-the-latest-year
-1483140519

10. https://www.ice.gov/removal-statistics

11. http://www.wsj.com/articles/remittances-to-latin-america-caribbean-hit-68-3
    -billion-in-2015-1455598863; http://www.migrationpolicy.org/article/remittances
    -united-states-context
12. See, e.g., Douglas S. Massey, Jorge Durand & Nolan J. Malone, *Beyond Smoke and Mirrors: Mexican Immigration in an Era of Economic Integration* (2002), chap. 4; Raúl Hernández-Coss, "The U.S.–Mexico Remittance Corridor Lessons on Shifting from Informal to Formal Transfer Systems," *World Bank Working Paper* no. 47 (2005); Luin Goldring, "Family and Collective Remittances to Mexico: A Multi-Dimensional Typology," 35 *Development and Change* 799 (2004); Dilip Ratha, "Workers' Remittances: An Important and Stable Source of External Development Finance," in *Global Development Finance* 157 (2003).
13. https://www.healthcare.gov/immigrants/immigration-status/
14. http://www.dhs.gov/sites/default/files/publications/ois_lpr_fr_2013.pdf, table 2.
15. https://www.dhs.gov/immigration-statistics/lawful-permanent-residents
16. https://www.dhs.gov/immigration-statistics/nonimmigrant
17. Many immigration advocates and scholars prefer to call them undocumented or unauthorized non-citizens. E.g., Julie Turowitz, "In Colorado, Calls to Change a Restaurant's Name from 'Illegal Pete's,'" *New York Times*, November 16, 2014.
18. http://www.wsj.com/articles/number-of-illegal-immigrants-in-u-s-holds-steady-at
    -11-million-1474394518
19. Robert Warren & Don Kerwin, "Beyond DAPA and DACA: Revisiting Legislative Reform in Light of Long-Term Trends in Unauthorized Immigration to the United States," 3 *Journal of Migration and Human Security* 80, 83 (2015).
20. Ibid. at 87.
21. Ibid. at 90, fig. 5.
22. http://www.pewresearch.org/fact-tank/2014/11/18/5-facts-about-illegal
    -immigration-in-the-u-s/
23. Warren & Kerwin, "Beyond DAPA and DACA," at 84.
24. Neil Shah, "Wave of Immigrants to U.S. Resurges," *Wall Street Journal*, October 9, 2014.
25. Estimate in email to author from Jeffrey Passell, Pew Hispanic Center, October 27, 2015.
26. Warren & Kerwin, "Beyond DAPA and DACA," at 93, fig. 8.
27. http://www.pewhispanic.org/2011/12/01/unauthorized-immigrants-length-of
    -residency-patterns-of-parenthood/
28. http://www.migrationpolicy.org/research/profile-us-children-unauthorized
    -immigrant-parents
29. Ibid.
30. http://www.pewhispanic.org/2011/12/01/unauthorized-immigrants-length-of
    -residency-patterns-of-parenthood/, at 98–99.
31. http://www.pewhispanic.org/2015/03/26/testimony-of-jeffrey-s-passel
    -unauthorized-immigrant-population/
32. https://www.unlocktalent.gov/files/Employee-Engagement-and-Global-Satisfaction
    -Trends.pdf
33. Karen Manges Douglas & Rogelio Saenz, ""The Criminalization of Immigrants and the Immigration Industrial Complex," 142 *Daedalus* 199 (2013). For the large legal literature on crimmigration, see Peter H. Schuck, "Immigrant Criminals in Over-

crowded Prisons: Rethinking an Anachronistic Policy," 27 *Georgetown Immigration Law Journal* 597, 605, n 32 (2013). See also Ingrid V. Eagly, "Criminal Justice for Noncitizens: An Analysis of Variation in Local Enforcement," 88 *NYU Law Review* 1126 (2013).

34. https://www.congress.gov/bill/114th-congress/house-bill/2029/text

35. http://www.cbp.gov/sites/default/files/documents/BP%20Budget%20History %201990–2013.pdf; http://immigrationpolicy.org/sites/default/files/docs /borderenforcement.pdf

36. https://www.cbp.gov/sites/default/files/documents/BP%20Staffing%20FY1992 -FY2015.pdf

37. http://www.immigrationpolicy.org/just-facts/growth-us-deportation-machine; https://www.dhs.gov/sites/default/files/publications/FY15-BIB.pdf

38. http://www.humanrightsfirst.org/resource/us-immigration-court-ballooning -backlog-requires-action

39. Marisa Abrajano & Zoltan L. Hafnal, *White Backlash: Immigration, Race, and American Politics* (2015).

40. See Jennifer Chacon, "Who Is Responsible for U.S. Immigration Policy?" 14 *American Bar Association: Insights on Law and Society*, http://www.americanbar.org /publications/insights_on_law_andsociety/14/spring-2014/who-is-responsible-for-u -s—immigration-policy-.html

41. http://www.wsj.com/articles/pew-poll-americans-favor-legalizing-people-unlawfully -in-u-s-1433426401

42. William Galston, " 'Building a Wall' May Keep Republicans from the White House," *Brookings*, March 29, 2016.

43. http://www.nytimes.com/2015/11/17/us/politics/gop-governors-vow-to-close-doors -to-syrian-refugees.html?_r=0

44. http://immigrationreform.com/2015/11/30/sen-sessions-releases-list-of-vetted -refugees-who-were-implicated-in-terrorism-this-year/?utm_source=ET&utm _medium=email&utm_campaign=Top512032015

45. For a comprehensive review of public opinion on these issues, including attitudes toward multiculturalism, see Jack Citrin and David O. Sears, *American Identity and the Politics of Multiculturalism* (2014), chaps. 5 and 6.

46. http://www.pewhispanic.org/2015/09/28/chapter-4-u-s-public-has-mixed-views-of -immigrants-and-immigration/

47. http://www.brookings.edu/blogs/fixgov/posts/2016/06/24-prri-survey-white -working-class-immigration-galston#.V27e3MrnSI8.mailto. For an analysis of the role of economic concerns, see J. Citrin, D. P. Green, C. Muste, & C. Wong, "Public Opinion toward Immigration Reform: The Role of Economic Motives," 59 *Journal of Politics* 2 (May 1997), pp. 858–81.

48. http://www.gallup.com/poll/171962/decrease-immigration-increase.aspx

49. http://www.nytimes.com/2016/02/19/us/politics/us-expands-restrictions-on-visa -waiver-program-for-visitors.html

50. http://bigstory.ap.org/urn:publicid:ap.org:40acc163f5d245ce940e7571d0f54bd4

51. William Galston, "Republicans and Democrats Divided on Important Issues for a Presidential Nominee," *Brookings*, June 3, 2015.

52. M. Levy, M. Wright, & J. Citrin, "Mass Opinion and Immigration Policy in the United

States: Reassessing Clientilistic and Elite Perspectives," 14 *Perspectives on Politics* 3 (September 2016), pp. 660–80.

53. T. Alexander Aleinikoff, "Good Aliens, Bad Aliens and the Supreme Court," in Lydio F. Tomasi, ed., *In Defense of the Alien* (1986).

54. http://www.migrationpolicy.org/article/refugees-and-asylees-united-states

55. http://www.theatlantic.com/politics/archive/2015/09/the-surprising-optimism-of -african-americans-and-latinos/401054/

56. Emily Ryo, "Less Enforcement, More Compliance: Rethinking Unauthorized Migration," 62 *UCLA Law Review* 622 (2015), part 4.

57. INA, Sec. 275, 8 U.S.C.A. Sec. 1325.

58. For an analysis of the multiple reasons for public opposition to both legal and illegal immigration, see M. Wright, M. Levy, & J. Citrin, "Public Attitudes toward Immigration Policy across the Legal/Illegal Divide: The Role of Categorical and Attribute-Based Decision-Making," 38 *Political Behavior* 1 (January 2016), pp. 229–53.

59. Ronald B. Rapoport, Alan I. Abramowitz, & Walter J. Stone, "Why Trump Was Inevitable," *New York Review of Books*, June 23, 2016.

60. Shibley Telhami, "Measuring the Backlash against the Muslim Backlash," *Brookings*, July 12, 2016.

61. Wright, Levy, & Citrin, "Public Attitudes toward Immigration Policy," pp. 229–53.

62. Julie Hirschfield Davis, "Genial Force behind Bitter Opposition to Immigration Overhaul," *New York Times*, December 3, 2014.

63. INA, Sec. 274A, 8 U.S.C.A. Sec. 1324a.

64. I develop this point in Peter H. Schuck, "Law and the Study of Migration," in *Migration Theory: Talking across Disciplines*, 2d ed., ed. C. Brettell & J. Hollifield (2007).

65. http://www.nytimes.com/2016/09/20/us/flaws-in-fingerprint-records-allowed -hundreds-to-become-us-citizens.html?_r=0}

66. http://www.nytimes.com/2015/10/15/us/aclu-accuses-border-patrol-of -underreporting-civil-rights-complaints.html?_r=0

67. http://www.aei.org/publication/corruption-makes-securing-americas-borders-even -harder/?utm_source=paramount&utm_medium=email&utm_content=AEI TODAY&utm_campaign=012815

68. http://bestplacestowork.org/BPTW/rankings/detail/HS00

69. http://bestplacestowork.org/BPTW/rankings/overall/large

70. https://www.ice.gov/sites/default/files/documents/Report/2016/sevis-bythenumbers -0416.pdf

71. Alison Smale, "German Leader Denounces Anti-Immigrant Surge," *New York Times*, December 15, 2014, A4.

72. http://www.latimes.com/local/political/la-me-pc-gov-jerry-brown-signs-bills-to -help-immigrants-20150810-story.html?wpsrc=slatest_newsletter&sid=5388f3a6dd 52b8e41100764e

73. E.g., Julia Preston, "Lack of Consensus in Legislatures Slows Tough Measures on Immigration," *New York Times*, March 14, 2011, A13.

74. E.g., *Arizona v. United States*, 132 S. Ct. 2492 (2012).

75. James Rice, "Looking Past the Label: An Analysis of the Measures Underlying 'Sanctuary Cities,'" p. 2 n. 13, on file with author (citing Marc R. Rosenblum, *Federal-Local Cooperation on Immigration Enforcement Frayed; Chance for Improvement Exists*, Migration Policy Institute (July 2015), http://www.migrationpolicy.org/news/ federal

-local-cooperation-immigration-enforcement-frayed-chance-improvement-exists (stating that "more than 360 jurisdictions have passed laws to formally limit their co-operation with U.S. Immigration and Customs Enforcement").

76. Ibid. at 13, n. 85 (citing Morgan Smith & Jay Root, "Jails Refused to Hold Thousands of Immigrants for Feds," *Texas Tribune* (January 15, 2016), http://www.texastribune.org/2016/01/15/34-texas-counties-declined-hold-deportable-immigra/. ICE did not start collecting data on declined detainers until January 2014. See U.S. Department of Homeland Security, Law Enforcement Systems and Analysis: Declined Detainer Outcome Report (2014), available at http://cis.org/sites/cis.org/files/Declined%20detainers%20report_0.pdf).

77. https://alpha.phila.gov/news/mayor/mayor-kenney-signs-executive-orders/

78. http://sanfrancisco.cbslocal.com/2014/04/06/immigration-deportation-trust-act/

79. http://www.washingtonpost.com/local/md-politics/hogan-has-decided-state-will-cooperate-with-feds-on-undocumented-detainees/2015/08/12/c46b0a2c-4126-11e5-8e7d-9c033e6745d8_story.html

80. http://www.ibtimes.com/immigration-reform-north-carolina-governor-mccrory-signs-law-banning-sanctuary-cities-2160711

81. http://www.sessions.senate.gov/public/index.cfm?p=news-releases&id=DE306843-2AB4-4433-983E-F47CB270BFBE

82. Schuck, *Diversity in America*, appendix 1.

83. http://www.aei.org/publication/why-immigration-is-a-big-deal-to-conservatives/

84. http://www.rasmussenreports.com/public_content/politics/current_events/immigration/immigration_update

85. See generally, Adam B. Cox & Eric A. Posner, "The Rights of Migrants: An Optimal Contact Framework," 84 *NYU Law Review* 1403 (2009).

86. F. Blau & C. Mackie, eds., *The Economic and Fiscal Consequences of Immigration* (2016).

87. www.migrationpolicy.org/research/through-immigrant-lens-piaac-assessment-competencies-adults-united-states

88. George Borjas, "Immigration and Globalization: A Review Essay," 53 *Journal of Economic Literature* 961 (2015).

89. James P. Smith & Barry Edmonston, eds., *The New Americans: Economic, Demographic, and Fiscal Effects of Immigration* (1997).

90. Giovanni Peri et al., "Foreign and Native Skilled Workers: What Can We Learn from H-1B Lotteries?" May 2015, http://www.nber.org/papers/w21175

91. http://www.pewhispanic.org/files/2015/03/2015-03-26_unauthorized-immigrants-passel-testimony_REPORT.pdf

92. William H. Frey, *Diversity Explosion: How New Racial Demographics Are Remaking America* (2014).

93. http://fiscalpolicy.org/wp-content/uploads/2015/01/Bringing-Vitality-to-Main-Street.pdf

94. See Simonetta Longhi, Peter Nijkamp, & Jacques Poot, "A Meta-Analytic Assessment of the Effect of Immigration on Wages," 19 *Journal of Economic Surveys* 451 (2005).

95. "Wages of Mariel," *The Economist*, July 23, 2016, p. 24.

96. George J. Borjas, Richard B. Freeman, & Lawrence F. Katz, "How Much Do Immigration and Trade Affect Labor Market Outcomes?" Brookings Papers on Economic Ac-

tivity, pp. 1–90 (1997). See also http://www.nationalreview.com/article/416118/give-me-your-tired-arguments-your-poor-reasoning-steven-camarota.

97. See, e.g., Mary C. Waters, *Black Identities: West Indian Immigrant Dreams and American Realities* (1999).

98. Peter H. Schuck, "Immigration," in Peter H. Schuck & James Q. Wilson, eds., *Understanding America: The Anatomy of an Exceptional Nation* (2008), p. 350.

99. Edward D. Kleinbard, *We Are Better Than This: How Government Should Spend Our Money* (2014), chap. 3.

100. Robert I. Lerman, "U.S. Wage Inequality Trends and Recent Immigration," 89 *American Economic Review* 23 (1999).

101. Alan K. Simpson & Bruce A. Morrison, "A Way Out on Immigration Reform," http://www.nytimes.com/2015/03/18/opinion/a-way-out-on-immigration-reform.html?emc=eta1

102. Abbe R. Gluck, Anne Joseph O'Connell, & Rosa Po, "Unorthodox Lawmaking, Unorthodox Rulemaking," 115 *Columbia Law Review* 1789 (2015).

103. http://www.migrationpolicy.org/article/little-debate-congress-enacts-broad-range-immigration-changes-spending-bill

104. See John Bound et al., "Finishing Degrees and Finding Jobs: U.S. Higher Education and the Flow of Foreign IT Workers," NBER Working Paper No. 20505.

105. http://assets.law360news.com/0769000/769256/rule.pdf

106. See, e.g., Hal Salzman, "What Shortages? The Real Evidence about the STEM Workforce," 29 *Issues in Science and Technology* 58 (2013).

107. Peter H. Schuck & John E. Tyler, "Making the Case for Changing U.S. Policy Regarding Highly-Skilled Immigrants," 38 *Fordham Urban Law Journal* 327 (2010–2011).

108. https://www.uscis.gov/working-united-states/permanent-workers

109. https://www.uscis.gov/news/alerts/uscis-completes-h-1b-cap-random-selection-process-fy-2017

110. http://www.renewoureconomy.org/wp-content/uploads/2013/07/university-letter.pdf

111. http://www.uspto.gov/web/offices/ac/ido/oeip/taf/us_stat.htm

112. http://www.nytimes.com/times-insider/2015/06/23/disney-has-no-comment-on-the-recent-reversal-of-layoffs/

113. http://www.nytimes.com/2015/09/30/us/temporary-visas-meant-to-import-talent-help-ship-jobs-abroad.html?emc=eta1&_r=0

114. http://www.nytimes.com/2015/11/11/us/large-companies-game-h-1b-visa-program-leaving-smaller-ones-in-the-cold.html?_r=0

115. Neil G. Ruiz & Mark Muro, "Obama's Overshadowed Start-Up Gambit," *Brookings*, November 26, 2014.

116. Albertina Antognini, "Family Unity Revisited: Divorce, Separation, and Death," 66 *South Carolina Law Review* 1 (2014) (reviewing rules on family-based admissions).

117. Alan Hyde, "The Law and Economics of Family Unification," 29 *Georgetown Immigration Law Journal* 355 (2014).

118. Former House immigration subcommittee chair Bruce Morrison thinks that this could be done for all permanent visa categories simply by regulation. Email to author dated October 27, 2014 and attached legal analysis.

119. http://www.migrationpolicy.org/research/hybrid-immigrant-selection-systems -next-generation-economic-migration-schemes, at p. 30.

120. http://www.migrationpolicy.org/article/top-10–2014-issue-9-points-system-dead -long-live-points-system

121. Email from Philip Martin to author, dated December 14, 2014.

122. Philip Martin, "Hired Farm Workers," *Choices*, 2d quarter 2012.

123. http://www.nytimes.com/roomfordebate/2011/08/17/could-farms-survive-without -illegal-labor/the-costs-and-benefits-of-a-raise-for-field-workers

124. Tom Hertz & Philip Martin, "Theme Overview: Immigration and Agriculture," *Choices*, 2nd quarter 2012.

125. Martin, "Hired Farm Workers"; Wallace E. Huffman, "The Status of Labor-Saving Mechanization in U.S. Fruit and Vegetable Harvesting," *Choices*, 2nd quarter 2012.

126. Zahniser et al., "Analyzing the Effects of Immigration Reforms on Agriculture," *Choices* (2012), http://www.choicesmagazine.org/choices-magazine/theme-articles /immigration-and-agriculture/analyzing-the-effects-of-immigration-reforms-on -agriculture

127. See ibid.

128. https://www.dhs.gov/sites/default/files/publications/LPR%20Flow%20Report% 202014_508.pdf

129. http://www.statista.com/statistics/188105/annual-gdp-of-the-united-states-since -1990/

130. http://www.wsj.com/articles/u-s-visa-program-attracts-11-million-applicants -1415250362

131. Schuck, *Diversity in America*, 123–31.

132. On an increasingly important subgroup of investor visas, see Eliot Brown, "Funding U.S. Builders: Visa Seekers," *Wall Street Journal*, December 10, 2014, C1.

133. http://www.nytimes.com/2014/12/14/business/some-of-the-rich-collect-art-others -collect-passports.html?_r=0

134. Ron Nixon, "Program That Lets Foreigners Write a Check, and Get a Visa, Draws Scrutiny," *New York Times*, March 15, 2016.

135. See, e.g., Edward P. Lazear, "An Immigration Game Plan for the New Congress," *Wall Street Journal*, December 4, 2014.

136. http://www.migrationpolicy.org/article/mexican-immigrants-united-states

137. Nancy Foner, ed., *One Out of Three: Immigrant New York in the Twenty-First Century* (2013).

138. http://www.ustr.gov/countries-regions/americas/mexico

139. https://travel.state.gov/content/visas/en/law-and-policy/bulletin/2016/visa -bulletin-for-may-2016.html

140. Samuel P. Huntington, *Who Are We? The Challenges in American Identity* (2004). See also Lawrence M. Mead, "Immigration: The Cultural Dimension," New York University, Department of Politics, unpublished manuscript, September 2009.

141. http://www.pewhispanic.org/2013/02/04/the-path-not-taken/

142. Peter H. Schuck, *Citizens, Strangers, and In-Betweens: Essays on Immigration and Citizenship (1998)*, chap. 12 (review of Thomas Sowell, *Migrations and Culture*), especially pp. 268–72.

143. See, e.g., Michael A. Olivas, "Review Essay—The Arc of Triumph and the Agony of

Defeat: Mexican Americans and the Law," 60 *Journal of Legal Education* 354 (2010).

144. Ibid., chap. 14 (review of Peter Brimelow, *Alien Nation: Common Sense about America's Immigration Disaster* [1995]).

145. http://www.nytimes.com/2015/02/02/us/law-favoring-cuba-arrivals-is-challenged.html?_r=0

146. http://www.nytimes.com/2016/02/13/us/as-cubans-and-central-americans-enter-us-the-welcomes-vary.html?emc=eta1&_r=0

147. http://www.nytimes.com/2016/01/10/world/americas/cubans-fearing-loss-of-favored-status-in-us-rush-to-make-an-arduous-journey.html?login=email

148. http://travel.state.gov/content/dam/visas/SIVs/Report%20of%20the%20Afghan%20SIV%20Program%20%E2%80%93%20April%202015.pdf

149. http://www.wsj.com/articles/number-of-illegal-immigrants-in-u-s-holds-steady-at-11-million-1474394518

150. Immigration and Nationality Act, Sec. 249.

151. http://www.pewhispanic.org/files/2014/09/2014-09-03_Unauthorized-Final.pdf

152. Some other immigration law scholars also doubt its legality. E.g., http://balkin.blogspot.com/2014/11/concerns-about-troubling-presidential.html; http://www.lawfareblog.com/2014/11/president-obamas-immigration-plan-rewriting-the-law/

153. http://www.migrationpolicy.org/research/daca-three-year-mark-high-pace-renewals-processing-difficulties-evident

154. http://www.uscis.gov/humanitarian/refugees-asylum/refugees/country-refugee parole-processing-minors-honduras-el-salvador-and-guatemala-central-american-minors-cam

155. Warren & Kerwin, "Beyond DAPA and DACA," at 95–98.

156. *United States v. Texas*, 136 S.Ct. 1120. A lower court decision rejecting the challenge on standing and other grounds is *Crane v. Johnson*, 783 F.3d 244 (5th Cir. 2015).

157. http://www.nytimes.com/2016/05/20/us/andrew-hanen-immigration-texas-court.html

158. http://www.washingtontimes.com/news/2015/mar/19/23-dreamers-obama-amnesty-snared-criminal-dragnet/

159. http://www.grassley.senate.gov/sites/default/files/judiciary/upload/2015-04-17%20USCIS%20to%20CEG%20%28DACA%20for%20Gang%20Member%29.pdf

160. http://www.wsj.com/articles/conservativesfightprovisiontoencouragesome immigrantstoenlist1431016422

161. E.g., David A. Martin, http://balkin.blogspot.com/2014/11/concerns-about-troubling-presidential.html; Peter H. Schuck, http://www.nytimes.com/2014/11/22/opinion/the-impeachment-of-obama-on-immigration-may-be-legal-but-its-wrong.html?module=Search&mabReward=relbias%3Aw%2C%7B%221%22%3A%22RI%3A7%22%7D

162. *United States v. Texas*, No. 15–674, 136 S. Ct. 1539 (2016).

163. Congressional Research Service, "Amount of the Child Tax Credit and Earned Income Tax Credit for a Hypothetical Family, 2011–2014," dated February 25, 2015.

164. http://oversight.house.gov/wp-content/uploads/2015/03/Mr.-Rector-Testimony-Bio-TNT.pdf

165. http://www.cnsnews.com/sites/default/files/documents/Responses%20to%20

Questions%20from%20Grassley-Johnson-Sessions%2002.26.15%20%283%29
.pdf

166. http://www.wsj.com/articles/illegal-immigrants-get-public-health-care-despite
-federal-policy-1458850082

167. Associated Press, "Obama Promises Action on Immigration," *New York Times: News
Clips*, November 5, 2014; Alan Rappeport, "Boehner Says Obama Risks 'Burning
Himself' on Immigration," *New York Times*, November 6, 2014.

168. http://www.nytimes.com/2015/11/17/us/politics/gop-governors-vow-to-close-doors
-to-syrian-refugees.html?_r=0

169. http://jmhs.cmsny.org/index.php/jmhs/article/view/41

170. 132. S. Ct. 2492 (2012).

171. See generally Carrie Byrne Hessick & Gabriel J. Chin, *Strange Neighbors: The Role
of States in Immigration Policy* (2014).

172. http://immigrationreform.com/2015/10/01/52-percent-of-california-drivers
-licenses-going-to-noncitizens/?utm_source=ET&utm_medium=email&utm
_campaign=Top510022015

173. http://www.cnsnews.com/blog/melanie-hunter/new-york-state-will-let-some
-illegal-aliens-teach-practice-medicine

174. Jack Healy & Julie Turkewitz, "Unauthorized Immigrants' Access to Driver's Licenses Is at Risk," *New York Times*, February. 12, 2015, A17.

175. http://www.newschannel10.com/story/31227044/new-mexico-legislature-sends
-real-id-bill-to-governor

176. http://wwlp.com/2016/03/09/massachusetts-may-issue-licenses-to
-undocumented-immigrants/

177. Peter H. Schuck, "Taking Immigration Federalism Seriously," 57 *University of Chicago Legal Forum* 57 (2007).

178. See, e.g., Cristina M. Rodríguez, "The Significance of the Local in Immigration Regulation," 106 *Michigan Law Review*.

179. Michael J. Trebilcock, "The Law and Economics of Immigration," 5 *American Law
and Economics Review* 271 (2003).

180. http://cis.org/High-Cost-of-Resettling-Middle-Eastern-Refugees

181. http://cis.org/immigrant-welfare-use-2011

182. http://cis.org/immigrant-families-accounted-for-42-percent-of-medicaid-growth
-since-2011

183. E.g., Michael Fix, ed., *Immigrants and Welfare: The Impact of Welfare Reform on
America's Newcomers* (2009).

184. Jennifer Medina, "Arriving as Pregnant Tourists, Leaving with American Babies,"
New York Times, March 28, 2011.

185. Peter H. Schuck & Rogers M. Smith, *Citizenship without Consent: Illegal Aliens in
the American Polity* (1985).

186. http://judiciary.house.gov/_cache/files/9504b34f-9f28-4e49-b31d-7d5a4e86d6c9
/feere-testimony.pdf, April 29, 2015.

187. http://www.nytimes.com/2010/08/14/opinion/14schuck.html?module=Search&ma
bReward=relbias%3Ar%2C%7B%221%22%3A%22RI%3A8%22%7D

188. http://judiciary.house.gov/index.cfm/hearings?ID=E7872029-9B7E-4A62-A9E9
-1C035179C7F4

189. http://fcd-us.org/resources/demographic-impacts-repealing-birthright-citizenship

190. https://www.uscis.gov/news/fact-sheets/naturalization-fact-sheet

191. http://www.nytimes.com/2015/09/18/us/white-house-campaign-legal-immigrants -citizenship.html?_r=0

192. Schuck, *Citizens, Strangers, and In-Betweens*, at 192–93.

193. Julia Preston, "More Latinos Seek Citizenship to Vote against Trump," *New York Times*, March 7, 2016.

194. Liav Orgad, "Creating New Americans: The Essence of Americanism under the Citizenship Test," 47 *Houston Law Review* 1227, 1283–84 (2011).

195. Liav Orgad, *The Cultural Defence of Nations: A Liberal Theory of Majority Rights* (2015). See also email to author from Orgad, December 10, 2014.

196. Peter H. Schuck, "Whose Membership Is It Anyway? Comments on Gerald Neuman," 35 *Virginia Journal of International Law* 321 (1994).

197. See generally, Peter J. Spiro, *At Home in Two Countries: The Past and Future of Dual Citizenship* (2016).

198. Ibid; see also Schuck, *Citizens, Strangers, and In-Betweens*, chap. 10.

199. Spiro, *At Home in Two Countries*, at 68–69.

200. Laura Saunders, "Expatriations Hit Record," *Wall Street Journal*, February 6–7, 2016, B2.

201. https://www.dhs.gov/sites/default/files/publications/ois lpr pe 2013.pdf

202. http://jmhs.cmsny.org/index.php/jmhs/article/view/54

203. Different methodologies produce different numbers. See Robert Warren & Donald Kerwin, "The US Eligible-to-Naturalize Population: Detailed Social and Economic Characteristics," 3 *Journal of Migration and Human Security* 306 (2015). http:// jmhs.cmsny.org/index.php/jmhs/article/view/54

204. Waters & Pineau, *The Integration of Immigrants into American Society*, chap. 4.

205. http://www.pewhispanic.org/2013/02/04/the-path-not-taken/

206. Ibid., at 163–64.

207. Ibid., chap. 8.

208. http://www.wsj.com/articles/u-s-army-expands-immigrant-recruitment-program -1428529606

209. *Evenwel v. Abbott*, 136 S. Ct. 1120 (2016).

210. Peter Spiro, *Beyond Citizenship: American Identity after Globalization* (2008); Linda Bosniak, *The Citizen and the Alien: Dilemmas of Contemporary Membership* (2008).

211. Even fairly liberal regimes sometimes do so. See, e.g., W. Rogers Brubaker, "Citizenship Struggles in Soviet Successor States," 26 *International Migration Review* 269 (1992).

212. Peter H. Schuck, http://eudo-citizenship.eu/commentaries/citizenship-forum /citizenship-forum-cat/1268-the-return-of-banishment-do-the-new -denationalisation-policies-weaken-citizenship?showall=&start=2

213. See, e.g., Audrey Macklin, http://eudo-citizenship.eu/commentaries/citizenship -forum/1268-the-return-of-banishment-do-the-new-denationalisation-policies -weaken-citizenship

214. Patrick Weil, *The Sovereign Citizen: Denaturalization and the Origins of the American Republic* (2013).

215. *Afroyim v. Rusk*, 387 U.S. 253 (1967).

216. *Vance v. Terrazas*, 444 U.S. 252 (1980).

217. Stephen H. Legomsky & Cristina Rodriguez, *Immigration and Refugee Law & Policy*, 6th ed. (2015), 1368.

218. Adam B. Cox & Eric A. Posner, "The Second Order Structure of Immigration Law," 59 *Stanford Law Review* 809 (2007).

219. For some crude estimates, see http://www.wsj.com/articles/the-costs-of-mass -deportation-1458342018

220. http://www.nytimes.com/2016/05/20/us/politics/donald-trump-immigration.html

221. http://www.nytimes.com/politics/first-draft/2016/03/29/hard-line-on -immigration-resonates-less-with-young-republicans-survey-shows/

222. Galston, "'Building a Wall' May Keep Republicans from the White House."

223. Peter H. Schuck, "Law and the Study of Migration," in C. Brettell & J. Hollifield, eds., *Migration Theory: Talking across Disciplines*, 2d ed. (2008), 248–49.

224. https://www.uscis.gov/sites/default/files/USCIS/Outreach/PED-Credible_Fear _Workload_Report_Summary_POE_and_Inland_Caseload_through_2015-09 .pdf

225. http://www.gao.gov/products/GAO-16-50

226. The interpretation of immigration as a case of the support of concentrated interests trumping diffuse mass opposition is reviewed and modified in M. Levy, M. Wright, & J. Citrin, "Mass Opinion and Immigration Policy in the United States: Reassessing Clientilistic and Elite Perspectives," 14 *Perspectives on Politics* 3 (September 2016), pp. 660–80.

227. http://papers.ssrn.com/sol3/papers.cfm?abstract_id=2685372

228. For a detailed account, see David A. Martin, "Resolute Enforcement Is Not Just for Restrictionists: Building a Stable and Efficient Immigration Enforcement System," 30 *Journal of Law & Politics* 437–57 (2014).

229. See Thomas J. Miles & Adam B. Cox, "Does Immigration Enforcement Reduce Crime?: Evidence from Secure Communities," 57 *Journal of Law & Economics* 937 (2014) (finding little or no effect on the crime rate).

230. Peter H. Schuck, "Three States Short of a Secure Community," *New York Times*, June 22, 2011, A27.

231. http://papers.ssrn.com/sol3/papers.cfm?abstract_id=2658265

232. http://judiciary.house.gov/index.cfm/2015/6/goodlatte-implementation-of-priority -enforcement-program-endangers-our-communities; http://www.fairus.org /legislative-updates/legislative-update-6-30-2015#3

233. http://www.migrationpolicy.org/research/understanding-potential-impact -executive-action-immigration-enforcement

234. http://www.nytimes.com/2015/07/08/us/san-francisco-murder-case-exposes -lapses-in-immigration-enforcement.html

235. http://www.cnn.com/2015/07/10/us/san-francisco-killing/

236. http://www.usatoday.com/story/news/politics/2015/07/23/house-bill-sanctuary -cities/30581643/. Despite this threatened punishment, the San Francisco Board of Supervisors unanimously voted to keep its Sanctuary City law, though clarifying that police can notify ICE officials of defendants being charged with a violent crime and who were convicted of a violent crime within the past seven years. http://www .usnews.com/news/us/articles/2016-05-24/san-francisco-to-consider-immigrant -sanctuary-protections

237. http://www.latimes.com/nation/la-na-ohio-immigration-20150729-story.html

238. http://www.nytimes.com/2015/09/24/us/los-angeles-rethinks-deportation-of -inmates.html?_r=0

239. http://www.wsj.com/articles/u-s-says-deportations-rose-2-in-the-latest-year -1483140519

240. http://www.immigrantjustice.org/immigration-detention-bed-quota-timeline

241. http://www.nytimes.com/2015/06/15/us/texas-detention-center-takes-toll-on -immigrants-languishing-there.html

242. Julia Preston, "Detention Center Presented as Deterrent to Border Crossings," *New York Times*, December 15, 2014, A18.

243. Mark Metcalf, "Built to Fail: Deception and Disorder in America's Immigration Courts," Center for Immigration Studies, May 2011.

244. http://www.oig.dhs.gov/assets/Mgmt/2015/OIG_15-22_Feb15.pdf

245. http://www.washingtontimes.com/news/2015/jun/3/3700-illegal-immigrant -threat-level-1-criminals-re/?page=1

246. http://www.grassley.senate.gov/sites/default/files/judiciary/upload/2015-05-28 %20ICE%20to%20CEG%20and%20Flake%20%28Altimirano%29.pdf

247. http://immigrationreform.com/2016/04/29/ice-director-fudges-numbers-on -released-criminal-aliens/?utm_source=ET&utm_medium=email&utm _campaign=Top505062016

248. http://www.nytimes.com/2015/08/23/us/judge-increases-pressure-on-us-to -release-migrant-families.html; http://www.migrationpolicy.org/article/fierce -opposition-court-rulings-place-future-family-immigration-detention-doubt

249. https://www.oig.dhs.gov/assets/Mgmt/2015/OIG_15-85_May15.pdf

250. https://www.aclu.org/legal-document/humanitarian-crisis-migrant-deaths-us -mexico-border

251. John Leland, "Fleeing Violence in Honduras, A Teenage Boy Seeks Asylum in Brooklyn," *New York Times*, December 5, 2014, MB1.

252. http://www.washingtonexaminer.com/12509-illegal-kids-already-over-border-in -second-wave-just-1-in-6-returned/article/2561883

253. http://www.nbcnews.com/storyline/immigration-border-crisis/more-10-000 -unaccompanied-minors-apprehended-u-s-border-last-n478316

254. http://www.nytimes.com/2016/01/29/us/politics/us-placed-immigrant-children -with-traffickers-report-says.html?smid=nytcore-iphone-share&smprod=nytcore -iphone&_r=0

255. https://www.cbp.gov/newsroom/stats/southwest-border-unaccompanied-children /fy-2016

256. Zachary Gochenour, "Coyotes: The Industrial Organization of Human Smuggling" (2015), available at SSRN: http://ssrn.com/abstract=2630787

257. Thomas Main, *Homelessness in New York City* (2016).

258. *Sale v. Haitian Centers Council, Inc.*, 509 U.S. 155 (1993).

259. This problem is analyzed in Schuck, "Immigrant Criminals in Overcrowded Prisons," part IV.C.

260. E.g., http://www.dhs.gov/immigration-statistics-publications

261. Martin, "Resolute Enforcement Is Not Just for Restrictionists."

262. Ibid.

263. http://www.pewresearch.org/fact-tank/2015/02/24/is-u-s-fertility-at-an-all-time

-low-it-depends/; http://www.wsj.com/articles/u-s-birthrate-hits-turning-point
-1434513662

264. http://www.pewresearch.org/fact-tank/2015/03/09/u-s-immigrant-population
-projected-to-rise-even-as-share-falls-among-hispanics-asians/

265. http://www.pewsocialtrends.org/2012/12/14/census-bureau-lowers-u-s-growth
-forecast-mainly-due-to-reduced-immigration-and-births/

266. http://www.pewsocialtrends.org/2012/11/29/u-s-birth-rate-falls-to-a-record-low
-decline-is-greatest-among-immigrants/

267. Emilio A. Parrado & S. Philip Morgan, "Intergenerational Fertility Among Hispanic
Women: New Evidence of Immigrant Assimilation," 45 *Demography* 651 (2008).

268. Michael Lipsky, *Street-level Bureaucracy: Dilemmas of the Individual in Public Services* (1980), 33.

269. Smith, *Civic Ideals*, quoted in Schuck, *Diversity in America*, at 75.

270. Waters & Pineau, *The Integration of Immigrants into American Society*.

271. Francis D. Blau & Lawrence M. Kahn, "Immigrants and Gender Roles: Assimilation
vs. Culture," NBER Working Paper No. 21756 (2016).

272. http://www.brookings.edu/~/media/research/files/reports/2007/7
/useconomics%20haskins/07useconomics_haskins.pdf

273. See, e.g., Philip Kasinitz, John Mollenkopf, & Mary C. Waters, *Inheriting the City:
The Children of Immigrants Come of Age* (2008).

274. Waters & Pineau, *The Integration of Immigrants into American Society*.

275. Linda M. Williams, "Welcoming the Outsider: The Practices of Public Libraries toward Immigrants" (2015), available at http://papers.ssrn.com/sol3/papers.cfm
?abstract_id=2602407.

276. http://www.migrationpolicy.org/article/limited-english-proficient-population
-united-states

277. For discussion of these costs by the leading restrictionist group, see http://
immigrationreform.com/2016/04/06/by-the-numbers-how-the-immigration
-tsunami-is-overwhelming-our-schools/?utm_source=ET&utm_medium=email
&utm_campaign=Top504082016

278. http://www.migrationpolicy.org/article/mexican-immigrants-united-states
#Immigration Pathways and Naturalization

279. Jack Citrin & David O. Sears, *American Identity and the Politics of Multiculturalism* (2014), at 192.

280. Schuck, *Diversity in America*, at 109–23.

281. Waters & Pineau, *The Integration of Immigrants into American Society*.

282. Citrin & Sears, *American Identity and the Politics of Multiculturalism*, at 4–5.

283. https://www.nationalreview.com/nrd/articles/427929/race-class-health

284. For proposals by a leading pro-immigration research group, see http://
migrationpolicy.org/pubs/administrativefixes.pdf

285. For an exploration of such enforcement options, see Peter H. Schuck, "INS Detention and Removal: A White Paper," 11 Michael Lipsky, *Street-level Bureaucracy: Dilemmas of the Individual in Public Services* (1997), 667.

286. Emily Ryo, "Detained: A Study of Immigration Bond Hearings," *Law & Society Review* (forthcoming).

287. http://www.nytimes.com/2015/06/27/us/turning-the-granting-of-bail-into-a
-science.html?_r=0

288. http://www.nytimes.com/2015/06/15/us/texas-detention-center-takes-toll-on -immigrants-languishing-there.html

289. http://www.nytimes.com/2016/07/13/nyregion/naturalization-lottery-new-york -state.html?_r=0

290. http://www.manhattan-institute.org/html/what-works-english-language-learning -america-8212.html

CHAPTER 4. CAMPAIGN FINANCE

1. For the Canadian example, see http://www.nytimes.com/2015/08/03/world /americas/canadian-prime-minister-calls-federal-election.html.

2. "The Political System," in Peter H. Schuck & James Q. Wilson, eds., *Understanding America: The Anatomy of an Exceptional Nation* (2008), 20.

3. Samuel Issacharoff, Pamela S. Karlan, Richard H. Pildes, & Nathaniel Persily, *The Law of Democracy: Legal Structure of the Political Process* 5th ed. (2016), 385.

4. Richard H. Pildes, "Focus on Political Fragmentation, Not Polarization: Re-Empower Party Leadership," in *Solutions to Political Polarization in America*, N. Persily, ed., (2015), chap. 10.

5. E.g., Raymond J. La Raja & Brian F. Schaffner, *Campaign Finance and Political Polarization: When Purists Prevail* (2015), xiv.

6. For an analysis of such issues, see Thomas E. Mann & Norman Ornstein, *It's Even Worse Than It Looks: How the American Constitutional System Collided with the New Politics of Extremism* (2012).

7. E.g., *Williams-Yulee v. The Florida Bar*, 135 S. Ct. 1656 (2015); *Caperton v. A.T. Massey Coal Co.*, 556 U.S. 868 (2009).

8. See generally, Darrell M. West: *Billionaires: Reflections on the Upper Crust* (2014), chap. 3.

9. *FEC v. Wisconsin Right to Life, Inc.*, 551 U.S. 449 (2007).

10. *Citizens United v. FEC*, 558 U.S. 310 (2010).

11. *McCutcheon v. FEC*, 134 S. Ct. 1434 (2014).

12. *SpeechNOW.org v. FEC*, 599 F.3d 686 (D.C. Cir. 2010).

13. http://press.anu.edu.au/apps/bookworm/view/Corruption%3A+Expanding+the+fo cus/9901/ch03.html#toc_marker-13

14. Mark Grossman, *Political Corruption in America: An Encyclopedia of Scandals, Power, and Greed* (2003).

15. E.g., Lawrence Lessig, *Republic, Lost: How Money Corrupts Congress—and a Plan to Stop It* (2011), at 8.

16. http://www.nytimes.com/interactive/2015/06/02/us/politics/money-in-politics-poll .html?_r=0

17. Nathaniel Persily, "The Campaign Revolution Will Not Be Televised," 11 *American Interest* (2015).

18. Google Trends, http://www.google.com/trends/explore#q=%22campaign%20 finance%22%2C%20%22citizens%20united%22&geo=US&cmpt=q&tz=.

19. *Fed Policy and Campaign Spending Poll*, Reuters-Ipsos, May 22–24, 2012, at 4.

20. http://www.bloomberg.com/politics/articles/2015-09-28/bloomberg-poll -americans-want-supreme-court-to-turn-off-political-spending-spigot

21. http://cnsnews.com/news/article/schumer-citizens-united-worse-racial-segregation-case-plessy-v-ferguson

22. Richard Hasen, *Plutocrats United: Campaign Money, the Supreme Court, and the Distortion of American Elections* (2016), 7–9.

23. For an excellent, brief, general review of the contours of First Amendment doctrine as applied to politics, see Isssacharoff et al., *The Law of Democracy*, at 334–40.

24. Robert Post, *Citizens Divided: Campaign Finance Reform and the Constitution* (2014).

25. E.g., *Reed v. Town of Gilbert*, 135 S. Ct. 2218 (2015); Adam Liptak, "Court's Free-Speech Expansion Has Far-Reaching Consequences," *New York Times* (August 17, 2015), http://www.nytimes.com/2015/08/18/us/politics/courts-free-speech-expansion-has-far-reaching-consequences.html

26. *Citizens United v. Federal Election Comm'n*, 558 U.S. 310, 340 (2010).

27. This section borrows from the Federal Election Commission website, http://www.fec.gov/info/appfour.htm

28. For a tendentious account of the litigation's background by a participant, see https://www.aei.org/publication/the-struggle-to-preserve-a-free-political-system/?utm_source=paramount&utm_medium=email&utm_content=AEITODAY&utm_campaign=012915

29. 424 U.S. 1 (1976).

30. 424 U.S. at 23.

31. Samuel Issacharoff, "On Political Corruption," 124 *Harvard Law Review* 118, 119–20 (2010).

32. Issacharoff et al., *The Law of Democracy*, at 419.

33. Ibid., quoting from Frank J. Sorauf, *Inside Campaign Finance* (1992), 238.

34. Ibid.

35. http://www.wsj.com/articles/SB122512338741472357; Ryan Sager, "Buying 'Reform'; Media Missed Millionaires' Scam," *New York Post*, March 17, 2005, p. 33. See also remarks by Mark Schmitt, Director, Program on Political Reform, New America Foundation, at conference on Money and U.S. Politics, April 10, 2015, University of California at Berkeley.

36. Schmitt, ibid.

37. https://www.brennancenter.org/publication/secret-spending-states

38. http://www.fec.gov/pages/brochures/fecfeca.shtml#Disclosure

39. *McConnell v. FEC*, 540 U.S. 93 (2003).

40. http://www.barrypopik.com/index.php/new_york_city/entry/money_in_politics_is_like_water_flowing_downhill_unstoppable. See also, *McConnell v. FEC*, 540 U.S. 93, 224 (2003). ("Money, like water, will always find an outlet.")

41. http://prospect.org/article/when-super-pacs-go-dark-llcs-fuel-secret-spending

42. Issacharoff et al., *The Law of Democracy*, at 523–24.

43. Ibid. at 442.

44. *Citizens United v. Federal Election Comm'n*, 558 U.S. at 356–61.

45. http://www.nytimes.com/2016/12/09/us/politics/campaign-spending-donald-trump-hillary-clinton.html?emc=eta1&_r=0

46. http://thecaucus.blogs.nytimes.com/2012/11/01/labor-unions-to-have-128000-campaign-volunteers/

47. http://launionaflcio.org/2013/23844/volunteers-make-the-difference-in-city-elections.html

48. http://blogs.reuters.com/great-debate/2015/01/16/citizens-united-gives-freedom-of-speech-back-to-the-people/

49. Private communication from Nathaniel Persily.

50. https://www.opensecrets.org/pres12/#out

51. https://www.opensecrets.org/pres12/expenditures.php

52. https://www.opensecrets.org/overview/cost.php (additional calculations done by research assistant).

53. https://www.opensecrets.org/overview/incumbs.php (additional calculations done by research assistant).

54. https://www.opensecrets.org/bigpicture/b

55. https://www.opensecrets.org/overview/blio.php

56. http://www.wsj.com/articles/super-pac-donors-are-taking-charge-1451518976

57. https://www.opensecrets.org/bigpicture/index.php?cycle=2012

58. https://www.opensecrets.org/bigpicture/elec_stats.php?cycle=2012

59. https://www.opensecrets.org/bigpicture/donordemographics.php?cycle=2012&filter=A

60. http://www.loc.gov/law/help/campaign-finance/uk.php

61. https://nrf.com/media/press-releases/optimism-shines-national-retail-federation-forecasts-holiday-sales-increase-41

62. https://nrf.com/media/press-releases/holiday-shoppers-spend-more-31-billion-gift-cards-this-year-according-nrf

63. https://nrf.com/media/press-releases/gift-givers-plan-splurge-friends-family-this-holiday-

64. http://www.statista.com/statistics/243742/revenue-of-the-cosmetic-industry-in-the-us/

65. http://www.aei.org/publication/what-economic-lessons-about-medical-costs-can-we-learn-from-the-market-for-cosmetic-procedures/

66. http://www.the-numbers.com/market

67. https://www.washingtonpost.com/opinions/attack-ads-have-their-plus-sides/2014/08/26/c1150cd8-27eb-11e4-958c-268a320a60ce_story.html

68. Stephen Ansolabehere et al., "Why Is There So Little Money in U.S. Politics?" 17 *Journal of Economic Perspectives* 105 (2003). For an update on this, see email to author from Ansolabehere, July 6, 2016.

69. https://www.opensecrets.org/bigpicture/ptytots.php?cycle=2012

70. Lessig, *Republic, Lost,* at 233 (citing data published by Spencer Overton).

71. https://www.opensecrets.org/overview/donordemographics.php

72. https://www.opensecrets.org/pres12/bundlers.php

73. https://www.opensecrets.org/pres12/superpacs.php

74. https://www.opensecrets.org/pres12/bundlers.php?id=N00000286&cycle=2012

75. Bonica, Adam, Nolan McCarty, Keith T. Poole & Howard Rosenthal. "Why hasn't democracy slowed rising inequality?" 27 *Journal of Economic Perspectives* 3 (2013): 103–123.

76. Ibid.

77. Nicholas Confessore, Sarah Cohen, & Karen Yourish, "Here Are 120 million Monopoly Pieces, Roughly One for Every Household in the United States," *New York Times,* October 10, 2015.

78. McCarty, in *Solutions to Political Polarization in America*, at 139 (citing Michael Barber paper).

79. Michael J. Barber & Nolan McCarty, "Causes and Consequences of Polarization," in *Solutions to Political Polarization in America*, at 32–33.

80. Ian Vandewalker, "Outside Spending, Dark Money Dominate Toss-Up Senate Races," https://www.brennancenter.org/sites/default/files/analysis/Outside%20 Spending%20Since%20Citizens%20United.pdf

81. Hasen, *Plutocrats United*, at 3.

82. http://www.nytimes.com/2015/09/23/us/politics/scott-walkers-demise-shows-limits -of-super-pac-money-model.html?emc=eta1&_r=0

83. http://www.wsj.com/articles/super-pac-donors-are-taking-charge-1451518976

84. http://www.campaignfreedom.org/wp-content/uploads/2016/02/2016-02-10_Issue -Brief_Iowa-and-New-Hampshire-Results-Indicate-Moneys-Failure-to-Buy-the -2016-Election.pdf

85. http://www.nytimes.com/2016/03/10/us/politics/george-soros-and-other-liberal -donors-to-fund-bid-to-spur-latino-voters.html?smid=nytcore-iphone -share&smprod=nytcore-iphone

86. http://www.nytimes.com/2015/11/04/us/politics/small-donors-are-clicking-more -with-democrats-than-republicans.html?_r=0

87. Nicholas Confessore & Eric Lichtblau, "'Outsider' Presidential Candidates Prove Competitive in Fund-Raising," *New York Times*, October 15, 2015.

88. http://www.nytimes.com/politics/first-draft/2015/10/21/carl-icahn-supporter-of -donald-trump-plans-150-million-super-pac/; http://www.nytimes.com/aponline /2015/10/23/us/ap-us-gop-2016-trump-money.html

89. Maggie Haberman & Nich Corasaniti, "'Super Pac' Emerges to Support Donald Trump, Who Criticizes Such Groups," *New York Times*, April 6, 2016.

90. http://www.ncsl.org/research/elections-and-campaigns/citizens-united-and-the -states.aspx

91. Data in the rest of this paragraph are taken from Chisun Lee, Brent Furguson, & David Earley, *After* Citizens United: *The Story in the States*, Brennan Center for Justice (2014).

92. Twenty-five states have enacted a variety of public financing schemes that are used by candidates in contrast to the de facto abandoned presidential public financing program. http://www.ncsl.org/research/elections-and-campaigns/public-financing-of -campaigns-overview.aspx

93. See generally, Joanne B. Freeman, *Affairs of Honor: National Politics in the New Republic* (2001).

94. *Solutions to Political Polarization in America*, at 9.

95. https://www.washingtonpost.com/opinions/robert-j-samuelson-in-politics-money-is -speech/2014/04/04/075df4ec-bc18–11e3–9a05-c739f29ccb08_story.html

96. Issacharoff, "On Political Corruption," at 119 (quoting Richard Briffault).

97. 424 U.S. at 49.

98. See generally, Nathaniel Persily & Kelly Lammie, "Perceptions of Corruption and Campaign Finance: When Public Opinion Determines Constitutional Law," 153 *University of Pennsylvania Law Review* 119 (2004).

99. 558 U.S. at 294.

100. See Tribe's extended remarks on April 1, 2016, at https://www.youtube.com/watch?v=th6VIERsFGo&index=3&list=PL2q2U2nTrWq0ZIaDtqyrXAeEpru59iM-5

101. *McCutcheon v. Fed. Election Comm'n*, 134 S.Ct. 1434, 1438 (2014).

102. Ibid. at 1451.

103. Ibid. at 1465 (Breyer, J., dissenting).

104. 136 S. Ct. 2355 (2016).

105. http://usgovinfo.about.com/od/uscongress/a/congress-reluctant-to-punish-its-own.htm. For two recent examples, see Lessig, *Republic, Lost*, at 226–27.

106. 424 U.S. at 28.

107. E.g., Issacharoff, "On Political Corruption," at 129–34.

108. http://www.fec.gov/pages/brochures/fecfeca.shtml#anchor257909

109. *Randall v. Sorrell*, 548 U.S. 230 (2006).

110. Persily & Lammie, "Perceptions of Corruption and Campaign Finance."

111. Issacharoff, "On Political Corruption," at 129.

112. https://www.opensecrets.org/lobby/

113. Michael J. Graetz & Ian Shapiro, *Death by a Thousand Cuts: The Fight over Taxing Inherited Wealth* (2005), p. 240.

114. http://www.the-american-interest.com/2013/04/12/the-political-roots-of-inequality/

115. *McCutcheon v. Fed. Election Comm'n*, 134 S. Ct. 1434, 1467 (2014) (Breyer, J., dissenting).

116. See, e.g., Hasen, *Plutocrats United*.

117. http://www.nytimes.com/2015/10/17/us/politics/filings-reveal-hillary-clinton-leads-money-race.html?_r=0

118. http://www.nytimes.com/2016/03/16/upshot/measuring-donald-trumps-mammoth-advantage-in-free-media.html?emc=eta1

119. Lessig, *Republic, Lost*, at 233.

120. For a probing analysis of this issue, see Adam M. Samaha, "Regulation for the Sake of Appearance," 125 *Harvard Law Review* 1563 (2012). Samaha discusses its application to campaign finance law in Part IV.A.

121. See Persily & Lammie, "Perceptions of Corruption and Campaign Finance," at 142.

122. Samuel Issacharoff & Pamela S. Karlan, "The Hydraulics of Campaign Finance Regulation," 77 *Texas Law Review* 1705, 1713–14 (1999).

123. *FEC v. Colorado Republican Federal Campaign Committee*, 533 U.S. 431 (2001).

124. http://www.nytimes.com/2015/10/30/us/politics/fec-panel-delays-a-decision-on-spending-in-16-races.html?emc=eta1&_r=0

125. http://www.nytimes.com/2015/10/01/us/politics/as-carly-fiorina-surges-so-does-the-work-of-her-super-pac.html?_r=0

126. http://www.nytimes.com/politics/first-draft/2015/10/22/clinton-super-pac-responded-to-benghazi-hearings-with-research-center-and-a-flurry-of-news-releases/?_r=0

127. http://www.nytimes.com/2015/12/23/us/politics/as-tv-ad-rates-soar-super-pacs-pivot-to-core-campaign-work.html?_r=0

128. http://www.wsj.com/articles/super-pac-donors-are-taking-charge-1451518976

129. http://harvardlawreview.org/2015/03/working-together-for-an-independent-expenditure/#stq=&stp=1

130. http://www.wsj.com/article_email/california-considers-tough-campaign-finance -rules-1444602199-lMyQjAxMTI1NDE5MzQxODMxWj

131. http://www.nytimes.com/2015/10/12/us/politics/nonprofit-masks-dark-money-ads -backing-marco-rubio.html?emc=eta1

132. "Incumbents Nearly Always Win," *Open Secrets*, https://www.opensecrets.org /resources/dollarocracy/02.php

133. See https://www.opensecrets.org/bigpicture/reelect.php?cycle=2012

134. *Solutions to Political Polarization in America*, at 13.

135. 425 U.S. 1, 31–32 (1976).

136. *Citizens United v. FEC*, 558 U.S. 310, 340 (2010).

137. *First National Bank of Boston v. Bellotti*, 435 U.S. 765 (1978).

138. Issacharoff et al., *The Law of Democracy*, at 471–73 (distinguishing *First National Bank of Boston v. Bellotti*).

139. 558 U.S. at 318.

140. 494 U.S. 652 (1990).

141. http://www.nytimes.com/2015/09/30/us/politics/big-donors-seek-larger-roles-in -presidential-campaigns.html?smid=nytcore-iphone-share&smprod=nytcore -iphone

142. https://www.aeaweb.org/articles.php?doi=10.1257/089533003321164976

143. http://www.wsj.com/articles/big-obama-donors-stay-on-sidelines-in-2016-race -1447375429

144. "The Effects of Campaign Finance Spending Bans on Electoral Outcomes," https://polsci.umass.edu/people/faculty/ray-la-raja/recent-publications

145. https://www.opensecrets.org/parties/

146. Ibid.

147. https://www.aeaweb.org/articles.php?doi=10.1257/089533003321164976, pp. 112–17.

148. Email to author from Professor Stephen Ansolabehere, September 15, 2015.

149. http://scholar.princeton.edu/sites/default/files/mgilens/files/gilens_and_page _2014_-testing_theories_of_american_politics.doc.pdf

150. Kay Scholzman et al., *The Unheavenly Chorus: Unequal Political Voice and the Broken Promise of American Democracy* (2012).

151. http://www.nytimes.com/2015/04/16/upshot/big-money-from-super-pacs-is -eroding-the-power-of-parties.html

152. For my own defense of factions, see Peter H. Schuck, "Against (and for) Madison: An Essay in Praise of Factions," in Schuck, *The Limits of Law: Essays on Democratic Governance* (2000), chap. 7.

153. Nathaniel Persily, "Stronger Parties as a Solution to Polarization," in *Solutions to Political Polarization in America*, at 124.

154. For gridlock's definition, see Nathaniel Persily, ed., *Solutions to Political Polarization in America* (2015), 7–8.

155. http://www.hazlet.org/cms/lib05/nj01000600/centricity/domain/188/toward%20 a%20more%20responsible%20two-party%20system%20(pdf).pdf

156. 561 U.S. 186 (2010).

157. Abby K. Wood & Douglas M. Spencer, "In the Shadows of Sunlight: The Effects of Transparency on State Political Campaigns" *Election Law Journal*, 15 (June 2016).

158. Raymond J. La Raja, "Political Participation and Civic Courage: The Negative Effect of Transparency on Making Small Campaign Contributions," 36 *Political Behavior* 753 (2014).

159. http://www.brennancenter.org/blog/budget-bill-blocks-agencies-considering -tougher-rules

160. http://prospect.org/article/when-super-pacs-go-dark-llcs-fuel-secret-spending

161. https://www.theguardian.com/commentisfree/2016/apr/19/donald-trump -facebook-election-manipulate-behavior

162. Persily, "The Campaign Revolution Will Not Be Televised," http://www.the -american-interest.com/2015/10/10/the-campaign-revolution-will-not-be-televised/

163. See Hasen, *Plutocrats United*, chap. 6

164. http://www.brookings.edu/~/media/Research/Files/Reports/2015/04/political -realism-rauch/political-realism-rauch.pdf?la=en. The quotations from Rauch's essay that follow are taken from ibid. at 2.

165. *O'Keefe v. Chisholm,* 769 F.3d 936, 941 (7th Cir. 2014), cert. denied 135 S. Ct. 2311 (2015).

166. http://www.brookings.edu/~/media/Research/Files/Reports/2015/06/futility -nostalgia-romanticism-new-political-realists-mann-dionne/new_political_ realists_mann_dionne.pdf

167. E.g., Burt Neuborne, *Madison's Music: On Reading the First Amendment* (2015).

168. Jacob S. Hacker & Paul Pierson, "Confronting Asymmetric Polarization," in *Solutions to Political Polarization in America,* chap. 3.

169. http://www.brookings.edu/research/papers/2014/11/24-why-critics-transparency -wrong-bass-brian-eisen

170. Pamela S. Karlan, "Elections and Change under 'Voting with Dollars,'" 91 *California Law Review* 705 (2003); David A. Strauss, "What's the Problem? Ackerman and Ayres on Campaign Finance Reform," 91 *California Law Review* 723, 741 (2003).

171. Morris P. Fiorina, Samuel J. Abrams, & Jeremy C. Pope, *Culture War? The Myth of a Polarized America* 3d ed. (2010), 209.

172. Tribe, https://www.youtube.com/watch?v=th6VIERsFGo&index=3&list=PL2q2U2 nTrWq0ZIaDtqyrXAeEpru59iM-5.

173. http://www.nytimes.com/2015/10/30/us/politics/fec-panel-delays-a-decision-on -spending-in-16-races.html?emc=eta1&_r=0

174. http://www.loc.gov/law/help/campaign-finance/comparative-summary.php

175. http://www.fec.gov/pages/brochures/pubfund.shtml

176. E.g., *Arizona Free Enterprise Club's Freedom Club PAC v. Bennett,* 564 U.S. 721 (2011); *Davis v. FEC,* 554 U.S. 724 (2008).

177. Issacharoff et al., *The Law of Democracy,* at 559, 576.

178. See ibid., at 580–83.

179. *Voting with Dollars: A New Paradigm for Campaign Finance* (2003).

180. http://www.latimes.com/opinion/op-ed/la-oe-0202-goldberg-party-paper-tigers -20160202-column.html

181. http://www.seattletimes.com/seattle-news/politics/seattle-initiative-puts-spotlight -on-campaign-financing/

182. Ibid. at 731.

183. Ibid. at 733–34.

184. *Arizona Free Enterprise Club's Freedom Club PAC v. Bennett,* 564 U.S. 721 (2011).

185. See Issacharoff et al., *The Law of Democracy*, at 577–79.

186. For a recent review of the arguments pro and con, see *Solutions to Political Polarization in America*, especially chaps. 8–11.

187. Persily, "Stronger Parties as a Solution to Polarization," in *Solutions to Political Polarization in America*, at 126.

188. Pildes, *Solutions to Political Polarization in America*, at 154–55.

189. The classic analysis is Nelson W. Polsby, *Consequences of Party Reform* (1982).

190. http://www.masspoliticsprofs.com/2014/07/10/who-were-those-delegates-anyway/

191. John C. Green, *The Faith Factor: How Religion Influences American Elections* (2007), table 7.9; http://www.centerforpolitics.org/crystalball/articles/republicans -2016-white-evangelicals-dominate-the-early-calendar/.

192. http://ballotpedia.org/Open_primary

193. Elaine C. Kamarck, "Solutions to Polarization," in *Solutions to Political Polarization in America*, at 97; Jonathan Rodden, "Geography and Gridlock in the United States," ibid. at 114; McCarty, ibid. at 139.

194. https://www.brookings.edu/research/the-state-of-state-parties-and-how -strengthening-them-can-improve-our-politics/

195. Nolan McCarty, "Reducing Polarization by Making Parties Stronger," in *Solutions to Political Polarization in America*.

196. Ibid. at 143.

197. However, Frances Lee has shown that parties' collective interests, as distinct from their ideologies, are a central cause of this polarization. *Beyond Ideology: Politics, Principles, and Partisanship in the U.S. Senate* (2009), 19.

198. E.g., Peter Levine, "The Waning Influence of American Political Parties," *The Conversation* (March 31, 2016), http://theconversation.com/the-waning-influence-of -american-political-parties-56875 (millennials uninterested in political parties); Pew Research Center, http://www.people-press.org/2011/11/03/section-1-how -generations-have-changed/ (shifts in political attitudes and voting trends).

199. http://www.wsj.com/article_email/jeb-bush-disclosure-on-his-campaign-bundlers -spurs-criticism-1444861910-lMyQjAxMTA1ODE1NTgxMzU4Wj

200. http://www.brookings.edu/~/media/research/files/reports/2010/1/14-campaign -finance-reform/0114_campaign_finance_reform.pdf

201. Remarks by Raymond La Raja and Brian Schaffner at Brennan Center for Justice book discussion, December 17, 2015.

202. Email to author from Jonathan Rauch, August 24, 2016.

CHAPTER 5. AFFIRMATIVE ACTION

1. For instance, gaps between black and white experiences extend to job prospects (http://qz.com/318356/white-americans-who-dont-finish-high-school-have-better -job-prospects-than-black-americans-who-went-to-college/); wealth (http://www .pewresearch.org/fact-tank/2014/12/12/racial-wealth-gaps-great-recession/); and community violence and resources (https://www.washingtonpost.com/news/wonk /wp/2016/05/09/whites-and-blacks-in-chicago-are-living-in-two-totally-different -cities/). However, the black-white gap in life expectancy has decreased in recent years (https://www.washingtonpost.com/news/to-your-health/wp/2015/11/06/the

-black-white-gap-in-life-expectancy-is-narrowing-as-african-americans-get
-healthier/).

2. See Amy L. Wax, "On Not Dreaming of Affirmative Action," 17 *Journal of Constitutional Law* 757 (2015).

3. See, e.g., Christopher Edley, Jr., quoted in William M. Leiter & Samuel Leiter, *Affirmative Action in Antidiscrimination Law and Policy: An Overview and Synthesis* 2d ed. (2009), at 394 n 362.

4. Peter Arcidiacono & Michael Lovenheim, "Affirmative Action and the Quality-Fit Tradeoff," 54 *Journal of Economic Literature* 3 (2016).

5. Nondiscrimination's psychological and philosophical contours are doubtless complex and opaque. Linda Hamilton Krieger, "Civil Rights Perestroika: Intergroup Relations after Affirmative Action," 86 *California Law Review* 1251, 1329 (1998) ("When a person is color-blind, there is simply much he will not see"). John Hasnas, "Equal Opportunity, Affirmative Action, and the Anti-Discrimination Principle: The Philosophical Basis for the Legal Prohibition of Discrimination," 71 *Fordham Law Review* 423, 429 (2002) ("utter lack of agreement on what it means to give this principle effect"). See Alexandra Kalev, Frank Dobbin, & Erin Kelly, "Best Practices or Best Guesses? Assessing the Efficacy of Corporate Affirmative Action and Diversity Policies," 71 *American Sociological Review* 589 (2006) (comparing the efficacy of various diversity programs in companies).

6. Alan Wolfe, "Strangled by Roots," *New Republic* 33 (May 28, 2001) (review of Gary Gerstle, *American Crucible: Race and Nation in the Twentieth Century* [2001]). A 2015 Gallup poll found that Americans' satisfaction with the way blacks are treated has declined to a 15-year low of 49% dissatisfaction. http://www.gallup.com/poll /184466/americans-satisfaction-blacks-treated-tumbles.aspx?g_source =satisfaction%20with%20way%20blacks%20treated&g_medium=search&g _campaign=tiles

7. Schuck, *Diversity in America*, 137–38.

8. Ibid.

9. This discussion of merit draws heavily, often verbatim, on Schuck, *Diversity in America*, at 152–56 and the sources cited there.

10. See, e.g., Lani Guinier, *Democratizing Higher: The Tyranny of the Meritocracy Education in America* (2015).

11. Thomas Espenshade, Chang Y. Chug, & Joan L. Walling, "Admission Preferences for Minority Students, Athletes, and Legacies at Elite Universities," 85 *Social Science Quarterly* 1422 (2004).

12. See, e.g., Wax, "On Not Dreaming of Affirmative Action."

13. This possibility reflects people's inability to determine the quality of certain goods, including likely academic performance, before the fact due to asymmetric information. George A. Akerlof, "The Market for 'Lemons': Quality Uncertainty and the Market Mechanism," 84 *Quarterly Journal of Economics* 488 (1970).

14. David A. Hollinger, *Postethnic America: Beyond Multiculturalism* (1995), 8.

15. Leiter & Leiter, *Affirmative Action in Antidiscrimination Law and Policy*, at 19–24.

16. Office of Management and Budget, "Standards for Maintaining, Collecting, and Presenting Federal Data on Race and Ethnicity," 81 *Federal Register* 67398 (September 30, 2016).

17. Kenneth Prewitt, *What Is Your Race? The Census and Our Flawed Efforts to Classify Americans* (2013).

18. E.g., Boris I. Bittker, *The Case for Black Reparations* (1973); Ta-Nehisi Coates, "The Case for Reparations," *Atlantic* (June 2014), http://www.theatlantic.com/magazine /archive/2014/06/the-case-for-reparations/361631/.

19. Peter H. Schuck, *Meditations of a Militant Moderate* (2006), chap. 6.

20. Akerlof, "The Market for 'Lemons.' "

21. The history is summarized in John D. Skrentny, *The Ironies of Affirmative Action: Politics, Culture, and Justice in America* (1996).

22. John D. Skrentny, *After Civil Rights: Racial Realism in the New American Workplace* (2014), 3–18.

23. Much of this section is taken from Schuck, *Diversity in America*, 140–43 and sources cited there.

24. *Griggs v. Duke Power Co.*, 401 U.S. 424 (1971).

25. E.g., *Wal-Mart v. Dukes*, 564 U.S. 338 (2011).

26. E.g., *Ricci v. DeStefano*, 557 U.S. 557 (2009).

27. *Fullilove v. Klutznick*, 448 U.S. 448 (1980).

28. *Adarand Constructors, Inc. v. Pena*, 515 U.S. 200 (1995). For a detailed analysis of these cases and related developments on affirmative action in the workplace and government contracting, see Leiter & Leiter, *Affirmative Action in Antidiscrimination Law and Policy*, chap. 3.

29. *City of Richmond v. Croson*, 488 U.S. 469 (1989).

30. *Parents Involved in Community Schools v. Seattle School District No. 1*, 551 U.S. 701 (2007).

31. *Schuette v. Coalition to Defend Affirmative Action*, 134 S. Ct. 1623 (2014).

32. *Metro Broadcasting, Inc. v. FCC*, 497 U.S. 547 (1990).

33. Jeffrey M. Jones, *In U.S.*, "Most Reject Considering Race in College Admissions," Gallup.com (July 24, 2013), http://www.gallup.com/poll/163655/reject-considering -race-college-admissions.aspx

34. 136. S. Ct. 2198 (2016).

35. http://www.gallup.com/poll/193508/oppose-colleges-considering-race-admissions .aspx

36. Paul M. Sniderman & Edward G. Carmine, *Reaching beyond Race* 145 (1997).

37. Loan Le & Jack Citrin, "Affirmative Action," in N. Persily, J. Citrin, & P. Egan, *Public Opinion and Constitutional Controversy* (2008), 163.

38. Ibid. at 165.

39. Ibid. at 166.

40. *Reaching beyond Race* (1997).

41. Douglas Belkin, "Asian-Americans Allege Harvard Admissions Bias," *Wall Street Journal*, May 16–17, 2015, at A3.

42. For my analysis of this concern, see Schuck, *Diversity in America*, at 182–86.

43. http://www.salon.com/2013/05/28/report_diversity_in_elite_professions_ stagnating/

44. S. Michael Gaddis, "Discrimination in the Credential Society: An Audit Study of Race and College Selectivity in the Labor Market," 2015 *Social Forces* 1451. http://sf .oxfordjournals.org/content/93/4/1451

45. Jonathan Rothwell, "Black Students at Top Colleges: Exceptions, Not the Rule," *Brookings*, February 3, 2015.
46. http://fivethirtyeight.com/features/race-gap-narrows-in-college-enrollment-but-not-in-graduation/
47. http://nces.ed.gov/fastfacts/display.asp?id=61
48. http://www.jbhe.com/news_views/65_blackfaculty.html
49. See *Richmond v. J.R. Croson*, 488 U.S. 469 (1989); *Adarand Constructors v. Pena*, 515 U.S. 200 (1995).
50. Schuck, *Diversity in America*, at 161.
51. Eric Schnapper, "Affirmative Action and the Legislative History of the Fourteenth Amendment," 71 *Virginia Law Review* 753 (1985).
52. See source cited in Schuck, *Diversity in America*, at 374 n 5.
53. Hugh Davis Graham, *Collision Course: The Strange Convergence and Affirmative Action Policy in America* (2002), 132.
54. Arcidiacono & Lovenheim, "Affirmative Action and the Quality-Fit Tradeoff," at 5.
55. Belkin, "Asian-Americans Allege Harvard Admissions Bias."
56. See Pew studies cited in Justice Alito's dissenting opinion in *Fisher II*, slip opinion at pp. 27–8, n 8.
57. http://www.nytimes.com/aponline/2015/06/11/us/politics/ap-us-multiracial-america.html?_r=0
58. See part II.C.3. of dissenting opinion of Alito, J. in *Fisher II*.
59. Derek Bok & William Bowen, *The Shape of the River* (1998).
60. Scott E. Carrell, Bruce I. Sacerdote, & James E. West, "From Natural Variation to Optimal Policy? The Importance of Endogenous Peer Group Formation," 81 *Econometrica* 855 (May 2013).
61. Orlando Patterson, *The Ordeal of Integration* 192–93 (1997).
62. *Grutter v. Bollinger*, 539 U.S. 306, 319–20 (2003).
63. Ibid. at 336–41.
64. Ibid. at 146–50.
65. Richard H. Sander & Stuart Taylor, Jr., *Mismatch: How Affirmative Action Hurts Students It's Intended to Help, and Why Universities Won't Admit It* (2012), 16–18.
66. Mark Perry, "Acceptance Rates at US Medical Schools in 2014 Reveal Ongoing Discrimination Against Asian-Americans and Whites," *American Enterprise Institute*, January 4, 2015.
67. Thomas J. Espenshade & Alexandria Walton Radford, *No Longer Separate, Not Yet Equal: Race and Class in Elite College Admissions and Campus Life* (2009), 93, 217.
68. Thomas J. Kane, "Racial and Ethnic Preferences in College Admissions" in *The Black-White Test Score Gap Gap*, C. Jencks & M. Philips, eds. (1998), 431–32. For a fuller analysis of the size of affirmative action preferences as they existed in the early 2000s, see Schuck, *Diversity in America*, at 146–50.
69. Arcidiacono & Lovenheim, "Affirmative Action and the Quality-Fit Tradeoff," at 12–13.
70. Terrance Sandalow, "Minority Preferences Reconsidered," 97 *Michigan Law Review* 1874, 1877 n 4 (1997); Lynn Letukas, "Nine Facts about the SAT That Might Surprise You," College Board Research: Statistical Report (2015) (SAT performance by Hispanics and African Americans slightly overpredicts future college and employment

performance). http://research.collegeboard.org/sites/default/files/publications/2015/1/sat-rumors-stat-report.pdf

71. https://secure-media.collegeboard.org/digitalServices/pdf/sat/total-group-2015.pdf; Charles Murray, "American High Schools Are Going to Hell. Unless You're Asian," *American Enterprise Institute*, September 22, 2015.

72. Tom Loveless, "No, the Sky Is Not Falling: Interpreting the Latest SAT Scores," *Brookings*, October 1, 2015.

73. *Parents Involved in Community Schools v. Seattle School District No. 1.*

74. http://www.nytimes.com/2015/12/16/opinion/what-israel-tells-us-about-affirmative-action-and-race.html?_r=0

75. Michael Kinsley, "The Spoils of Victimhood," *New Yorker* (March 27, 1995). http://www.newyorker.com/magazine/1995/03/27/the-spoils-of-victimhood.

76. Sander & Taylor, Jr., *Mismatch*, at 285.

77. 136. U.S. 2198 (2016).

78. Caroline Hoxby & Sarah Turner, "Expanding College Opportunities for High-Achieving, Low Income Students," SIEPR Discussion Paper No. 12–014 (2013).

79. Slip opinion at 40.

80. 539. U.S. at 343.

81. Thomas Sowell, *Affirmative Action around the World: An Empirical Study* (2004).

82. See sources cited in Schuck, *Diversity in America*, at 184.

83. E.g., Christopher Lasch, *The Revolt of the Elites and the Betrayal of Democracy* (1995), 79, 137. John S. Rosenberg, " 'Role-Model' Affirmative Action: Not Needed, Not Legal," *Minding the Campus* (February 25, 2014). http://www.mindingthecampus.org/2014/02/role-model_affirmative_action_/

84. Sander & Taylor, *Mismatch*.

85. Ibid. at 4.

86. Arcidiacono & Lovenheim, "Affirmative Action and the Quality-Fit Tradeoff," at 10.

87. Sander & Taylor, *Mismatch*, at 4.

88. Ben Backes, "Do Affirmative Action Bans Lower Minority College Enrollment and Attainment?" 47 *Journal of Human Resources* 435 (2012); Peter Hinrichs, "The Effects of Affirmative Action Bans on College Enrollment, Educational Attainment, and the Demographic Composition of Universities," 94 *Review of Economics and Statistics* 712, 721 (2012).

89. http://www.nytimes.com/2016/06/24/opinion/the-supreme-court-has-upheld-affirmative-action-so-lets-dump-mismatch-theory.html?_r=0

90. Arcidiacono & Lovenheim, "Affirmative Action and the Quality-Fit Tradeoff," at 17.

91. Ibid. at 5.

92. See dissenting opinion of Justice Alito in *Fisher II*.

93. Email to author from Sander, March 30, 2015.

94. Jack Citrin, "Affirmative Action in the People's Court," *Public Interest* 39, 43–44 (Winter 1996). Howard Schuman et al., *Racial Attitudes in America: Trends into Interpretations*, rev. ed. (1997), 182; Charlotte Steeth & Maria Krysan, "Affirmative Action and the Public, 1970–1995," 60 *Public Opinion Quarterly* 128, 132 (1996); Stuart Taylor, Jr., "Do African-Americans Really Want Racial Preferences?," *Atlantic* (December 1, 2002), http://www.theatlantic.com/politics/archive/2002/12/do-african-americans-really-want-racial-preferences/378113/.

95. http://www.gallup.com/poll/184772/higher-support-gender-affirmative-action -race.aspx?utm_source=alert&utm_medium=email&utm_content=morelink&utm _campaign=syndication

96. Bok & Bowen, *The Shape of the River*, at 341.

97. Douglas S. Massey, Margarita Mooney, Kimberly C. Torres, & Camille Z. Charles, "Black Immigrants and Black Natives Attending Selective Colleges and Universities in the United States," 113 *American Journal of Education* 243, 246–249 (2007).

98. Robert Lerner & Althea K. Nagai, *Pervasive Preferences: Racial and Ethnic Discrimination in Undergraduate Admissions across the Nation* (Center for Equal Opportunity, 2001).

99. http://www.gse.upenn.edu/pdf/cmsi/Changing_Face_HBCUs.pdf

100. Stephan Thernstrom & Abigail Thernstrom, "Racial Preferences: What We Now Know," 107 *Commentary* 49 (1999).

101. Lekan Oguntoyinbo, "The Influx of Latino Students at Historically Black Colleges," *Atlantic* (September 29, 2015), http://www.theatlantic.com/education/archive /2015/09/hbcus-more-latino-students/407953/

102. Diana Jean Schemo, "Black Colleges Lobby Hard to Lure the Best and Brightest," *New York Times*, March 8, 2001, A10; Pearl Stewart, "HBCUs Ramping Up, Revamping Recruiting Techniques," *Diverse: Issues in Higher Education* (August 14, 2014), http://diverseeducation.com/article/66386/. In fact, in 2014 the White House even announced a My Brother's Keeper initiative on historically black colleges and universities seeking to "promote the academic success of Black males at HBCUs through leadership, scholarship and civic engagement" (http://sites.ed.gov /whhbcu/2014/03/14/hbcus-are-my-brothers-keeper/).

103. Jack Citrin, "Affirmative Action in the People's Court," *Public Interest* 39, 43–44 (Winter 1996). Howard Schuman et al., *Racial Attitudes in America: Trends into Interpretations*, rev. ed. (1997), p. 182; Charlotte Steeth & Maria Krysan, "Affirmative Action and the Public, 1970–1995," 60 *Public Opinion Quarterly* 128, 132 (1996); Stuart Taylor, Jr., "Do African-Americans Really Want Racial Preferences?," *Atlantic* (December 1, 2002), http://www.theatlantic.com/politics/archive/2002/12 /do-african-americans-really-want-racial-preferences/378113/.

104. Peter H. Schuck, *Why Government Fails So Often, and How It Can Do Better* (2014).

CHAPTER 6. RELIGIOUS EXEMPTIONS FROM SECULAR POLICIES

1. See generally, Peter H. Schuck, *Diversity in America: Keeping Government at a Safe Distance* (2003), 3.

2. See ibid., pp. 274–76 on the Supreme Court's efforts to define what constitutes religion.

3. U.S. Constitution, Art. VI, Clause 3.

4. *Burwell v. Hobby Lobby Stores, Inc.*, 134 S. Ct. 2751 (2014).

5. *Obergefell v. Hodges*, 135 S. Ct. 2584 (2015).

6. William T. Cavanagh, *The Myth of Religious Violence: Secular Ideology and the Roots of Modern Conflict* (2009).

7. Shibley Telhami, "Measuring the Backlash against the Muslim Backlash," *Brookings*, July 12, 2016.

8. Richard N. Ostling, "America's Ever-Changing Religious Landscape," in *What's God Got to Do with the American Experiment?* E. J. Dionne, Jr., & John J. DiIulio, Jr., eds. (2000), 21–22.

9. Andrew Kohut, John C. Green, Scott Teeter, & Robert C. Toth, *The Diminishing Divide: Religion's Changing Role in American Politics* (2000), 63–64.

10. Patrick Healy & Julie Bosman, "G.O.P. Governors Vow to Close Doors to Syrian Refugees," *New York Times*, November 16, 2015, http://www.nytimes.com/2015/11/17/us /politics/gop-governors-vow-to-close-doors-to-syrian-refugees.html

11. https://www.washingtonpost.com/news/monkey-cage/wp/2016/08/15/white -christian-america-is-dying/?postshare=8481471277782400&tid=ss_mail

12. Pew Research Center, *Political Polarization in the American Public*, June 2014, http://www.people-press.org/2014/06/12/section-3-political-polarization-and -personal-life/#marrying-across-party-lines; see also Pew Research Center, *So, you married an atheist . . .* , June 2014, http://www.pewresearch.org/fact-tank/2014/06 /16/so-you-married-an-atheist.

13. Tamara Audi, "More Americans Support Mixing Religion and Politics," *Wall Street Journal*, September 22, 2014, http://www.wsj.com/articles/pew-survey-more -americans-support-mixing-religion-and-politics-1411401662

14. Steven D. Smith, *Getting over Equality: A Critical Diagnosis of Religious Freedom in America* (2001), 21.

15. About Santeria, "Why Is It Called Santeria?," http://www.aboutsanteria.com/what-is -santeria.html

16. Mary Ann Glendon, *Rights Talk: The Impoverishment of Political Discourse* (1991).

17. Robert Kagan, *Adversarial Legalism: The American Way of Law* (2003; 2d ed. forthcoming).

18. Peter H. Schuck, *Why Government Fails So Often and How It Can Do Better* (2014), chap. 9.

19. Ibid., chap. 4.

20. Schuck, *Diversity in America*, chap. 2.

21. Stanley Fish, *The Trouble with Principle* (1999), chap. 9.

22. Douglas Laycock, "Formal, Substantive, and Disaggregated Neutrality toward Religion," 39 *DePaul Law Review* 993 (1990).

23. 42. U.S.C. Sec. 2000bb-1.

24. For my analysis of a particular example, see Schuck, *Diversity in America*, at 280–82.

25. *Plyler v. Doe*, 457 U.S. 202 (1982).

26. 98. U.S. 145 (1878).

27. 374. U.S. 398 (1963).

28. 521. U.S. 507 (1997).

29. Marci A. Hamilton, *God vs. the Gavel* (2014).

30. Danielle Weatherby, "The Arkansas 'Mini-RFRA' Is Bad Policy," May 21, 2015, http://papers.ssrn.com/sol3/papers.cfm?abstract_id=2609154

31. *ACLU*, "Anti-LGBT Religious Exemption Legislation across the Country," aclu.org /anti-lgbt-religious-exemption-legislation-across-country#rfra16 (updated every Wednesday).

32. Hamilton, *God vs. the Gavel*, at 119.

33. 134. S. Ct. 2751 (2014).

34. Email to author from Prof. Richard Garnett, July 21, 2016 (attaching Lund's blog discussing such cases).

35. Christopher C. Lund, "RFRA, State RFRAs, and Religious Minorities," 53 *San Diego Law Review* (2016), 163, 164–65.

36. Elizabeth Sepper, "Reports of Accommodation's Death Have Been Greatly Exaggerated," 128 *Harvard Law Review Forum* 24, 30 (2014).

37. Kara Loewentheil, "The Satanic Temple, Scott Walker, and Contraception: A Partial Account of Hobby Lobby's Implications for State Laws," 9 *Harvard Law and Policy Review* 89 (2015).

38. Ira C. Lupu, "Moving Targets: Obergefell, Hobby Lobby, and the Future of LGBT Rights," 7 *Alabama Civil Rights & Civil Liberties Law Review* 1, 43 (2015).

39. *Obama Administrative Record for the LGBT Community*, September 2014, https://www.whitehouse.gov/sites/default/files/docs/lgbt_record_1.pdf; Lupu, "Moving Targets," at 12, 45.

40. 388 U.S. 1 (1967).

41. Lupu, "Moving Targets."

42. Katherine Peralta, "NBA's Silver: LGBT Law Must Change to Keep 2017 All-Star Game in Charlotte," *Charlotte Observer*, April 21, 2016, http://www.charlotteobserver.com/news/business/article73086142.html.

43. Lindsay Gibbs, "NCAA Adopts New Antidiscrimination Policies in the Wake of HB2," *Think Progress*, April 28, 2016, http://thinkprogress.org/sports/2016/04/28/3773410/ncaa-anti-discrimination-lgbt-hb2/.

44. Shane Ferro, "PayPal Won't Tolerate North Carolina's Discrimination, Scraps Expansion Plans," *Huffington Post*, April 5, 2016, http://www.huffingtonpost.com/entry/paypal-north-carolina_us_5703c95ae4b0a06d5806dedf.

45. Katy Steinmetz, "Salesforce CEO Marc Benioff: 'Anti-LGBT' Bills Are 'Anti-Business,'" *Time*, March 31, 2016, http://time.com/4276603/marc-benioff-salesforce-lgbt-rfra/.

46. http://www.nytimes.com/2016/09/15/sports/acc-championships-north-carolina-hb2.html

47. Ibid. at 31.

48. Ibid. at 32–33.

49. Ibid. at 45–46.

50. http://www.cnn.com/2016/07/09/us/massachusetts-governor-transgender-rights/

51. See Amer Phillips, "Mississippi's New Law of Allowing Refusal of Service to LGBT People Is the Most Sweeping Yet," *Washington Post*, April 5, 2016, https://www.washingtonpost.com/news/the-fix/wp/2016/04/05/mississippis-new-religious-freedom-law-is-the-most-sweeping-weve-seen-yet-heres-what-it-does/.

52. *Texas v. United States*, http://www.nytimes.com/2016/08/23/us/transgender-bathroom-access-guidelines-blocked-by-judge.html?_r=0

53. Moriah Balingit, "Another 10 States Sue Obama Administration over Bathroom Guidance for Transgender Students," *Washington Post*, July 8, 2016, https://www.washingtonpost.com/local/education/another-10-states-sue-obama-administration-over-bathroom-guidance-for-transgender-students/2016/07/08/a930238e-4533-11e6-88d0-6adee48be8bc_story.html

54. Peter H. Schuck, "A Bathroom of One's Own," *New York Times*, May 18, 2016, http://www.nytimes.com/2016/05/18/opinion/a-bathroom-of-ones-own.html?_r=0

55. 461. U.S. 574 (1983).

56. Schuck, *Diversity in America*, at 331–37.

57. Peter H. Schuck, *The Limits of Law: Essays on Democratic Governance* (2000), especially chap. 13.

58. Steven J. Heyman, "A Struggle for Recognition: The Controversy over Religious Liberty, Civil Rights, and Same-Sex Marriage," 14 *First American Law Review* 1 (2015).

59. Brief for Douglas Laycock et al. as Amici Curiae Supporting Petitioners, *Obergefell v. Hodges*, available at http://ssrn.com/abstract=2593623, p. 2. Emphasis added.

60. Douglas NeJaime & Reva B. Siegel, "Conscience Wars: Complicity-Based Conscience Claims in Religion and Politics," 124 *Yale Law Journal* 2516, 2577 (2015).

61. Sherif Girgis, "Nervous Victors, Illiberal Measures: A Response to Douglas NeJaime and Reva Siegel," *Yale Law Journal Forum*, March 16, 2016, http://www.yalelawjournal.org/pdf/Girgis_PDF_v7w4z24v.pdf.

62. 406 U.S. 205 (1972).

63. 505 U.S. 577 (1992).

64. 530 U.S. 290 (2000).

65. For my own take on this, see Peter H. Schuck, "What the President of Yale Should Have Said," *Minding the Campus*, November 15, 2015, http://www.mindingthecampus.org/2015/11/what-the-president-of-yale-should-have-said/

66. 321 U.S. 158 (1944). See also, Application of President and Directors of Georgetown Coll., 331 F.2d 1000 (D.C. Cir. 1964), cert. denied, 377 U.S. 978 (1964).

67. See, e.g., Richard W. Garnett, "Taking Pierce Seriously: The Family, Religious Education, and Harm to Children," 76 *Notre Dame Law Review* 109, 116–17 (2000).

68. Lisa Anderson, "*U.S. Women at Risk of FGM More Than Double since 2000: Research*," Reuters, February 6, 2015, http://www.reuters.com/article/2015/02/06/us-usa-women-fgm-idUSKBN0LA1CJ20150206.

69. Lupu, "Moving Targets," at 18.

70. *Christian Legal Society v. Martinez*, 561 U.S. 661 (2011).

71. 135. S. Ct. 853 (2015).

72. Ibid. at 31.

73. Roderick M. Hills, Jr., "Decentralizing Religious and Secular Accommodations," in *Institutionalizing Rights and Religion: Competing Supremacies* (L. Batnitzky & H. Dagan, eds.) (forthcoming).

74. Jeremy Waldron, *Law and Disagreement* (1999), 232.

75. 136. S. Ct. 1557 (2016).

76. Andrew Koppelman, "Gay Rights, Religious Accommodations, and the Purposes of Antidiscrimination Law," 88 *Southern California Law Review* 619 (2015). For a modified version, see http://papers.ssrn.com/sol3/papers.cfm?abstract_id=2791641.

77. Tamara Audi, "Utah and Mormons Walk a Complicated Line on Gay, Religious Rights," *Wall Street Journal*, November 10, 2015, http://www.wsj.com/articles/utah-and-mormons-walk-a-complicated-line-on-gay-religious-rights-1447197146

78. Robin Fretwell Wilson, "When Governments Insulate Dissenters from Social Change: What Hobby Lobby and Abortion Conscience Clauses Teach about Specific Exemptions," 48 *University of California Davis Law Review* 703 (2014).

79. E.g., NeJaime & Siegel, "Conscience Wars."

80. Lupu, "Moving Targets," at 2.

81. *Palko v. Connecticut*, 302 U.S. 319, 325 (1937).

CONCLUSION

1. http://www.nytimes.com/2016/07/01/health/transgender-population.html?_r=0

2. http://www.reuters.com/article/2007/08/28/us-world-firearms -idUSL2834893820070828 (citing Geneva-based Small Arms Survey 2007). See also James B. Jacobs, *Can Gun Control Work?* (2002).

INDEX